THE MEAL SCENES
IN LUKE-ACTS

THE SOCIETY OF BIBLICAL LITERATURE
MONOGRAPH SERIES

Editor
Sharon H. Ringe

Number 52
THE MEAL SCENES
IN LUKE-ACTS
An Audience-Oriented Approach

by
John Paul Heil

THE MEAL SCENES
IN LUKE-ACTS
An Audience-Oriented Approach

John Paul Heil

Society of Biblical Literature
Atlanta, Georgia

THE MEAL SCENES
IN LUKE-ACTS
An Audience-Oriented Approach

by
John Paul Heil

Library of Congress Cataloging-in-Publication Data

Heil, John Paul.
   The meal scenes in Luke-Acts : an audience-oriented approach / John Paul Heil.
      p.cm. — (Society of Biblical Literature monograph series ; no. 52)
   Includes bibliographical references and indexes.
   ISBN 0-88414-013-X (hardcover : alk. paper)
     1. Dinners and dining in the Bible. 2. Bible. N.T. Luke—Criticism, interpretation, etc. 3. Bible. N.T. Acts—Criticism, interpretation, etc. I. Title. II. Series.

BS2589.6.D56 H45 1999
226.4'06—dc21   99-056091

08 07 06 05 04 03 02 01 00 99   5 4 3 2 1

Printed in the United States of America
on acid-free paper

∞

TABLE OF CONTENTS

CHAPTER 1

AUDIENCE-ORIENTED APPROACH TO THE MEAL SCENES IN LUKE-ACTS

Eating and Drinking in Luke-Acts

References to eating and drinking occur frequently throughout Luke-Acts.[1] Indeed the theme of eating and drinking, food, and table fellowship seems to be a special Lukan concern.[2] This book seeks to present a narrative-critical investigation of the theme of eating and drinking in Luke-Acts by

---

[1] We shall treat Luke and Acts as a narrative unity. On the unity of Luke-Acts, see G. E. Sterling, *Historiography and Self-Definition: Josephos, Luke-Acts and Apologetic Historiography* (NovTSup 64; Leiden: Brill, 1992) 331-39; J. B. Green, *The Gospel of Luke* (NICNT; Grand Rapids: Eerdmans, 1997) 6-10. On the need for a more nuanced approach to the question of various unities (authorial, canonical, generic, narrative, and theological) in Luke-Acts, see M. C. Parsons and R. I. Pervo, *Rethinking the Unity of Luke and Acts* (Minneapolis: Fortress, 1993) and the review by J. B. Green in *CBQ* 57 (1995) 411-13.

[2] For recent discussions of eating and drinking in Luke-Acts, see R. J. Karris, *Luke: Artist and Theologian: Luke's Passion Account as Literature* (New York: Paulist, 1985) 47-78; H. Moxnes, "Meals and the New Community in Luke," *SEÅ* 51 (1986) 158-67; P. F. Esler, *Community and Gospel in Luke-Acts: The Social and Political Motivations of Lucan Theology* (SNTSMS 57; Cambridge: Cambridge University Press, 1987) 93-109; D. E. Smith, "Table Fellowship as a Literary Motif in the Gospel of Luke," *JBL* 106 (1987) 613-38; J. H. Neyrey, "Ceremonies in Luke-Acts: The Case of Meals and Table Fellowship," *The Social World of Luke-Acts: Models for Interpretation* (ed. J. H. Neyrey; Peabody: Hendrickson, 1991) 361-87; A. A. Just, *The Ongoing Feast: Table Fellowship and Eschatology at Emmaus* (Collegeville: Liturgical Press, 1993); P. K. Nelson, *Leadership and Discipleship: A Study of Luke 22:24-30* (SBLDS 138; Atlanta: Scholars Press, 1994) 62-74; D. L. Matson, *Household Conversion Narratives in Acts: Pattern and Interpretation* (JSNTSup 123; Sheffield: Sheffield Academic Press, 1996) 80-82; C. Heil, *Die Ablehnung der Speisegebote durch Paulus: Zur Frage nach der Stellung des Apostels zum Gesetz* (BBB 96; Weinheim: Beltz Athenäum, 1994) 271-72; C. Osiek and D. L. Balch, *Families in the New Testament World: Households and House Churches* (Louisville: Westminster John Knox, 1997) 45-46, 204-6.

focusing primarily on all of the actual meals or meal scenes.[3] That most of these scenes are unique to Luke-Acts underlines the distinctiveness of this theme. The many other Lukan references that have to do with eating and drinking, feasting and fasting, food and table fellowship, etc. will be considered insofar as they relate to these explicitly narrated meals. Although there are studies of various aspects of the theme of eating and drinking in Luke and/or Acts, our goal is a comprehensive, narrative-critical treatment of this theme in the whole of Luke and Acts.[4]

An Audience-Oriented Approach

The Authorial Audience

Our audience-oriented approach, as part of the broader category of narrative criticism, concentrates on the "authorial audience" of the text. The "authorial audience" refers to the hearers or readers the author envisions in

---

[3] Our narrative-critical approach to Luke-Acts is generally compatible with R. C. Tannehill, *The Narrative Unity of Luke-Acts* (FFNT; 2 vols; Philadelphia: Fortress, 1986, 1990); W. S. Kurz, "Narrative Approaches to Luke-Acts," *Bib* 68 (1987) 195-220; idem, *Reading Luke-Acts: Dynamics of Biblical Narrative* (Louisville: Westminster/Knox, 1993); J. A. Darr, *On Character Building: The Reader and the Rhetoric of Characterization in Luke-Acts* (Louisville: Westminster/Knox, 1992); idem, "Narrator as Character: Mapping a Reader-Oriented Approach to Narration in Luke-Acts," *Characterization in Biblical Literature* (*Semeia* 63; eds. E. S. Malbon and A. Berlin; Atlanta: Scholars Press, 1993) 43-60; idem, "'Watch How You Listen' (Lk. 8.18): Jesus and the Rhetoric of Perception in Luke-Acts," *The New Literary Criticism and the New Testament* (JSNTSup 109; eds. E. S. Malbon and E. V. McKnight; Sheffield: Sheffield Academic Press, 1994) 87-107; M. A. Powell, "Toward a Narrative-Critical Understanding of Luke," *Int* 48 (1994) 341-46; W. H. Shepherd, *The Narrative Function of the Holy Spirit as a Character in Luke-Acts* (SBLDS 147; Atlanta: Scholars Press, 1994).

[4] That a large number of the occasions for teaching in Luke-Acts are in a convivial setting suggests that relaxed mealtime would have been the most likely occasion for a publicly performed reading of Luke-Acts according to F. G. Downing, "Theophilus's First Reading of Luke-Acts," *Luke's Literary Achievement: Collected Essays* (JSNTSup 116; ed. C. M. Tuckett; Sheffield: Sheffield Academic Press, 1995) 91-95; P. J. J. Botha, "Community and Conviction in Luke-Acts," *Neot* 29 (1995) 150-51.

creating the text.[5] The author assumes that this audience possesses the social, cultural, historical, literary, rhetorical, and interpretive knowledge necessary to actualize the text's meaning and receive its communication.[6] For Luke-Acts it is presupposed that the audience values the authority and has a knowledge of the scripture contained in the Septuagint.[7] The authorial audience is thus equivalent to a contextualized "implied reader," the reader that is presupposed not only by the text but by the socio-historical and literary context of the text.[8] The authorial audience refers not to any real audience, past or present, but is a theoretical construct determined by the interrelation between the text and its context. This audience's interaction with the text is shaped by the historical location of its production and reception. For Luke-Acts the authorial audience refers to the author's image or conception of the community or communities for which he writes.[9]

---

[5] For the audience-oriented approach that we are following, see W. Carter and J. P. Heil, *Matthew's Parables: Audience-Oriented Perspectives* (CBQMS 30; Washington: Catholic Biblical Association, 1998) 8-14. For a recent description of an audience-oriented approach specifically to Luke-Acts, see S. J. Roth, *The Blind, the Lame, and the Poor: Character Types in Luke-Acts* (JSNTSup 144; Sheffield: Sheffield Academic Press, 1997) 56-79.

[6] On the knowledge and thought world of the implied author of Luke-Acts from a social science and narrative-critical perspective, see V. K. Robbins, "The Social Location of the Implied Author of Luke-Acts," *The Social World of Luke-Acts: Models for Interpretation* (ed. J. H. Neyrey; Peabody: Hendrickson, 1991) 305-32.

[7] On the Lukan authorial audience's knowledge of the Septuagint, see Roth, *The Blind*, 80-94.

[8] On the presupposed knowledge of the implied reader/audience of Luke-Acts, see J. B. Tyson, "The Implied Reader in Luke-Acts," *Images of Judaism in Luke-Acts* (Columbia: University of South Carolina Press, 1992) 19-41. On the socio-historical situation of Luke's audience, see Sterling, *Historiography*, 374-78; D. A. S. Ravens, *Luke and the Restoration of Israel* (JSNTSup 119; Sheffield: Sheffield Academic Press, 1995) 11-16.

[9] On the importance of considering the audience in interpreting Luke-Acts, see C. Cook, "The Sense of Audience in Luke: A Literary Examination," *New Blackfriars* 72 (1991) 19-30; J. O. York, *The Last Shall Be First: The Rhetoric of Reversal in Luke* (JSNTSup 46; Sheffield: JSOT, 1991) 164-66; R. Dillman, "Das Lukasevangelium als Tendenzschrift: Leserlenkung und Leseintention in Lk 1,1-4," *BZ* 38 (1994) 86-93.

Narrative Progressions

Our narrative-critical investigation takes seriously that reading or hearing a narrative engages the audience in a dynamic process. We will pay particular attention to how the authorial audience or implied reader responds to the narrative of Luke-Acts in the sequence in which it is read or heard. This will involve a consideration of various narrative progressions: (1) Each of the meal scenes, as narrative units in themselves, possesses its own narrative progression or plot that the audience follows in sequence from beginning to end. How does the audience move through, interact with, and respond to the particular narrative progression of each meal scene? (2) Each meal scene occurs at a particular point within the overall progression of the narrative. How does what the audience has already heard in the narrative affect the way it interacts with and responds to each meal scene? (3) How do the various meal scenes interrelate among themselves? What particular narrative progressions or thematic developments are operative among them? What do these particular progressions or developments among the meal scenes contribute to the overall narrative progression of Luke-Acts?

Pragmatics

Our audience-oriented investigation will aim at determining the pragmatics of the audience's interaction with and response to each Lukan meal scene. By pragmatics we mean what practical consequences emerge for the audience after it has heard and understood what each meal scene is communicating. What does each meal scene evoke from the authorial audience? What is the audience expected to do with this communication? What new thoughts, feelings, attitudes, or perspectives does the audience gain? What actions or behavior is the audience persuaded to adopt or practice? We will thus treat the meal scenes as rhetorical strategies or "speech acts" aimed at not only informing but persuading the audience to do something, to perform some activity.[10]

---

[10] For an explanation of speech act theory as applied to NT texts, see J. E. Botha, *Jesus and the Samaritan Woman: A Speech Act Reading of John 4:1-42* (NovTSup 65; Leiden: Brill, 1991); D. Neufeld, *Reconceiving Texts as Speech Acts: An Analysis of 1 John* (Biblical Interpretation Series 7; Leiden: Brill, 1994).

Preliminary Survey of the Meal Scenes in Luke-Acts

By "meal scene" we mean an integral narrative unit in which an actual meal involving the hospitality of eating and drinking provides the main framework or a dominant concern of the scene or unit and occurs as part of the narrated action. Meals or meal scenes occur within various literary genres, e.g., pronouncement stories (Luke 5:27-32; 5:33-39; 6:1-5, etc.), miracle story (Luke 9:10-17), parables (Luke 15:1-32; 16:19-31), summary (Acts 2:42-47). We do not include as meal scenes references to hypothetical meals not actually narrated (e.g. Luke 17:7-10), brief or passing references to eating and drinking in the rest of the narrative, and the many images for eating and drinking that appear throughout Luke-Acts, although all of these will be included as contributing to the overall narrative context of the actually narrated meals.[11] After considering the theme of eating and drinking in the preparatory narrative of Luke-Acts (Luke 1:1-4:44), we will treat the various meal scenes in the sequence in which they appear in the rest of Luke-Acts as follows:

Chapter 2 considers the narrated meal scenes which occur in Luke 5:27-6:5. Here eating and drinking form the narrative framework for a series of three pronouncement stories:[12] (1) After the tax collector Levi answered Jesus' call to follow him, he gave a great banquet for Jesus in his house. There was a great crowd of tax collectors and others reclining at the meal. This prompted the Pharisees and their scribes to question why Jesus' disciples eat and drink with tax collectors and sinners. The climax is Jesus' pronouncement that he has not come to invite the righteous but sinners to repentance (5:27-32). (2) At the same banquet the controversy continues with the question why the disciples of Jesus eat and drink while the disciples of John and of the Pharisees fast. The climax is Jesus' pronouncement contrasting old and new wine (5:33-39). (3) After the banquet the disciples were eating grain they picked on the sabbath. To the objecting Pharisees Jesus appeals to the example of David and those with him eating the bread that only the priests could eat. The climax is Jesus' pronouncement that the Son of Man is lord of the sabbath (6:1-5).

Chapter 3 deals with the meal scene in Luke 7:36-50 at which Jesus reclined in the house of one of the Pharisees after being invited to eat with him

---

[11] For a listing of these references and images, see Nelson, *Leadership and Discipleship*, 62 nn. 56-57.

[12] For a recent discussion of pronouncement stories, see V. K. Robbins, "Pronouncement Stories from a Rhetorical Perspective," *Forum* 4,2 (1988) 3-32.

(7:36). The scene includes Jesus' rebuke of the Pharisee for failing to offer him the usual meal hospitality: He did not give Jesus water for his feet; he did not give him a kiss; and he did not anoint his head with oil (7:44-46). Those reclining at the meal with Jesus question his forgiveness (7:49) of the sinful woman who washed, kissed, and anointed his feet.

Chapter 4 discusses the meal scene in Luke 9:10-17, Jesus' miraculously overabundant feeding of the crowds following him. Although the disciples want Jesus to dismiss the crowd so that they can go and find provisions for themselves, Jesus orders the disciples to feed them. But the disciples do not have more than five loaves and two fish (9:12-13). After the crowd reclined for a meal and Jesus blessed and broke the loaves and fish for the disciples to give to the crowd, not only did all eat to satisfaction but twelve baskets of leftover fragments were taken up (9:15-17).

Chapter 5 focuses upon the meal scene in Luke 10:38-42 in which a woman named Martha hospitably welcomed Jesus, while on his way to Jerusalem, into her home for a meal. While Martha was busy with all that is involved in the "service" (10:40) of the meal, her sister Mary chose the "best portion" (10:42) of the meal by sitting beside the Lord at his feet and listening to his word (10:39).

Chapter 6 concentrates on the meal scene in Luke 11:37-54, the second meal at which Jesus is the guest of a Pharisee (cf. 7:36-50). After Jesus accepted the Pharisee's invitation to dine with him and reclined for the meal in his home, the Pharisee was amazed that Jesus did not perform the prescribed washing before the meal (11:37-38). This provoked Jesus to severely denounce various practices of the Pharisees (11:39-44) as well as of the scholars of the Law (11:45-52). The scribes and Pharisees then acted with hostility toward him, plotting to entrap him in his speech (11:53-54).

Chapter 7 looks at the meal scene in Luke 14:1-24, the third meal at which Jesus is the guest of a Pharisee (cf. 7:36-50; 11:37-54). On a sabbath Jesus went into the house of one of the leading Pharisees to dine (14:1). The meal scene that follows includes: (1) Jesus' controversial healing of a man on the sabbath in which he again engages the scholars of the Law and the Pharisees (14:2-6); (2) Jesus' parable about humbly taking the last places at a wedding banquet, addressed to the invited guests who were choosing the places of honor at the meal (14:7-11); (3) Jesus' exhortation to the host of the meal to invite the poor who cannot repay him (14:12-14); (4) Jesus' parable about who will be blessed to dine in the kingdom of God, addressed to one of his fellow guests at the meal (14:15-24).

Chapter 8 begins with the complaint of the Pharisees and scribes that Jesus eats with tax collectors and sinners in Luke 15:1-2 and then moves to Jesus' response in the parables of the lost sheep in 15:3-7, of the lost coin in

15:8-10, and of the lost son and brother in 15:11-32 in which eating plays a prominent role. The joyful celebrations in the first two parables (15:3-10) imply festive meals. In the third parable the younger son finds himself in a famine dying from hunger and longing to eat what is fed to swine (15:14-17). The elder son refuses to participate in the father's feast for his returning brother for whom the fattened calf has been slaughtered (15:23-30).

Chapter 9 centers upon the meal scenes in the parable of the rich man and Lazarus in Luke 16:19-31. The parable begins with the meal scene in which the rich man dines sumptuously while Lazarus is starving at his gate (16:19-21) and concludes with the heavenly banquet scene in which Lazarus is reclining in the "bosom of Abraham" while the rich man is thirsting in the nether world (16:23-26).

Chapter 10 focuses on the implied meal Jesus shares with Zacchaeus, a chief tax collector and a rich man, within the hospitality of lodging at his house in Luke 19:1-10. After Jesus invites himself to stay in the house of Zacchaeus, which would include the sharing of meal fellowship, Zacchaeus welcomes him to the hospitality with joy (19:5-6). All grumble that Jesus has gone to stay in the house of a sinner, but Zacchaeus's conversion leads to Jesus' pronouncement that salvation has come to this house (19:7-9).

Chapter 11 treats Jesus' last supper with his disciples in Luke 22:7-38. This extensive meal scene includes: (1) the disciples' preparation for this last Passover meal following the authoritative instructions of Jesus (22:7-13); (2) the Passover meal itself in which Jesus shares with his disciples the bread he designates as his body and the cup he designates as the new covenant in his blood that will be shed for them (22:14-20); (3) Jesus' announcement that one of the disciples eating with him will betray him (22:21-23); (4) Jesus' analogy of table service to declare that he is among the disciples, who are disputing about who is the greatest among them, as one who serves and that they will eat and drink at his table in his kingdom (22:24-30); (5) Jesus' exhortation that after Peter has turned back from denying Jesus he must strengthen his brothers (22:31-34); (6) Jesus' instructions for the disciples to be prepared with money bag, sack, and sword for the scriptural fulfillment that he be counted among the wicked (22:35-38).

Chapter 12 concerns the meal in which the risen Jesus, who appears unrecognized to two disciples going away from Jerusalem to the village of Emmaus (24:13-27), is recognized in his breaking of the bread of the meal he shares with them (24:28-35).

Chapter 13 considers the meal in which the risen Jesus, who appears to the whole group of disciples gathered together in Jerusalem (24:36-40), takes a piece of baked fish offered by the assembly of his disciples and eats it in their presence (24:41-43).

Chapter 14 centers upon the meals that the newly baptized believers in Jerusalem shared as part of their communal life according to Acts 2:42-47.

Chapter 15 regards the theme of table fellowship between Jews and Gentiles in the encounter of Peter with Cornelius in Acts 10:1-11:18. While Peter was hungry and wished to eat he had a vision commanding him to eat the unclean animals God has now declared clean (10:10-16). Peter then showed meal hospitality to those sent to him from Cornelius (10:23). In his speech at the house of Cornelius Peter referred to the witnesses who ate and drank with Jesus after he rose from the dead (10:41). At Jerusalem the circumcised believers confronted him with the accusation that he ate with uncircumcised people (11:2-3). Peter then recounted the vision in which he was commanded to eat the unclean animals God has declared clean (11:4-10).

Chapter 16 examines the meal scene in which Paul revives Eutychus who fell to his death while Paul was speaking in Acts 20:7-12. A meal provides the framework for the scene. It begins with a reference to the "breaking of bread" on the first day of the week (20:7) and moves to Paul's announcement that there is still life in Eutychus, who was then taken away alive after Paul broke bread and ate (20:10-12).

Chapter 17 presents the final meal scene, which occurs during Paul's sea journey to Rome in Acts 27:33-38. After urging his fellow passengers, who had eaten nothing for fourteen days, to take some food for their survival, Paul himself took bread and ate it in front of them all (27:33-35). As a result they were encouraged to take some food themselves in order to be saved (27:36-38).

Overview of the Literary Structure of Luke-Acts

Before beginning our investigation it will be helpful to consider the overall literary structure of Luke-Acts and to note where the meal scenes fit within this structure.[13]
Gospel of Luke

I. Luke 1:1-4:44: Preparatory Narrative
  A. 1:1-4: Prologue
  B. 1:5-2:52: Infancy Narrative

---

[13] We adopt the literary structure for Luke-Acts developed and demonstrated by F. O'Fearghail, *The Introduction to Luke-Acts: A Study of the Role of Lk 1,1-4,44 in the Composition of Luke's Two-Volume Work* (AnBib 126; Rome: Biblical Institute, 1991) 9-84.

      1) 1:5-56: Birth Announcements, Call, and Visitation
        a) 1:5-25: Announcement of the Birth of John
        b) 1:26-38: Announcement of the Birth of Jesus and Call of Mary
        c) 1:39-56: Mary Visits Elizabeth (Magnificat: 1:46-55)
      2) 1:57-80: Birth and Growth of John (Benedictus: 1:67-79)
      3) 2:1-52: Birth and Growth of Jesus
        a) 2:1-21: Birth, Circumcision, and Naming of Jesus
        b) 2:22-39: Parents' Presentation of Jesus in the Temple
        c) 2:40-52: Jesus Found by Parents in the Temple
    C. 3:1-4:44: Ministries of John and Jesus
      1) 3:1-20: Ministry of John
      2) 3:21-4:44: Ministry of Jesus
        a) 3:21-38: Initiation of Jesus' Ministry
        b) 4:1-13: Devil's Temptation of Jesus
        c) 4:14-44: Anticipation of Jesus' Ministry

II. Luke 5:1-9:50: Ministry of Jesus in Galilee
    A. 5:1-6:11: Gathering Disciples
    B. 6:12-19: Choice of the Twelve
    C. 6:20-49: Sermon on the Plain
    D. 7:1-17: Healings in Capernaum and Nain
    E. 7:18-35: John's Delegation to Jesus and His Testimony about John
    F. 7:36-50: Meal with Sinful Woman and Pharisee
    G. 8:1-21: Jesus' Preaching Illustrated
    H. 8:22-56: Examples of Jesus' Salvific Miracles
    I. 9:1-50: Mission of the Twelve

III. Luke 9:51-19:48: Travel Narrative of Jesus on His Way to Jerusalem
    A. 9:51-10:37: (a) Introduction to the Travel Narrative
    B. 10:38-11:54: (b) Acceptance and Rejection
    C. 12:1-13:21: (c) Readiness for Judgment
    D. 13:22-14:24: (d) The Universality of Salvation
    E. 14:25-17:10: (c') Discipleship and Repentance
    F. 17:11-18:30: (b') The Kingdom of God
    G. 18:31-19:48: (a') Conclusion of the Travel Narrative[14]

IV. Luke 20:1-24:53: Ministry of Jesus in Jerusalem

---

[14] For an explanation of this chiastic arrangement, see O'Fearghail, *Introduction to Luke-Acts*, 59-61.

A. 20:1-21:38: Teaching in the Temple
    1) 20:1-44: The People Addressed
    2) 20:45-21:38: Disciples Addressed with the People
B. 22:1-23:54: Passion, Death, Burial
    1) 22:1-65: The Passover Feast
        a) 22:1-38: Jesus' Passover Meal with His Disciples
        b) 22:39-46: Jesus' Prayer on the Mount of Olives
        c) 22:47-53: Jesus' Betrayal by Judas and Arrest
        d) 22:54-65: Peter's Denial of Jesus
    2) 22:66-23:54: Day after the Passover Feast
        a) 22:66-71: Jesus' Trial before Sanhedrin
        b) 23:1-25: Jesus' Trial before Pilate and Herod
        c) 23:26-43: Jesus' Crucifixion
        d) 23:44-49: Jesus' Death
        e) 23:50-54: Jesus' Burial
C. 23:55-24:53: Resurrection, Mission, Ascension
    1) 23:55-24:12: Announcement of Resurrection to Women
    2) 24:13-35: Appearance of Risen Jesus to Emmaus Disciples
    3) 24:36-53: Appearance of Risen Jesus to Disciples in Jerusalem

Acts of the Apostles

I. Acts 1:1-26: Prologue
  A. 1:1-14: Recapitulation, Repetition, Introduction
  B. 1:15-26: Recomposition of the Twelve

II. Acts 2:1-8:3: In Jerusalem
  A. 2:1-4:31: Gift of the Holy Spirit and Preaching of the Apostles
  B. 4:32-5:42: Apostles and Their Witness
  C. 6:1-8:3: The Twelve and Stephen

III. Acts 8:4-21:17: Missionary Preaching
  A. 8:4-11:18: From Samaritans to Gentiles
    1) 8:4-40: Philip in Samaria
    2) 9:1-31: Paul's Conversion
    3) 9:32-11:18: Peter's Healing Ministry and Conversion of Cornelius
  B. 11:19-14:28: Turning to the Gentiles
    1) 11:19-12:25: Antioch, Peter's Deliverance, Death of Herod
    2) 13:1-14:28: Paul's First Journey Initiating His Gentile Mission
  C. 15:1-35: Council of Jerusalem
  D. 15:36-18:22: The Greek World

E. 18:23-21:17: Reassurance and Farewell

IV. Acts 21:18-28:31: To Rome
  A. 21:18-23:11: Paul in Jerusalem
  B. 23:12-26:32: Plot against Paul
  C. 27:1-28:31: Paul's Journey to Rome
    1) 27:1-28:16: Paul's Sea Voyage to Rome
    2) 28:17-31: Paul's Witness in Rome

Indicative of the extent and importance of the theme of eating and drinking in Luke-Acts, the meal scenes delineated and listed above occur in each of the main divisions of both Luke and Acts. After the preparatory narrative in Luke 1:1-4:44 the meal scenes in 5:27-6:11, 7:36-50, and 9:10-17 occur during Jesus' ministry in Galilee in 5:1-9:50. The meal scenes in 10:38-42, 11:37-54, 14:1-24, 15:1-32, and 16:19-31 appear in the travel narrative of Jesus on his way to Jerusalem in 9:51-19:48. The meal scenes in 22:7-38 and 24:28-35, 41-43 take place during Jesus' ministry in Jerusalem in 20:1-24:53. After the introductory section to Acts in 1:1-26 the meals in 2:42-47 occur in the Jerusalem section in 2:1-8:3. The meal scenes in 10:1-11:18 and 20:7-12 appear during the missionary preaching in 8:4-21:17. The final meal scene in 27:33-38 takes place during Paul's journey to Rome in 21:18-28:31.

The Authorial Audience and the Prologue (Luke 1:1-4)

The author of Luke-Acts (whom we will refer to as "Luke") progressively draws his audience into his narrative by means of an elegant prologue (1:1-4):[15]

---

[15] On Luke 1:1-4, see R. J. Dillon, "Previewing Luke's Project from His Prologue (Luke 1:1-4)," *CBQ* 43 (1981) 205-27; Tannehill, *Narrative Unity*, 1.9-12; D. L. Bock, "Understanding Luke's Task: Carefully Building on Precedent (Luke 1:1-4)," *Criswell Theological Review* 5 (1991) 183-201; O'Fearghail, *Introduction to Luke-Acts*, 85-116; D. P. Moessner, "The Meaning of ΚΑΘΕΞΗΣ in the Lukan Prologue as a Key to the Distinctive Contribution of Luke's Narrative among the 'Many'," *The Four Gospels 1992: Festschrift Frans Neirynck* (BETL 100; ed. F. Van Segbroeck, et al; Leuven: Leuven University Press, 1992) 1513-28; S. M. Sheeley, *Narrative Asides in Luke-Acts* (JSNTSup 72; Sheffield: JSOT, 1992) 115-16, 165-66; Sterling, *Historiography*, 339-46; L. Alexander, *The Preface to Luke's Gospel: Literary Convention and Social Context in Luke 1.1-4 and Acts 1.1* (SNTSMS 78; Cambridge: Cambridge University Press, 1993) 102-42; Kurz, *Reading Luke-Acts*, 41-44; Dillman, "Lukasevangelium," 86-93; Shepherd, *Holy Spirit*, 102-

First, he invites the audience to identify with the "us" (ἡμῖν) among whom the "deeds" or "events" (πραγμάτων) about which many in the past have attempted to compile a narrative "have been brought to fulfillment" (πεπληροφορημένων) by God (divine passive), that is, they have fulfilled prophetic promises in accord with God's providential plan (1:1).[16] That these deeds have already been brought to fulfillment so that they are now in a state of accomplishment "among us," as expressed by the perfect passive participle πεπληροφορημένων, means they have a continuing relevance for the audience.[17]

Second, Luke includes his audience along with himself among the "us" (ἡμῖν), those who have been the recipients of the tradition about these divinely accomplished deeds as handed down "to us" by those who from the beginning were eyewitnesses and became ministers of the word (1:2). As communicators of the deeds brought to their fulfillment among us by God, the ministers of "the word" (τοῦ λόγου) are thus ministers of the word of God.[18]

Third, Luke, himself functioning as a "minister of the word," envisions an audience represented by an individual he addresses as the most excellent "Theophilus" (literally, friend or lover of God) (1:4).[19] By his own comprehensive, accurate, and orderly narrative (1:3) Luke wants to impart to Theophilus the assurance, certainty, or reliability (ἀσφάλειαν) concerning the

---

13; I. J. du Plessis, "Applying the Results of Social-Historical Research to Narrative Exegesis: Luke as a Case Study," *Neot* 30 (1996) 343-44.

[16] J. T. Squires, *The Plan of God in Luke-Acts* (SNTSMS 76; Cambridge: Cambridge University Press, 1993) 23-24.

[17] S. E. Porter, *Verbal Aspect in the Greek of the New Testament, with Reference to Tense and Mood* (Studies in Biblical Greek 1; New York: Lang, 1993) 395; K. L. McKay, *A New Syntax of the Verb in New Testament Greek: An Aspectual Approach* (Studies in Biblical Greek 5; New York: Lang, 1994) 61.

[18] J. A. Fitzmyer, *The Gospel According to Luke I-IX* (AB 28; Garden City: Doubleday, 1981) 295; F. Bovon, *Das Evangelium nach Lukas (Lk 1,1-9,50)* (EKKNT 3; Zürich: Benziger, 1989) 37.

[19] The reference to God in the name "Theophilus" is the only explicit reference to God in the Lukan prologue, although God's activity is implicit throughout.

"words" or "deeds" (λόγων) in which he has already been instructed (1:4),[20] presumably by other ministers of the word (λόγου) (1:2).[21] Luke thus wants his audience to experience through his own narrative "the assurance" concerning (περὶ) the deeds or words (λόγων) in which they have already been instructed by others (1:4), that is, concerning (περὶ) the deeds (πραγμάτων) that have been brought to fulfillment by God among us (1:1).[22] Luke's own narrative will assure and make his audience certain of the continuing effect of these deeds done by God among us.[23]

Eating and Drinking in the Preparatory Narrative (Luke 1:1-4:44)

John will never drink wine or strong drink (1:15)

The audience encounters Luke's first reference to eating and drinking in the very first scene of the infancy narrative, the announcement of the birth of John (1:5-25). The angel of the Lord informs the priest Zechariah that the son he is to name John "will never drink either wine or strong drink" (1:15).[24] From its presumed familiarity with the OT the audience knows that God forbade priests to drink any wine or strong drink in preparation for their priestly service (Lev 10:9), that those taking the Nazirite vow dedicating one

---

[20] There is a close, almost synonymous, relation between God's "word" and "deed" in the biblical tradition; see R. F. O'Toole, *The Unity of Luke's Theology: An Analysis of Luke-Acts* (GNS 9; Wilmington: Glazier, 1984) 87. On the meaning of παρακολουθέω in 1:3, see D. P. Moessner, "'Eyewitnesses,' 'Informed Contemporaries,' and 'Unknowing Inquirers': Josephus' Criteria for Authentic Historiography and the Meaning of παρακολουθέω," *NovT* 38 (1996) 105-22.

[21] The "words" (λόγων) then would include various forms of instruction of the "word" (λόγου) of God; see Sterling, *Historiography*, 345 n. 170.

[22] The words, "the assurance" (τὴν ἀσφάλειαν), occur in an emphatic position at the conclusion of the periodic sentence comprising the prologue (1:4) and express the purpose of the entire Lukan narrative. See Fitzmyer, *Luke I-IX*, 289; Green, *Luke*, 45.

[23] B. C. Frein, "Narrative Predictions, Old Testament Prophecies and Luke's Sense of Fulfilment," *NTS* 40 (1994) 22-37.

[24] The double negative in "he will never drink" (οὐ μὴ πίῃ) expresses "prophetic" emphasis; see M. Zerwick, *Biblical Greek* (Rome: Biblical

to God shall abstain from wine and strong drink (Num 6:3), that the mother of Samson was not to drink wine or strong drink because her son was to be consecrated as a Nazirite to God from the womb and deliver Israel from the Philistines (Judg 13:4-5, 7), and that Hannah had drunk neither wine nor strong drink (1 Sam 1:15) when she promised to give to God her yet to be born son, the priestly prophet Samuel, as one who will drink neither wine nor strong drink in accord with the Nazirite vow (1 Sam 1:11). That John will observe the ascetical practice of never drinking wine or strong drink indicates to the audience that he, like important priestly, prophetic, and salvific figures before him, is specially consecrated to play a significant role in God's plan of salvation.[25]

God has filled the hungry with good things (1:53)

In her Magnificat of praise to God Mary, the lowly handmaiden from Nazareth in Galilee whom God chose to be the mother of his Son Jesus, proclaimed that God "has filled the hungry with good things, but the rich he has sent away empty" (1:53). God's reversal of the rich and the hungry associates the hungry with the poor, the expected opposite of the rich. The hungry, those who lack nourishment and long for it, parallel the lowly whom God has lifted up in contrast to the powerful whom God has thrown down from their thrones (1:52). That God "has filled the hungry with good things" makes the audience aware that what God has done for his physically and spiritually hungry people in the past, as remembered from Psalm 106:9 (LXX), where God "filled the hungry soul with good things," God is now doing for his "hungry" people Israel and the descendants of Abraham (1:54-55) represented by the lowly Mary. The audience looks forward to how God will reverse the fortunes of the hungry and the rich in the story of the yet to be born Jesus, and is alerted to a spiritual and metaphorical as well as a physical

---

Institute, 1963) 149-50.

[25] R. E. Brown, *The Birth of the Messiah: A Commentary on the Infancy Narratives in the Gospels of Matthew and Luke* (ABRL; New Updated ed; New York: Doubleday, 1993) 273-74; I. H. Marshall, *The Gospel of Luke* (Grand Rapids: Eerdmans, 1978) 57; Fitzmyer, *Luke I-IX*, 325-26; Bovon, *Lukas*, 1.55-56; J. Nolland, *Luke 1-9:20* (WBC 35A; Dallas: Word Books,

and literal use of "hunger" which God himself satisfies with "good things," a symbol for material as well as spiritual benefits.[26]

The newborn Jesus was placed in a manger (2:7, 12, 16)

That Mary placed the newborn Jesus in a manger (φάτνη, 2:7), a feeding trough for animals, begins to indicate in a very subtle symbolical and ironical way for the audience how God will "fill the hungry with good things" (1:53) in and through Jesus. Familiar with the irony of Isaiah 1:3 (LXX) according to which a donkey knows the manger (φάτνην) of its lord but the people of Israel do not know God as their "manger," the one who feeds and nourishes them, Luke's audience experiences the similar irony of Jesus being placed in a manger, symbolic of the God who nourishes his people, although there is no place for Jesus in the lodgings of the people (2:7). The feeding trough in which Jesus lies (2:12, 16) serves as the sign by which God makes known to lowly shepherds (2:15) and through them to all the people (2:10, 17) the birth of their savior, Christ the Lord (2:11), through whom God will feed his hungry people.[27]

1989) 30.

[26] A. Plummer, *The Gospel According to S. Luke* (ICC; Edinburgh: Clark, 1922) 33; D. P. Seccombe, *Possessions and the Poor in Luke-Acts* (SNT(SU) 6; Linz: Fuchs, 1982) 77-81; Tannehill, *Narrative Unity*, 1.26-30; S. Farris, *The Hymns of Luke's Infancy Narratives: Their Origin, Meaning and Significance* (JSNTSup 9; Sheffield: JSOT, 1985) 121-26; York, *Last Shall Be First*, 44-55; J. B. Green, "The Social Status of Mary in Luke 1,5-2,52: A Plea for Methodological Integration," *Bib* 73 (1992) 457-72; M. Coleridge, *The Birth of the Lukan Narrative: Narrative as Christology in Luke 1-2* (JSNTSup 88; Sheffield: JSOT, 1993) 91-95; V. K. Robbins, "Socio-Rhetorical Criticism: Mary, Elizabeth and the Magnificat as a Test Case," *The New Literary Criticism and the New Testament* (JSNTSup 109; eds. E. S. Malbon and E. V. McKnight; Sheffield: Sheffield Academic Press, 1994) 164-209. We remain unconvinced by Robbins's contention that the lowliness of Mary (1:48) refers to her becoming pregnant outside of marriage rather than to her pre-pregnancy low status as a handmaiden from Nazareth in Galilee.

[27] Brown, *Birth*, 418-31, 668-81; Fitzmyer, *Luke I-IX*, 394-96, 408; Marshall, *Luke*, 106-7; Nelson, *Leadership and Discipleship*, 67; Coleridge, *Birth*, 133-53; M. L. Strauss, *The Davidic Messiah in Luke-Acts: The Promise and Its Fulfillment in Lukan Christology* (JSNTSup 110; Sheffield: Sheffield

The prophetess Anna worshiped with fasting (2:37)

The ascetical practice of not drinking wine or strong drink predicted of the yet to be born John (1:15) is complemented by the fasting of the venerable prophetess Anna.[28] That "she did not leave the temple, but worshiped with fastings (νηστείαις) and prayers (δεήσεσιν) night and day" (2:37) places her in the position of the physically and spiritually "hungry" whom God is now filling with good things (1:53) in the birth of Jesus.[29] Anna's temple piety and prophetic role supplements that of the righteous and devout Simeon, who was "awaiting the consolation of Israel" as he prophesied about Jesus (2:25). Her continual fastings coupled with prayers of supplication to God (2:37) indicate to the audience that she too is awaiting God's messianic salvation for her people and equip her for her prophetic role of speaking about Jesus to all those "awaiting the redemption of Jerusalem" (2:38).[30]

John urges the sharing of food with the needy (3:11)

John urged the crowds coming out to be baptized by him (3:7) with the baptism of repentance for the forgiveness of sins (3:3) to "do" the fruits

---

Academic Press, 1995) 108-17.

[28] On the various meanings of fasting in early Judaism and in the NT, see G. Feeley-Harnik, *The Lord's Table: The Meaning of Food in Early Judaism and Christianity* (Washington: Smithsonian Institution, 1994) 89-92; J. F. Wimmer, *Fasting in the New Testament: A Study in Biblical Theology* (New York: Paulist, 1982) 111-16.

[29] J. Zmijewski, "νηστεύω," *EDNT* 2.466: "The idea that the effectiveness of prayer can be enhanced through fasting can be found already in the OT....For the Jews (esp. the Pharisees) fasting was included along with prayer and almsgiving among the most important works of godliness." See also U. Schoenborn, "δέομαι," *EDNT* 1.286-87.

[30] On Anna in 2:36-38, see Brown, *Birth*, 466-68, 688-89; Coleridge, *Birth*, 178-83; J. K. Elliott, "Anna's Age (Luke 2:36-37)," *NovT* 30 (1988) 100-102; M. Wilcox, "Luke 2,36-38: 'Anna Bat Phanuel, of the Tribe of Asher, a Prophetess..': A Study in Midrash in Material Special to Luke," *The Four Gospels 1992: Festschrift Frans Neirynck* (BETL 100; ed. F. Van Segbroeck, et al; Leuven: Leuven University Press, 1992) 1571-79; B. E. Reid, *Choosing the Better Part?: Women in the Gospel of Luke* (Collegeville: Liturgical Press, 1996) 90-95; R. M. Price, *The Widow Traditions in Luke-Acts: A Feminist-Critical Scrutiny* (SBLDS 155; Atlanta: Scholars Press, 1997)

worthy of repentance (3:8). To the crowds who asked, "What then shall we do?" (3:10), John replied, "Let the one who has two tunics share with one who has none, and let the one who has food do likewise" (3:11). Through this reply to the crowds John challenges the Lukan audience to a repentance that calls them to share their material possessions including their food with those in need.

Jesus overcomes the devil's temptation to feed himself (4:1-4)

"Full of the Holy Spirit" (4:1), Jesus returned from the Jordan river where he had been baptized (cf. 3:3) and had received the Holy Spirit (3:21-22). He was led (ἤγετο) by the Spirit in the wilderness (ἐρήμῳ), tested (πειραζόμενος) for forty days by the devil, and he did not eat anything during these days so that when they were completed he was hungry (4:1-2). This develops Jesus' solidarity with the sinful situation of his people as he relives the experience of the ancestors of his people who sinned in the wilderness. Through their knowledge of the OT the audience recalls how the Lord God led (ἤγαγέν) the people of Israel in the wilderness (ἐρήμῳ) for forty years,[31] in order to test (ἐκπειράσῃ) them and to determine what is in their heart, whether they will keep his commandments or not, by letting them hunger before feeding them with manna (LXX Deut 8:2-3). As one disciplines his son (υἱὸν) so the Lord God will discipline his people Israel (LXX Deut 8:5).[32] Similarly, since God declared Jesus to be his beloved Son (υἱός) in whom God is well pleased (3:22; see also 3:38), the devil tests Jesus' sonship: "If you are the Son (υἱός) of God, command this stone to become bread!" (4:3). Unlike Israel who proved to be God's unfaithful "son" and sinned while hungry in the wilderness (Pss 78:17-31; 106:13-14), Jesus proves to be God's faithful Son, overcoming the devil's temptation by quoting God's scriptural word, "Not by bread alone will a person live!" (LXX Deut 8:3 in 4:4).[33]

47-61.

[31] On the correspondence between forty years and forty days, see Num 14:34; Ezek 4:6 and Wimmer, *Fasting*, 38.

[32] For the background on Israel as "son" of God, see B. Gerhardsson, *The Testing of God's Son (Matt 4:1-11 & Par)* (ConBNT 2; Lund: Gleerup, 1966) 20-24; Wimmer, *Fasting*, 35.

[33] Gerhardsson, *Testing*, 36-53; Wimmer, *Fasting*, 31-51; S. R. Garrett, *The Demise of the Devil: Magic and the Demonic in Luke's Writings* (Minneapolis: Fortress, 1989) 38-43; R. L. Brawley, "Canon and Community: Intertextuality, Canon, Interpretation, Christology, Theology, and Persuasive Rhetoric in Luke 4:1-13," *SBLASP* 31 (1992) 419-34; C. A. Kimball, *Jesus' Exposition of the Old Testament in Luke's Gospel* (JSNTSup 94; Sheffield:

Although he was hungry (ἐπείνασεν, 4:2), Jesus, filled by God with the Holy Spirit (3:22; 4:1), refused to abuse his special sonship by satisfying his hunger himself and thus remained faithful to the God who fills the hungry (πεινῶντας) with good things (1:53). In solidarity with the sinfulness of the people he demonstrates how they can overcome their sinfulness through the power of the Holy Spirit. By actualizing, through the guiding power of the Holy Spirit, God's written word that "not by bread alone will a person live!" (4:4), Jesus functions as both model and mediator for the audience, who identifies with the people. They can overcome their sinfulness by following the example of Jesus through the power of the Holy Spirit with which he will baptize them (3:16). As the Son who overcame the devil through the Holy Spirit and remained faithful to God, Jesus prophetically calls and enables every person (ἄνθρωπος, 4:4) in the audience to live by faith in the God who satisfies not only physical hunger but the hunger that bread alone cannot satisfy.

Jesus healed Simon's mother-in-law and she "served" them (4:39)

After leaving the public realm of the synagogue where he exorcized a man with the spirit of an unclean demon (4:31-37) through the power of the Holy Spirit that continues to accompany him (3:22; 4:1, 14, 18, 36), Jesus entered into the private domain of the house of Simon, whose mother-in-law was incapacitated with a severe fever (4:38). By rebuking her demonic fever so that it left her (4:39), Jesus gave her, like the exorcized man, a personal experience of the salvation he has been equipped to bring through the Spirit (4:18).[34] Her personal experience of salvation includes the restoration of her

---

JSOT, 1994) 80-97; Shepherd, *Holy Spirit*, 130-34; P. Grelot, "Les tentations de Jésus," *NRT* 117 (1995) 501-16.

[34] On Jesus' healing miracles as personal experiences of salvation, see J. P. Heil, "Interpreting the Miracles of Jesus," *McKendree Pastoral Review* 3 (1986) 21-31; idem, "Miracles," *HarperCollins Bible Dictionary*, 687-89. See also J. J. Pilch, "Sickness and Healing in Luke-Acts," *The Social World of Luke-Acts: Models for Interpretation* (ed. J. H. Neyrey; Peabody: Hendrickson, 1991) 181-209; J. T. Carroll, "Jesus as Healer in Luke-Acts," *SBLASP* 33 (1994) 269-85; idem, "Sickness and Healing in the New Testament Gospels," *Int* 49 (1995) 130-42. On the role of the Spirit in Jesus' healings in Luke, see M. Turner, "The Spirit and the Power of Jesus' Miracles in the Lucan Conception," *NovT* 33 (1991) 124-52; idem, "The Spirit of Prophecy and the Power of Authoritative Preaching in Luke-Acts: A Question of Origins," *NTS* 38 (1992) 66-88; R. P. Menzies, "Spirit and Power in Luke-

communal role of extending meal hospitality to this newly arrived guest and the others in the house as she gratefully "served" (διηκόνει) them at table (4:39).[35] As her "serving" at a meal can also have the meaning of "serving" in a more comprehensive sense, this healed woman acts as a model for the audience to likewise "serve" Jesus and the community in gratitude for their own personal experiences of the salvation Jesus brings them. Serving at a meal is thus a Lukan paradigm for Christian service in general.[36]

Summary

Luke's preparatory narrative (1:1-4:44) has introduced the audience to certain aspects of the theme of eating and drinking: That John will not drink wine or strong drink, indicating his consecration to God, helps to prepare the audience for the significant role he will play in God's plan of salvation (1:15). Mary's proclamation that God has filled the hungry with good things in the birth of Jesus (1:53) opens the audience to the metaphorical meaning of God satisfying those who "hunger." That the newborn Jesus was placed in a feeding trough (2:7, 12, 16) begins to symbolize how God will feed his "hungry" people, including the audience, through Jesus. The prophetess Anna's fasting allows her to recognize God's salvation in Jesus and proclaim it to the audience (2:37). John urged the audience to share the food God gives them with those in need (3:11). The Spirit-equipped Jesus acts as model and mediator for the audience, to whom he will give the Holy Spirit (3:16), so that they, like him, can live by faith in the God who satisfies not only physical but spiritual hunger (4:1-4). By serving a meal, Simon's mother-in-law provides a paradigm for the audience to serve Jesus and the Christian community in gratitude for the salvation Jesus imparts to them (4:39).

Acts: A Response to Max Turner," *JSNT* 49 (1993) 11-20.

[35] K. E. Corley, *Private Women, Public Meals: Social Conflict in the Synoptic Tradition* (Peabody: Hendrickson, 1993) 119-21.

[36] BAGD, 184; A. Weiser, "διακονέω," *EDNT* 1.302-4; Fitzmyer, *Luke I-IX*, 549-50. See also R. J. Karris, "Women and Discipleship in Luke," *CBQ* 56 (1994) 1-20; Matson, *Household Conversion*, 56-58; Reid, *Women*.

CHAPTER 2

CONTROVERSIAL MEALS OF JESUS AND HIS DISCIPLES
LUKE 5:27-6:5

Having heard the preparatory narrative with its various references to eating and/or drinking (1:5-4:44), the audience encounters the first meal scenes as part of the narrative progression in which Jesus begins to gather disciples (5:1-6:11), the progression that introduces the main Lukan narrative with Jesus' ministry in Galilee (5:1-9:50). The opening section of Jesus gathering disciples divides into two parallel progressions. Each begins with a call to discipleship (5:1-11 and 5:27-28), contains accounts of Jesus' healing and teaching activity (5:12-25 and 5:29-6:10), and concludes with parallel formulations that represent brief pauses in the narrative (5:26 and 6:11).[1] The audience encounters the first Lukan meal scenes, in which eating and/or drinking provide the narrative framework for three successive pronouncement stories (5:27-32, 5:33-39, and 6:1-5), at the beginning of this second parallel progression (5:27-6:11).

Jesus and His Disciples Eat with the Sinful
at Levi's Great Banquet (5:27-32)

27 Then after this he went out and observed a tax collector by the name of Levi sitting at the tax office, and he said to him, "Follow me!" 28 Leaving behind everything, he arose and followed him.

29 Then Levi gave a great banquet for him in his house, and a large crowd of tax collectors was there and others who were reclining with them. 30 The Pharisees and their scribes were grumbling to his disciples, saying, "Why do you eat and drink with tax collectors and sinners?"

31 But Jesus replied and said to them, "Those who are healthy have no need of a physician, but those who are sick. 32 I have not come to invite the righteous but sinners to repentance!"[2]

Levi abandons tax collecting to follow Jesus (5:27-28)

The words, "then after this" (καὶ μετὰ ταῦτα, 5:27), introduce the audience to a new scene by breaking the pattern in which the three previous

---

[1] "They were filled (ἐπλήσθησαν) with awe" and "they were glorifying (imperfect tense) God" in 5:26; "they were filled (ἐπλήσθησαν) with rage" and "they were discussing (imperfect tense) among themselves" in 6:11; see O'Fearghail, *Introduction to Luke-Acts*, 45.

[2] I shall employ my own translation of the Greek text throughout the book.

scenes were each introduced and connected by the verb "it happened" (ἐγένετο, 5:1; καὶ ἐγένετο, 5:12, 17). After Jesus called his first followers (5:1-11), healed a leper (5:12-16), and both healed and pronounced the divine forgiveness of the sins of a paralytic (5:17-26), he went out and observed a tax collector by the name of Levi sitting at the tax office (5:27). The audience has already heard that even tax collectors came to John to be baptized (3:12) with his baptism of repentance for the forgiveness of sins (3:3). When they asked John what they should do (3:12) to "produce fruits worthy of repentance" (3:8), he said to them, "Stop collecting more than what is prescribed for you!" (3:13). The audience knows that Levi, as a tax collector (τελώνης), that is, an agent employed by a chief tax collector (ἀρχιτελώνης, see 19:2) to collect various tolls, tariffs, duties, and customs from his fellow Jews for the Roman government, is a member of a group notoriously dishonest and corrupt because they collect more than they should, but at least some of whom are open to repentance from their sinfulness.[3]

Whereas tax collectors willing to repent came to John, who challenged them to demonstrate their repentance by being honest within their profession (3:12-13), Jesus takes the initiative with the tax collector Levi, as he observes him "sitting at the tax office" in the business of collecting, and orders him to an even more radical repentance by leaving his sinful profession entirely. Jesus simply issues Levi the succinctly authoritative invitation, "Follow me!" (5:27).

Levi promptly and without question accepted Jesus' challenging invitation as he left behind everything (καταλιπὼν πάντα) involved in the sinfulness of his tax collecting profession, "arose" from his position of "sitting" at the tax office, and followed him (ἠκολούθει αὐτῷ) (5:28). This reminds the audience of the call of the first followers of Jesus (5:1-11). Simon Peter, who confessed to Jesus that he was a sinful man (5:8), together with his fellow fishermen, James and John (5:10), similarly manifested a radical repentance as they left everything (ἀφέντες πάντα) involved in their fishing profession and followed him (ἠκολούθησαν αὐτῷ) (5:11). By these parallels the audience realizes that Levi has joined the group of disciples whom Jesus will empower to "catch people" (5:10) now that they have turned away from their sinfulness and toward Jesus by abandoning their professions and following him. Since John's baptism of repentance was for the forgiveness of sins (3:3; cf. 1:77) and Jesus has just demonstrated his divine authority to forgive sins in his healing of the paralytic (5:24), the audience deduces that Jesus has forgiven the sins of the repentant Levi.

---

[3] On tax collectors, see Fitzmyer, *Luke I-IX*, 469-70; H. Merkel, "τελώνης," *EDNT* 3.348-50; J. R. Donahue, "Tax Collector," *ABD* 6.337-38.

Pharisees question why the disciples eat and drink with the sinful (5:29-30)

In apparent appreciation for what Jesus has done for him in calling him to be his follower and forgiving his sinfulness, Levi, acting as host, extends the hospitality of meal fellowship to Jesus, his honored guest, by giving a great banquet for him in his own house (5:29).[4] That a great crowd of tax collectors was there and others who were reclining with them (5:29) not only adds to the magnitude and festivity of this "great" banquet but underlines the close bond of unity, friendliness, hospitality, and peace with God and with one another that the fellowship of this festive meal creates among the participants. Others were reclining and thus sharing table fellowship "with them" ($\mu\varepsilon\tau$' $\alpha\dot{\nu}\tau\hat{\omega}\nu$), that is, *with* Jesus, Levi, and the great crowd of tax collectors.[5] Since the audience has experienced that tax collectors, although notoriously sinful (3:13), have all repented in the narrative to this point, the presence of a great crowd of tax collectors and others at this feast for Jesus would appear to be favorable. Indeed, Levi may be seen as beginning to fulfill Jesus' promise of empowering those who follow him to "catch people" (5:10).

The Pharisees, who, together with teachers of the law, had come from every village of Galilee, and Judea, and Jerusalem (5:17), and who, together with the scribes, had objected to Jesus extending the divine forgiveness of sins to a paralytic (5:21), now, together with their scribes, were grumbling to the disciples of Jesus (5:30).[6] This is the first use in the narrative of the

---

[4] That Levi "left behind everything" (5:28) refers to "everything" involved in his profession as a tax collector and obviously does not include his house; see Plummer, *Luke*, 159-60; Matson, *Household Conversion*, 81.

[5] On the significance of sharing table fellowship in the ancient world and in the NT, see D. E. Smith, "Table Fellowship," *ABD* 6.302-4. On the table fellowship in 5:27-32, see D. B. Gowler, *Host, Guest, Enemy, and Friend: Portraits of the Pharisees in Luke and Acts* (New York: Lang, 1991) 202-3.

[6] On the Pharisees and scribes in general, see G. Baumbach, "Φαρισαῖος," *EDNT* 3.415-17; idem, "γραμματεύς," *EDNT* 1.259-60; A. J. Saldarini, "Scribes," *ABD* 5.1012-16, esp. 1015 on the scribes in Luke-Acts; idem, "Pharisees," *ABD* 5.289-303. On the characterization of the Pharisees in Luke-Acts, see J. T. Carroll, "Luke's Portrayal of the Pharisees," *CBQ* 50 (1988) 604-21; M. A. Powell, "The Religious Leaders in Luke: A Literary-Critical Study," *JBL* 109 (1990) 93-110; J. D. Kingsbury, "The Pharisees in Luke-Acts," *The Four Gospels 1992: Festschrift Frans Neirynck* (BETL 100; ed. F. Van Segbroeck, et al; Leuven: Leuven University Press, 1992) 1497-512; Gowler, *Host*; Darr, *Character Building*, 85-126.

expression "disciples" for the followers of Jesus (5:1-11, 27-28), and the audience now learns that they also have been participating in the meal fellowship of this great banquet. That the Pharisees and their scribes were grumbling to Jesus' disciples rather than directly to him underscores the close association between Jesus and his disciples. Their "grumbling" (ἐγόγγυζον) at Jesus' disciples recalls for the audience how Israelites of the wilderness generation similarly resisted the leadership of God and Moses and Aaron by "grumbling" against them.[7]

The complaint of the Pharisees and their scribes against Jesus' disciples, "Why do you eat and drink with tax collectors and sinners?" (5:30), raises the issue of the close bond of table fellowship shared "with" (μετὰ) tax collectors and sinners.[8] In referring to tax collectors and "sinners," whereas the narrator had referred to tax collectors and "others" (5:29), the Pharisees and their scribes reveal their negative attitude, in contrast to the audience's positive attitude, toward those participating in the meal fellowship of this great banquet. Ironically, the disciples themselves have recognized their own sinfulness (5:8-10) and repented in following Jesus (5:11, 27-28). But meal fellowship establishes a close religious and social bond among the participants, so that for the Pharisees and their scribes it is against God's will to share such fellowship with publicly recognized sinners. Their complaint serves as the pointed objection from opponents that characterizes the literary genre of controversy or pronouncement stories.

Jesus has not come to invite the righteous but sinners to repentance (5:31-32)

Although the Pharisees and their scribes grumbled to his disciples, Jesus himself, their primary target, answers them with the authoritative pronouncement that climaxes this pronouncement story. He begins to explain to his opponents and to the audience his participation in meal fellowship with tax collectors and sinners by stating that "those who are healthy have no need of a physician (ἰατροῦ), but those who are sick" (5:31). Jesus, whom the audience has previously heard refer to himself as a physician (ἰατρέ, 4:23),

---

[7] LXX Exod 15:24; 16:2, 7-9, 12; 17:3; LXX Num 11:1; 14:2, 27, 29, 36; 16:11; 17:6, 20, 25. See also A. J. Hess, "γογγύζω," *EDNT* 1.256-57; Gowler, *Host*, 199; Darr, *Character Building*, 96.

[8] On the significance of the term "sinners" here, see D. A. Neale, *None But the Sinners: Religious Categories in the Gospel of Luke* (JSNTSup 58; Sheffield: JSOT, 1991) 110-34.

places the tax collectors and sinners into the same category as those he has healed (4:31-40; 5:12-16), especially the paralytic whose healing included Jesus' declaration of the divine forgiveness of his sins (5:17-26).[9] Jesus' sharing of meal fellowship with tax collectors and sinners is part of his ministry of bringing God's healing and forgiveness to those who are sick and sinful.[10]

Jesus concludes his authoritative pronouncement with an expression of the purpose of his mission from God: "I have not come to invite the righteous but sinners to repentance!" (5:32). This statement about Jesus' definitive "coming" (ἐλήλυθα), expressed in the perfect tense denoting a past act with continuing effect, resonates with and develops previous references the audience has heard about the purpose of Jesus' being "sent" on his mission by God.

Applying a reading from Isaiah to himself in the synagogue at Nazareth (4:16-21), Jesus declared that the Spirit of the Lord has sent him to proclaim to captives "liberty" "forgiveness" (ἄφεσιν) (Isa 61:1 in 4:18) and to send away the oppressed "with liberty" or "with forgiveness" (ἐν ἀφέσει) (Isa 58:6 in 4:18), to proclaim the Lord's year of favor (4:19).[11] To the crowds trying to prevent Jesus from leaving them (4:42), he announced that it was divinely necessary (δεῖ) for him to bring the good news of the kingdom of God to other cities also, because "for this purpose I was sent" by God (divine passive)

---

[9] R. Leivestad, "ἰατρός," *EDNT* 2.171.

[10] On the close interrelationship and the common demonic origin of sin and sickness in the apocalyptic-eschatological milieu of the NT, see Heil, "Interpreting the Miracles," 18-21; idem, "Miracles," 640; A. Oepke, "νόσος," *TDNT* 4.1094-95.

[11] The use of the perfect tense for "he has sent" (ἀπέσταλκέν) denotes a present state: "He has sent me and I am here." See M. Zerwick and M. Grosvenor, *A Grammatical Analysis of the Greek New Testament* (vol. 1; Rome: Biblical Institute, 1974) 186. On the meaning of the word ἄφεσις here, see H. Leroy, "ἀφίημι," *EDNT* 1.182: "In connection with Isa 61:1; 58:6 (LXX), Luke 4:18 (bis) uses the word in the sense of *liberation*; yet this is also conceived as *forgiveness*." See also C. Spicq, "ἄφεσις," *Theological Lexicon of the New Testament* (3 vols.; Peabody: Hendrickson, 1994) 1.238-44; L. T. Johnson, *The Gospel of Luke* (SacPag 3; Collegeville: Liturgical Press, 1991) 79; Fitzmyer, *Luke I-IX*, 533; Tannehill, *Narrative Unity*, 1.65-66, 105 R. F. O'Toole, "Does Luke Also Portray Jesus as the Christ in Luke 4,16-30?" *Bib* 76 (1995) 498-522; R. I. Denova, *The Things Accomplished Among Us: Prophetic Tradition in the Structural Pattern of Luke-Acts* (JSNTSup 141; Sheffield: Sheffield Academic Press, 1997) 136-37.

(4:43). Carrying out his mission, Jesus gave the paralytic, made "captive" and "oppressed" by his demonic sickness and sinfulness, an experience of the kingdom of God and of the Lord's year of favor by healing his illness and forgiving or liberating (ἀφέωνταί, 5:20, 23; ἀφεῖναι, 5:21; ἀφιέναι, 5:24) him from his sins.[12] Jesus shares meal fellowship with tax collectors and sinners because he has not "come," that is, not been sent by God, to invite the righteous but sinners to the repentance that enables them to experience the healing forgiveness (cf. 3:3; 1:77) of God's kingdom.

Because of the banquet context the audience hears the connotation of "invite to a banquet" in the Greek verb καλέω, "call," used here by Jesus, which sometimes carries this meaning as it will later in the narrative (7:39; 14:7-10, 12-13, 16-17, 24).[13] Although Levi acted as host when he gave the great banquet for him (5:29), Jesus now speaks as the host who has come in the past (perfect tense) and invited sinners such as Levi (5:27-28) and Simon Peter and his companions (5:8-11) to celebrate their repentance and forgiveness in the meal fellowship of this great banquet, as an anticipation of the great eschatological or messianic banquet.[14] As the audience knows from Isaiah 55:1-7, sinners are invited to repent and receive God's abundant forgiveness in a great eschatological banquet offered by God: "You who are thirsty come to the water...drink wine and milk...eat good things...Let the wicked leave behind his ways and the lawless man his plans and turn to the Lord, and receive mercy, for he will generously forgive your sins" (LXX Isa 55:1-2, 7).

That Jesus has not come to invite the righteous but sinners to repentance (5:32) not only explains to the grumbling Pharisees and their scribes his and his disciples' participation in this great banquet, but also serves as a provocative invitation for these opponents to partake of the great eschatological banquet by repenting of their sinfulness. That Jesus has come and is now here so that his past coming has a continuing effect, as expressed by the perfect tense of the Greek verb, ἐλήλυθα, means that he is still inviting sinners to repent. Although the Pharisees and their scribes may consider themselves righteous in not sharing meal fellowship with tax collectors and sinners, Jesus has not come to invite the righteous. This is a surprising reversal

---

[12] On the "Lord's year of favor" (4:19) and the "kingdom of God" (4:43) as very closely related, if not synonymous, see Tannehill, *Narrative Unity*, 1.68.

[13] J. Eckert, "καλέω," *EDNT* 2.241.

[14] D. E. Smith, "Messianic Banquet," *ABD* 4.788-91, esp. p. 789 on Luke 5:29-32; J. F. Priest, "Messianic Banquet," *IDBSup*, 591-92.

for the audience, since previously in the narrative "righteous" has been a positive attribute (1:6, 17; 2:25). Instead Jesus is inviting his opponents to repent of their sinfulness, like the crowds, tax collectors, soldiers (3:7-14), and disciples (5:1-11, 27-28), in order to join in the meal fellowship they so highly value in the eschatological banquet he will host.[15]

Pragmatics of the Meal Scene in Luke 5:27-32

1) By identifying with Levi, the audience gains a *model for the trust, radical repentance, and gratitude involved in becoming a disciple of Jesus.* Like Levi, the audience is invited to trust in Jesus' powerful command to follow him by leaving their sinfulness behind and gratefully receiving the divine forgiveness Jesus bestows, in order to become fully committed disciples of Jesus.

2) By identifying with Jesus and his disciples in contrast to the Pharisees and their scribes, the audience acquires a *strategy for calling others to repentance.* Rather than dissociating themselves, like the Pharisees and their scribes, from those they consider sinful or inferior, the audience may imitate Jesus and his disciples by sharing meal fellowship and socializing with public sinners and outcasts as a way of leading them to the repentance that will prepare them for the meal fellowship of the great eschatological banquet.

3) By identifying with the Pharisees and their scribes, the audience *realizes the danger of exclusivity.* The exclusivity of the superior minded Pharisees and their scribes warns the audience not to exclude themselves from the continual need to humbly repent of their own sinfulness. If the audience, like the Pharisees and their scribes, exclude others they deem inferior from the close religious and social contact epitomized by the sharing of meal fellowship, they risk excluding themselves from the ultimate meal fellowship of God's great final feast that Jesus will host.

The Disciples Will Fast After They Feast with the Bridegroom (5:33-39)

33 They then said to him, "The disciples of John fast often and offer prayers, likewise also those of the Pharisees, but yours eat and drink." 34 Jesus said to them, "You cannot make the wedding guests fast while the

---

[15] On the theme of repentance in 5:27-32, see Ravens, *Luke,* 144-45; P. Böhlemann, *Jesus und der Täufer: Schlüssel zur Theologie und Ethik des Lukas* (SNTSMS 99; Cambridge: Cambridge University Press, 1997) 102-4.

bridegroom is with them, can you?[16] *35 But the days will come, and when the bridegroom is taken away from them, then they will fast in those days."*

36 He also told them a parable: "No one tears a patch from a new garment and puts it onto an old garment. Otherwise, he will tear the new and the patch from the new will not match the old. 37 And no one puts young wine into old wineskins. Otherwise, the young wine will burst the skins and it will be spilled, and the skins will be ruined. 38 But young wine must be put into new wineskins! 39 Yet no one drinking old desires young, for he says, 'The old is good.'"

The disciples will fast when Jesus, the bridegroom, is taken from them (5:33-35)

Continuing the scene of Levi's great banquet, "they," that is, the Pharisees and their scribes, who grumbled to his disciples about eating and drinking with tax collectors and sinners (5:30), now complain directly to Jesus about his disciples eating and drinking rather than fasting and praying: "The disciples of John fast often and offer prayers, likewise also those of the Pharisees, but yours eat and drink" (5:33). The audience learns that the disciples of the John who "will never drink either wine or strong drink" (1:15) follow in his ascetical footsteps. That they fast (νηστεύουσιν) often and offer prayers (δεήσεις) reminds the audience of the prophetess Anna, who "did not leave the temple, but worshiped with fastings (νηστείαις) and prayers (δεήσεσιν) night and day" (2:37) in supplication and preparation for God's messianic salvation (2:25, 38).[17] By fasting frequently while praying, John's disciples are likewise preparing for the coming salvation of God announced by their master (3:3-6). Since even the Pharisees' own disciples fast and pray to supplicate and prepare for God's future salvation, why are the disciples of Jesus "eating and drinking," feasting rather than fasting?

Jesus once again counters his opponents' objection with a superior pronouncement (cf. 5:31), beginning with a provocative question that forces them to admit and the audience to realize that his disciples' feasting is most appropriate, since they are celebrating the presence in the person of Jesus of the salvation the fasting disciples are supplicating and awaiting: "You cannot

---

[16] "Wedding guests" renders the literal "sons of the bridal chamber." Fitzmyer, *Luke I-IX*, 598: "The use of 'son' expresses the close relationship of the wedding guests so designated to the groom because of the role that they played in attending him on his wedding occasion."

[17] On the fasting and prayers of Anna, see chapter 1.

make the wedding guests fast while the bridegroom is with them, can you?" (5:34). Within the context of Levi's great banquet Jesus indicates the arrival of the great messianic, eschatological banquet that is sometimes pictured as a joyous wedding feast (Isa 54:5-55:5), inasmuch as God is often portrayed as the bridegroom of his people (Hos 2:18, 21; Ezek 16:7-8; Isa 54:5-8; 62:5; Jer 2:2). Since the end-time wedding banquet has now arrived with Jesus as the bridegroom, his disciples, as the wedding guests, must joyously celebrate by feasting rather than fasting.

As long as Jesus, the bridegroom, is with them ($\mu\epsilon\tau$' $\alpha\grave{v}\tau\hat{\omega}\nu$), the disciples, the wedding guests, must appropriately celebrate by eating and drinking (5:34). But, as Jesus predicts, the days will come when the bridegroom is taken away from them ($\grave{\alpha}\pi$' $\alpha\grave{v}\tau\hat{\omega}\nu$) and then they will appropriately fast in those days (5:35). This begins to prepare the audience for the future absence of Jesus and endorses for them, who live in the days when Jesus is absent, the practice of fasting. But the fasting of the disciples of Jesus and hence of the audience will be essentially new and different from that of the disciples of John and those of the Pharisees (5:33). As wedding guests who have already celebrated the presence of the bridegroom by feasting, the disciples and the audience will mark the absence of the bridegroom by fasting in supplication and preparation for the completion of God's eschatological wedding banquet that they have already anticipated.

Jesus parabolically affirms the feasting that brings a new kind of fasting (5:36-39)

Jesus extends his prevailing pronouncement by telling a parable that further explains and provokes: "No one tears a patch from a new garment and puts it onto an old garment. Otherwise, he will tear the new and the patch from the new will not match the old" (5:36).[18] The new garment represents the new situation of the disciples of Jesus feasting while the bridegroom is with them. The old garment represents the old situation of the disciples of John and those of the Pharisees fasting in supplication and preparation for God's future salvific activity. To force the disciples of Jesus, the wedding guests, to fast while Jesus, the bridegroom, is with them would be like trying to repair the old garment with a patch from the new garment. Both would suffer harm. The

---

[18] In 4:23 "parable" means proverb, but here it means similitude or metaphorical comparison. For a fuller explanation of the term and its various meanings, see Fitzmyer, *Luke I-IX*, 600; G. Haufe, "$\pi\alpha\rho\alpha\beta o\lambda\acute{\eta}$," *EDNT* 3.15-16.

new garment would be torn and the old garment would not be repaired with the proper match. By eating and drinking while Jesus is with them but fasting when he will be taken away from them, the disciples of Jesus preserve both the new garment by appropriately feasting and the old garment by appropriately fasting in supplication and preparation for God's future salvific activity they have already tasted.

The parable progresses from clothing imagery to that of drinking wine, befitting the context of the eschatological wedding banquet: "And no one puts young wine into old wineskins. Otherwise, the young wine will burst the skins and it will be spilled, and the skins will be ruined" (5:37). The young wine, like the new garment, represents the new situation of feasting with the presence of the bridegroom, while the old wineskins, like the old garment, represent the old situation of fasting in the absence of God's salvation. But the incompatibility of the new and the old now becomes even more precarious. For the disciples of Jesus to fast while the bridegroom is with them would be like putting "young" (νέον), not yet fully fermented, wine into old wineskins.[19] Not only will the young wine that bursts the old wineskins be spilled and lost, but the old wineskins will also be completely ruined. The disciples conserve the young wine by feasting while Jesus, the bridegroom, is with them as well as the old wineskins by fasting when he is absent.

Moving from a focus on old wineskins (5:37) to new wineskins, the parable, with an emphatic "but" (ἀλλὰ), exclaims the need for new behavior in view of the new salvific situation: "But young wine must be put into new wineskins!" (5:38). It is not a question of merely preserving both the new feasting and the old fasting, but of recognizing the arrival and the significance of the new salvific situation. The young, fresh wine that represents the new feasting must be put into new wineskins that represent a new kind of fasting, a fasting that "contains" or takes into account the significance of the young wine that has now arrived with Jesus, the bridegroom of God's eschatological wedding banquet.

With a third introductory "no one" (οὐδεὶς, 5:36, 37, 39) the parable reaches its climactic conclusion: "Yet no one drinking old desires young, for he says, 'The old is good.'" (5:39).[20] Ironically, the imagery of drinking aged wine now characterizes the old kind of fasting. That no one who drinks old wine from old wineskins he considers to be good wishes to try young wine in

---

[19] G. Schneider, "νέος," EDNT 2.462-63; BAGD, 536.

[20] For a comparison with the Gospel of Thomas, see G. J. Riley, "Influence of Thomas Christianity on Luke 12:14 and 5:39," HTR 88 (1995) 232-34.

new wineskins explains for the audience why the disciples of John and those of the Pharisees are content to fast (5:33) in preparation for God's coming salvation rather than to feast in recognition that God's salvation has already arrived in the person of Jesus as the bridegroom of God's wedding banquet (5:34). While the drinking of the aged wine, the old kind of fasting, is affirmed as good, the audience realizes that the drinking of the young wine, the new kind of fasting that follows upon the feasting, is even better. The disciples of Jesus and those in the audience willing to drink the young, yet to be fermented, wine in new wineskins look forward, by their fasting while the bridegroom is absent (5:35), to the "fermentation" and consummation of God's salvation that already began when the bridegroom of the wedding banquet was present.

It has been suggested that Luke 5:29-39 exhibits features of the Hellenistic banquet symposium, with which the audience would be familiar.[21] The participants of a symposium include a host notable for wealth or status, a chief guest distinguished by wisdom and insight, and other guests, including intruders. A symposium begins with the invitation of the chief guest, followed by a *fait divers*, an incident that sparks a dispute, and concludes with a discussion in which the insight of the chief guest prevails. Levi functions as the wealthy host of the symposium who invites Jesus as the chief guest to a great banquet with a crowd of tax collectors and others as fellow guests (5:29). The Pharisees and scribes serve as the intruders, whose grumbling points out the eating of Jesus and his disciples with tax collectors and sinners as the *fait divers* (5:30). After Jesus responds with insight and wisdom (5:31-32), the symposium setting continues with a further objection by the intruders involving the disciples' eating and drinking (5:33). It concludes with more insightful pronouncements by Jesus, the chief guest (5:34-39).[22]

Pragmatics of the Meal Scene in Luke 5:33-39

Jesus' potent pronouncement (5:34-35) with its parabolic extension (5:36-39) calls for the audience to look upon the old kind of fasting practiced

---

[21] Sterling, *Historiography*, 370-71.

[22] On the features of the Hellenistic symposium, see E. S. Steele, "Luke 11:37-54--A Modified Hellenistic Symposium?" *JBL* 103 (1984) 380-81; Nelson, *Leadership*, 52-54; Darr, *Character Building*, 32-33; R. Garrison, *The Graeco-Roman Context of Early Christian Literature* (JSNTSup 137; Sheffield: Sheffield Academic Press, 1997) 41-47. On the theme of table fellowship in Luke 5:27-39, see Just, *Ongoing Feast*, 130-38.

by the disciples of John and those of the Pharisees (5:33) as good, since it appropriately supplicates and prepares for God's future salvation. The disciples of Jesus, however, who feasted by eating and drinking while Jesus was with them as the bridegroom of God's eschatological wedding banquet, but who will fast when he is taken away from them, model for the audience a new and even better kind of fasting. Because Jesus has already been present as the bridegroom, the audience can practice *a new fasting that is a joyous, hopeful, and assured anticipation of God's final fulfillment of the wedding feast that Jesus has already inaugurated.*

The Disciples Eat Grain Picked on the Sabbath (6:1-5)

1 While he was going through grainfields on a sabbath, his disciples were picking and eating the ears of grain, rubbing them in their hands. 2 Some of the Pharisees said, "Why are you doing what is not lawful on the sabbath?"

3 Replying to them, Jesus said, "Have you not even read what David did when he was hungry, he and those with him? 4 How he entered into the house of God and, taking the loaves of presentation, ate and gave to those with him, even though it was not lawful for anyone to eat them but the priests alone?"

5 Then he said to them, "Lord of the sabbath is the Son of Man!"

Pharisees object to the disciples picking and eating grain on the sabbath (6:1-2)

Resuming the pattern of the introductory ἐγένετο, literally, "it happened" (cf. 5:1, 12, 17), a new scene begins with a temporal notice, "on a sabbath," and a shift in setting as Jesus was going through grainfields and his disciples were picking and eating the ears of grain, rubbing them in their hands (6:1). This scene is closely connected to the two previous scenes by the thematic progression of the disciples eating while with Jesus. The audience has experienced the disciples along with Jesus "eating and drinking" with tax collectors and sinners (5:30), "eating and drinking" rather than fasting while with Jesus, the bridegroom (5:33-34), and now "eating" while with Jesus on a sabbath.

Since Deuteronomy 23:25-26 (LXX) states that one entering into the harvest of his neighbor may collect ears of grain (στάχυς) in his hands (ἐν ταῖς χερσίν) but not put a sickle to the harvest, and may eat (φάγῃ) his fill of grapes while in his neighbor's vineyard but not collect them in a basket, the audience knows that the disciples, who were eating (ἤσθιον) the ears of grain (στάχυας), rubbing them in their hands (ταῖς χερσίν), were not stealing from anyone or taking more than they need, but satisfying their hunger in a divinely approved way. However, by "picking" and "rubbing" they were doing work not permitted on the sabbath, the sacred day of rest, even during the time of harvest (Exod 34:21). Accordingly, some of the Pharisees object, "Why are you doing what is not lawful on the sabbath?" (6:2).[23]

Introducing another controversy, this objection provides yet another link to the previous scenes. The audience has heard the "scribes and the Pharisees" question Jesus' authority to extend the divine forgiveness of sins to the paralytic (5:21). The "Pharisees and their scribes" grumbled to the disciples about eating and drinking with tax collectors and sinners (5:30). "They," that is, the Pharisees and their scribes, complained to Jesus that his disciples eat and drink rather than fast (5:33). And now "some of the Pharisees" object that the disciples and Jesus are doing what is not lawful, that is, not in accord with God's will, on the sabbath (6:2).[24]

Jesus counters the Pharisees with the example of David (6:3-4)

Once again coming to the defense of his disciples (cf. 5:30-31, 33-34), Jesus, who, as the audience has heard, will fulfill the messianic promises associated with his ancestor David (1:27, 32, 69; 2:4, 11; 3:31), counters the objection of the Pharisees with an authoritative scriptural example of this important figure from the salvation history of Israel. With a sarcastic denigration of the objecting Pharisees' scriptural knowledge, "Have you not even read *this*?," Jesus' counter question applies what David "did" ($\dot{\varepsilon}\pi o\dot{\iota}\eta\sigma\varepsilon\nu$) in 1 Samuel 21:2-7, when he and those with him were hungry (6:3), to his opponents' question of why "you are doing" ($\pi o\iota\varepsilon\hat{\iota}\tau\varepsilon$) what is not lawful on the sabbath (6:2). The emphasis that not only David but his companions, "he and those with him," were hungry directs the focus of the Pharisees and of the audience away from the disciples and Jesus doing what is unlawful on the sabbath to the disciples doing what is necessary to satisfy their hunger while with Jesus, the messianic descendant of David, on the sabbath.

Continuing his counter question, Jesus recounts how David entered into the house of God and, taking the sacred "loaves of presentation," the twelve

---

[23] On the significance of the sabbath as a sacred day of worship and rest based on God's rest after creation (Gen 2:1-3), see D. A. Glatt and J. H. Tigay, "Sabbath," *HarperCollins Bible Dictionary*, 954-55; G. F. Hasel, "Sabbath," *ABD* 5.849-56.

[24] On the characterization of the Pharisees in 6:1-5, see Gowler, *Host*, 206-10.

loaves of the "bread of the Presence" set out continually before God as a pledge that sacrifices would continue eternally,[25] ate the loaves himself and gave them to those with him. These were the loaves that it was not lawful for anyone to eat except the priests alone (6:4), when they were replaced with fresh loaves every sabbath (Lev 24:5-9).[26] The audience is to deduce that just as those with David, because they were *with* this scripturally important figure, were allowed to satisfy their hunger by eating loaves "it is not lawful" (6:2) for anyone to eat except the priests alone (on the sabbath), so the disciples with Jesus, because they are *with* the messianic descendant of David, are allowed to satisfy their hunger by doing the work "it is not lawful" (6:4) to do on the sabbath. That it is in accord with God's salvific will as recorded in scripture for the disciples, like those with David, those "with him" (μετ' αὐτοῦ, 6:3-4), to eat on the sabbath because they are with Jesus complements their eating rather than fasting because Jesus, the eschatological bridegroom, is now "with them" (μετ' αὐτῶν, 5:34).

Jesus pronounces his lordship as the Son of Man over the sabbath (6:5)

Jesus climaxes his two unanswered counter questions (6:3-4) with a striking pronouncement that overrides the Pharisees' complaint (6:2) as he said to them, "Lord of the sabbath is the Son of Man!" (6:5). When Jesus declared the divine forgiveness of the paralytic's sins, the audience for the first time in the narrative heard Jesus refer to himself as the Son of Man, an apocalyptic messianic title based on the heavenly figure who functions as an agent of God's kingdom and leader of God's people in Daniel 7.[27] After the scribes and Pharisees accused him of blasphemy, insisting that no one can forgive sins except God alone (5:21), Jesus healed the paralytic so that his opponents may

---

[25] H. Balz, "ἄρτος," *EDNT* 1.160.

[26] On the meaning and background of the "loaves of presentation," see Fitzmyer, *Luke I-IX*, 609.

[27] On the background, meaning, and use of this much disputed term, see C. C. Caragounis, *The Son of Man: Vision and Interpretation* (WUNT 38; Tübingen: Mohr-Siebeck, 1986) 232-50. See also my review of Caragounis in *CBQ* 49 (1987) 665-66. For a discussion of Jesus as the Son of Man in Luke, see C. M. Tuckett, "The Lukan Son of Man," *Luke's Literary Achievement: Collected Essays* (JSNTSup 116; ed. C. M. Tuckett; Sheffield: Sheffield Academic Press, 1995) 198-217, especially p. 216, where he notes how the author never explains the Son of Man title, presupposing his audience's knowledge of its meaning.

know that he, as the Son of Man, a heavenly figure, has divine authority "on the earth" to forgive sins (5:24). Similarly, that Jesus, as the Son of Man, is *lord* over the divine institution of the sabbath, with "lord" (κύριός) as the emphatic introduction to the pronouncement, indicates to the audience that, as the heavenly Son of Man now on earth, Jesus has divine authority to allow his disciples to do the work of satisfying their hunger on the sabbath.

That Jesus, as the Son of Man, is lord of the sabbath means much more for the audience than Jesus being an exception to, being above, or abrogating the law of the sabbath. It means he has the divine authority to begin to fulfill the eschatological hope rooted in the original meaning of the sabbath. As a commemoration of the day on which God rested and set apart as a sacred time after he completed the work of creation (Gen 2:1-3; Exod 20:8-11), every sabbath anticipated the final, unending Sabbath, the sacred time of rest, relaxation, restoration, and refreshment, toward which all of creation was oriented as its consummation.[28] By allowing his disciples to satisfy their hunger and thus restore and refresh themselves after doing the work of picking and rubbing the grain on the sabbath, Jesus, demonstrating his lordship over the sabbath, enables them to experience and anticipate the restoration and refreshment that begins to fulfill the true meaning of the sabbath.[29]

That Jesus has come as the Son of Man, who is lord of the sabbath in the sense of beginning to fulfill the true meaning of the sabbath as a sacred time anticipating the eschatological time of salvation, accords well with what the audience has heard previously about Jesus' messianic mission. The time of the eschatological wedding banquet is anticipated with the presence of Jesus as the bridegroom (5:34). Jesus has been sent to announce the good news of the arrival of the eschatological time of God's kingdom (4:43). On a sabbath (4:16) Jesus declared that the spirit of the Lord has anointed him to proclaim the "year of the Lord's favor" (4:19), an expression of the eschatological time of salvation with associations to the jubilary and sabbatical years that are

---

[28] E. Lohse, "σάββατον," *TDNT* 7.8.

[29] Bovon, *Lukas*, 1.270-71; Nolland, *Luke 1-9:20*, 258. In the next unit of the narrative (6:6-11) Jesus further demonstrates his lordship over the sabbath in terms of fulfilling its original meaning. Before he heals a man with a withered hand on the sabbath, he asks the scribes and Pharisees whether "it is lawful" (cf. 6:2, 4), that is, in accord with God's salvific will for the sabbath, to do good or to do evil on the sabbath, to save life or destroy it (6:9). See also 13:16; 14:3.

closely connected to the concept of the sabbath as a sacred time of God's salvific rest and liberation.[30]

Pragmatics of the Meal Scene in Luke 6:1-5

The Pharisees who object to the disciples doing the work of satisfying their hunger on the sabbath present the audience with a negative model. Unlike the Pharisees, the audience must not allow legal, cultural, or religious practices, such as the prohibition of work on the sabbath, to deprive human beings of such basic and fundamental needs as the satisfaction of their hunger. The audience must realize that *the satisfaction of hunger not only overrides the prohibition against working on the sabbath but actually fulfills the divine intention for the sabbath observance as a sacred time of rest, relaxation, restoration, and refreshment.*

The disciples who are allowed to do the work of satisfying their hunger on the sabbath because they are with Jesus, the messianic descendant of David, provide a positive model for the audience. They invite the audience to experience Jesus, the heavenly Son of Man with divine authority on earth, as *the lord of the sabbath who allows people to satisfy their hunger as an anticipation of the eschatological time of salvific rest and refreshment he has inaugurated.*

Summary

The first three Lukan meal scenes, which are also controversial pronouncement stories (5:27-6:5), begin to demonstrate a variety of dimensions to the theme of eating and drinking in Luke-Acts. It includes the issue of sharing meal fellowship with social outcasts, the religious practice of fasting, and the question of satisfying one's hunger on the sabbath.

The first meal scene (5:27-32) focuses upon the dimension of meal fellowship as Jesus and his disciples eat and drink with tax collectors and sinners at Levi's great banquet, which results in the complaining of the

---

[30] C. J. H. Wright, "Sabbatical Year," *ABD* 5.857-61, especially pp. 860-61 on the eschatological hope associated with the sabbatical year. On the jubilee year associations in 4:16-21, see Kimball, *Jesus' Exposition of the Old Testament*, 109-11. See also R. B. Sloan, *The Favorable Year of the Lord: A Study of Jubilary Theology in the Gospel of Luke* (Austin: Schola, 1977); S. H. Ringe, *Jesus, Liberation, and the Biblical Jubilee* (OBT 19; Philadelphia: Fortress, 1985).

Pharisees and their scribes. Jesus' pronouncement invites the audience to share meal fellowship and socialize with public sinners and outcasts as a way of leading them to the repentance that will prepare them for the meal fellowship of the great eschatological banquet. The audience must not exclude themselves from the continual need to humbly *repent* of their own sinfulness in order to share in the *inclusive meal fellowship* of God's great final feast that Jesus will host.

The second meal scene (5:33-39) concerns the disciples eating and drinking while with Jesus rather than fasting. Jesus' pronouncement with its parabolic extension calls for the audience to look upon the old kind of fasting as good, since it appropriately supplicates and prepares for God's future salvation. But the disciples of Jesus, who feasted by eating and drinking while Jesus was with them as the bridegroom of God's eschatological wedding banquet, but who will fast when he is taken away from them, model for the audience a *new and even better kind of fasting*. The audience can practice a new fasting that joyfully anticipates God's final fulfillment of the wedding feast that Jesus, as the bridegroom, has already inaugurated.

The third meal scene (6:1-5) centers upon the disciples satisfying their hunger while with Jesus on the sabbath. The audience must not allow legal, cultural, or religious practices, such as the prohibition of work on the sabbath, to deprive human beings of such basic and fundamental needs as the *satisfaction of their hunger*, which not only overrides the prohibition against working on the sabbath, but actually fulfills the divine intention of the sabbath observance as a sacred time of rest and refreshment. Jesus' pronouncement invites the audience to experience him as the lord of the sabbath, who allows people to satisfy their hunger as an anticipation of the eschatological time of salvific rest and refreshment he has inaugurated.

CHAPTER 3

JESUS' FIRST MEAL WITH A PHARISEE
LUKE 7:36-50

After encountering the theme of eating and drinking in the sermon on the plain (6:20-49) and in Jesus' testimony about John (7:24-35), the audience hears the next Lukan meal scene, a meal with a sinful woman and a Pharisee (7:36-50), during Jesus' ministry in Galilee (5:1-9:50).[1]

The Theme of Eating and Drinking in the Sermon on the Plain (6:21, 25)

In the second of the four beatitudes (6:20-22) that introduce the sermon on the plain, addressed not only to the disciples (6:20, 17) but to the great crowd of the people from both Jewish ("all of Judea and Jerusalem") and Gentile ("Tyre and Sidon") territory (6:17), Jesus announces: "Blessed are those who hunger now, for you will be satisfied" (6:21).[2] "Those who hunger now" are closely associated with and further specify "the poor" who are blessed by God in the first beatitude because theirs is the kingdom of God (6:20). That the poor (οἱ πτωχοί) already experience the blessing of the kingdom of God develops what the audience has heard Jesus previously state about his mission to bring good news to the poor (πτωχοῖς, 4:18) and to bring the good news of the kingdom of God (4:43). The "poor," grouped with and further described as captives, blind, and oppressed (4:18), refers not only to those who are economically needy but to those who are physically afflicted, socially outcast, lowly, humiliated, and completely dependent upon God's salvific activity.[3]

---

[1] For a discussion of the literary structure in which these next references to eating and drinking occur, see O'Fearghail, *Introduction to Luke-Acts*, 45-46.

[2] For a recent comprehensive treatment of the sermon on the plain, see H. D. Betz, *The Sermon on the Mount: A Commentary on the Sermon on the Mount, Including the Sermon on the Plain (Matthew 5:3-7:27 and Luke 6:20-49)* (Hermeneia; Minneapolis: Fortress, 1995) 571-640.

[3] H. Merklein, "πτωχός," *EDNT* 3.194: "The context in Luke 6:21 suggests that actual poor people are meant. The blessing follows the line of OT and Jewish thinking, according to which the poor stand under God's special protection, though it hardly intends to carry forth the prophetic social criticism directly. It is, rather, a proclamation that exposes the insufficiency of any earthly system of values for the presently commencing eschatological events." See also Seccombe, *Possessions*, 87-93; Marshall, *Luke*, 249; York, *Last Shall Be First*, 97-98; W. E. Pilgrim, *Good News to the Poor: Wealth and Poverty in Luke-Acts* (Minneapolis: Augsburg, 1981) 74-77; D. J. Ireland, *Stewardship and the Kingdom of God: An Historical, Exegetical, and Contextual Study of*

In the person of Jesus and his salvific ministry the poor already experience the kingdom of God (cf. 4:21) that they will inherit fully in the future (6:20). The poor include those afflicted with sickness (4:31-41; 5:12-26) and sinfulness (5:17-26), especially those present for the sermon (6:17-19), who have personally experienced the kingdom of God in the healing and forgiveness that Jesus brings. The poor include those social outcasts, such as the tax collectors and sinners, who have experienced the kingdom of God in their sharing of meal fellowship with Jesus (5:29-32), the bridegroom of the eschatological wedding banquet (5:34). And the poor include the disciples, who are closely related to the sick (4:38-39), who are aware of their own sinfulness (5:8), and who have abandoned everything in their professions to follow Jesus and thus experience the kingdom of God in and with him (5:11, 27-28).

But these "poor ones" are further specified as "those who hunger now," those who lack satisfying nourishment whether physical or spiritual and long for it. They are blessed now for their hunger will eventually be fully satisfied by God (divine passive) (6:21). Although the poor have begun to experience the kingdom of God, they still "hunger" or long for God's full and final salvation. That Jesus, as the Son of Man who is lord of the sabbath (6:5), allowed his disciples, who hungered ($\dot{\varepsilon}\pi\varepsilon$ίνασεν) like David and those with him (6:3), to eat on the sabbath (6:1), which anticipates the time of eschatological salvation, helps to confirm for the audience his promise that those who hunger ($\pi\varepsilon\iota\nu\hat{\omega}\nu\tau\varepsilon\varsigma$) now will be finally satisfied by God. Their hunger will be satisfied by God's final wedding banquet, because the bridegroom of that banquet has already appeared in the person of Jesus (5:34), whose disciples eat and drink (5:33, 29) in anticipation of that ultimate banquet.

In the second of the four woes (6:24-26), which follow and antithetically parallel the four beatitudes, Jesus announces: "Woe to you, those who are filled up now, for you will hunger" (6:25). "Those who are filled up now" further delineate "the rich," who are unfortunate in the first woe because they already have their consolation (6:24). As the opposite of "the poor" (6:20; 4:18), "the rich" include not only those who are economically prosperous, but those who are socially elite, materially satisfied, religiously complacent, self-sufficient, and independent of God. That the rich already have their consolation ($\pi\alpha\rho\dot{\alpha}\kappa\lambda\eta\sigma\iota\nu$) means they are comfortable with their present status and closed to God's future salvific activity, unlike the poor, such as Simeon, who was longing for God's future consolation ($\pi\alpha\rho\dot{\alpha}\kappa\lambda\eta\sigma\iota\nu$) of

the Parable of the Unjust Steward in Luke 16:1-13 (NovTSup 70; Leiden: Brill, 1992) 168-75.

Israel (2:25). Jesus' promise that those who are hungry (πεινῶντες) now will be satisfied (6:21) and his woes to the rich (πλουσίοις, 6:24), as those who are filled up (ἐμπεπλησμένοι) now, but who will hunger (πεινάσετε) later (6:25), develop the dramatic reversal of expectations the audience heard Mary introduce in her Magnificat: God "has filled (ἐνέπλησεν) the hungry (πεινῶντας) with good things, but the rich (πλουτοῦντας) he has sent away empty" (1:53).[4]

Jesus' beatitude and corresponding woe regarding hunger continue to indicate how the Lukan theme of eating and drinking has a spiritual and metaphorical as well as a material and literal dimension. Jesus' authoritative pronouncement that those who hunger now are blessed because they will be satisfied by God (6:21) encourages, comforts, and assures not only those in the audience who are physically hungry, but especially those who are spiritually hungry, that they will receive God's full and final salvation. His threat that those who are filled up now are unfortunate because they will hunger later (6:25) warns the audience that material riches, including food and drink, cannot fully and finally satisfy. It challenges all in the audience, whether rich or poor, to become those who hunger now for the material and spiritual satisfaction that only God can give, so that they will not be hungry later but fully and finally satisfied.

The Theme of Eating and Drinking in Jesus' Testimony about John (7:33-34)

In his application of the parable comparing "this generation," those like the Pharisees and lawyers who reject God's plan for themselves by not being baptized by John (7:30),[5] to children sitting in the marketplace (7:31-32) Jesus states: "For John the Baptist has come neither eating bread nor drinking wine, and you say, 'He has a demon.' The Son of Man has come eating and drinking, and you say, 'Look, a glutton and a drunkard, a friend of tax collectors and sinners'" (7:33-34). The dismissal of John's ascetic lifestyle of eating no bread and drinking no wine as demonic corresponds to the children's

---

[4] See chapter 1 on 1:53. See also Tannehill, *Narrative Unity*, 1.208; York, *Last Shall Be First*, 55-62; Betz, *Sermon*, 586.

[5] York, *Last Shall Be First*, 121. On the characterization of the Pharisees here, see Darr, *Character Building*, 100-101; Gowler, *Host*, 215-18. On the functions of the narrative aside in 7:29-30, see Sheeley, *Narrative Asides*, 114-15.

refusal to weep when a dirge is sung to them.[6] The rejection of Jesus' festive eating and drinking corresponds to the children's refusal to dance when the flute is played for them (7:32).[7]

The audience knows that John's ascetical abstention from food and wine indicates not that he has a demon (7:33) but that he has a special role to play in God's plan of salvation. It was divinely determined before his birth that he "will never drink either wine or strong drink" (1:15). That John and his disciples fast (5:33) accords with his preaching a baptism of repentance for the forgiveness of sins in preparation for God's coming salvation (3:3-6). John's not eating food and not drinking wine is evidence of his own penitence that invites the audience to repent of their sins and prepare for the kingdom of God which Jesus announces and inaugurates (cf. 7:28).

That Jesus has come as the Son of Man, eating and drinking (7:34), recalls for the audience that, as the Son of Man, he is lord of the sabbath, who allowed his disciples to eat and satisfy their hunger on the sabbath (6:1-5). Although Jesus festively eats and drinks in table fellowship with tax collectors and sinners (5:27-32), so that he can be called their "friend," the audience knows that his feasting is not for the purpose of overindulging in gluttony and drunkenness.[8] He has come to invite sinners to repentance (5:32) for the celebration of the eschatological wedding banquet that has begun with his presence as the "bridegroom" (5:34). Complementing John's not eating and drinking in God's plan (cf. 7:30), Jesus' eating and drinking likewise invites

---

[6] Bread and wine are stock terms for food and drink; see Fitzmyer, *Luke I-IX*, 680-81.

[7] On the various ways to interpret the parable in 7:31-32, see, in addition to the commentaries, O. Linton, "The Parable of the Children's Game: Baptist and Son of Man (Matt. XI.16-19=Luke VII.31-5): A Synoptic Text-Critical, Structural and Exegetical Investigation," *NTS* 22 (1975-76) 159-79, esp. 173; W. J. Cotter, "The Parable of the Children in the Marketplace, Q (Lk) 7:31-35: An Examination of the Parable's Image and Significance," *NovT* 29 (1987) 289-304; Neale, *None But the Sinners*, 137-40.

[8] The charge that Jesus was a "glutton and a drunkard" (7:34) may allude to Deuteronomy 21:20 where it designates a rebellious son deserving of death. On the use of φίλος (friend) for Jesus here and its occurrence in the rest of Luke-Acts, see A. G. Brock, "The Significance of φιλέω and φίλος in the Tradition of Jesus Sayings and in the Early Christian Communities," *HTR* 90 (1997) 396-401. Brock notes that in Luke-Acts the term "friend/s" frequently occurs "with references to common meals, hospitality, or alliances" (p. 399).

the audience to repent of their sins in order to share in the inclusive meal fellowship of God's end-time banquet that has begun with Jesus.[9]

Jesus' Meal with a Sinful Woman and Simon the Pharisee (7:36-50)

36 One of the Pharisees asked him to eat with him, and he entered into the house of the Pharisee and reclined at table. 37 And behold a woman, who was a sinner in the city, having learned that he was at table in the house of the Pharisee, brought in an alabaster jar of perfumed ointment. 38 And standing behind him at his feet, weeping, she began to bathe his feet with her tears and was drying them with the hair of her head and was affectionately kissing his feet and anointing them with the perfumed ointment. 39 When the Pharisee who had invited him saw it, he said to himself, "If this man were a prophet, he would know who and what sort of woman this is who is touching him, that she is a sinner."

40 Replying, Jesus said to him, "Simon, I have something to say to you." "Teacher," he said, "Say it." 41 "A certain creditor had two debtors; one owed five hundred denarii, and the other fifty. 42 When they could not repay, he excused both. Which of them then will love him more?" 43 Replying, Simon said, "I suppose the one for whom he excused more." He said to him, "You have judged rightly."

44 Then turning to the woman, he said to Simon, "Do you see this woman? I entered into your house; water you did not give me for my feet,[10] but she has bathed my feet with her tears and dried them with her hair. 45 A kiss you did not give me, but she from the time I entered has not ceased affectionately kissing my feet. 46 With oil you did not anoint my head, but she has anointed my feet with perfumed ointment. 47 Therefore, I tell you, her sins, which were many, have been forgiven, for she has loved greatly. The one to whom little is forgiven, loves little."

---

[9] For a possible source of 7:18-35, see T. L. Brodie, "Again Not Q: Luke 7:18-35 as an Acts-Oriented Transformation of the Vindication of the Prophet Micaiah (1 Kings 22:1-38)," *IBS* 16 (1994) 2-30. On eating and drinking in 7:33-34, see Matson, *Household Conversion*, 80-81.

[10] For the translation, "water you did not pour upon my feet," see O. Hofius, "Fusswaschung als Erweis der Liebe: Sprachliche und sachliche Anmerkungung zu Lk 7,44b," *ZNW* 81 (1990) 171-77.

48 He said to her, "Your sins are forgiven." 49 Then the fellow guests began to say among themselves, "Who is this man who even forgives sins?" 50 But he said to the woman, "Your faith has saved you; go in peace."[11]

---

[11] Recent discussions of 7:36-50 include J. J. Kilgallen, "John the Baptist, the Sinful Woman, and the Pharisee," *JBL* 104 (1985) 675-79; idem, "A Proposal for Interpreting Luke 7,36-50," *Bib* 72 (1991) 305-30; idem, "Forgiveness of Sins (Luke 7:36-50)," *NovT* 40 (1998) 105-16; L. Ramaroson, "'Le premier, c'est l'amour' (Lc 7,47a)," *ScEs* 39 (1987) 319-29; D. A. S. Ravens, "The Setting of Luke's Account of the Anointing: Luke 7.2-8.3," *NTS* 34 (1988) 282-92; B. L. Mack, "The Anointing of Jesus: Elaboration Within a Chreia," *Patterns of Persuasion in the Gospels* (FFNT; eds. B. L. Mack and V. K. Robbins; Sonoma: Polebridge, 1989) 100-104; Gowler, *Host*, 219-26; Neale, *None But the Sinners*, 140-47; J. L. Resseguie, "Automatization and Defamiliarization in Luke 7:36-50," *Literature & Theology* 5 (1991) 137-50; York, *Last Shall Be First*, 118-26; Darr, *Character Building*, 32-35, 101-3; G. Lafon, "Le repas chez Simon," *Études* 377 (1992) 651-60; Corley, *Private Women*, 121-30; J. Delobel, "Lk 7,47 in Its Context: An Old Crux Revisited," *The Four Gospels 1992: Festschrift Frans Neirynck* (BETL 100; ed. F. Van Segbroeck, et al; Leuven: Leuven University Press, 1992) 1581-90; Just, *Ongoing Feast*, 151-55; E. R. Thibeaux, "'Known To Be a Sinner': The Narrative Rhetoric of Luke 7:36-50," *BTB* 23 (1993) 151-60; T. Cavalcanti, "Jesus, the Pentitent Woman, and the Pharisee," *Journal of Hispanic/Latino Theology* 2 (1994) 28-40; I. R. Kitzberger, "Love and Footwashing: John 13:1-20 and Luke 7:36-50 Read Intertextually," *Biblical Interpretation* 2 (1994) 190-206; R. Meynet, "'Celui à qui est remis peu, aime un peu..' (Lc 7,36-50)," *Greg* 75 (1994) 267-80; T. K. Seim, *The Double Message: Patterns of Gender in Luke-Acts* (Nashville: Abingdon, 1994) 88-96; R. C. Tannehill, "Should We Love Simon the Pharisee?: Hermeneutical Reflections on the Pharisees in Luke," *CurTM* 21 (1994) 424-33; B. E. Reid, "'Do You See This Woman?': Luke 7:36-50 as a Paradigm for Feminist Hermeneutics," *BR* 40 (1995) 37-49; idem, *Women*, 107-23; du Plessis, "Applying the Results," 351-52; D. A. Lee, "Women as 'Sinners': Three Narratives of Salvation in Luke and John," *AusBR* 44 (1996) 1-15; Matson, *Household Conversion*, 63-64; Price, *Widow Traditions*, 101-26; J. M. Arlandson, *Women, Class, and Society in Early Christianity: Models from Luke-Acts* (Peabody: Hendrickson, 1997) 158-68.

A sinful woman extends extraordinary hospitality to Jesus in a Pharisee's house (7:36-39)

Since the Pharisees have rejected God's plan for themselves by not being baptized (7:30) with John's baptism of repentance (3:3), it is surprising for the audience that one of the Pharisees now asks Jesus, considered to be a glutton ($\phi\acute{\alpha}\gamma o\varsigma$) and a drunkard, who eats and drinks as a friend of tax collectors and sinners (7:34), to eat ($\phi\acute{\alpha}\gamma\eta$) with him (7:36). The invitation alerts the audience to the beginning of a banquet symposium, in which the Pharisee, a religious leader, functions as the host and Jesus as the chief guest. That Jesus enters into the house of the Pharisee and reclines at table (7:36) for a meal recalls for the audience how he earlier was in the house of the tax collector Levi for a great banquet symposium (5:29).[12] To the Pharisees and scribes who complained about his eating and drinking with tax collectors and sinners at that banquet (5:30) Jesus announced that he has come to call sinners to repentance (5:32). Has Jesus accepted the invitation to eat with this Pharisee in order to call him to repentance?

The words "and behold" ($\kappa\alpha\grave{\iota}$ $\grave{\iota}\delta o\grave{\upsilon}$) draw the audience's attention to a certain woman who was a "sinner in the city" (7:37), strongly suggesting that she is a publicly known prostitute.[13] Having learned that Jesus, considered to be a friend of sinners (7:34), was at table, this woman, publicly known as a sinner "in the city," dares to come to Jesus privately "in the house of the Pharisee," bringing in an alabaster flask of perfumed ointment (7:37). Not having been invited as a guest, she plays the role of an intruder to the symposium.[14] Tension is already aroused for the audience, since Pharisees have previously objected to Jesus' meal fellowship with sinners (5:30; cf. 7:34).

That the woman was "standing behind" Jesus "at his feet" rather than facing him not only corresponds to his position of reclining on a couch facing the table, but begins to describe her extremely humble, shameful, and loving

---

[12] The characters involved in a symposium include a socially respected host, a chief guest noted for wisdom and insight, and other guests, including intruders. A symposium begins with the host's invitation of the chief guest, followed by a *fait divers*, an incident that sparks a dispute, and concludes with a discussion in which the insight of the chief guest prevails. On the similarities of Luke 5:29-39 to the features of the Hellenistic banquet symposium, see chapter 2.

[13] Corley, *Private Women*, 38-39, 124.

[14] On intruders as a feature of symposia, see Nelson, *Leadership*, 53.

gestures of unconventional and extraordinary hospitality focused on the feet of Jesus (7:38). Since the verb "weep" (κλαίω) has occurred previously in the narrative with the meaning of being sad and sorrowful, lamenting and mourning (6:21, 25; 7:13, 32), the audience would understand the woman's weeping as an expression of repentant sorrow for her sinfulness rather than a weeping for joy.[15] That she began to bathe his feet with her tears of sorrowful repentance and was drying them with the hair of her head and was affectionately kissing his feet and anointing them with the perfumed ointment accords with the fundamental meaning of repentance (μετάνοια) as not only a turning away from sinfulness in sorrow and shame but also a humble turning toward and radical acknowledgment of God, or in this case God's agent, Jesus.[16] As the audience knows, Jesus was not only sent by God to call sinners to repentance (5:32) but has the authority to pronounce God's forgiveness of sins (5:20-24). The repentant woman seeks that forgiveness.

The highly unusual way in which the woman performs customary practices of hospitality toward Jesus as the chief guest at this banquet symposium expresses both the humble shame of her repentance and her loving recognition of Jesus' significance as God's agent of forgiveness. Usurping one of the hospitable practices for which the host was responsible, she personally performs the customary task of a household servant to bathe the feet of a guest, yet she does it very intimately from her own body, with her own tears of repentance.[17] She completes this humble task by drying "his feet" with the hair of "her head," an honored part of her own body, disgracefully letting down her hair in the public presence of men.[18] Rather than giving Jesus a simple and conventional kiss of greeting on the cheek, she was affectionately kissing "his feet," expressing both her humble repentance and loving acknowledgment of Jesus.[19] Instead of the normal hospitable practice of

---

[15] In the NT κλαίω never means weeping for joy; see BAGD, 433; H. Balz, "κλαίω," *EDNT* 2.293-94; *contra* Fitzmyer, *Luke I-IX*, 689: "It could also have been a weeping for joy at the realization of the forgiveness of her sins by God that she has already received."

[16] H. Merklein, "μετάνοια," *EDNT* 2.415-19.

[17] Seim, *Double Message*, 94: "...it would indeed have been the host's duty to see that some of the services mentioned were offered to the guest, but it would have been the servant's duty to carry them out....Her actions lie within the area for which a host had responsibility..."

[18] Gowler, *Host*, 223.

[19] The verb for "kiss" here is not the simple φιλέω, but the intensified καταφιλέω, "kiss affectionately"; see Zerwick and Grosvenor, *Grammatical Analysis*, 1.202-3.

anointing Jesus on the head with ordinary olive oil, she was anointing his feet with the fragrant perfumed ointment she had brought in, further indicating both the humility of her repentance and her exuberant appreciation of the worthiness of Jesus. The double mention of the perfumed ointment (7:37, 38), the personal possession that she brought in, frames the very personal and profuse gestures of humble, repentant devotion that involve the parts of her own body.[20]

The striking and startling gestures of the woman function as the *fait divers* of the banquet symposium, the incident that instigates the topic of dispute.[21] The designation of the Pharisee as the one "who had invited him" reminds the audience that, although the woman performed the customary acts of hospitality, the Pharisee is the host who invited "him," Jesus, and not the intruding woman. When the Pharisee saw the woman's gestures, he made a judgment privately, "to himself," about both Jesus and the woman. Although the audience heard Jesus exclaimed as a "great prophet" (7:16) after he raised the only son of the widow (7:16), the Pharisee doubts whether Jesus is a prophet. If he were truly a prophet he would certainly have the insight to know who and what sort of woman this is. The Pharisee sees in the woman's hospitable gestures not loving repentance but the contaminating "touch" of one who is a sinner (7:39).

Jesus replies to the Pharisee's disdain for the sinful woman with a parable (7:40-43)

Whereas the woman remains anonymous, Jesus addresses the Pharisee by his name of Simon, initiating the discussion by informing him that he has something to say to him. This begins the irony for the audience of Jesus

---

[20] Resseguie, "Automatization and Defamiliarization," 141: "The paratactic construction and threefold repetition of *kai* (*and*) allow each of her actions to be foregrounded and to stand out with lavish individuality. 'She began to wet his feet with her tears, *and* she dried them with the hair of her head, *and* kissed his feet *and* anointed them with ointment.' Additionally, the imperfect tense dismisses any notion that her actions are merely perfunctory or unintentional; rather it stresses her effusive and deliberate behaviour ('she *was kissing* his feet and she *was anointing* them with oil'). Furthermore, the phrase, 'and with her hair of her head she dried' his feet, confirms the extraordinary circumstances of her unconventional activity."

[21] Darr, *Character Building*, 32-33; Gowler, *Host*, 219-20.

demonstrating the prophetic insight Simon thinks he lacks.[22] Although Simon may think Jesus does not know who and what kind of woman is touching him (7:39), he knows who Simon is and what he is thinking privately about Jesus and the woman. Simon's reply to Jesus, "Teacher (Διδάσκαλε), say it" (7:40), indicates his willingness to learn from Jesus and possibly begins to open him to repentance. As the audience recalls, the tax collectors willing to repent similarly addressed John the Baptist, "Teacher (Διδάσκαλε), what should we do?" (3:12).

In his role as teacher Jesus presents Simon with a parable of a creditor who had two debtors with debts that differed greatly in monetary value--one owed five hundred denarii, and the other fifty (7:41). Since neither could repay, he excused the debts of both. Jesus allows Simon to answer for himself the question, "Which of them then will love him more?" (7:42).[23] Although betraying a hint of hesitation, Simon demonstrates that he has learned the point of the parable from the "teacher" as he replies with the obvious answer, "I suppose the one for whom he excused more." Jesus immediately affirms his correct answer: "You have judged rightly" (7:43).

That Jesus has forced Simon to judge rightly that the debtor who was excused more will love the creditor more gives Simon the basis for rectifying his wrong judgments about Jesus, the woman, and himself. Although Simon thinks Jesus is no prophet because he does not know the woman is a sinner (7:39), the parable (7:41-43) invites him to compare Jesus with the creditor who forgives debtors (sinners). Although Simon thinks the woman is a sinner, the parable invites him to compare her with the debtor (sinner) who loves the creditor (Jesus) more for being forgiven more. Since Simon thinks that he is not a sinner like the woman, the parable invites him to realize that he compares with neither debtor who was forgiven.[24] The parable enables the audience to

---

[22] Resseguie, "Automatization and Defamiliarization," 143. For the definition of irony and other examples of it in Luke, see J. P. Heil, "Reader-Response and the Irony of Jesus Before the Sanhedrin in Luke 22:66-71," *CBQ* 51 (1989) 271-84; idem, "Reader-Response and the Irony of the Trial of Jesus in Luke 23:1-25," *ScEs* 43 (1991) 175-86.

[23] Although some interpret the verb "will love" (ἀγαπήσει) as meaning "will thank" or "will be grateful to," the more literal sense of "love" should be retained; see Fitzmyer, *Luke I-IX*, 690. "Love" here means much more than "thankfulness" or "gratitude" for the forgiveness of the debts; it refers to a personal acknowledgment of and devotion to the generous creditor.

[24] Nolland, *Luke 1-9:20*, 359; Kilgallen, "Interpreting Luke 7,36-50," 309-14.

realize that Simon needs to repent and be forgiven as a sinner in order to know and love Jesus and in order to appreciate the repentance of other sinners such as the woman.

Jesus points the Pharisee to the woman's great love leading to her forgiveness (7:44-47)

Turning to the woman, Jesus, as teacher (7:40), continues his instruction as he bids Simon, who saw (ἰδὼν) the woman's gestures as the touch of a sinner (7:39), to take a closer look: "Do you see (βλέπεις) this woman?" (7:44). With an emphatic "your" Jesus reminds Simon that "I entered into *your* house" (εἰσῆλθόν σου εἰς τὴν οἰκίαν, 7:44), underscoring that Simon is the host who invited Jesus as a guest (7:39) "into the house of the Pharisee" (7:36, 37).[25] Jesus then draws a stark contrast between "this woman," an uninvited intruder who welcomed Jesus with extraordinary acts of hospitality, and Simon, the host who failed to acknowledge Jesus with even the most ordinary acts of hospitality. Although Jesus entered into "your" (σου), Simon's, house, Simon did not give "me" (μοι), Jesus, the customary water for washing the feet, "but she" (αὕτη δὲ) has bathed "my feet" with her tears of repentance and dried them with her hair (7:44). Simon did not give "me" (μοι), Jesus, a customary kiss of welcome on the cheek, "but she" (αὕτη δὲ) from the time Jesus entered has not ceased affectionately kissing "my feet" (7:45).[26] Simon did not anoint "my" (μου), Jesus', head with the customary oil, "but she" (αὕτη δὲ) anointed "my feet" with perfumed ointment (7:46).[27] In contrast to the woman Simon's utter failure to show any recognition or "love" for the person of Jesus, the forgiving creditor of the parable (7:41-43), confirms for the audience that he corresponds to neither debtor who was forgiven.[28]

---

[25] Gowler, *Host*, 225.

[26] Note the contrast between the simple "kiss" (φίλημά) that Simon neglects and the "affectionate kissing" (καταφιλοῦσά) of the woman.

[27] Note the contrast between the simple oil (ἐλαίῳ) that Simon neglects and the perfumed ointment (μύρῳ) of the woman.

[28] Resseguie, "Automatization and Defamiliarization," 144-45: "...the emphatic position given to the demonstrative pronoun strengthens the contrast between her welcomed behaviour and Simon's neglectful behaviour...Even Jesus' hyberbole, '*from the time I entered* she *did not cease* to kiss my feet, does not characterize the woman's action as excessive, but rather accentuates her extraordinary attentiveness and Simon's total failure...Simon failed to give water for the *feet*, a kiss (for the *cheek*), and oil for the *head*. On the other hand, she wet his *feet*, kissed his *feet*, and anointed his *feet*. The contrast

After the words, "therefore, I tell you," completing the "something I have to say to you" (7:40), Jesus informs Simon that the woman's sins, although they were many, have been forgiven, for she has loved greatly. His further statement that "the one to whom little is forgiven, loves little" confirms that the woman has been forgiven much because her lavish gestures of hospitality indicate that she already loves Jesus much (7:47).[29] Although in the parable (7:41-43) the debtor (sinner) forgiven more "will love" (ἀγαπήσει, 7:42) the forgiving creditor more, the woman has remarkably anticipated her forgiveness since she already "has loved greatly" (ἠγάπησεν πολύ, 7:47) Jesus. Not only will she continue to love Jesus after being forgiven, but she has already loved him by repenting and seeking forgiveness. This woman to whom much is forgiven, loves Jesus much, whether before or after being forgiven.[30]

This further calls for Simon to "judge rightly" (7:43) about Jesus, the woman, and himself. Jesus does indeed have the prophetic knowledge of who and what sort of woman this is who is touching him (7:39), namely, that she is a great sinner whose touching of Jesus demonstrates her great love for him that leads to her many sins being forgiven. It also makes Simon realize that he has not loved Jesus at all, not even a little, since he has not been forgiven even a little. The audience realizes that Simon must repent of his own sinfulness and be forgiven, if even a little, in order to experience who Jesus really is by loving him.[31]

Jesus pronounces the forgiveness of the woman's sins (7:48-50)

After informing Simon that the woman's sins have been forgiven, Jesus declares to the woman, "Your sins have been forgiven" (7:48). Jesus not only has the prophetic knowledge that the woman's sins have been forgiven by God (divine passive), but he has the divine authority to pronounce God's forgiveness of her sins. Jesus' forgiveness of the woman's sins echoes for the

---

emphasizes Simon's failure to do even the minimal, conventional acts which begin in a humble position with the feet and work up to the head, while the woman gives complete, extraordinary, and humble attentiveness to Jesus."

[29] Note that "the one to whom little is forgiven, loves little" does not refer to Simon, who has not loved Jesus even a little nor been forgiven even a little.

[30] An interpretation that sees the woman's loving gestures (7:37-38) as the grateful response to her forgiveness previous to the story undermines the climactic pronouncement of her forgiveness by Jesus.

[31] Meynet, "'Celui à qui est remis peu,'" 267-80.

audience his pronouncement to the paralytic, "Your sins have been forgiven you" (5:20), which demonstrated that Jesus, as the heavenly Son of Man, has the divine authority to forgive sins on the earth (5:24). The audience knows that although it is John's role to give his people knowledge of salvation through forgiveness of their sins (1:77) and to preach a baptism of repentance for the forgiveness of sins (3:3), it is Jesus who actually pronounces the divine forgiveness of sins.

That Jesus, as the chief guest of the banquet, pronounces the woman's forgiveness advances the symposium's discussion among the fellow guests. The question they began to ask among themselves (λέγειν ἐν ἑαυτοῖς), "Who is this man (οὗτός) who even forgives sins (ἁμαρτίας)?" (7:49), raises to a new level Simon's doubt about the identity and significance of Jesus when he said to himself (ἐν ἑαυτῷ λέγων), "If this man (οὗτος) were a prophet" he would know that the woman touching him is a sinner (ἁμαρτωλός) (7:39). Their question recalls for the audience the question of the scribes and Pharisees after Jesus pronounced the forgiveness of the paralytic's sins, "Who is this who speaks blasphemies? Who can forgive sins except God alone?" (5:21). Although the audience can answer these questions, having heard that Jesus, as the Son of Man, is God's agent who has the authority on earth to pronounce the divine forgiveness of sins (5:24), the real question for the audience, the fellow guests, and Simon as a representative of the Pharisees who have not repented (7:30) is whether they, like the woman, will acknowledge and experience who Jesus is by repenting, being forgiven, and loving Jesus.[32]

Jesus' final words of dismissal to the woman complete her personal experience of the peace (1:79) and salvation that, as the audience recalls, John was to make known to his people by the forgiveness of their sins (1:77): "Your faith has saved you; go in peace" (7:50). She individually experiences the "peace on earth" (2:14) that the birth of Jesus as a "savior" who is Christ the Lord brings (2:10). Similar to Simeon, who asked God to dismiss him "in peace" (2:29) after he saw in the infant Jesus "the salvation" God had prepared in the sight of all peoples (2:30), the woman is dismissed "in peace" by the Jesus who gave her an experience of that salvation. She individually experiences "the salvation" John prepared all flesh to see in the person of Jesus (3:6).

Jesus provides Simon and the audience with an additional interpretation of the woman's unusual gestures of hospitality (7:37-38). They demonstrate not only the great love (7:47) but the faith that brings her forgiveness. Her

---

[32] On Simon as an open, teachable character with whom the audience identifies, see Tannehill, "Should We Love Simon the Pharisee?" 432-33.

exemplary faith echoes for the audience that of the gentile centurion whose faith won Jesus' healing of his slave (7:9). That her faith (πίστις) has saved her recalls for the audience how Jesus forgave the sins of the paralytic after he saw the faith (πίστιν) of those bringing the paralytic to him (5:20). Jesus' focus on her faith completes the sharp contrast between the woman and Simon, who lacks the faith that Jesus is a prophet (7:39), and between the woman and the fellow guests, who have raised the question of who Jesus as the forgiver of sins is, but have not yet believed in him like the woman. The faith in Jesus that saved the sinful woman and brought her peace with God and Jesus by the forgiveness of her sins begs to be imitated by the fellow guests, by Simon and his fellow Pharisees, who have thwarted God's plan for themselves (7:30), and by the audience.[33]

Jesus' dismissal of the woman completes the surprising and ironic reversal of expected roles in this meal scene.[34] Although Simon is the host who invited Jesus as the chief guest of the banquet, the uninvited woman has extended to Jesus the acts of hospitality that the host has neglected. Now Jesus plays the role of the host and transforms the uninvited woman into an honored guest as he bestows upon her the kind of fellowship or communion with God and with one another that participation in Jewish meals as social and religious events was expected to create. That the woman's faith in Jesus as the forgiver of sins "has saved" her and placed her in a present state of salvation (σέσωκέν, in the perfect tense expressing the continuing effect of a past act) so that she can go "in peace" (ἐις εἰρήνην) (7:50) means that Jesus, the "bridegroom" of the eschatological wedding banquet (5:34), has extended meal fellowship to her in the form of the eschatological salvation and peace that he brings. The "peace" she now experiences corresponds to the Jewish concept of *shalom*, which refers not just to an absence of hostility but to a state of overall well-being that comes from God and includes being in harmony, concord, or fellowship with one's fellow human beings.[35]

By generously forgiving the repentant woman's many sins and dismissing her with salvation and peace, Jesus, the chief guest, has granted the uninvited woman the meal hospitality and fellowship that Simon, the host, has refused her. Jesus thus implicitly invites his fellow guests, Simon and his fellow Pharisees, who refuse to share meal fellowship with public sinners (5:30; 7:34), as well as the audience, not to disdain the woman as a public

---

[33] On the important role of faith in Jesus for the story, see Kilgallen, "Interpreting Luke 7,36-50," 326-29.

[34] York, *Last Shall Be First*, 125-26.

[35] V. Hasler, "εἰρήνη," *EDNT* 1.395-96; Fitzmyer, *Luke I-IX*, 224-25.

sinner (7:37, 39) but to forgive and accept her as God and Jesus have forgiven and accepted her.

Pragmatics of the Meal Scene in Luke 7:36-50

1) The sinful woman serves as a model for the audience to imitate her humble faith in Jesus' authority and willingness to forgive as well as her repentant love of the person of Jesus, in order to experience true meal fellowship with him by receiving the salvation and peace he grants to repentant sinners. That her many sins were forgiven encourages all in the audience who are aware of their sinfulness, no matter how great their sins, *to seek and receive the divine forgiveness of Jesus.*

2) Simon the Pharisee serves as a model for all in the audience to ask themselves whether they have a sinfulness of which they are unaware or refuse to acknowledge. Jesus invites Simon and the audience, once they have recognized their need to be forgiven, to turn to Jesus with the faith that he can and will forgive them. Then they can realize who Jesus really is by loving him for his forgiveness and experiencing the *new meal fellowship of God's salvation and peace that he brings.*

3) Jesus calls Simon the Pharisee and the audience to allow others, like the sinful woman, the opportunity to repent of their sinfulness, no matter how great, and receive God's forgiveness from Jesus. They are urged *to acknowledge and welcome into the end-time meal fellowship of God's salvation and peace those repentant sinners Jesus has forgiven.*

CHAPTER 4

OVERABUNDANT FEEDING OF CROWDS
LUKE 9:10-17

After references to the theme of eating and drinking in the story of Jesus raising the daughter of Jairus (8:40-56) and in the mission of the twelve (9:1-6), the audience meets the next Lukan meal scene, the miraculously overabundant feeding of crowds by Jesus and his disciples within his ministry in Galilee (9:10-17).

Jesus Commands That the Daughter of Jairus Be Given Something to Eat (8:55)

After Jesus called to the dead daughter of Jairus, "Child, arise!" (8:54), her spirit returned and she immediately arose. That he then ordered that she be given something to eat (8:55) completes her miraculous restoration to life as it confirms her return to the realm of the living where people eat and drink. She may again participate in meal fellowship. But that Jesus, the one who called her back to life, also ordered that she be given something to eat continues to illustrate for the audience the close connection between eating and drinking and salvation in the kingdom of God. That Jesus enables her to eat again coincides with and complements her return to the community of the living as a personal experience of the salvation he brings.[1]

Jesus Tells the Twelve Apostles Not To Take Bread on Their Mission (9:3)

After Jesus sent the twelve apostles (cf. 6:13; 8:1) to preach the kingdom of God and to heal with the power and authority he gave them (9:1-2), he directed them not to take anything for the journey, neither walking stick, nor bag, nor bread, nor money, nor a second tunic (9:3). He impresses upon them and the audience not only the urgency of their mission but that they are to be radically dependent upon God to supply their physical needs through the hospitality of those who welcome them into their homes (9:4-5). In commanding them not to take bread ($\check{\alpha}\rho\tau o\nu$) Jesus teaches them to imitate his own total dependence upon God. When the devil tested whether Jesus is the Son of God by urging him to command a stone to become bread ($\check{\alpha}\rho\tau o\varsigma$), Jesus overcame the test by quoting God's word in Deuteronomy 8:3, "A person does not live on bread ($\check{\alpha}\rho\tau\varphi$) alone" (4:3-4).

---

[1] Bovon, *Lukas*, 1.473: "Essen bedeutete damals weiterleben, sich daran freuen und Gemeinschaft erleben."

Miraculously Overabundant Feeding of Crowds by Jesus and His Disciples (9:10-17)

10 When the apostles returned, they recounted to him what they had done. Taking them along he withdrew privately to a city called Bethsaida. 11 When the crowds learned of this, they followed him. Welcoming them he spoke to them about the kingdom of God, and cured those who had need of healing. 12 As the day began to decline, the twelve approached and said to him, "Dismiss the crowd, so that they may go into the surrounding villages and farms to lodge and find provisions; for we are in a deserted place here." 13 But he said to them, "You give them something to eat." They said, "We have no more than five loaves and two fish, unless we ourselves are to go and buy food for all this people." 14 For there were about five thousand men. Then he said to his disciples, "Make them recline in groups of about fifty each." 15 They did so and made them all recline. 16 Then taking the five loaves and the two fish, and looking up to heaven, he blessed them, broke them, and kept giving them to the disciples to set before the crowd. 17 All ate and were satisfied, and what was left over to them was taken up, twelve baskets of fragments.[2]

Jesus welcomes the crowds who followed him and the apostles to Bethsaida (9:10-11)

When the twelve Jesus chose from his disciples and named "apostles" (6:13) returned from the mission on which he sent (9:2) them, they recounted to him what they had done (9:10). "What they had done" refers to their preaching and proclaiming the good news of the kingdom of God as well as healing the sick (9:1-2, 6). Jesus gave them the power and authority (9:1) to participate in his own ministry of healing (cf. 4:36, 40; 5:17, 24; 6:18-19; 7:21), and sent them as apostles ("sent ones") to extend the mission of preaching and proclaiming the good news of the kingdom of God--the same mission he himself has been sent on by God (cf. 4:18, 43-44; 6:20; 8:1).[3]

After Herod the tetrarch heard "all that was happening" (9:7), he raised the question of the correct and more profound identity of Jesus, "Who then is

---

[2] On 9:10-17 see, in addition to the commentaries: Tannehill, *Narrative Unity*, 1.216-19; Just, *Ongoing Feast*, 156-64; A. Seethaler, "Die Brotvermehrung--ein Kirchenspiegel?" *BZ* 34 (1990) 108-12.

[3] L. Feldkämper, *Der betende Jesus als Heilsmittler nach Lukas* (VeröFfentlichungen Des Missionspriesterseminars St. Augustin bei Bonn 29; St. Augustin, West Germany: Steyler, 1978) 114.

this about whom I hear such things?," and sought to see him (9:9). "Such things" and "all that was happening" include the immediately preceding preaching and healing by the apostles (9:1-6), "what they had done" (9:10). This suggests to the audience that the question of the true identity of Jesus is to be answered on the basis not only of Jesus' own deeds but also those of his apostles.

Whereas Jesus, together with the twelve, had been going around to city and village preaching and proclaiming the good news of the kingdom of God (8:1), and whereas the twelve had been going from village to village proclaiming the good news and healing everywhere (9:6), now Jesus, taking along his twelve apostles, "withdrew privately to a city called Bethsaida" (9:10). That they withdrew "privately" means they withdrew from the crowds to whom they have been preaching and healing, the many crowds who have been coming to Jesus to hear him and be healed (5:15; 6:19; 8:4), the crowds who have been pressing in upon him (8:42, 45).[4] Rather than to "city and village" (8:1) or "village to village" (9:6), they go to the single city named Bethsaida.

Although Jesus withdrew privately with his twelve apostles, the crowds learned of it and followed him. Rather than further withdrawing from the crowds, Jesus received them favorably, welcoming them hospitably. In welcoming ($\dot{\alpha}\pi o\delta\epsilon\xi\dot{\alpha}\mu\epsilon\nu o\varsigma$) them (9:11) Jesus reciprocates the hospitable reception that the crowd gave him earlier, when they welcomed ($\dot{\alpha}\pi\epsilon\delta\dot{\epsilon}\xi\alpha\tau o$) him after he returned from the region of the Gerasenes, for they were all waiting for him (8:40). After Jesus sent his twelve apostles out to preach the kingdom of God and cure ($\dot{\iota}\dot{\alpha}\sigma\theta\alpha\iota$) with the power and authority he gave them to heal ($\theta\epsilon\rho\alpha\pi\epsilon\dot{\upsilon}\epsilon\iota\nu$) (9:1-2), they went around from village to village proclaiming the good news and healing ($\theta\epsilon\rho\alpha\pi\epsilon\dot{\upsilon}o\nu\tau\epsilon\varsigma$) everywhere (9:6). Now Jesus continues to exercise the same mission he gave his apostles, as he himself continues to speak (imperfect tense) to the crowds about the kingdom of God (cf. 4:43; 8:1), and continues to cure ($\dot{\iota}\dot{\alpha}\tau o$, imperfect tense) those who had need of healing ($\theta\epsilon\rho\alpha\pi\epsilon\dot{\iota}\alpha\varsigma$) (9:11).

---

[4] For a discussion of the role of the crowds in Luke-Acts as compared to ancient Greek novels, see R. S. Ascough, "Narrative Technique and Generic Designation: Crowd Scenes in Luke-Acts and in Chariton," *CBQ* 58 (1996) 69-81.

The twelve urged Jesus to dismiss the crowd to find food for themselves (9:12)

That "the day began to decline" (9:12) suggests to the audience the time of the evening meal and the crowd's need for overnight hospitality. The twelve's urging of Jesus to "dismiss" (9:12) the crowd contradicts Jesus' hospitable "welcoming" (9:11) of them. That the twelve expect the crowd to go into the surrounding villages (εἰς τὰς κύκλῳ κώμας) and farms to lodge and find provisions (9:12) indicates to the audience their failure to extend to the crowd the same kind of hospitality they expected to receive from those who welcomed them into their homes, when Jesus sent them on their mission from village to village (κατὰ τὰς κώμας) without provisions (9:3-5). A dismissal of the crowd into the surrounding villages and farms would scatter them and destroy their communal unity around the hospitable Jesus in the single city of Bethsaida.

The twelve's motivation for dismissing the crowd to find food, "for we are in a deserted (ἐρήμῳ) place here" (9:12), reminds the audience of the situation of the people of Israel after their exodus from Egypt, when they were wandering in the desert without food. The whole assembly of Israel grumbled against Moses and Aaron, wishing they had died by the hand of the Lord in Egypt where they ate their fill of bread, "for you have led us into this desert (ἔρημον) to kill this whole assembly with famine" (LXX Exod 16:3; see also Exod 16:1, 10, 14, 32). They did not think God could provide them the hospitality of a meal in the desert: "Surely God cannot prepare a table in the desert (ἐρήμῳ)?..Surely he cannot give bread or prepare a table for his people?" (LXX Ps 77:19-20). Similarly, the twelve do not expect that Jesus can provide the crowds he has welcomed, taught, and healed the hospitality of a meal in a deserted place.[5]

The twelve have only five loaves and two fish to feed all the people (9:13)

Rather than dismissing the crowd to find food for themselves, Jesus emphatically challenges his twelve apostles to return the favor of hospitality they had recently received on their mission (9:3-5). He spoke not to the crowd they want him to dismiss but to *them*: "*You* (ὑμεῖς) give them something to eat" (9:13). Jesus' command that the twelve give (Δότε) the large crowd

---

[5] Note that Bethsaida (9:1) is considered to be in a deserted area and that the twelve do not think the crowds can find enough lodging and food there, but must go into the surrounding villages.

something to eat recalls for the audience the command of the man who brought Elisha, the "man of God," and his servant twenty barley loaves, "Give (Δότε) to the people (τῷ λαῷ) and let them eat" (4 Kgdms 4:42). When the servant questioned how he could give this before a hundred men, he heard the repeated command, "Give (Δὸς) to the people (τῷ λαῷ) and let them eat, for the Lord says, 'They will eat and they will have some left'" (4 Kgdms 4:43).

Similarly, the twelve point out that they do not have enough food for the people. In contrast to Jesus' emphasis that "*you*" (ὑμεῖς) give them something to eat, they reply that "*we*" (ἡμῖν) have no more than five loaves and two fish--even less than twenty barley loaves, unless "*we* (ἡμεῖς) ourselves" are to go and buy food for all this people (9:13). Their "unless" (εἰ μήτι, expecting a negative answer) suggests that Jesus surely does not expect that they, whom he instructed to take no money for their mission (9:3), can purchase enough food. Their designation of the "crowd" (cf. 9:11, 12) as "all this people" (πάντα τὸν λαὸν τοῦτον) underlines their lack of food for so many people. It enhances the audience's association of this "people" with the "people" fed with only twenty barley loaves in the Elisha story. Their reference to the crowd as a "people" (λαός) further indicates the crowd's communal unity. They are not just an amorphous crowd of assorted individuals but a unified community, a "people." That they are a λαός resonates with the previous occurrences of this term in the narrative, which allude to the salvation historical "people of God," who stand in continuity with the chosen people of Israel of old.[6]

The twelve make the five thousand recline in groups of fifty (9:14-15)

The narrator's aside, "for there were about five thousand men" (9:14), further explains to the audience the twelve's dismay about feeding such a large crowd. "All this people" (9:13) includes about five thousand men. Whereas in the Elisha story there were only twenty loaves for a hundred men (4 Kgdms 4:43), here both the insufficient amount of bread and the number of people are intensified, as there are only five loaves for five thousand men. The reference to the large number of five thousand not only underlines the twelve's inability to feed such a quantity, but also further defines the crowd as a large but countable community of "people" whose number includes about five thousand men.

Continuing his hospitable welcome of the people (9:11), Jesus begins to serve as the host of a meal, as he told his disciples to make the people recline

---

[6] See Luke 1:10, 17, 21, 68, 77; 2:10, 32; 3:15, 18, 21; 6:17; 7:1, 16, 29; 8:47; H. Frankemölle, "λαός," *EDNT* 2.340-42.

in groups of about fifty each (9:14). This prepares the audience for a great and festive banquet scene with emphasis upon the communal intimacy of meal fellowship. That the disciples are to make them recline (κατακλίνατε) means they are to make the people lie down or sit down specifically to eat a meal.[7] In the previous meal scene Jesus himself entered into the house of a Pharisee and reclined at table (κατεκλίθη) as a guest of a meal (7:36). The groups (κλισίας) of about fifty each refer to dining groups, to groups of people gathered together specifically to share meal fellowship.[8] The crowd that includes about five thousand men are thus to be divided, ordered, and unified into smaller groups of about fifty each, appropriate for sharing the intimacy of meal fellowship. That the disciples obeyed Jesus and made "all" recline (κατέκλιναν) places this entire large crowd of people into their proper positions as guests for a vast banquet with Jesus and his disciples as their hosts (9:15).

Jesus gave the food to the disciples to set before the people (9:16)

Acting as the host, Jesus took the five loaves and the two fish (9:16), the insufficient amount of food provided by his disciples (9:13).[9] He then looked up to heaven (9:16), the heaven that the audience recalls opened when Jesus was praying during his baptism, allowing the holy Spirit to descend upon him (3:21-22). The voice of God then came from heaven and announced that "you are my beloved Son, with you I am well pleased" (3:22). Jesus thus looks to heaven as the source of his Father's divine Spirit which gave him the power (δύναμις) to perform his previous miracles of healing and expelling unclean spirits.[10] His "looking up to heaven" (ἀναβλέψας εἰς τὸν οὐρανὸν) as part of his prayer over the food resonates with Job 22:26-27 (LXX): "Then you shall have boldness before the Lord, looking up to heaven (ἀναβλέψας εἰς τὸν οὐρανὸν) cheerfully. When you pray to him, he will hear you..."

---

[7] BAGD, 411. The verb for "recline" here, κατακλίνω, occurs only in Luke in the NT.

[8] See 3 Macc 6:31; EDNT 2.300-301; BAGD, 436.

[9] Marshall, Luke, 361: "The language used to describe his action indicates the usual action of the host at a meal, taking the food, giving thanks for it, and distributing it."

[10] Note especially Luke 4:14: "Jesus returned in the power (δυνάμει) of the Spirit into Galilee." See also 4:18, 36; 5:17; 6:19; 8:46; 9:1; Bovon, Lukas, 1.472.

In accord with Jewish meal practice Jesus blessed the loaves and fish before he broke them into pieces for distribution (9:16).[11] That he blessed them while looking up to heaven means that he called down God's gracious power upon them from heaven, the source of that power. The blessing of heavenly power upon the broken pieces enables Jesus to "keep giving" (ἐδίδου) the broken pieces to the disciples (9:16), indicating to the audience the miraculous multiplication of the food.[12] That Jesus kept giving the food to the disciples "to set before" the crowd (9:16) underlines for the audience the hospitable dimension of this meal, as the verb "to set before" (παραθεῖναι) refers to the serving of food as a sign of hospitality.[13]

The audience realizes that Jesus has transformed the twelve disciples, who urged him to dismiss the crowd whom they could not provide with the hospitality of a meal in the desert (9:12), into his agents of hospitality. As the host he not only directed them to make the crowd recline as his guests for a meal in convenient dining groups (9:14), but kept giving them, who could provide only five loaves and two fish (9:13), enough food to set before the entire crowd of his dinner guests. The twelve disciples Jesus earlier empowered to preach and heal everywhere (9:1-2, 6) he now empowers to provide "all this people" (9:13) the hospitality of a marvelous meal.

After all ate and were satisfied, there were twelve baskets of leftovers (9:17)

That "all" (πάντες) that is, "all" (πάντα) this people (9:13) who include about five thousand men (9:14), "all" (ἅπαντας) whom the disciples made recline for the meal (9:15), ate and were satisfied (9:17) further confirms the miraculous multiplication of the insufficient amount of food Jesus blessed.[14] That all ate and were satisfied (ἐχορτάσθησαν) begins to fulfill for

---

[11] H. Patsch, "εὐλογέω," *EDNT* 2.79: "...Jesus says the blessing...before he breaks the bread, in the same way as the father in the Jewish household." J. Wanke, "κλάω," *EDNT* 2.296: "The Gospels place Jesus in the role of the Jewish head of the household when he breaks bread at the feeding of the crowd."

[12] "Kept giving" translates the imperfect tense of ἐδίδου, which expresses duration and perhaps repetition; see Zerwick and Grosvenor, *Grammatical Analysis*, 1.212; Nolland, *Luke 1-9:20*, 444.

[13] P. Trummer, "παρατίθημι," *EDNT* 3.22. See also Luke 10:8; 11:6; Acts 16:34; 1 Cor 10:27.

[14] Marshall, *Luke*, 363: "Luke places πάντες in an emphatic position."

the hungry crowd what the audience heard Jesus promise in his beatitudes: "Blessed are those who hunger now, for you will be satisfied (χορτασθήσεσθε, divine passive)" (6:21). This recalls for the audience how in the OT God abundantly satisfied and promised to satisfy his people in the future with food: "In the days of famine they will be satisfied (χορτασθήσονται, divine passive)" (LXX Ps 36:19); "he (God) satisfied (ἐχόρτασεν) them with honey from the rock" (LXX Ps 80:17); "I (God) will abundantly bless her provisions; I will satisfy (χορτάσω) her poor with bread" (LXX Ps 131:15). God is once again abundantly satisfying his people with food through Jesus and his twelve apostles.

Not only did all the people eat to satisfaction, but they had more than enough, an overabundance. That twelve baskets of fragments were left over to them after all ate (ἔφαγον) and were satisfied (9:17) reminds the audience of the overabundance provided by God in the Elisha miracle. Elisha's servant was told to give the mere twenty loaves to the people that they may eat, "for the Lord says, 'They will eat (Φάγονται) and have some left.' And they ate (ἔφαγον) and had some left according to the word of the Lord" (4 Kgdms 4:43-44). But Jesus has outdone the Elisha miracle. Whereas Elisha, through the miraculous power of God, fed a hundred men with twenty loaves and had some left, Jesus, after calling down God's blessing from heaven, feeds a crowd that includes about five thousand men with only five loaves and two fish and provides twelve baskets of leftovers. Jesus' hospitable and festive feeding not only to satisfaction but to overabundance of such a large crowd of the people of Israel suggests to the audience that this miraculous meal in the desert is a unique anticipation of the eschatological, messianic banquet, at which there is expected to be an overabundance of food and drink (Isa 25:6-8; 55:1-2; Jer 31:14; Joel 2:24-26; Amos 9:13-15).

The twelve baskets of fragments or broken pieces (κλασμάτων) underline Jesus' miraculous multiplication of the food, as they greatly exceed the amount of the original five loaves and two fish Jesus broke (κατέκλασεν) for distribution (9:16). That there are twelve baskets of leftover fragments means that there is one basket of overabundant food for each of the twelve apostles (9:12, 10). The number "twelve" symbolically alludes to the division of the people of Israel into twelve tribes based on the twelve sons of Jacob/Israel. Although most of these tribes disappeared in the course of history, it was expected that in the end-time, messianic age of salvation the people of Israel would be reconstituted by a renewed division into twelve tribes.[15] This suggests to the audience that Jesus has empowered his twelve

---

[15] T. Holtz, "δώδεκα," *EDNT* 1.362-63.

apostles to feed not only this particular crowd of the people of Israel but future crowds as well. Indeed, Jesus has provided his twelve apostles with twelve baskets of abundant food, enough to feed the renewed twelve tribes of the people of Israel in the messianic kingdom of God, which Jesus and his twelve apostles are bringing about by teaching, healing, and hospitably feeding the people (9:1-2, 6, 11).

Herod raised for the audience the question of Jesus' true identity based on the preaching and miraculous healings of both Jesus and his apostles (9:9). Although some thought Jesus was John the Baptist raised from the dead (9:7), Herod dismissed this identification, because he himself had beheaded John (9:9). Others thought Jesus was Elijah or one of the prophets of old (9:8). But Jesus' empowerment of his apostles to overabundantly feed the vast crowd reveals to the audience that Jesus surpasses the prophet Elijah, who multiplied food for only a widow and her son (1 Kgs 17:7-16), as well as Elijah's prophetic successor, Elisha, who wondrously fed a hundred men with twenty loaves (2 Kgs 4:42-44). Peter, as spokesman for the twelve who experienced Jesus' miraculously overabundant feeding of the people as a unique anticipation of the messianic banquet of God's kingdom, confesses the more profound identity of Jesus: "You are the Christ of God!" (9:18-20).

Relation of Luke 9:10-17 to Previous Meal Scenes

1) The overabundant feeding develops the *theme of the arrival of the eschatological messianic banquet of the kingdom of God with the person of Jesus*. In the first Lukan meal scene (5:27-32) Levi, who repented by turning away from his sinful tax collecting profession and becoming a follower of Jesus (5:27-28), served as host and Jesus as the honored guest of a "great banquet" which began to hint at the arrival of the messianic banquet. At this "great banquet" Jesus shared the hospitality of meal fellowship with such outcasts as tax collectors and sinners in order to call them to repentance (5:29-32), so that they may experience the messianic salvation that he brings by the divine forgiveness of their sins (1:77; 3:2; 5:24). The disciples eat and drink rather than fast because of the presence of Jesus as the "bridegroom" of the eschatological wedding banquet (5:33-34). Because the disciples are with Jesus, the messianic Son of Man who is lord of the sabbath, they eat grain picked on the sabbath, anticipating the end time meal of rest and refreshment that the sabbath foreshadows (6:1-5). Now Jesus and his twelve apostles serve as the hospitable hosts and the crowd of people as the honored guests of a miraculously overabundant meal that anticipates the abundance of salvific benefits in the messianic banquet of God's kingdom.

2) The overabundant feeding develops the *role of the disciples in the meal scenes*. Along with Jesus the disciples were guests who shared meal

fellowship with tax collectors and sinners at Levi's great banquet (5:30). They eat and drink rather than fast because they are guests of Jesus, the bridegroom (5:34). They ate picked grain on the sabbath as guests of Jesus, the Son of Man who is lord of the sabbath (6:1-5). Jesus sent out his twelve chosen disciples to be guests dependent upon the hospitality of those whom they heal and to whom they preach (9:3-4). Now Jesus has transformed the twelve into hosts, so that they may give the crowd of people an experience of the kingdom of God (9:2, 11) by hospitably feeding them as an additional part of their mission of healing them and bringing to them the good news of God's kingdom (9:1-6).

3) The overabundant feeding *broadens the scope of those who have participated in the meals*. Whereas Jesus has shared meal fellowship with a large crowd of tax collectors and sinners (5:27-32), with his disciples (5:33-6:5), and with Simon the Pharisee, a sinful woman, and other guests (7:36-50), he now hospitably feeds a vast crowd of the people of Israel which includes about five thousand men.

4) The overabundant feeding develops the *salvific benefits received from Jesus in the meal scenes*. At Levi's great banquet Jesus offered tax collectors, sinners, the Pharisees, and their scribes the opportunity to repent in order to experience the salvation of forgiveness (5:27-32). He allowed his disciples to celebrate his presence as the bridegroom by feasting rather than fasting (5:33-39). He permitted his disciples to do the work of satisfying their hunger on the sabbath and thus experience the salvific refreshment the sabbath anticipates (6:1-5). At the meal with Simon the Pharisee he bestowed divine forgiveness and salvific peace upon a lovingly repentant sinful woman (7:36-50). Now he feeds a huge crowd with a physical satisfaction and overabundance that anticipates their complete satisfaction, physical and spiritual, in the kingdom of God (1:53; 4:4; 6:21).

5) The overabundant feeding develops the *reciprocal dynamics of hospitality at work in the meal scenes*. Jesus not only accepted hospitality as the honored guest at Levi's great banquet, but also offered hospitality by functioning as a physician to those who are sick, calling sinners to repentance (5:27-32). Although Jesus accepted Simon the Pharisee's offer of meal hospitality, it was the sinful woman, an uninvited intruder, rather than Simon, who acted as the true host by welcoming Jesus with loving gestures of hospitality. Jesus reciprocated her hospitality by pronouncing the divine forgiveness of her sins and dismissing her in the salvific peace her faith won for her (7:36-50). By welcoming the crowd and overabundantly feeding them, Jesus reciprocates the hospitality the crowd extended to him when they welcomed him upon his return from the region of the Gerasenes (8:40). He also teaches his twelve apostles, previous recipients of his special meal

hospitality (5:33-6:5), to reciprocate the meal hospitality they received from those who welcomed them during their mission (9:3-4), as he empowers them to overabundantly feed the crowd.

Pragmatics of the Meal Scene in Luke 9:10-17

1) The audience experiences the more profound messianic identity and character of Jesus that surpasses his identification as John the Baptist, Elijah, or one of the prophets of old (9:7-9), and that complements his character as a healer and preacher of the good news of the kingdom of God. As followers of Jesus like the crowd, the audience is called to believe in the Jesus who warmly welcomes them as his guests to share in the meal hospitality of the messianic banquet in the kingdom of God that he is inaugurating. They are to realize that Jesus has the miraculous divine power not only to heal them but *to overabundantly satisfy both their physical and spiritual hunger.*

2) Although the audience may think, like the twelve apostles, that they do not have the resources to welcome and feed the vast crowds of hungry people in the world, they are called to place their faith in the Jesus who has inaugurated the end-time messianic banquet. They are to trust in his miraculous divine power to enable them not only to heal and proclaim the good news of the kingdom of God, but to provide hungry people with the kingdom's hospitality by both *materially and spiritually feeding them to an overabundant satisfaction.*

3) Jesus not only teaches but empowers the audience *to graciously reciprocate the hospitality* they can expect to receive as his apostles sent into the world.

CHAPTER 5

JESUS' MEAL WITH MARTHA AND MARY
LUKE 10:38-42

The audience meets the next reference to the theme of eating and drinking (10:7-8) in Jesus' instructions for the mission of the seventy-two disciples in the introductory section (9:51-10:37) of the travel narrative in which Jesus makes his way to Jerusalem (9:51-19:48). The next meal scene, Jesus' meal with the sisters Martha and Mary (10:38-42), occurs at the beginning of the second section of the travel narrative (10:38-11:54).[1]

Jesus Instructs the Seventy-Two To Eat and Drink What They Are Offered (10:7-8)

While on his way to Jerusalem Jesus instructs the seventy-two he sent out before him to remain in the same household that has accepted their greeting of peace (10:6-7). They are to accept the meal hospitality they are offered by eating and drinking what the household has, for the laborer is worthy of his pay. They are not to move from house to house. Rather, in whatever town they enter that welcomes them, they are to eat what is set before them (10:7-8).[2] This develops for the audience the theme of meal hospitality offered to those Jesus sends on a mission. The twelve apostles were not to take bread on their mission, but to depend on the hospitality of those who welcome them (9:3-4). So also the seventy-two are to depend upon and graciously accept the meal hospitality they are offered by the households that welcome them.[3]

Jesus' Meal in the Home of Martha and Her Sister Mary (10:38-42)

38 As they were going along, he entered into a certain village, and a certain woman by the name of Martha welcomed him. 39 She had a sister named Mary, who sat alongside at the feet of the Lord and was listening to his word.

---

[1] For a discussion of these sections of the travel narrative, see O'Fearghail, *Introduction to Luke-Acts*, 54-56.

[2] D. P. Moessner, *Lord of the Banquet: The Literary and Theological Significance of the Lukan Travel Narrative* (Minneapolis: Fortress, 1989) 139: "But when the Seventy(-two) are told to remain in the same house before moving ahead to another town, the reasoning is now clear. They are to establish a 'banquet fellowship' where the presence of the coming King is celebrated and anticipated as the 'eating and drinking' of salvation."

[3] For a detailed discussion of the household mission of the seventy-two, see Matson, *Household Conversion*, 26-52.

40 But Martha was completely preoccupied over much service. She came up and said, "Lord, does it not concern you that my sister has left me alone to do the serving? Tell her then to help me."

41 But the Lord said to her in reply, "Martha, Martha, you are worried and troubled over many things. 42 But one thing is necessary.[4] *For Mary has chosen the best portion, which will not be taken away from her."*[5]

---

[4] For the choice of this reading over its variants, see B. M. Metzger, *A Textual Commentary on the Greek New Testament* (New York: United Bible Societies, 1971) 153-54; J. A. Fitzmyer, *The Gospel According to Luke X-XXIV* (AB 28A; Garden City: Doubleday, 1985) 894. Some have argued that the longer reading, "a few things are necessary or one" (ὀλίγων δέ ἐστιν χρεία ἤ ἑνός), is not a conflation, but to be preferred as the more difficult reading. See G. D. Fee, "'One Thing Needful?' Luke 10:42," *New Testament Textual Criticism: Its Significance for Exegesis: Essays in Honour of Bruce M. Metzger* (eds. E. J. Epp and G. D. Fee; Oxford: Clarendon, 1981) 61-75; idem, "The Use of Greek Patristic Citations in New Testament Textual Criticism: The State of the Question," *Studies in the Theory and Method of New Testament Textual Criticism* (SD 45; eds. E. J. Epp and G. D. Fee; Grand Rapids: Eerdmans, 1993) 356-57; Corley, *Private Women*, 138-40; J. L. North, "ὀλίγων δέ ἐστιν χρεία ἤ ἑνός (Luke 10.42): Text, Subtext and Context," *JSNT* 66 (1997) 3-13.

[5] On 10:38-42, in addition to the commentaries, see B. Witherington, *Women in the Ministry of Jesus: A Study of Jesus' Attitude to Women and Their Roles as Reflected in His Earthly Life* (SNTSMS 51; Cambridge: Cambridge University Press, 1984) 100-103; E. J. Via, "Women, the Discipleship of Service, and the Early Christian Ritual Meal in the Gospel of Luke," *St. Luke's Journal of Theology* 29 (1985) 37-60; J. Brutscheck, *Die Maria-Marta Erzählung: Eine redaktionskritische Untersuchung zu Lk 10, 38-42* (BBB 64; Frankfurt: Hanstein, 1986); idem, "Lukanische Anliegen in der Maria-Marta Erzählung: Zu Lk 10,38-42," *Geist und Leben* 62 (1989) 84-96; E. Schüssler Fiorenza, "A Feminist Critical Interpretation for Liberation: Martha and Mary: Lk. 10:38-42," *Religion and Intellectual Life* 3 (1986) 21-36; idem, "Theological Criteria and Historical Reconstruction: Martha and Mary: Luke 10:38-42," *Center for Hermeneutical Studies Protocol Series* 53 (1987) 1-12; Tannehill, *Narrative Unity* 1.136-38; J. R. Donahue, *The Gospel in Parable: Metaphor, Narrative, and Theology in the Synoptic Gospels* (Philadelphia: Fortress, 1988) 134-39; F. Beydon, "A temps nouveau, nouvelles questions: Luc 10,38-42," *Foi et Vie* 88 (1989) 25-32; R. W. Wall, "Martha and Mary (Luke 10.38-42) in the Context of a Christian Deuteronomy," *JSNT* 35 (1989) 19-35; L. Alexander, "Sisters in Adversity: Retelling Martha's Story," *Women in the Biblical Tradition* (Studies in

Martha welcomed Jesus and her sister Mary was listening to him (10:38-39)

Jesus' determined journey to Jerusalem (9:51-62), which has seemingly been at a standstill (10:1-37), begins to move again. The travel notice, "as they were going (πορεύεσθαι) along" (10:38), reminds the audience of the beginning of the journey, when Jesus and his disciples (cf. 10:23) were going (πορευομένων) on the way (9:57), after Jesus had "set his face" to go (πορεύεσθαι) to Jerusalem since the days of his being taken up were being fulfilled (9:51). Jerusalem was the place where he would fulfill his exodus from suffering and death to heavenly glory (9:31). He had sent messengers "before his face," and going (πορευθέντες), they entered into a Samaritan village to prepare for him (9:52). But the Samaritans did not receive him, because "his face was going" (πορευόμενον) to Jerusalem (9:53), so Jesus and his disciples went (ἐπορεύθησαν) into another village (9:56).

In contrast to the Samaritans who did not receive (ἐδέξαντο) Jesus with hospitality because he was going to Jerusalem (9:53), after his messengers entered (εἰσῆλθον) into their village (κώμην) to prepare for him (9:52), Martha warmly welcomed (ὑπεδέξατο) him as a guest into the hospitality of her home after he entered (εἰσῆλθεν) into her village (κώμην) while on his way to Jerusalem (10:38). Martha extends to Jesus the kind of hospitality, which implies a meal, that he instructed his disciples to depend upon while on their missionary journeys (9:3-4; 10:7-8). She continues for the audience the theme of neighborly hospitality demonstrated by the good Samaritan, who proved to be a true neighbor by caring for a traveling Jew victimized by robbers (10:34-37).

That Martha's sister Mary "sat alongside at the feet of the Lord" (10:39) places her in a position not only of a guest at the meal along with Jesus and his disciples, but also of a disciple herself, attentively and zealously sitting at the feet of the master, receptive and ready to learn (cf. 8:35; Acts 22:3).[6]

Women and Religion 31; ed. G. J. Brooke; Lewiston: Mellen, 1992) 167-86; Corley, *Private Women*, 133-44; Darr, "'Watch How You Listen'," 101-2; Seim, *Double Message*, 97-112; I. M. Fornari-Carbonell, *La escucha del huésped (Lc 10,38-42): La hospitalidad en el horizonte de la communicación* (Institución San Jerónimo 30; Estella: Verbo Divino, 1995); W. Carter, "Getting Martha Out of the Kitchen: Luke 10:38-42 Again," *CBQ* 58 (1996) 264-80; Matson, *Household Conversion*, 69-70; Reid, *Women*, 144-62; Price, *Widow Traditions*, 175-90.

[6] R. Bergmeier, "πούς," *EDNT* 3.143: "Pupils 'sit at the *feet*' of the teacher." See also Marshall, *Luke*, 452; Witherington, *Women*, 101; Fitzmyer, *Luke X-XXIV*, 893: "Her position is that of a listening disciple."

For a woman to join the male guests at a meal as well as to assume the role of a disciple was very unusual for first-century Palestinian Judaism.[7] But Mary's position as a disciple of Jesus is confirmed for the audience as she "was listening to his word" (10:39).

That Mary was listening (ἤκουεν) to the word of Jesus in the position of a disciple while Jesus is on his final journey to Jerusalem alerts the audience to her obedience of God's heavenly pronouncement to the disciples at the transfiguration of Jesus. After Jesus was speaking with the heavenly Moses and Elijah about his exodus from earthly to heavenly life which he was about to fulfill in Jerusalem (9:31), God thundered: "This is my chosen Son; listen (ἀκούετε) to him!" (9:35). God is emphatically directing the disciples, who saw the heavenly glory of Jesus but did not hear the conversation about his exodus (9:31-32), to listen to the words Jesus has just spoken before his temporary transfiguration into a heavenly figure. After Peter confessed Jesus to be the Christ of God (9:20), Jesus told his disciples that it is divinely necessary for him as the Son of Man to suffer many things and be rejected by the elders, chief priests, and scribes, and be killed, but raised on the third day (9:22). Mary is listening to the word of Jesus that includes a call for disciples to realize that Jesus will attain heavenly glory only after his rejection, suffering, and death.

That the disciple Mary is attentively hearing the word (λόγον) of Jesus (10:39) reminds the audience of Jesus' own extremely strong insistence upon his disciples' attentive hearing of the "words" that predict his suffering and death, shortly after God's command to hear his chosen Son at the transfiguration (9:35): "You (emphatic ὑμεῖς) place these words (τοὺς λόγους τούτους, cf. 9:28) into your ears: The Son of Man is going to be delivered into the hands of men" (9:44).[8] There follows, however, the narrator's emphatic expression of the disciples' dramatic failure to understand these words: "But they did not understand this saying, and its meaning was concealed from them so that they could not comprehend it. They were even afraid to ask him about this saying" (9:45). By attentively listening to the word of Jesus in the context of a meal, Mary, a female disciple, is in a position to understand the necessity of Jesus' journey to suffer and die in Jerusalem, which the male disciples are unable to understand at this point.

But listening to the word of Jesus on his final journey to Jerusalem involves more than understanding the divine necessity of his suffering and

---

[7] Marshall, *Luke*, 452; Witherington, *Women*, 101; Corley, *Private Women*, 135.

[8] On the emphasis, see Zerwick and Grosvenor, *Grammatical Analysis*, 1.215.

death. After Jesus' first prediction of his rejection, suffering, death, and resurrection (9:22) he invited his audience not to be ashamed of his "words" that call them to actively follow him: "Then he said to all: 'If anyone wishes to come after me, let him deny himself and take up his cross daily and follow me. For whoever wishes to save his life will lose it, but whoever loses his life for my sake will save it. What does it profit a person to gain the whole world but lose or forfeit himself? For whoever is ashamed of me and these words of mine, the Son of Man will be ashamed of, whenever he comes in his glory and in the glory of the Father and of the holy angels'" (9:23-26). By attentively listening to the word (λόγον) of Jesus (10:39) on his way to Jerusalem, Mary is in a position not only to understand the necessity of his suffering and death but to avoid being ashamed of "these words of mine" (τοὺς ἐμοὺς λόγους, 9:26) by putting them into practice, appropriating the suffering and death of Jesus into her daily life as a disciple.

Sitting at the feet of Jesus and listening to his word does not make Mary an ideal model of passive contemplation or silent subordination for the audience, since the word of Jesus demands the action of putting it into practice.[9] The audience knows of Jesus' insistence that hearing must include doing his words. If Mary not only hears the words of Jesus but does them, she will be like a person building her house on a foundation of rock (6:47-48). But if she hears the words of Jesus and does not do them, she will be like a person

---

[9] On Mary as a model of silent submissiveness and therefore of Luke's denigration of women disciples, see Schüssler Fiorenza, "Feminist Critical Interpretation," 21-36; idem, "Theological Criteria," 1-12. For a recent favorable assessment of Schüssler Fiorenza's interpretation, see Corley, *Private Women*, 136-42. Interpretations that see in Mary the denigration of women disciples fail to consider adequately the narrative context of the story with Jesus' insistence that hearing must include doing the word. The figures of Mary and Martha, as well as the actions of hearing and doing the word, are not antithetical but complementary; Feldkämper, *Der betende Jesus*, 185: "Das 'Hören' ist die Voraussetzung des 'Tuns,' und nur im 'Tun' bewährt und bewahrheitet sich das 'Hören'." See also J. Nolland, *Luke 9:21-18:34* (WBC 35B; Dallas: Word Books, 1993) 603. For an argument that the Mary-Martha story is concerned with the integration of women into Jesus' ministry of the word, rather than with the relation between action and contemplation, see Carter, "Martha," 264-80. For the state of the question on whether Luke is positive or negative toward women as disciples, and for suggestions that he is even more positive than previously thought, see Karris, "Women and Discipleship," 1-20.

building a house without a foundation (6:49). Mary's hearing the word of
Jesus gives her the opportunity to embrace it with a generous and good heart
and bear fruit through perseverance (8:15). By not only hearing but doing the
word of God that Jesus speaks (5:1; 8:11), Mary can be a sister in Jesus' true
family (8:21). Hearing the word of Jesus as a disciple enables Mary to
represent Jesus himself by not only hearing but speaking the word. Jesus said
to his disciples: "Whoever hears you hears me, and whoever rejects you rejects
me, but whoever rejects me rejects the one who sent me" (10:16). Hearing the
word of Jesus as a disciple associates Mary with the disciples whom Jesus
pronounces blessed because they now see and hear what many kings and
prophets longed to see "but did not see it, and to hear but did not hear it"
(10:24).[10]

Martha was preoccupied with the service of meal hospitality (10:40)

While Mary was sitting at the feet of the Lord, attentively listening to
his word (10:39), Martha "was completely preoccupied over much service"
(10:40) in preparing the meal for her guests.[11] The audience views Martha's
extreme concern with the hospitality of meal "service" ($\delta\iota\alpha\kappa\sigma\nu\acute{\iota}\alpha\nu$) as quite
natural and legitimate, since this is the way women have responded to Jesus
previously. After Jesus healed Simon Peter's mother-in-law, she gratefully
"served" ($\delta\iota\eta\kappa\acute{\sigma}\nu\epsilon\iota$) them at table (4:39), an important part of the more general
"service" involved in discipleship.[12] The many women who accompanied
Jesus and the twelve apostles on their journey of preaching and proclaiming the
good news of the kingdom of God (8:1-2) "served" ($\delta\iota\eta\kappa\acute{\sigma}\nu\sigma\upsilon\nu$) them from
their own possessions (8:3), which included but was not limited to serving

---

[10] For this connection, see Darr, "'Watch How You Listen'," 87-105.

[11] Note how the redundance and alliteration of the Greek make this an
emphatically strong expression: $\pi\epsilon\rho\iota\epsilon\sigma\pi\tilde{\alpha}\tau\sigma$ $\pi\epsilon\rho\grave{\iota}$ $\pi\sigma\lambda\lambda\grave{\eta}\nu$ $\delta\iota\alpha\kappa\sigma\nu\acute{\iota}\alpha\nu$, literally,
"she was over-occupied over much service." See W. Köhler, "$\pi\epsilon\rho\acute{\iota}$," EDNT
3.72; see also "$\pi\epsilon\rho\iota\sigma\pi\acute{\alpha}\sigma\mu\alpha\iota$," EDNT 3.76.

[12] On the service of Peter's mother-in-law in 4:39, see chapter 1. On
Martha's service referring to the more general service involved in the
leadership and ministry of a disciple, see Carter, "Martha," 268-76.

meals.[13] Furthermore, Martha's concern for the hospitality of serving a meal associates her with the service of Jesus and the twelve apostles, who provided the hospitality of an overabundant meal for the huge crowd as part of their mission of proclaiming the kingdom of God (9:10-17). As the host, Jesus himself took, blessed, and broke the five loaves and two fish (9:16), and he directed his disciples to share with him the tasks of meal hospitality by making the crowd recline (9:14) and by setting before the crowd the food he had miraculously multiplied (9:16).

The narrator's statement to the audience about Martha's preoccupation with all of the "service" (διακονίαν) involved in preparing the meal is reinforced by Martha's pleading question and request as she came up to Jesus and said, "Lord, does it not concern you that my sister has left me alone to do the serving (διακονεῖν)? Tell her then to help me" (10:40). Martha, with her question introduced by οὐ, expects Jesus to agree with her.[14] She appeals not only to Jesus' concern that her sister has inappropriately left her alone to do all the work of serving but to his authority as Lord to tell Mary to help her because she is her sister.[15] But Martha's point that Mary is her sister rings ironic for the audience, who has heard Jesus tell those who informed him that his mother and his brothers wanted to see him (8:19-20): "My mother and my brothers are those who are hearing and doing the word of God" (8:21). By hearing the word of Jesus, which is the word of God (5:1; 8:11), Mary is appropriately acting as a sister of Jesus, not just of Martha (cf. 14:26).

---

[13] Fitzmyer, *Luke I-IX*, 698; Bovon, *Lukas*, 1.400; Nolland, *Luke 1-9:20*, 367; idem, *Luke 9:21-18:34*, 604; Corley, *Private Women*, 110-19; Witherington, *Women*, 118: "Being Jesus' disciples did not lead these women to abandon their traditional roles in regard to preparing food, serving, etc. Rather, it gave these roles new significance and importance, for now they could be used to serve the Master and the family of faith. The transformation of these women involved not only assuming new discipleship roles, but also resuming their traditional roles for a new purpose."

[14] On this grammatical expectation, see Zerwick and Grosvenor, *Grammatical Analysis*, 1.222.

[15] On Martha and Mary as partners in ministry, see Carter, "Martha," 275-76. Note how the alliteration of the Greek (μέλει...μου μόνην με) emphasizes the concern (μέλει) Jesus should have for Martha because Mary is "my" (μου) sister who has left "me" (με) alone (μόνην).

Mary has chosen the best portion of the meal (10:41-42)

The "Lord" (cf. 10:40) whose authoritative consideration and command Martha sought indicates his affectionate yet chiding concern for all that she is doing to prepare the meal as he begins his reply by repeating her name: "Martha, Martha, you are worried and troubled over many things" (10:41).[16] That Martha is "worried" (μεριμνᾷς) reminds the audience of the "worries" (μεριμνῶν) that choke those who have heard the word of God (8:14). Jesus' remark that Martha is not only "worried" but also "troubled," "disturbed," or "agitated" (θορυβάζῃ) over many things (περὶ πολλά) reinforces the narrator's report to the audience that Martha was completely preoccupied over much (περιεσπᾶτο περὶ πολλὴν) service for the meal (10:40).[17] The "many things" include all the details involved in the "much" service of preparing the meal and imply that Martha is very concerned to provide a number of dishes or courses for a special meal of hospitality.[18]

In contrast to Martha's worry and agitation over "many things" with an implication of many courses or dishes for the meal, Jesus insists that "one thing is necessary" with an implication that only one dish or course is

---

[16] For other expressions in Luke-Acts of Jesus' affectionate and/or reproachful concern for individuals by repeating their names, see Luke 22:31 (Simon); Acts 9:4; 22:7; 26:14 (Saul); see also Plummer, *Luke*, 291. Note how the alliteration of "Martha, Martha, you are worried" (Μάρθα Μάρθα, μεριμνᾷς, 10:41) counters the alliteration of the "concern" that "my" sister has left "me alone" (μέλει...ἡ ἀδελφή μου μόνην με, 10:40).

[17] This is the only occurrence in the NT of the verb θορυβάζω; see G. Schneider, "θόρυβος," *EDNT* 2.153-54. Its unusualness led scribes to replace it in some manuscripts with the more common and synonymous τορυβάζω; see Plummer, *Luke*, 291-92; Marshall, *Luke*, 453; Fitzmyer, *Luke X-XXIV*, 894. It is a strong expression that Johnson (*Luke*, 174) translates as "you are putting yourself in an uproar." Corley (*Private Women*, 140) overinterprets when she sees a "communal connotation" in the verb because its cognates are used elsewhere in Luke-Acts in a communal context.

[18] Plummer, *Luke*, 292. Although Marshall (*Luke*, 453) does not think that "many things" necessarily refers to a number of courses or dishes, the context of preparing an especially hospitable meal for Jesus, the "Lord" (10:40, 41), and the contrast with Mary's choice of the "best portion" (10:42) of the meal strongly imply it.

necessary for the meal (10:42).[19] The play on the essential elements of the meal continues as Jesus indicates to Martha that he is not concerned that her sister has left her alone and that he will not tell her to help serve the meal (10:40), for (γὰρ) Mary has chosen the "best portion,"[20] the best course or dish of the meal, which will not be taken away from her (10:42).[21] By listening to the word of Jesus (10:39) on his way to Jerusalem, Mary has chosen the best "portion," the one necessary course or dish of the meal.[22] But Jesus' insistence that one thing is "necessary" (χρεία), listening to his word, reminds the audience of the key content of that word which God (9:35) and Jesus (9:44) have insistently urged the disciples to heed, namely, that it is "necessary" (δεῖ), in accord with God's plan, that Jesus go to Jerusalem to suffer, be rejected by the Jewish authorities, and be killed, before being raised on the third day (9:22; cf. 9:44). The necessary part of the meal is to hear the word of Jesus about the necessity of his suffering and death, which the disciples do not yet understand (9:45).

By declaring that Mary has chosen the best portion of the meal by listening to his word, Jesus affirms her position, although she is a woman, not only as a disciple but as a guest of the meal. In alliterative and ironic contrast to Martha, who is troubled and worried (Μάρθα Μάρθα, μεριμνᾷς, 10:41) about providing many dishes as the hospitable hostess of the meal, Mary, as a guest, has calmly chosen the best portion (Μαριὰμ...μερίδα, 10:42), the one

---

[19] A. Sand, "χρεία," *EDNT* 3.473: "In Luke 10:42, by putting ἑνός in first position and appropriately rendering the text, the contrast between 'one' and 'many' comes even more clearly to expression: Only one thing is necessary, which is to hear the word."

[20] "Best" portion is literally "good" portion, but the positive degree of the adjective is often used for the superlative when speaking of a group or class of things, in this case, the many courses or dishes of the meal. See Zerwick, *Biblical Greek*, 48-49; Fitzmyer, *Luke X-XXIV*, 894.

[21] On the significance of the γὰρ in 10:42, J. J. Kilgallen ("A Suggestion Regarding *Gar* in Luke 10,42," *Bib* 73 [1992] 255-58) notes that "a reason is being given for something unexpressed but real in the dialogue between Martha and Jesus. Jesus has not forgotten Martha's request to him, nor its 'justification'; he answers her in the elliptical way that a Greek *gar* permits" (p. 258).

[22] Fitzmyer, *Luke X-XXIV*, 894: "The word *meris*, 'part,' is used in the LXX for a portion of food (Gen 43:34; Deut 18:8; 1 Sam 1:4), but also for 'portion' in a higher sense (Pss 16:5; 119:57)."

necessary dish, of the meal Jesus is hosting.[23] Despite Martha's earnest request that Jesus tell Mary to help her serve the meal she is hosting, Jesus assures her that the best portion, listening to his word, of the meal he is hosting "will not be taken away" from Mary by Jesus, Martha, or anyone else, including God.[24]

Mary's choice of the best portion ($\mu\epsilon\rho\acute{\iota}\delta\alpha$) that will not be taken away from her (10:42) complements the lawyer's question to Jesus, "What must I do to inherit ($\kappa\lambda\eta\rho o\nu o\mu\acute{\eta}\sigma\omega$) eternal life?" (10:25). The audience knows that the words "portion" or "part" ($\mu\epsilon\rho\acute{\iota}\varsigma$; $\mu\acute{\epsilon}\rho o\varsigma$) and "inheritance" or "share" ($\kappa\lambda\eta\rho o\nu o\mu\acute{\iota}\alpha$; $\kappa\lambda\tilde{\eta}\rho o\varsigma$) are often used together and synonymously in the biblical tradition to express the acquisition of eschatological promises.[25] By listening to the word of Jesus on his way to Jerusalem, Mary is choosing the best "portion" and thus doing what is necessary, in addition to loving God and one's neighbor as oneself (10:26-28), to "inherit," that is, to acquire her portion or share, of eternal life.[26] The audience realizes that before a disciple can serve Jesus like Martha, he or she must first listen to the word of Jesus like Mary, the word that calls disciples to a service that recognizes the necessity of his suffering and death before his resurrection (9:22, 35, 44). Such service includes following him by denying oneself and taking up one's cross daily in order to save one's life (9:23-25) and inherit eternal life (10:25).

Relation of Luke 10:38-42 to Previous Meal Scenes

1) The Martha and Mary meal scene advances the *theme of Jesus as the bringer of the eschatological banquet.* Although the bridegroom of the end

---

[23] Darr ("'Watch How You Listen'," 102) also notes the alliterative word play between Martha being "worried" ($\mu\epsilon\rho\iota\mu\nu\tilde{\alpha}\varsigma$) and Mary's "portion" ($\mu\epsilon\rho\acute{\iota}\delta\alpha$), and draws a relation to the "worries" ($\mu\epsilon\rho\iota\mu\nu\tilde{\omega}\nu$) that choke the growth of the word like thorns in the explanation of the parable of the sower in 8:14.

[24] The verb, "will not be taken away," can also be understood as a divine passive. According to Marshall (*Luke*, 454) the "best portion" is Mary's "inalienable right and possession, guaranteed by Jesus."

[25] See, for example, Ps 15:5 (LXX): "The Lord is the portion ($\mu\epsilon\rho\acute{\iota}\varsigma$) of my inheritance ($\kappa\lambda\eta\rho o\nu o\mu\acute{\iota}\alpha\varsigma$) and of my cup; You are the one who restores my inheritance ($\kappa\lambda\eta\rho o\nu o\mu\acute{\iota}\alpha\nu$) to me." See also J. H. Friedrich, "$\kappa\lambda\eta\rho o\nu o\mu\acute{\epsilon}\omega$," *EDNT* 2.298-99; idem, "$\kappa\lambda\tilde{\eta}\rho o\varsigma$," *EDNT* 2.299-300; H. Balz, "$\mu\epsilon\rho\acute{\iota}\varsigma$," *EDNT* 2.409; G. Nebe, "$\mu\acute{\epsilon}\rho o\varsigma$," *EDNT* 2.409-10.

[26] Plummer, *Luke*, 290; Feldkämper, *Der betende Jesus*, 185.

time wedding banquet has arrived in the person of Jesus so that the disciples must feast rather than fast (5:33-34), the days are coming when the bridegroom will be taken away from them (5:35), which points to Jesus' suffering, rejection, and death. As the bridegroom and the host of the overabundant meal which prefigures the final messianic meal (9:10-17), Jesus acts as the host who offers Mary the one necessary dish, the best portion of the meal (10:42), namely, his word about the necessity of his suffering, death, and resurrection in Jerusalem (9:22, 35, 44). It is by his death and resurrection that Jesus will bring about the ultimate banquet of the kingdom of God.

2) The Martha and Mary story promotes the *theme of discipleship in the meal scenes*. In the overabundant feeding story (9:10-17) Jesus transformed his disciples, who had been guests at previous meals (5:30, 34; 6:1-5; 9:3-4), into his fellow hosts whom he miraculously empowered to serve the crowds a magnificent meal of hospitality as an additional part of their mission of healing and preaching the good news of God's kingdom (9:1-6). But in order for them to become "hosts" who serve Jesus as his disciples, like Martha, they must first become "guests," like Mary, who choose the best portion of his meal, the one necessary dish (10:42), by listening to his word about the necessity of his suffering, death, and resurrection. The word of Jesus calls for disciples to serve him by denying themselves, taking up their cross daily, following him, and losing their lives for his sake in order to save them (9:22-24) and inherit eternal life (10:25).

3) The meal involving the sisters Martha and Mary develops the *role of women in the meal scenes*. Martha stands in the line of those women who have previously "served" Jesus with meal hospitality (4:39; 8:2-3). But in contrast to the Samaritans who refused to receive Jesus (9:52) and as an example of the kind of hospitality his disciples are to depend upon in their mission (10:7-8), Martha is the first to welcome Jesus into her home and prepare a meal of hospitality for him while he is on his way to suffer, die, and be raised in Jerusalem (10:38, 40). The repentant sinful woman performed humble and loving gestures of hospitality focused on the feet of Jesus at a meal (7:38) and in return received his divine forgiveness (7:47-49) and salvific peace (7:50). Similarly, Mary humbly sits at the feet of Jesus, attentively listening to his word, and thus chooses the best portion, the one necessary dish, as a guest of his meal (10:42). By listening to the word of God that Jesus speaks, Mary, the sister of Martha, acts also as a sister of Jesus (8:21).

4) The Martha and Mary story develops the *salvific benefits Jesus offers in the meal scenes*. At Levi's great banquet Jesus offered the opportunity to repent in order to experience salvific forgiveness (5:27-32). His presence as the bridegroom allowed his disciples to feast rather than fast (5:33-39). He permitted his disciples to do the work of satisfying their hunger on the sabbath

(6:1-5). At the meal with Simon the Pharisee he bestowed divine forgiveness and salvific peace upon a repentant sinful woman (7:36-50). He fed a huge crowd with an overabundance that points to their complete physical and spiritual satisfaction in the kingdom of God (9:10-17). And now Mary has chosen and Martha is offered the best portion of his meal, the one necessary dish, listening to his word about the necessity of his salvific death and resurrection in Jerusalem. By listening to the word of Jesus as the best portion of the meal, Mary illustrates what Jesus proclaimed to the devil at his temptation: "Not by bread alone will a person live!" (LXX Deut 8:3 in 4:4).[27]

5) The Martha and Mary episode continues the *dual role of Jesus as both the guest and the host* of previous meal scenes. Levi invited Jesus as a guest to a great banquet, which anticipates the messianic wedding feast that Jesus as the bridegroom is hosting (5:27-6:5). Simon the Pharisee invited Jesus to his home as the chief guest of a symposium banquet, but Jesus usurped the role of the host from Simon as he treated the uninvited sinful woman as a welcome guest to whom he extended forgiveness and whom he dismissed in salvific peace in accord with the hospitality of meal fellowship (7:36-50). Although Martha welcomes Jesus as a guest for a meal, Mary relates to Jesus as the host who provides the best portion, the one necessary dish of the meal.

Pragmatics of the Meal Scene in Luke 10:38-42

1) Warmly welcoming Jesus and hospitably serving him as a disciple by preparing a meal for him on his way to Jerusalem, Martha presents all in the audience, both men and women, with a model for them to imitate. The audience is encouraged *to welcome and hospitably serve their fellow Christians*, who represent Jesus himself (10:16) when they are engaged in continuing his ministry of bringing the kingdom of God to others (10:1-12).

2) Mary demonstrates to the audience the necessity of attentively *listening to the word of Jesus in order to serve him properly as a disciple.* Before one can hospitably serve Jesus, he or she must first choose the "best portion," the one necessary dish, of the messianic banquet he is hosting by listening to his word. Listening to the word of Jesus includes not only understanding the divine necessity of his suffering and death in Jerusalem before being raised (9:22, 35, 44). It also calls all in the audience to follow Jesus by denying themselves, taking up their cross daily, and losing their lives for his sake in order to save them (9:23-25) and inherit eternal life (10:25).

---

[27] On Luke 4:4, see chapter 1.

3) Indicating the complementarity of hearing and doing the word of God that Jesus speaks (5:1; 6:46-49; 8:15), Martha and Mary demonstrate to the audience that *women as well as men can become disciples and members of Jesus' family*, by not only hearing but doing the word of God (8:21). All who wish to serve Jesus are invited to become his guests and choose the best portion of the banquet he is hosting by hearing and doing his word.

4) That Jesus was hospitably welcomed and given a meal by Martha encourages the audience to depend upon the hospitality of those to whom they bring the good news of the kingdom of God (10:1-12). But like Jesus and Mary they must be focused not on the many things involved in hospitality but on the one necessary thing, the word of Jesus. Proclaiming the good news of the kingdom of God and serving Jesus as a disciple must be informed by *the word of Jesus about the divine necessity of his suffering and death* before being raised and bringing about the ultimate banquet of the kingdom of God.

CHAPTER 6

JESUS' SECOND MEAL WITH A PHARISEE
LUKE 11:37-54

Immediately after the meal scene with Martha and Mary (10:38-42) the theme of eating and drinking appears again when Jesus teaches his disciples how they are to pray (11:1-13). The audience encounters the next meal scene, Jesus' second meal with a Pharisee (11:37-54), at the conclusion of the second section of the travel narrative (10:38-11:54) of Jesus on his way to Jerusalem (9:51-19:48).[1]

The Theme of Eating and Drinking in Jesus' Teaching about Prayer (11:1-13)

The meal scene with Martha and Mary began as Jesus was going to Jerusalem and entered into a certain village (κώμην τινά) where a certain (τις) woman named Martha welcomed him (10:38). Similarly, when Jesus was praying in a certain place (τόπῳ τινὶ), in correspondence to his having sent the seventy-two to every city and place (τόπον) where he was about to come (10:1), a certain one (τις) of the disciples asked him to teach them to pray, just as John taught his disciples (11:1). As Mary was listening to the word of Jesus (10:39) so the disciples are listening to Jesus teach them how they are to pray.[2]

The disciples are to pray that God, whom Jesus teaches them to address as "Father" (11:2), keep giving them daily their necessary bread (11:3).[3] Jesus teaches his disciples and the audience to imitate his faithful dependence upon God as the Father, who fills the hungry with good things (1:53). When tested as the Son of God (3:22, 38), Jesus did not command the stone to become bread (4:3), but remained faithfully dependent upon the Father, who satisfies not only physical hunger but the hunger that bread alone cannot satisfy: "Not by bread alone will a person live!" (LXX Deut 8:3 in 4:4). That Jesus, after

---

[1] For a discussion of the second section of the travel narrative, see O'Fearghail, *Introduction to Luke-Acts*, 55-56.

[2] On the teaching about prayer in 11:1-13, see Feldkämper, *Der betende Jesus*, 178-205; Tannehill, *Narrative Unity*, 1.237-40; F. Plymale, *The Prayer Texts of Luke-Acts* (New York: Lang, 1991) 50-56; Shepherd, *Holy Spirit*, 141-43.

[3] For the translation "our necessary (ἐπιούσιον) bread" or "the bread that we need" and discussions of other possible meanings of the difficult word ἐπιούσιος, see Marshall, *Luke*, 459-60; Fitzmyer, *Luke X-XXIV*, 904-6; Johnson, *Luke*, 177-78; C. Müller, "ἐπιούσιος," *EDNT* 2.31-32.

praying to his Father by looking up to heaven, blessed the bread and fish and kept giving (ἐδίδου) them to the disciples to place before the crowd (9:16) bolsters his instruction for the disciples and the audience to pray that God keep giving (δίδου) them daily the bread they need (11:3). That Jesus is on his way to suffer, die, and be raised in Jerusalem when he teaches the disciples and the audience to pray that God keep giving them their necessary bread daily (καθ' ἡμέραν, 11:3) reminds them of their dependence upon God for the sustenance they need to deny themselves, take up their cross daily (καθ' ἡμέραν), and follow him (9:23).

Jesus assures his disciples and the audience that their prayer for God to keep giving them daily the bread they need will certainly be answered (11:9-10). Just as a friend will give a persistent friend three loaves (ἄρτους) he needs for the sake of hospitality (11:5-8), so God will give those who ask the bread (ἄρτον) they need (11:3). Just as a father will not give his son a poisonous snake or scorpion if he asks for a fish or egg to eat (11:11-12), so the heavenly Father will not give anything harmful but rather the Holy Spirit to those who ask him (11:13).

Jesus Dines with Another Pharisee (11:37-54)

37 While he was speaking, a Pharisee invited him to dine with him; so he entered and reclined at table. 38 When the Pharisee saw this, he was surprised that he did not first wash before the meal. 39 But the Lord said to him, "Now you Pharisees clean the outside of the cup and of the dish, but the inside of you is full of greed and wickedness. 40 Fools! Did not the one who made the outside also make the inside? 41 But as to the things that are inside give alms, and behold everything is clean for you! 42 But woe to you Pharisees! For you pay tithes on mint and rue and every herb, but neglect justice and the love of God. These things one ought to do, without neglecting the others. 43 Woe to you Pharisees! For you love the front seat in the synagogues and greetings in the marketplaces. 44 Woe to you! For you are like unmarked tombs over which people walk without knowing it."

45 One of the lawyers said to him in reply, "Teacher, in saying these things you are also insulting us." 46 So he said, "Woe also to you lawyers! For you burden people with burdens hard to bear, but you yourselves will not touch the burdens with one of your fingers. 47 Woe to you! For you build the tombs of the prophets, but your fathers killed them. 48 Therefore you are witnesses and approve the deeds of your fathers, for they killed them, and you build. 49 And for this reason the wisdom of God said, 'I will send to them prophets and apostles, and some of them they will kill and persecute,' 50 so that the blood of all the prophets shed from the foundation of the world may be

avenged on this generation, 51 from the blood of Abel to the blood of
Zechariah who perished between the altar and the sanctuary. Yes, I tell you, it
will be avenged on this generation! 52 Woe to you lawyers! For you have taken
away the key of knowledge. You yourselves did not enter and you hindered
those entering."

53 When he went out of there, the scribes and the Pharisees began to be
deeply hostile and to interrogate him about many things, 54 plotting to trap
him in something he might say.[4]

Jesus denounces the Pharisees (11:37-44)

While Jesus was speaking to the crowds (11:14, 29) about the failure of
"this wicked generation" to repent (11:29-32), a Pharisee invited him to dine
with him. So Jesus entered his home and reclined at table (11:37). This
presents the audience with Jesus' next encounter with a Pharisee after he
similarly entered the house of Simon the Pharisee and reclined at table after he
invited Jesus to eat with him (7:36). A Pharisee, in accord with his status as a
religious leader, again functions as the socially respected host and Jesus, who
has been addressing the crowds with wisdom and insight (11:14-36), again
functions as the prominent guest of another banquet symposium.[5]

When the Pharisee saw Jesus recline at table, he was surprised that he
did not first wash or "immerse himself" before the meal (11:38).[6] Like the
startling gestures of the sinful woman toward Jesus in his first meal with a
Pharisee (7:37-39), his surprising disregard of the ritual washing before a meal
functions as the *fait divers* that sparks the dispute of this banquet symposium.
The Jewish ceremonial cleansing before meals was thought to remove defiling
impurities and to place one in a state of holiness in preparation for the

---

[4] On 11:37-54, in addition to the commentaries, see Steele, "Luke
11:37-54," 379-94; H. Moxnes, *The Economy of the Kingdom: Social Conflict
and Economic Relations in Luke's Gospel* (Philadelphia: Fortress, 1988) 109-
26; Darr, *Character Building*, 103-5; Gowler, *Host*, 226-35; idem,
"Hospitality and Characterization in Luke 11:37-54: A Socio-Narratological
Approach," *The Rhetoric of Pronouncement* (*Semeia* 64; ed. V. K. Robbins;
Atlanta: Scholars Press, 1994) 213-51; Matson, *Household Conversion*, 65-67.

[5] On the features of the Hellenistic banquet symposium, see chapter 2
on Luke 5:29-39. See also Smith, "Table Fellowship," 614-23.

[6] On the Pharisees' practice of immersion before eating, see A. I.
Baumgarten, *The Flourishing of Jewish Sects in the Maccabean Era: An
Interpretation* (JSJSup 55; Leiden: Brill, 1997) 98-99.

religious dimension, the sharing of food as a gift of God, that was part of meal fellowship (cf. Matt 15:1-2; Mark 7:1-5).[7] But the audience experiences the irony that whereas the Pharisee is surprised that Jesus did not wash or, literally, was not "baptized" (ἐβαπτίσθη) in preparation for union with God in the meal, the Pharisees and lawyers rejected the plan of God for themselves by not being baptized (βαπτισθέντες) with John's baptism (βάπτισμα) of repentance (7:29-30; 3:3).

In his response to the surprised Pharisee Jesus, as "the" authoritative "lord" (ὁ κύριος), addresses all the Pharisees about their concern for the ritual cleanness involved in meals. He points out the ironic contradiction that while the Pharisees cleanse the outside of the cup and of the dish used in the meal, the inside of their own persons is full of grasping greed and wickedness (11:39). As the chief guest of the symposium the Lord Jesus sharpens the issue from a concern for his external and ritual impurity to a concern for the internal and moral impurity of these religious leaders. That the inside of the Pharisees is full of wickedness (πονηρίας) links them to this wicked (πονηρά) generation that seeks a sign (11:29; cf. 11:16), but fails to repent at the sign given them in Jesus as the Son of Man, who is greater than Solomon and Jonah (11:29-32). That the inside of them is full of greed and wickedness means that the "light" within them has become darkness (11:35). The "eye" that gives light to the inside of their whole body is not sound, sincere, or pure (ἁπλοῦς), not focussed on God with single-mindedness and on others with generosity (11:34).[8] Rather, they are focussed selfishly upon what they can grasp for themselves, as the inside of them is full of greed (ἁρπαγῆς).[9] Full of wickedness (πονηρίας), their "eye" is evil or envious (πονηρὸς), so that their whole body is impure, defiled in darkness (11:34).[10]

---

[7] F. Hauck, "καθαρός," *TDNT* 3.416: "Uncleanness is not just a lack of cleanness. It is a power which positively defiles."

[8] On the meaning of "sound eye" (ὀφθαλμός ἁπλοῦς) as a simple, sincere, and single-minded focus on God with a connotation of generosity, see Spicq, "ἁπλότης, ἁπλοῦς," *Theological Lexicon*, 1.170-71; T. Schramm, "ἁπλοῦς," *EDNT* 1.123-24; BAGD, 86.

[9] S. R. Garrett, "'Lest the Light in You Be Darkness': Luke 11:33-36 and the Question of Commitment," *JBL* 110 (1991) 103: "Jesus' denunciation of the Pharisees...serves as a counterexample to the behavior that Jesus promotes in the saying about the single eye: the Pharisees' duplicity and internal corruption are the antithesis of integrity, of single-minded commitment to the will of God."

[10] On the meaning of "evil eye" (ὀφθαλμός πονηρὸς) as one that looks with envy or jealousy upon others, see BAGD, 599; Schramm, "ἁπλοῦς," 124; M. Völkel, "ὀφθαλμός," *EDNT* 2.552.

Jesus, who has a wisdom greater than that of Solomon (11:31), then addresses these supposedly wise and intelligent religious leaders as "fools" (11:40), as those who refuse to acknowledge their own proper dependence upon God.[11] With a poignant question introduced with οὐχ, expecting an affirmative answer, Jesus leads the Pharisees to admit and the audience to realize that the one who made the outside of cups, dishes, and human beings-- the main concern of their ritual cleanness--also made the inside of cups, dishes, and human beings, which they are neglecting in their concern for ritual purity (11:40). The God they are trying to please with their ritual cleanness cares about not only external but internal holiness.[12]

Jesus then exhorts the Pharisees and the audience to a repentance that purifies both externally and internally. With regard to purifying "the things that are inside," the food and drink inside dishes and cups as well as the greed and wickedness inside the Pharisees themselves, they must give alms so that "everything," the inside and outside of cup, dishes, and themselves, is "clean" (καθαρὰ) for them (11:41), who are so concerned with cleansing (καθαρίζετε) the outside of cup and dish (11:39). That their giving of alms includes sharing with those in need the food and drink that are inside their dishes and cups accords with John the Baptist's exhortation to produce the fruits worthy of repentance by sharing clothes and food with those who have none (3:8, 11). By giving alms to the poor the Pharisees may cleanse themselves externally and internally, ritually and morally, by transforming the grasping selfishness and envy of their greed and wickedness into a selfless and compassionate concern for the needy.[13]

Addressing the Pharisees with a "woe" (οὐαὶ), which warns them of exclusion from eschatological salvation, Jesus continues to call them to repentance.[14] Although they obey the laws for tithing so meticulously that they pay tithes to please God even on such small food items as "mint and rue and every herb," nevertheless they ironically neglect the bringing about of justice for their fellow human beings as well as the love of God. They should continue to "do these things," that is, scrupulously pay tithes, which support

---

[11] On the biblical meaning of "fools" (ἄφρονες) here, see D. Zeller, "ἀφροσύνη," EDNT 1.184-85; Marshall, Luke, 495: "The word characterises the Pharisees as ungodly men in their false piety."

[12] On God as the Maker in question, see Fitzmyer, Luke X-XXIV, 947; Marshall, Luke, 495; Johnson, Luke, 189.

[13] On the merit of almsgiving as a charitable deed in the OT and Jewish theology, see F. Staudinger, "ἐλεημοσύνη," EDNT 1.428-29.

[14] H. Balz, "οὐαί," EDNT 2.540; Fitzmyer, Luke I-IX, 636.

not only the temple establishment for the worship of God but also the poor in the community.[15] But they should not neglect "the others," that is, their own doing of justice for the poor as well as their own love for God (11:42). Jesus calls them and the audience to convert by adding their personal commitment in working for social justice and loving God to their more impersonal paying of tithes. By compassionately doing justice for their neighbor coupled with a wholehearted love of God, they can inherit eternal life (10:25-28) rather than the "woe" of God's condemnation.

With another "woe to you Pharisees!," Jesus accuses these religious leaders, who have neglected the love (ἀγάπην) of God (11:42), of loving (ἀγαπᾶτε) rather the front seats of honor in the synagogues, places of public worship, and respectful greetings in the marketplaces, areas of social business (11:43).[16] They are more interested in receiving the honor and respect from others that comes with their status as leaders than in a genuine religious and social leading of others by giving them justice and bringing them to a sincere love of God. After a quickly added third but abbreviated "woe to you!," Jesus compares the Pharisees to unmarked tombs over which people walk without knowing it (11:44). Contact with a tomb, even unwittingly, rendered one ritually impure (Num 19:16). Ironically, those honoring and greeting the Pharisees are unwittingly being defiled by them. Ironically, the Pharisees, rather than leading people to the ritual cleanness with which they are so meticulously concerned (11:38-40), are actually contaminating them with their own hidden and deadly impurity. With these final two woes Jesus implicitly calls the Pharisees and the audience to repent by seeking not adulation from others but authentic leadership of and service to others.

Jesus denounces the lawyers (11:45-52)

In accord with the symposium format other guests are present, the "lawyers" or scribes, a professional group of experts in the law responsible for

---

[15] On the meaning and background of tithing, see Marshall, *Luke*, 496-98; Fitzmyer, *Luke X-XXIV*, 948; Johnson, *Luke*, 189; J. C. Wilson, "Tithe," *ABD* 6.578-80.

[16] On the "front seats" in synagogues as places of honor, see "πρωτοκαθεδρία," *EDNT* 3.187: "As a rule the learned sat in the synagogues not with the congregation (in the center of the room), but rather before the Torah shrine on a platform facing the people, or on benches at the side walls....elevated seats visible to all and sought for reasons of prestige."

the details of Pharisaic piety Jesus has just condemned.[17] The audience recalls that the lawyers were coupled with the Pharisees as those who rejected the plan of God for themselves by not being baptized with John's baptism of repentance (7:30). Previously a certain (τις) lawyer had stood up to test Jesus and said, "Teacher, what must I do to inherit eternal life?" (10:25). Now, similarly, a certain one (τις) of the lawyers enters into the symposium's controversy as he said to Jesus in reply, "Teacher, in saying these things you are also insulting us" (11:45).

To the lawyer, who objects that Jesus is insulting not only the Pharisees but "also us," the lawyers (11:45), Jesus promptly includes them in his scathing denunciation of Jewish leaders, "Woe also to you lawyers!" (11:46). Although they oppress the people who look to them for religious leadership with burdens hard to bear by adding to the written Torah their own legal interpretations and teachings, they themselves will not touch the burdens with one of their fingers (11:46) to help the people fulfill such strenuous obligations to God. Just as Jesus urged the lawyer who tested him (10:25) to imitate the compassion of the Samaritan who mercifully helped an unfortunate traveler (10:37), so in this first "woe" to the lawyers he implicitly calls them to convert by transforming their stern style of leadership into a compassionate assistance of people to fulfill the religious burdens they lay upon them.

Jesus' second "woe to you!" (11:47), while addressed to the lawyers, does not explicitly mention them (cf. 11:46, 52) and so may be more broadly focused to include the Pharisees. The accusation that follows takes the form of a chiasm in which the middle (c) term unites the builders of the tombs of the prophets (a) with the fathers who killed them (b):
(a) For you build the tombs of the prophets,
(b) but your fathers killed them (11:47).
(c) Therefore you are witnesses and approve the deeds of your fathers,
(b) for they killed them,
(a) and you build (11:48).
Although they build tombs as memorials (μνημεῖα) presumably to preserve the memory and thus honor the prophets sent to speak God's word to them, their own fathers or ancestors were the ones who dishonored the prophets by not heeding but killing them (11:47).[18] Ironically, by building memorial tombs,

---

[17] Fitzmyer, *Luke X-XXIV*, 949; Marshall, *Luke*, 499-500; H. Hübner, "νομικός," *EDNT* 2.470-71.

[18] M. Völkel, "μνημεῖον," *EDNT* 2.434: "Μνημεῖον can always be translated as *grave* in the NT; it perhaps retains something of the original meaning *memorial* in Matt 23:29 and Luke 11:47."

they are bearing witness to or "memorializing" and approving not the messages of the prophets but the deeds of their ancestral fathers who murdered them. That the verb "you build" stands at the end of the sentence with its object (implicitly the tombs) left provocatively unexpressed links the "building" more closely to the "killing" (11:48). Their ancestors killed and they build upon the killing by building the tombs of the prophets they fail to heed.

"For this reason" (διὰ τοῦτο), that is, because they have killed the prophets of old,[19] God will send them more prophets so that they may continue to fulfill God's plan as predicted by the personified "wisdom of God" (cf. 7:35) quoted by Jesus: "I will send to them prophets and apostles, and some of them they will kill and persecute" (11:49).[20] As the audience knows, these additional prophets include both John the Baptist, a prophet (1:76; 7:26, 28) who was imprisoned (3:20) and killed (9:7, 9), and Jesus, a prophet (4:24; 7:16; 9:19) who was persecuted (4:29) and will be killed (9:22, 31, 44). Furthermore, the apostles sent by the wisdom of God include the twelve disciples Jesus chose and named apostles (6:13; 9:10). Jesus, filled with a wisdom of God (2:40, 52) greater than that of Solomon (11:31), is thus warning the audience that the twelve apostles and others he has sent to continue his mission (9:1-6; 10:1-12), including the members of the audience who identify with them, can expect to be mistreated, persecuted, and even killed by their religious leaders, for this is what their ancestral fathers did to the prophets of old (6:22-23; 10:3).

Jesus warns the lawyers and the Pharisees that if they continue to kill rather than listen to the prophets God sends them, then the blood of all the prophets shed from the foundation of the world will be avenged (by God, divine passive) on "this generation" (11:50).[21] The blood of all the prophets

---

[19] On διὰ τοῦτο as forming a close link with the preceding woes, see Marshall, *Luke*, 502: "The sense is: 'Because of your attitude to the old prophets, wisdom has prophesied that (further) messengers will be sent to Israel, so that, when you have killed them, you in this generation may undergo the full judgment that Israel deserves.'"

[20] On "the wisdom of God" here, see Marshall, *Luke*, 503: "The reference is to 'divine wisdom'...This fits in with the way in which wisdom is personified in the OT and Judaism; she is capable of speaking to men (e.g. Pr. 1:20-33; 8) and sends messengers to them (Wis. 7:27; Lk. 7:35)." See also H. Hegermann, "σοφία," *EDNT* 3.258, 261.

[21] On "avenged on" or "required of" (ἐκζητηθῇ) here, see Fitzmyer, *Luke X-XXIV*, 950: "An OT expression is used (see Gen 9:5; 42:22; 2 Sam 4:11; Ps 9:13; Ezek 3:18, 20) to formulate the debt that will be demanded of 'this generation' so that the deaths of the prophets of old will be avenged."

begins with the blood of Abel, the first person murdered in the OT (Gen 4:1-15) and loosely understood here to be a prophet.[22] His blood "cried out" to God from the soil (Gen 4:10) to be avenged. It concludes with the blood of Zechariah who perished in the very temple of God's presence between the altar and the sanctuary. The spirit of God had possessed this Zechariah, son of Jehoiada the priest, to prophesy against the people, who failed to convert from their idolatry at the warnings of the prophets God sent them (2 Chr 24:17-22). They conspired to put him to death, who, as he was dying, said, "May the Lord see and avenge" (2 Chr 24:22). Concluding his second woe to the lawyers, Jesus reinforces his warning that God will avenge the deaths of his prophets by repeating, "Yes, I tell you, it will be avenged on this generation!" (11:51).

As the audience recalls, the lawyers and Pharisees, who rejected God's plan for themselves by not being baptized with John's baptism of repentance (7:30; 3:3), are part of "this generation" (7:31) who welcome neither the prophet John nor the prophet Jesus (7:31-35). They are part of "this wicked generation" that seeks a sign, but no sign will be given it except the sign of the prophet Jonah. Just as Jonah became a sign to the Ninevites, so Jesus as the Son of Man will be a sign to "this generation." The queen of the south will rise at the judgment with the men of "this generation" and condemn them, for she came from the ends of the earth to hear the wisdom of Solomon (1 Kgs 10:1-10), but something greater than Solomon is here. The Ninevites will rise at the judgment with "this generation" and condemn it, for they repented at the preaching of the prophet Jonah, but something greater that Jonah is here (11:29-32). By warning the lawyers and Pharisees that the murders of all the prophets will be avenged on them as part of "this generation" (11:50, 51), Jesus is calling them and the audience to repent by heeding his preaching as a prophet greater than Jonah and filled with a wisdom greater than that of Solomon.[23]

With his third woe to the lawyers Jesus denounces them as leaders who possess an authoritative knowledge of God's law and will. Rather than

---

[22] Marshall, *Luke*, 506; Fitzmyer, *Luke X-XXIV*, 951: "Though Abel was not a prophet, the use of this saying by Luke fits his general view of the OT in which most of it is regarded as some sort of prophecy."

[23] For scriptural background and parallels in Jewish apocalyptic literature to "this generation" as the last generation before the end and the approaching judgment, see V. Hasler, "γενεά," *EDNT* 1.241. For a recent discussion of 11:47-51, see S. Cunningham, *'Through Many Tribulations': The Theology of Persecution in Luke-Acts* (JSNTSup 142; Sheffield: Sheffield Academic Press, 1997) 100-105.

utilizing their expert knowledge to lead themselves and others, they have taken away the "key of knowledge" that opens the way into the salvation of God's kingdom.[24] Not only did they not enter but they hindered those entering (11:52). This final woe calls the lawyers and the audience to repent by using their knowledge as a "key" to open the way for themselves and others into the kingdom of God that Jesus, who offers a wisdom greater than that of Solomon (11:31), is bringing about.[25]

The scribes and Pharisees plot to trap Jesus (11:53-54)

When Jesus went out of the banquet symposium in the house of the Pharisee, his threatening woes that called for repentance produce an intense animosity toward him. The scribes and the Pharisees began to be deeply hostile and to interrogate Jesus about many things, plotting to trap him in something he might say (11:53-54).[26] That the lawyers (11:45-52) are now referred to by their alternate designation of "scribes" reminds the audience that it was "the scribes and Pharisees" who questioned (5:21), grumbled against (5:30), and scrutinized (6:7) Jesus.[27] Their deeply hostile plotting to trap Jesus in his speech advances their becoming enraged and discussing among themselves what they might do to Jesus (6:11), after they scrutinized him to see if he would heal on the sabbath, so that they might find something with which to accuse him (6:7). They are ironically fulfilling Jesus' prediction that they will continue to persecute and kill the prophets and apostles sent to them by the

---

[24] Marshall, *Luke*, 507: "The key consists of the knowledge of God and leads to the knowledge of God." In 1:77 John the Baptist is "to give his people knowledge of salvation through the forgiveness of their sins."

[25] That the kingdom of God is to be entered here is implicit. See Marshall, *Luke*, 507; F. G. Untergassmair, "κλείς," *EDNT* 2.296-97. The kingdom of God that has arrived with Jesus has been explicitly mentioned in 4:43; 6:20; 7:28; 8:1, 10; 9:2, 11, 27, 60, 62; 10:9, 11; 11:20. See also Matt 23:13.

[26] Literally, they were "drawing from his mouth" (ἀποστοματίζειν) concerning many things, plotting to trap him in something "from his mouth" (ἐκ τοῦ στόματος αὐτοῦ).

[27] There is no clear distinction between "lawyer" (νομικός) and "scribe" (γραμματεύς) in Luke; see Hübner, "νομικός," 471; Baumbach, "γραμματεύς," 259. Lawyers are coupled with Pharisees in 7:30; 11:37-52; 14:3, whereas scribes are coupled with Pharisees in 5:21, 30; 6:7; 11:53; 15:2.

wisdom of God (11:49).[28] Jesus' second meal with a Pharisee has resulted in a profound hostility toward him on the part of the scribes and Pharisees that greatly increases the narrative's dramatic tension for the audience.

Relation of Luke 11:37-54 to Previous Meal Scenes

1) Jesus' second meal with a Pharisee develops the *theme of Jesus calling the scribes and Pharisees to repentance in the context of a meal*. After the scribes and Pharisees grumbled against Jesus and his disciples for eating and drinking with tax collectors and sinners at Levi's banquet (5:30), Jesus ironically called these righteous religious leaders to recognize their own sinfulness and repent: "I have not come to call the righteous but sinners to repentance" (5:32). Rather than repent, they eventually sought to accuse Jesus (6:7) and in their rage discussed what they might do to him (6:11). In Jesus' first meal with a Pharisee (7:36-50) he invited Simon the Pharisee to repent by recognizing his need to be forgiven like the sinful woman (7:47). Now, in his second meal with a Pharisee (11:37-54), Jesus, with a salvo of scathing woes, calls the Pharisees and lawyers to repent of their sinful ways as religious leaders. Rather than repent, they become extremely hostile and plot to trap him in his speech (11:53-54).

2) Jesus' second meal with a Pharisee advances the *theme of proper leadership*. In the first meal scenes (5:27-6:5) Jesus began to exhibit his inclusive and compassionate style of leadership. He shared meal fellowship with social outcasts and public sinners to call them to repentance (5:27-32). He allowed his disciples to feast rather than fast (5:33-39) and to do the work necessary to satisfy their hunger on the sabbath (6:1-5). In his first meal with a Pharisee (7:36-50) Jesus modeled for Simon the Pharisee a type of leadership that allows others, like the sinful woman, the opportunity to repent of their sinfulness, no matter how great, and receive God's forgiveness. In the miraculously overabundant meal (9:10-17) Jesus empowered his disciples to a hospitable leadership that enables them not only to heal and proclaim the good news of the kingdom of God, but to nourish people with the overabundance he provided. In his second meal with a Pharisee Jesus calls the Pharisees and lawyers to a more authentic and compassionate leadership. They are to lead

---

[28] For a possible allusion between the "plotting" (ἐνεδρεύοντες) of the scribes and Pharisees against Jesus and the "plotting" (ἐνεδρεύσωμεν) of opponents against the suffering just one in Wisdom 2:12, see P. Doble, *The Paradox of Salvation: Luke's Theology of the Cross* (SNTSMS 87; Cambridge: Cambridge University Press, 1996) 208-9.

others to holiness by giving alms to the poor and hungry (11:39-41), by being concerned with social justice and the love of God (11:42), by being unconcerned with the honor of their status (11:43-44), by helping people to carry the legal burdens they lay upon them (11:46), by heeding God's prophets (11:47-51), and by using their knowledge to lead themselves and others into the kingdom of God (11:52).

3) Jesus' second meal with a Pharisee promotes the *theme of discipleship*. In the Martha and Mary meal scene (10:38-42) Martha hospitably welcomes Jesus while Mary epitomizes the ideal disciple by sitting at the feet of Jesus and attentively listening to the word of the master (10:39). In stark contrast the scribes and Pharisees, inhospitably hostile to Jesus in his second meal with a Pharisee, are interrogating him about many things, plotting to trap him in his word (11:53-54). The word of Jesus that Mary is listening to includes the necessity of his suffering, death, and resurrection. It calls for disciples to deny themselves, take up their cross daily, follow him, and lose their lives for his sake in order to save them (9:22-24). That the hostile scribes and Pharisees will continue to kill and persecute the prophets and apostles God sends them (11:49) ominously reminds the audience that disciples, as apostles of Jesus, can expect to suffer the same fate as the prophet Jesus.

Pragmatics of the Meal Scene in Luke 11:37-54

1) The Pharisees and lawyers present the audience with negative models of leadership they are not to emulate. Unlike the hostile scribes and Pharisees (11:53-54) the audience is to heed Jesus' threatening woes exhorting them to a *profound repentance*. Rather than greedily grasping things from others to serve and satisfy themselves like the Pharisees, the audience is urged *to give alms selflessly and compassionately to the poor and hungry*, and thereby cleanse themselves both externally and internally, ritually and morally (11:39-41).

2) Unlike the Pharisees the audience must not allow a meticulous and detailed observance of religious obligations to dispense or distract them from a more personal commitment *to work for social justice* and to love God in a sincere and wholehearted way (11:42).

3) Rather than seek human honor and adulation in their social relations like the Pharisees (11:43), the audience should seek *to serve and edify* instead of corrupting and defiling those with whom they come into contact (11:44).

4) Unlike the lawyers or scribes who refuse to help those they burden with religious obligations, the audience must not only teach people how they can best serve God and one another but *compassionately assist them* to fulfill such teachings (11:46).

5) Rather than failing to honor the prophets of the past like the Pharisees and lawyers, the audience must learn *to recognize, welcome, and heed the prophets currently speaking God's word to them* (11:47-51).

6) Sent as disciples and apostles of Jesus to proclaim the good news of the kingdom of God, the audience can expect *to be rejected, persecuted, and even killed like Jesus*. But they can be encouraged that God will vindicate his rejected prophets and apostles (11:47-51).

7) Unlike the lawyers the audience must use the knowledge of God's will revealed to them by Jesus, who has a wisdom greater than that of Solomon (11:31), as a "key" *to open the way for themselves and others into the kingdom of God* that Jesus is bringing about (11:52).

CHAPTER 7

JESUS' THIRD MEAL WITH A PHARISEE
LUKE 14:1-24

The theme of eating and drinking next appears in the third section of the travel narrative (12:1-13:21) when Jesus teaches about anxiety over eating and drinking (12:13-34) and about readiness for the eschatological meal (12:35-48). The fourth section of the travel narrative (13:22-14:24) begins with the theme of who will eat and drink at the eschatological meal (13:22-30) and concludes with the next meal scene, Jesus' third meal with a Pharisee (14:1-24).[1]

Anxiety about Eating and Drinking in This Age (12:13-34)

After Jesus cautioned the crowd and thus the audience to guard against all ruthless greed, because one's life does not consist in an abundance of possessions (12:15), he told them a parable (12:16-21) to illustrate his point.[2] A rich man had gathered so much grain and goods that he said to himself, "You have many good things stored up for many years; rest, eat, drink, be merry!" (12:19).[3] But God called him a "fool" and informed him that his life would be taken away from him that very night, so that he prepared for himself in vain (12:20).[4] Jesus' conclusion, "Thus it is for the one who stores up treasure for himself but is not rich toward God" (12:21), warns the audience to live by trusting in God and sharing with others.[5]

---

[1] For a discussion of the third and fourth sections of the travel narrative, see O'Fearghail, *Introduction to Luke-Acts*, 56-57.

[2] On 12:13-21, see M. Làconi, "Ricchi davanti a Dio (Lc 12,13-21)," *Sacra Doctrina* 34 (1989) 5-41.

[3] A. J. Malherbe, "The Christianization of a *Topos* (Luke 12:13-34)," *NovT* 38 (1996) 133: "Luke represents the insatiably covetous rich man as a hedonist. The man calls on his soul to take its rest, eat, drink, be merry (ἀναπαύου, φάγε, πίε, εὐφραίνου). With some variations, this motto was widely associated with the licentious or hedonistic life that held out no prospect for existence after death." See also Marshall, *Luke*, 524; Fitzmyer, *Luke X-XXIV*, 973; Johnson, *Luke*, 199.

[4] On a "fool" as one who refuses to acknowledge dependence on God, see Zeller, "ἀφροσύνη," 184-85.

[5] Johnson, *Luke*, 199: "Wealth with respect to God has two levels of meaning for Luke: the first is the response of faith, the second is the disposition of possessions in accordance with faith, which means to share them with others rather than accumulating them for one's self." See also Fitzmyer, *Luke X-XXIV*, 974.

In contrast to the foolish rich man, who was concerned to accumulate food to eat and drink for himself, for his own "life" (12:19), which "life" God will take from him (12:20), Jesus exhorts his disciples and thus the audience not to worry for their "life," what they will eat, or for their body, what they will wear (12:22), for "life" is more than food and the body more than clothing (12:23; cf. 4:4). If God feeds the ravens and clothes the lilies, they can have faith that God will certainly feed and clothe them (12:24-28). They are not to seek what to eat and what to drink and not be anxious, for the Father knows they need these things (12:29-30). They are rather to seek his kingdom and these things will be given to them as well (12:31).[6]

Eating and Drinking and Readiness for the Eschatological Banquet (12:35-48)

In a striking reversal of expected roles Jesus promises his disciples and thus the audience that if they are ready for his return at the end of time, he, although the Lord, will serve them, the servants, food at the eschatological banquet: "Blessed are those servants whom the Lord will find watching when he comes. Amen I say to you, he will gird himself, make them recline, and come and serve them" (12:37). Being ready for the return of Jesus as Lord involves the audience in a proper stewardship over food: "Who is the faithful and prudent steward whom the Lord will set over his servants to give them their food allowance at the proper time? Blessed is that servant whom his Lord will find doing thus when he comes" (12:42-43). Through the parallelism, "doing thus" (12:43), that is, feeding one's fellow servants, delineates what it means to be "watching" (12:37) when Jesus returns. On the other hand, if the audience abuses their fellow servants and abuses food by "eating and drinking and getting drunk" (12:45), they will not be ready and thus lose their eschatological reward by being placed with the unfaithful (12:46).[7]

---

[6] On 12:22-31, see R. J. Dillon, "Ravens, Lilies, and the Kingdom of God (Matthew 6:25-33/Luke 12:22-31)," *CBQ* 53 (1991) 605-27; O. Wischmeyer, "Matthäus 6,25-34 par: Die Spruchreihe vom Sorgen," *ZNW* 85 (1994) 1-22; J. N. Jones, "'Think of the Lilies' and Prov 6:6-11," *HTR* 88 (1995) 175-77.

[7] On eating and drinking as a negative symbol in both 12:16-21 and 12:42-46, see Smith, "Table Fellowship," 624-25. With regard to the effect of such texts on the audience, he notes: "These texts thus function both as a warning and as an assurance to the faithful. They are assured that those who feast luxuriously now will eventually be judged, and they are warned lest they fall into the same trap" (p. 624).

Those Who Will Eat and Drink at the Eschatological Banquet (13:22-30)

Continuing his teaching in towns and villages as he makes his way to Jerusalem (13:22), Jesus warns the audience that the kind of meal fellowship consisting in merely eating and drinking before him (13:26) without responding to his appeals for repentance (13:3,5; cf. 5:30) will not guarantee entrance into the kingdom of God. Indeed, those evildoers who have only a superficial familiarity with Jesus and his teaching will be cast out of the kingdom (13:28). But others who do repent will come from the east and the west and from the north and the south and will recline to eat and drink at the eschatological banquet in the kingdom of God (13:29).

Jesus Again Dines with a Pharisee (14:1-24)

1 When he went into the house of one of the leading Pharisees on a sabbath to dine, they were watching him closely. 2 Just then a certain man who had dropsy was in front of him. 3 Responding, Jesus said to the lawyers and Pharisees, "Is it lawful to heal on the sabbath or not?" 4 But they were silent. So after taking hold of him, he healed and dismissed him. 5 Then he said to them, "If a son or ox of any of you falls into a cistern, will he not immediately pull it out on a sabbath day?" 6 But they were not able to reply to these things.

7 Then he told a parable to those who had been invited, noticing how they chose the places of honor. He said to them, 8 "When you are invited by someone to a wedding feast, do not recline at the place of honor, lest one more honorable than you has been invited by him. 9 Then the one who invited you and him will come and say to you, 'Give your place to this one,' and then you will begin with shame to take the lowest place. 10 Rather, when you are invited, go and recline at the lowest place, so that when he who invited you comes he will say to you, 'Friend, move up higher.' Then you will have honor before all of your fellow guests. 11 For everyone who exalts himself will be humbled, but the one who humbles himself will be exalted."

12 Then he told the one who had invited him, "When you give a lunch or dinner, do not call your friends or your brothers or your relatives or wealthy neighbors, lest they invite you back and you have repayment. 13 Rather, when you give a banquet, invite the poor, the crippled, the lame, the blind. 14 And you will be blessed, because they cannot repay you, for you will be repaid at the resurrection of the righteous."

15 One of the fellow guests on hearing these things said to him, "Blessed is anyone who will dine in the kingdom of God!" 16 He replied to him, "A certain man gave a great dinner and invited many. 17 At the time of the dinner he sent his servant to tell those invited, 'Come, for it is already prepared.' 18 But they all alike began to excuse themselves. The first said to him, 'I have purchased a field and must go out and see it; I ask you, hold me excused.' 19 And another said, 'I have purchased five yoke of oxen and am going to test them; I ask you, hold me excused.' 20 And another said, 'I have married a wife and therefore cannot come.' 21 So the servant arrived and reported these things to his master. Then the master of the house became angry and said to his servant, 'Go out quickly into the streets and lanes of the city and bring in here the poor and crippled and blind and lame.' 22 The servant said, 'Master, what you ordered has been done, and there is still room.' 23 The master then said to the servant, 'Go out into the roads and fences and force people to come in, so that my house may be filled. 24 For I tell you, none of those invited will taste my dinner.' "[8]

---

[8] On 14:1-24, in addition to the commentaries, see X. de Meeûs, "Composition de Lc., XIV et genre symposiaque," *ETL* 37 (1961) 847-70; Donahue, *Gospel in Parable*, 140-46; Moxnes, *Economy of the Kingdom*, 127-38; T. Noël, "The Parable of the Wedding Feast: A Narrative-Critical Interpretation," *Perspectives in Religious Studies* 16 (1989) 17-27; B. B. Scott, *Hear Then the Parable: A Commentary on the Parables of Jesus* (Minneapolis: Fortress, 1989) 161-74, esp. 163-65; R. L. Rohrbaugh, "The Pre-Industrial City in Luke-Acts: Urban Social Relations," *The Social World of Luke-Acts: Models for Interpretation* (ed. J. H. Neyrey; Peabody: Hendrickson, 1991) 125-49; York, *Last Shall Be First*, 78-80, 133-45; Darr, *Character Building*, 106-8; Gowler, *Host*, 241-50; R. C. Tannehill, "The Lukan Discourse on Invitations (Luke 14,7-24)," *The Four Gospels 1992: Festschrift Frans Neirynck* (BETL 100; ed. F. Van Segbroeck, et al; Leuven: Leuven University Press, 1992) 1603-16; W. Braun, "Symposium or Anti-Symposium? Reflections on Luke 14:1-24," *Toronto Journal of Theology* 8 (1992) 70-84; idem, *Feasting and Social Rhetoric in Luke 14* (SNTSMS 85; Cambridge: Cambridge University Press, 1995); J. A. Sanders, "The Ethic of Election in Luke's Great Banquet Parable," *Luke and Scripture: The Function of Sacred Tradition in Luke-Acts* (eds. C. A. Evans and J. A. Sanders; Minneapolis: Fortress, 1993) 106-20; Just, *Ongoing Feast*, 171-80; W. G. Carey, "Excuses, Excuses: The Parable of the Banquet (Luke 14:15-24) Within the Larger Context of Luke," *IBS* 17 (1995) 177-87; Matson, *Household Conversion*, 67-69; Roth, *The Blind*, 179-83.

Jesus heals a man with dropsy on the sabbath (14:1-6)

In the introduction to Jesus' third meal with a Pharisee the audience encounters a progression in the dramatic tension of the previous meals with Pharisees. Whereas Jesus was explicitly invited to the earlier meals (7:36; 11:37), now, although an invitation may be implied, none is narrated, as Jesus merely "went into the house" (14:1). This already begins to highlight for the audience Jesus' superior authority and control of the situation as the chief guest in another banquet symposium. In addition, Jesus now dines in the house not of just any Pharisee but of one of the leading Pharisees. And the meal now is not just any meal but takes place during the sacred time of the sabbath (14:1; cf. 7:36; 11:37).

That they were closely watching (παρατηρούμενοι) him on the sabbath (14:1) when a certain man suffering from the disease of dropsy was in front of him (14:2) recalls for the audience how the scribes and Pharisees closely watched (παρετηροῦντο) him to see if we would heal a man with a withered right hand on the sabbath, so that they might find something with which to accuse him (6:7). After Jesus healed that man, they became enraged and discussed among themselves what they might do to Jesus (6:11). Their enmity against him intensified at the end of his second meal with Pharisees, as they began to be deeply hostile and to interrogate him about many things, plotting to trap him in something he might say (11:53-54). The audience knows, then, that this close scrutiny of him now is part of the hostile attempt to accuse him of something by ensnaring him in his speech.

The abrupt appearance of a certain man with dropsy during the sabbath meal serves as the *fait divers* that initiates the controversy of this banquet symposium. His immediate introduction, "and behold a certain man" (καὶ ἰδοὺ ἄνθρωπός τις, 14:2), recalls for the audience the similar introduction of the sinful woman who served as the *fait divers* in Jesus' first meal with a Pharisee, "and behold a certain woman" (καὶ ἰδοὺ γυνὴ ἥτις, 7:37). It also recalls the previous introduction in one of the synagogues where Jesus was teaching of the woman who likewise was in need of healing on the sabbath, "and behold a woman" (καὶ ἰδοὺ γυνὴ, 13:11). When the man with dropsy suddenly appears before Jesus on the sabbath, then, the audience already knows that Jesus has healed on the sabbath a man with an unclean spirit (4:31-37), a man with a withered right hand (6:6-11), and a severely crippled woman (13:10-17).

Dropsy is "an abnormal accumulation of serous fluids in connective tissues or cavities of the body accompanied by swelling, distention, or defective circulation. It is usually symptomatic of more serious problems."[9]

---

[9] Fitzmyer, *Luke X-XXIV*, 1041. See also Marshall, *Luke*, 578-79. This is the only instance in the NT of Jesus healing someone with dropsy.

Dropsy has a "paradoxical symptom, namely the unquenchable craving for drink though the body is inflated with fluid, a craving which, when indulged, serves not to ease but to feed the disease."[10] In the Greco-Roman world familiar to Luke and his audience dropsy was thought to be the consequence of gluttonous behavior. It often served as a metaphor for insatiable greed or craving desire.[11] The physically dropsical man in need of healing serves also as a subtle metaphor characterizing the morally dropsical Pharisees, who are also ironically in need of healing by repenting of the greed and craving selfish desires of which Jesus has accused them (11:39, 43; see also 12:15).

The answer to Jesus' question to the lawyers and Pharisees looking to trap him in his speech, "Is it lawful to heal on the sabbath or not?" (14:3), is obvious by now. It is not only "lawful," in accord with God's will, but most appropriate for Jesus to heal on the sabbath. Restoring health accords with the nature of the sabbath as a sacred time of rest, refreshment, and restoration that anticipates God's final restoration at the end of time.[12] Liberating one from an oppressive disease on the sabbath accords with Jesus' mission, announced on a sabbath (4:16), to proclaim liberty to captives and restoration of sight to the blind, to let the oppressed go free, and to proclaim the year of the Lord's favor (4:18-19). Jesus has already liberated on the sabbath someone oppressed by an unclean spirit (4:31-37). With his divine authority as "lord of the sabbath" (6:5) Jesus healed the man with the withered hand on the sabbath, because "it is lawful," it appropriately accords with God's will and Jesus' mission, to do good rather than evil and to save life rather than destroy it on the sabbath (6:9). "It was necessary," in accord with God's salvific will that Jesus' mission of liberation is now actualizing, that the woman oppressed by a spirit of infirmity, in bondage to Satan for eighteen years, be set free on the day of the sabbath (13:16, 12). So the audience knows that indeed "it is lawful" for Jesus to heal the man oppressed with dropsy on the sabbath.

Despite the obvious answer to Jesus' question the lawyers and Pharisees remain silent (14:4), heightening the dramatic tension of the scene. They refuse to acknowledge Jesus' authority as lord of the sabbath to heal the man with dropsy lawfully and most appropriately on the sabbath. The audience experiences the irony that, rather than providing his opponents with something with which to entrap and accuse him (6:7; 11:53-54), the question that comes out of the mouth of Jesus closes their mouths. As the chief guest of this

---

[10] Braun, *Feasting*, 32.

[11] For literary examples and a full discussion of the evidence, see Braun, *Feasting*, 22-42.

[12] Lohse, "σάββατον," 8. See chapter 2 on 6:1-5.

banquet symposium Jesus continues to demonstrate his superiority over his inimical hosts.

Despite their obstinate silence Jesus performed the work of healing on the sabbath as he took hold of the man, healed, and dismissed him (14:4). That he "healed" him continues the "healings" (13:32) Jesus must accomplish in accord with God's plan that he die in Jerusalem rather than flee, at the warning of the Pharisees, the murderous intent of Herod (13:31-33). Jesus completed the healing as he "dismissed" (ἀπέλυσεν) the man with its connotation of "releasing" or "setting him free" of the oppressive disease of dropsy. Just as Jesus appropriately liberated on the sabbath the crippled woman bound by Satan (13:16), "Woman, you are set free (ἀπολέλυσαι) of your infirmity" (13:12), so he appropriately liberated the man oppressed by dropsy on the sabbath. The audience realizes that Jesus, although a guest, performs as the hospitable host. He dismisses the man with a salvific benefit from the sabbath meal, a sabbath benefit the hosting lawyers and Pharisees are unwilling to grant.

When Jesus healed the crippled woman on the sabbath, he not only defended his action but appealed for those objecting, and thus for the audience, to share his compassionate care and concern for the needy woman. They routinely free their animals from their mangers and lead them to drink on the sabbath (13:15), rather than making them wait for a work day (13:14). Surely they must have the same concern not to make a fellow human being and Israelite, "this daughter of Abraham," who has already been bound by Satan for eighteen years, wait another day to benefit from the divine healing power now present in Jesus (4:18-19; 5:17; 6:18-19) to free her from bondage most appropriately on the day of the sabbath (13:16). With a similar poignant analogy in the form of a powerful rhetorical question Jesus again defends himself and appeals for the lawyers and Pharisees, and thus for the audience, to share his compassion for the urgent healing of the man with dropsy. Just as they would not wait but "immediately," even on the sabbath day, rescue their own son or even an animal who fell into a cistern (14:5), so they must allow Jesus to rescue this fellow human being from dropsy now, even and most appropriately on the sabbath.[13]

The hosting lawyers and Pharisees, who remained silent after Jesus' first question (14:3-4), now are so overwhelmed by the powerful words of their guest that "they were not able to reply to these things" (14:6). The audience realizes that Jesus has continued to frustrate the plot of his opponents

---

[13] For a discussion of the text-critical problem involving the reading "son or ox" in 14:5, see Metzger, *Textual Commentary*, 164.

to ensnare him in his speech (11:53-54). Ironically the superior speech of the chief guest of this sabbath meal has rendered his hosts speechless and powerless to accuse him at this point. In the process of healing the man with physical dropsy on the sabbath Jesus' powerful rhetorical questions (14:3, 5) have provided his hosting lawyers and Pharisees the opportunity to be healed themselves, on the sabbath and during this sabbath meal, of their moral "dropsy," their craving selfish desires. He invited them and thus the audience to repent of their selfishness by sharing his compassion for a fellow human being in urgent need of healing on the sabbath. But that they were not able (οὐκ ἴσχυσαν) to reply reminds the audience of Jesus' previous warning that many will seek to enter the kingdom of God but not be able (οὐκ ἰσχύσουσιν, 13:24).

Jesus tells a parable about taking places of honor at meals (14:7-11)

After his hosts had watched him closely (14:1), Jesus in turn noticed how those who had been invited to the sabbath meal were choosing the places of honor, literally, the "first places" (14:7). This provides a second *fait divers* for the symposium, as it occasions Jesus' telling of a parable to those invited. That they were choosing the first places (πρωτοκλισίας) of honor at the banquet reminds the audience that Jesus castigated the Pharisees in his previous meal with them because they love the first seat (πρωτοκαθεδρίαν) of honor in the synagogues (11:43). The Pharisees' love of the first seat of honor for their self-glorification is part of their moral "dropsy," their craving selfish desire. In choosing the first places of honor for their self-glorification, the guests demonstrate that they, like the host Pharisees, need the remedy from their dropsical, selfish behavior that Jesus' parable offers.

Jesus' parable contrasts two ways of reclining in places of honor as guests at a wedding feast. Jesus warns against reclining immediately in the first place of honor. One more honorable than you may have been invited, so that you will be forced to yield your place in shame and take the lowest place (14:8-9). The paradox of bringing shame upon oneself by seeking for oneself a place of honor resembles the paradoxical symptom of dropsy, craving the drink that worsens the swelling with fluid. Rather, Jesus recommends reclining at the lowest place, so that when the host comes he will call you to a higher place. Then you will have honor before all of your fellow guests (14:10).[14]

---

[14] On the important social values of honor and shame here, see Gowler, *Host*, 248-49; B. J. Malina and J. H. Neyrey, "Honor and Shame in Luke-Acts: Pivotal Values of the Mediterranean World," *The Social World of Luke-Acts: Models for Interpretation* (ed. J. H. Neyrey; Peabody: Hendrickson, 1991) 25-65.

Instead of selfishly grasping honor for yourself, have the humility of allowing your host to bestow it upon you.[15]

But the previous narrative leads the audience to compare the humble behavior recommended for a place of honor at the parable's wedding feast to the humility needed to recline with honor at the eschatological wedding feast. The audience has already heard Jesus refer to himself as the "bridegroom" of the eschatological wedding feast (5:34). Jesus' miraculously overabundant feeding of five thousand anticipates the eschatological banquet he will host (9:10-17). Jesus exhorted his disciples and thus the audience to await his return at the end of time like servants awaiting the return of their master from a wedding feast (12:36). If they are vigilant when he comes, he will gird himself, make them recline at the eschatological (wedding) feast, and come and serve them (12:37). Being forced to take the lowest or last ($\check{\epsilon}\sigma\chi\alpha\tau o\nu$) place at the parable's wedding feast (14:9) reminds the audience of Jesus' warning about being excluded from the eschatological banquet (13:28). Many will come from the east and the west and from the north and the south and will recline at the final banquet in the kingdom of God (13:29). For "some are last ($\check{\epsilon}\sigma\chi\alpha\tau o\iota$) who will be first, and some are first who will be last ($\check{\epsilon}\sigma\chi\alpha\tau o\iota$)" (13:30).

The antithetical aphorism concluding the parable (14:11) confirms that it offers not just prudent advice for how the social elite can avoid embarrassment at wedding feasts but calls for the humility necessary for all in the audience to recline at the ultimate wedding feast in the kingdom of God.[16] Everyone who "exalts" himself, like those who seek the first places of honor in the parable, "will be humbled" by God (divine passive), but the one who "humbles" himself, like those who take the last place at the wedding feast in the parable, "will be exalted" by God (divine passive).[17] They will be among the "last" who will recline at the final wedding banquet in the kingdom of God

---

[15] For similarities to this parable in Hellenistic literature, see Braun, *Feasting*, 45-53. Note also the close similarity in Prov 25:6-7.

[16] Tannehill, *Narrative Unity*, 1.184; York, *Last Shall Be First*, 135-36. Braun (*Feasting*, 44, 53-54, 179) denies a metaphorical dimension to the parable and sees it directed primarily at the social behavior of the wealthy urban elite. His fine treatment of the unity and coherence of Luke 14:1-24 suffers from a narrow focus which generally neglects the context of the passage within the larger Lukan narrative.

[17] On 14:11 as an expression of divine reversal, see York, *Last Shall Be First*, 78-80, 108-9. Fitzmyer (*Luke X-XXIV*, 1047) notes an allusion to Ezek 21:31 (LXX).

(13:30). As the audience recalls, Mary in her Magnificat praised the God who "exalted" the "humble" (1:52), which is parallel to God's filling the hungry with good things (1:53).[18] With his poignant parable (14:8-11) Jesus calls those invited to the sabbath meal (14:7) and also the audience to humble themselves in dependence upon God in their social interaction in order to be cured of their dropsical self-seeking, so that God will exalt them in places of honor at the eschatological wedding feast Jesus will host.

Jesus tells his host to invite to dinner those who cannot repay (14:12-14)

Complementing his sage instructions to the guests about their banquet behavior, Jesus addresses the host, the Pharisee who invited him, about his banquet behavior in a formally parallel way. He *told* the guests, "*When* you are invited by someone to a wedding feast, *do not* recline at the place of honor, *lest* one more honorable than you has been invited by him" (14:8). Similarly, he *told* the host, "*When* you give a lunch or dinner, *do not* call your friends or your brothers or your relatives or wealthy neighbors, *lest* they invite you back and you have repayment" (14:12). Just as Jesus advised the guests not to seek honor for themselves by taking the first places at banquets, so he now advises the host not to seek honor for himself by inviting to banquets those who can and will reciprocate.[19]

Jesus further advised the guests, "*Rather, when* you are invited, go and recline at the lowest place, so that when he who invited you comes he will say to you, 'Friend, move up higher.' Then *you will have honor* before all of your fellow guests. *Because* everyone who exalts himself will be humbled, but the one who humbles himself will be exalted" (14:10-11). Similarly, he further advised the host, "*Rather, when* you give a banquet, invite the poor, the crippled, the lame, the blind.[20] And *you will be blessed, because* they cannot

---

[18] On the biblical atttiude of humbling oneself in dependence upon God, see Spicq, "ταπεινός," *Theological Lexicon*, 3.369-71; H. Giesen, "ταπεινός," *EDNT* 3.333; idem, "ταπεινόω," *EDNT* 3.334-35.

[19] On the cultural commonplace of reciprocal banquet hospitality involving the bestowal and repayment of social honor, see Braun, *Feasting*, 55-57. He notes that "reciprocity was a central 'law' of Greco-Roman social interactions. With regard to meals it was simply expected in Luke's culture" (p. 57 n. 41). See also Rohrbaugh, "Pre-industrial City," 141; Garrison, *Graeco-Roman Context*, 45.

[20] Note the use of three different words, "lunch" (ἄριστον), "dinner" (δεῖπνον) (14:12), and "banquet" (δοχὴν) (14:13), to cover the variety of meal types.

repay you, for you will be repaid at the resurrection of the righteous" (14:13-14).[21] Just as Jesus instructed the guests to humble themselves by assuming the last places at banquets in order to be honored by the host and ultimately exalted with honor by God at the eschatological banquet, so he now instructs the host to humble himself by inviting those who cannot repay him with a banquet, so that he will be blessed and repaid by God (with the ultimate banquet?) at the eschatological resurrection of the righteous.[22]

But the audience experiences a conceptual progression through the formal parallelism. Jesus invites the host to cure his dropsical, selfish craving for social honor not only by humbling himself, like the guests, but also by demonstrating a selfless care and concern for those who are socially and economically unfortunate. He challenges the hosting Pharisee to shatter social expectations by inviting to his banquets not those with whom he is socially bonded by friendship, familial ties, similar affiliations, or economic status, not his wealthy neighbors (14:12), but those who are socially marginal, the poor and the physically disabled (14:13).[23] Urging the host to demonstrate humility and compassion by extending meal fellowship to the physically disabled--the crippled, the lame, and the blind (14:13), Jesus further persuades the Pharisees and lawyers and thus the audience to the appropriateness of his compassionate healing of the man with dropsy during the sabbath meal (14:1-6).

Through recall of the previous narrative the audience can see that Jesus' challenge at this sabbath meal for the hosting Pharisee to invite the *poor*, the *crippled*, the *lame*, and the *blind* to his banquets (14:13) instead of *rich* neighbors (14:12) draws him into Jesus' own mission and ministry. On a sabbath in the synagogue at Nazareth Jesus announced his mission. The Spirit of the Lord anointed him to proclaim good news to the *poor* and sent him to

---

[21] On the formal parallelism between 14:7-11 and 14:12-14, see Noël, "Wedding Guest," 20-21; York, *Last Shall Be First*, 138-39; Braun, *Feasting*, 16 n. 30.

[22] Braun (*Feasting*, 54 n. 34) denigrates the eschatological reward as merely an ideal used "to criticize and amend current social arrangements and moral attitudes." He understands the "resurrection of the righteous" not as the resurrection of the dead but as a "rising" in juxtaposition with "lowliness" (p. 61 n. 52). He does not, however, explain what it would then mean to be repaid at the rising of the righteous from lowliness.

[23] Braun, *Feasting*, 56-57; Roth, *The Blind*, 181-82: "to exhort the Pharisee to provide hospitality to these groups is to imply that the Pharisee has overlooked Scripture, specifically, scriptural mandates for generosity to the poor, the blind, and the lame."

announce the return of sight to the *blind* as part of his announcement of the arrival of the sabbatical "year of the Lord's favor" (4:18-19). He declared the *poor* blessed, because theirs is the kingdom of God (6:20), but woe to the *rich*, who have received their consolation (6:24). As the "one to come," the bringer of God's eschatological kingdom (7:19-20), Jesus' ministry of healing gave the sick and disabled personal experiences of that kingdom. He healed many of their diseases, sufferings, and evil spirits, and granted sight to many who were *blind* (7:21). He told the disciples of John to report to him what they have seen and heard Jesus do: the *blind* see again, the *lame* walk, *lepers* are cleansed, the *deaf* hear, the *dead* are raised, the *poor* have good news proclaimed to them (7:22). Jesus challenges the host and the audience to share in his ministry by bestowing the honor of meal fellowship upon the poor and disabled in order to be blessed and repaid by God in the eschatological resurrection of the righteous (14:14).

Jesus tells a parable about those invited to a great dinner (14:15-24)

One of Jesus' fellow guests on hearing "these things," Jesus' preceding appeals to both the guests (14:7-11) and the host (14:12-14) of this sabbath banquet, exclaims, "Blessed ($\mu\alpha\kappa\acute{\alpha}\rho\iota\sigma\varsigma$) is anyone who will dine in the kingdom of God!" (14:15). This exuberant exclamation makes explicit for the audience the previous implicit references to the eschatological banquet. It confirms that if the host invites the poor and disabled to his banquets, he will be blessed ($\mu\alpha\kappa\acute{\alpha}\rho\iota\sigma\varsigma$) and repaid by God in the resurrection of the righteous (14:14) by dining at the eschatological banquet. It also makes explicit the implication that the guests who humble themselves at banquets will be exalted by God (14:11) by being among the "last" who will recline at the final banquet in the kingdom of God (13:30). It accords with Jesus' own pronouncement that blessed ($\mu\alpha\kappa\acute{\alpha}\rho\iota\sigma\iota$) are those servants who will be ready whenever he comes at the end of time, as he will make them recline and serve them himself at the eschatological banquet (12:37; cf. 12:38, 43).

Jesus elaborates upon the exuberant exclamation by his fellow guest (cf. 11:27-28) at this sabbath meal, as he tells a story about a certain man who gave a great dinner and invited many (14:16). The immediate reference to a "great dinner" to which many are invited after the exclamation about dining in the kingdom of God (14:15) alerts the audience to a parabolic story comparing the "great dinner" to the eschatological banquet in the kingdom of God. Levi's great banquet ($\delta o\chi\grave{\eta}\nu \mu\varepsilon\gamma\acute{\alpha}\lambda\eta\nu$) anticipated (5:29) and now the parabolic great dinner ($\delta\varepsilon\hat{\iota}\pi\nu o\nu \mu\acute{\varepsilon}\gamma\alpha$) characterizes God's great eschatological banquet. The "certain man" who at the time of the dinner sent his servant to tell those invited, "Come, for it is already prepared" (14:17), characterizes Jesus as the host, who through his ministry is inviting many, including the Pharisees and lawyers, to repent in order to dine at the great dinner in the kingdom of God that has already arrived (cf. 5:30, 34; 7:36-50; 11:37-54; 12:37; 13:22-30).

The mention of a certain man who invited (ἐκάλεσεν) many to the great dinner (14:16) leads the audience to compare this host, who characterizes Jesus as the host of the great eschatological dinner, with the host who invited (κεκληκότι) Jesus and other guests to the sabbath meal (14:12). The mention of those invited (κεκλημένοις) to the great dinner (14:17) guides the audience to a comparison with those invited (κεκλημένους) to the sabbath meal (14:7). And the mention of the servant (δοῦλον), whom the host sent (ἀπέστειλεν) to announce to those who had been invited that the great dinner is now ready (14:17), steers the audience to a comparison with the disciples. They have just recently been characterized as servants (δοῦλοι) awaiting the return of Jesus as their master (12:22, 37-47) and as the host who will serve them the eschatological meal (12:37). Jesus previously sent (ἀπέστειλεν) his disciples to continue his mission and ministry by announcing the arrival of the kingdom of God (9:2; 10:1, 9, 11). The parable of the great dinner thus communicates a threefold message to the Lukan audience as they identify in turn with the host, with the invited guests, and with the servant.[24]

All of those invited to the great dinner began to excuse themselves because of their selfish preoccupation and craving, "dropsical" desire to acquire property and increase their wealth and social status. Their excuses characterize them as members of the wealthy urban elite, bent on taking possession of a purchase or acquisition.[25] The first "purchased" a field and must go out of the city in which he lives apparently as a wealthy absentee landlord to inspect it and attend to the business of possessing it (14:18). Another "purchased" five yoke of oxen and was going to test his new acquisition (14:19). That he could buy in one transaction and needed this many animals for plowing indicates that he is the wealthy owner of a large amount of

---

[24] Tannehill ("Discourse on Invitations," 1616) discusses reading the parable both from the viewpoint of the host and the guests. He suggests but does not develop reading it also from the the viewpoint of the servant.

[25] For a more detailed socio-economic discussion of these excuses, see Rohrbaugh, "Pre-industrial City," 142-43; Braun, *Feasting*, 73-80.

land. Another "married" and thus acquired a wife, which involved accruing and maintaining additional wealth, and could not come (14:20).[26]

The invited guests who excuse themselves from the great dinner (14:18-20) provide the Pharisees and lawyers invited as guests of the sabbath meal (14:7), and the audience as they identify with them, a point of comparison. Will they, who are concerned to acquire positions of honor at banquets (14:7-10), fail to be blessed with the honor of dining in the kingdom of God (14:15), because their dropsical preoccupation with acquiring possessions and wealth leads them to reject Jesus' invitation to dine at the great eschatological dinner? For the audience as they identify with the host of the sabbath meal (14:12-14), the guests who excuse themselves from the great dinner demonstrate a failure of the system of social reciprocity. The host and audience are warned that those they invite to their banquets may be so preoccupied with their own wealthy social status that not only will they not repay the invitation (14:12), but they may even dishonor and humiliate their hosts by rejecting it.[27] For the audience as they identify with the disciples, characterized by the servant, whom the host sent with the invitation that the great dinner is ready (14:17), the rejection by those invited warns of the rejection they may encounter in being sent by Jesus to proclaim the arrival of the kingdom of God (9:2; 10:1, 9, 11).

That Jesus refers to the host of the great dinner as the "master of the house" or the "householder" ($οἰκοδεσπότης$), who became angry when the servant reported to him the rejection by the invited guests (14:21), enhances the different ways in which the audience identifies with and relates to the host. The audience can see themselves in the parable's householder and empathize with his anger over the rejection of his invitation, since Jesus has already told the disciples and thus the audience to be as ready for his final coming as the householder ($οἰκοδεσπότης$), who does not know when a thief will come to

---

[26] Braun, *Feasting*, 77: "Especially among the wealthy élite, primary among motives for marriage was the generation of legitimate sons as heirs to ensure that property remained in the family. Another motive, slightly lesser perhaps, was the attraction of a large dowry (wealth) to which came attached the added benefit of a manager of household chores (labour)...it is fair to say that acquiring a wife in the first place was governed more by forces that regulated the flow of wealth than by noble fancies for friendship."

[27] On the social dishonor and shame involved in the host's rejection by his wealthy peers, see Braun, *Feasting*, 100-113.

break into his house (12:39-40).[28] The audience can also see Jesus in the parable's householder, since he has already compared himself to the householder (οἰκοδεσπότης) who locked the door of the house and would not allow those who have only a superficial familiarity through eating and drinking with him to enter and recline at the eschatological banquet in the kingdom of God (13:25-29).

The angry householder directs his servant to go out quickly into the city's "streets" (πλατείας), the broader streets or squares serving as normal places for communication with the non-elite, and "lanes" (ῥύμας), the narrow streets and alleys where the poorest of the non-elite people lived, and bring to the dinner the poor and crippled and blind and lame (14:21).[29] Rather than seeking revenge on the originally invited, socially elite guests for the shame and dishonor of refusing his dinner invitation, the householder demonstrates a complete social conversion as he totally rejects the system of social reciprocity and surprisingly initiates a beneficent and non-reciprocal social interaction with the non-elite.[30] The "poor and crippled and blind and lame" are precisely the same socially non-elite and lowly groups Jesus has just urged the host of the sabbath meal to invite to his banquets instead of those who can repay him (14:12-13).

The social conversion of the parable's householder provides the host of the sabbath meal and thus the audience a model for their own social conversion. They are called to reject completely the system of social reciprocity and invite to their banquets society's poor and disabled (14:12-14), because these are the kind of people upon whom Jesus himself, characterized by the householder, will bestow the blessing of dining at the great eschatological dinner (14:15). The invitation of the poor and disabled calls the guests of the sabbath meal and thus the audience to further humble themselves. They are not only to take the last places at banquets (14:7-11) but to identify and associate themselves with the lowly poor and disabled if they hope to be blessed and exalted with honor by dining at the great eschatological dinner (14:15). That the parable's householder (Jesus) directs the servant (disciples)

---

[28] On the host's response of anger, Braun (*Feasting*, 114) comments that it is "a typical response of righteous indignation at being defamed without the warrant of one's actions or intentions. Outrage in the face of insult indeed is demanded by the honour-shame code itself." See also York, *Last Shall Be First*, 142.

[29] Rohrbaugh, "Pre-industrial City," 144.

[30] On the social conversion of the householder, see Braun, *Feasting*, 113-21.

to bring in the poor and disabled provides the audience a model for not being discouraged by the rejection of their announcement that the kingdom of God has arrived (10:1-12) but to turn to those who are better disposed to accept and appreciate it.

The "servant" then addresses the householder as "master" or "lord" (14:22) and "the lord" in turn replies to the "servant" (14:23). This further enhances for the audience the characterization of the disciples as the "servant" and of Jesus as "the lord" (see 12:36-47). The servant informs the master that what he ordered has been done and yet "there is still room" (14:22). This means there is still room for the originally invited guests who refused to come (14:18-20). But rather than turn to them, the master directs the servant to go into the "roads" (ὁδοὺς) outside of the city and the "fences" or "hedges" (φραγμοὺς) that surround properties beyond the city limits and force those of the lowest social position to come in, "so that my house may be filled" (14:23).[31] That the master will even "force" the outcasts who are unwilling to come because they do not belong socially, but does not bother to force the social elite who are unwilling to come underlines the master's social conversion and determination to exclude the original guests.[32] This is confirmed by his solemn pronouncement, "For I tell you, none of those invited will taste my dinner" (14:24).

For the Pharisee who hosts the sabbath meal, and the audience as they identify with him, the master continues to provide a model for their resolute rejection of the system of social reciprocity. After they have invited the poor and disabled of society, they are not to turn again to the wealthy and social

---

[31] BAGD, 865: "Vagabonds and beggars frequent the hedges and fences around houses." Rohrbaugh, "Pre-industrial City," 145: "...those just outside the walls usually included ethnic groups, tanners, and traders (along with the more commonly noted beggars and prostitutes), many of whom would have had business in the city (serving the needs of the elite) that required proximity to it. But they were not allowed to live inside the city walls." See also Braun, *Feasting*, 88-97.

[32] Braun, *Feasting*, 95: "...Luke opts for the most forceful language of invitation of the entire episode at this point. 'Make them enter by force of insistent persuasion' (ἀνάγκασον εἰσελθεῖν)." Rohrbaugh, "Pre-industrial City," 145: "Strong were the sanctions preventing those living immediately outside the walls from coming into the city for reasons other than business. Such people would have immediately understood the invitation as an inexplicable breach of the system. Considerable compulsion would be required to induce them to attend the supper."

elite and force them to come to their dinners. Instead, they are to invite and force those of lowest status in society to take their place. The Pharisees and lawyers invited (κεκλημένους) to the sabbath meal (14:3, 7), and the audience as they identify with them, are further warned that they may be among those invited (κεκλημένων) to the great dinner who will not taste it (14:24). If they continue to exalt themselves in their self-absorbing refusal of Jesus' invitation to the great dinner, they risk being humbled (14:11) by the loss of the blessing of dining in the kingdom of God (14:15). But if they humble themselves in association with the lowest of society, they will be exalted with the blessed honor of tasting the great dinner. The disciples, characterized by the servant, and the audience as they identify with them, are further encouraged to overcome the rejection of their invitation to the kingdom's great dinner that Jesus is already hosting by turning away from the selfish rich and toward the poor and lowly.[33]

Relation of Luke 14:1-24 to Previous Meal Scenes

1) Jesus' third meal with a Pharisee develops the *theme of Jesus calling the Pharisees and scribes/lawyers to repentance* in the context of a meal (5:32). In Jesus' first meal with a Pharisee (7:36-50) he invited Simon the Pharisee to repent by recognizing his need to be forgiven like the sinful woman (7:47). In his second meal with a Pharisee (11:37-54), Jesus called the Pharisees and lawyers to repent of their sinful ways as religious leaders. Rather than repent, they became extremely hostile and plotted to trap him in his

---

[33] The use of the plural "you" in the master's final pronouncement, "For I tell you (ὑμῖν)" (14:24) promotes the audience's identification with both the servant (disciples) of the parable and the guests (Pharisees and lawyers) invited to the sabbath meal. On the level of the parable the master addresses the plural "you" to the singular "servant," representative of the group of servants or disciples, who have just recently been characterized by the use of both the plural "servants" (12:37) and the singular "servant" (12:43, 45-47). On the level of the sabbath meal Jesus, as the master and host of the great eschatological dinner, addresses the plural "you" to the Pharisees and lawyers (14:3), his host (14:12) and fellow guests (14:7, 15). The warning, "I tell you, none of those invited will taste my dinner" (14:24) replies directly to the exclamation uttered by one of the fellow guests, "Blessed is anyone who will dine in the kingdom of God!" (14:15). But on the level of the Lukan narrative the implied audience hears Jesus address them directly with the plural "you."

speech (11:53-54). Now, in his third meal with a Pharisee (14:1-24), Jesus invites the Pharisees and lawyers to a complete conversion from their "dropsical," selfish system of social reciprocity. His healing of a man with dropsy calls them to abandon their hostility toward him by recognizing his superior authority and sharing his compassionate care to heal a fellow human being even on the sabbath (14:1-6). He urges them to repent of their selfish seeking of the first places of honor at banquets by humbly taking the last places, so that God will exalt them with honor at the eschatological banquet (14:7-11). He directs them to repent of their selfish seeking of social reciprocity by inviting to their banquets the poor and disabled, who cannot repay them, so that they may be repaid by God at the resurrection of the righteous (14:12-14). He warns that unless they repent of their selfish preoccupation with possessions (14:18-20) and associate with the poor, the sick, and the lowly, they will be excluded from the blessing of tasting the great dinner in the kingdom of God (14:15-24).

2) Jesus' third meal with a Pharisee continues to call the Pharisees and scribes/lawyers to a more *authentic and compassionate leadership*. In his first meal with a Pharisee (7:36-50) Jesus modeled for Simon the Pharisee a type of leadership that allows people like the sinful woman the opportunity to repent of their sinfulness and receive God's forgiveness. Now, in his third meal with a Pharisee Jesus models for the lawyers and Pharisees a type of leadership that allows people like the man with dropsy the opportunity to be healed of his disease even and especially on the sabbath (14:1-6). In his second meal with a Pharisee (11:37-54) Jesus exhorted the Pharisees and lawyers to give alms to the poor and hungry (11:39-41). Now, in the third meal he exhorts them to invite the poor, the disabled, and the socially non-elite to their banquets (14:13, 21, 23). Whereas he then warned them to be concerned with social justice and the love of God (11:42), he now goads them to a complete social conversion by turning away from the wealthy and toward the poor (14:12-13, 18-23). He advised them not to seek social honor by taking the first seats in synagogues (11:43). And now he instructs them to humble themselves socially by taking the lowest rather than the highest places of honor at banquets (14:7-11).

3) Jesus' third meal with a Pharisee advances the *theme of discipleship* in the meal scenes. In the miraculously overabundant meal Jesus empowered his disciples to continue his mission by not only healing and proclaiming the good news of the kingdom of God, but by nourishing people with an overabundance that anticipates the great eschatological banquet in the kingdom of God (9:10-17). Now, he encourages them that when his mission and ministry is rejected by the wealthy and social elite, they are to invite society's poor, disabled, and lowly to dine at the great dinner in the kingdom of God (14:15-24).

Pragmatics of the Meal Scene in Luke 14:1-24

1) Jesus calls the Pharisees and lawyers and thus the audience to a repentance that recognizes his power and authority not only to heal a man with dropsy on the sabbath, but to heal them of their moral dropsy, their craving desires to acquire wealth and honor for themselves. They can begin to allow Jesus to heal their dropsical selfishness by sharing his compassionate concern to heal the dropsical man even and especially on the sabbath, a sacred time to celebrate and experience God's refreshing liberation from the oppression of disease (14:1-6) that has now arrived with Jesus (4:18-21). Jesus warns the audience *to avoid a preoccupation with acquiring wealth and status in society* which will exclude them from the blessing of dining at the great banquet he will host in the kingdom of God (14:18-20, 24).

2) Jesus urges the audience not to selfishly seek social honor for themselves but *to humble themselves in their social behavior*, so that God will exalt them with the ultimate honor and blessing of dining at the eschatological banquet in the kingdom of God (14:7-11, 15).

3) Jesus challenges the audience not to selfishly seek the honor that society's wealthy can repay them but *to reject completely the system of social reciprocity*. They are to bestow the honor of inviting to their banquets society's poor, sick, and lowly, who cannot repay them. God will repay them at the eschatological resurrection of the righteous with the blessed honor of dining at the kingdom's great final banquet (14:12-24).

4) Jesus encourages the audience, sent to continue his mission and ministry by inviting people into the kingdom of God that has now arrived with Jesus, to overcome the rejection of their invitation by turning to those who are better disposed to appreciate and accept it, those who are *not selfishly absorbed with acquiring possessions and social honors* (14:15-24).

CHAPTER 8

MEALS CELEBRATING THE FINDING OF THE LOST
LUKE 15:1-32

The fifth section of the travel narrative (14:25-17:10) contains the next occurrence of the theme of eating and drinking. After the Pharisees and the scribes complain that Jesus welcomes and eats with sinners (15:1-2), he tells three parables in which implicit (15:3-10) and explicit (15:11-32) festive meals celebrate the joy of finding what was lost.[1]

Festive Meals Celebrating the Finding of the Lost (15:1-32)

1 All the tax collectors and the sinners were coming near to him to hear him. 2 But both the Pharisees and the scribes kept grumbling, saying, "This man welcomes sinners and eats with them."

3 So he addressed to them this parable: 4 "Which one of you, having a hundred sheep and losing one of them, does not leave the ninety-nine in the wilderness and go after the lost one until he finds it? 5 And finding it, he sets it upon his shoulders rejoicing. 6 And coming into the house, he calls together friends and neighbors, saying to them, 'Rejoice with me, for I have found my sheep that was lost.' 7 I tell you that in just the same way there will be more joy in heaven over one sinner who repents than over ninety-nine righteous who have no need of repentance.

8 Or what woman having ten silver coins, if she loses one silver coin, does not light a lamp, sweep the house, and search carefully until she finds it? 9 And when she finds it, she calls together friends and neighbors, saying, 'Rejoice with me, for I have found the silver coin that I lost.' 10 In just the same way, I tell you, there is joy among the angels of God over one sinner who repents."

11 Then he said, "A certain man had two sons. 12 The younger of them said to his father, 'Father, give me the share of the property that will come to me.' So he divided his estate between them. 13 Not many days later, gathering everything, the younger son traveled to a distant country and there he squandered his property, living dissolutely. 14 When he had spent everything, a severe famine took place throughout that country, and he began to be in need. 15 So he went and attached himself to one of the citizens of that country, who sent him into his fields to feed pigs. 16 He longed to satisfy his hunger from the pods the pigs were eating, but no one gave him anything. 17 Coming to himself, he said, 'How many hired workers of my father have more than

---

[1] On the fifth section of the travel narrative, see O'Fearghail, *Introduction to Luke-Acts*, 57.

enough food, while I am dying of hunger here. 18 I will get up and go to my father and I will say to him, "Father, I have sinned against heaven and before you. 19 I am no longer worthy to be called your son; treat me as one of your hired workers."'

20 So getting up he went to his father. But while he was still a long way off, his father saw him and was filled with compassion. He ran and threw his arms around his neck and kissed him affectionately. 21 The son said to him, 'Father, I have sinned against heaven and before you, I am no longer worthy to be called your son.' 22 But the Father said to his servants, 'Quick! Bring out the finest robe and put it on him; give him a ring for his hand and sandals for his feet. 23 Bring the fatted calf and slaughter it; let us eat and celebrate, 24 for this son of mine was dead but has come back to life, he was lost but has been found.' Then they began to celebrate.

25 Now the older son was in the field and as he came and approached the house, he heard music and dancing. 26 He called to one of the servant boys and asked what it was all about. 27 He said to him, 'Your brother has come and your father has slaughtered the fatted calf, because he has got him back safe and sound.' 28 Then he became angry and refused to go in. So his father went out and pleaded with him. 29 Replying he said to his father, 'Look, for all these years I have been serving you and have never disobeyed your command; yet you never gave me even a young goat so that I might celebrate with my friends. 30 But when this son of yours came, who devoured your estate with prostitutes, you slaughtered for him the fatted calf!' 31 Then he said to him, 'Child, you are always with me, and everything that is mine is yours. 32 But it was necessary to celebrate and rejoice, for this brother of yours was dead but has come to life, and he was lost but has been found.'"[2]

---

[2] Recent additions to the extensive literature on 15:1-32 include R. D. Aus, "Luke 15:11-32 and R. Eliezer Ben Hyrcanus's Rise to Fame," *JBL* 104 (1985) 443-69; Donahue, *Gospel in Parable*, 146-62; G. Scobel, "Das Gleichnis vom verlorenen Sohn als metakommunikativer Text: Überlegungen zur Verständigungsproblematik in Lukas 15," *Freiburger Zeitschrift für Philosophie und Theologie* 35 (1988) 21-67; Scott, *Hear Then the Parable*, 99-125; G. W. Ramsey, "Plots, Gaps, Repetitions, and Ambiguity in Luke 15," *Perspectives in Religious Studies* 17 (1990) 33-42; R. Couffignal, "Un père au coeur d'or: Approches nouvelles de Luc 15,11-32," *RevThom* 91 (1991) 95-111; idem, "Du jumelage des paraboles: Approches nouvelles de Luc XV,3-10," *BLE* 94 (1993) 3-18; Neale, *None But the Sinners*, 154-58; Gowler, *Host*, 250-56; B. Heininger, *Metaphorik, Erzählstruktur und Szenisch-Dramatische Gestaltung in den Sondergutgleichnissen bei Lukas* (NTAbh 24; Münster: Aschendorff, 1991) 140-66; K.-W. Niebuhr, "Kommunikationsebenen im Gleichnis vom verlorenen Sohn," *TLZ* 116 (1991)

Jesus eats with sinners (15:1-2)

Jesus concluded his teaching about the cost of discipleship (14:25-35) with the exhortation, "Whoever has ears *to hear*, let him *hear*" (14:35). Then all the tax collectors and the sinners were coming near to him "*to hear*" him (15:1). A hyperbolic "all" of the tax collectors and the sinners are thus strongly attracted to Jesus' teaching, receptive to hearing more of it. The audience knows that tax collectors willing to repent came to John, who challenged them to demonstrate their repentance with honesty in their profession (3:12-13). At the command of Jesus the tax collector Levi exhibited an even more radical repentance by abandoning his profession entirely to become a disciple (5:27-28).[3]

That the Pharisees and the scribes kept grumbling, "This man welcomes sinners and eats with them" (15:2) reminds the audience of their similar complaint at the great banquet Levi hosted for Jesus and a large crowd of tax collectors. Whereas at Levi's banquet they were grumbling (ἐγόγγυζον, 5:30), they are now still grumbling (διεγόγγυζον), expressed with a more intensive form of the verb. Whereas at Levi's banquet they complained that the disciples and Jesus were "eating and drinking" as fellow guests along with the tax

481-94; K. E. Bailey, *Finding the Lost: Cultural Keys to Luke 15* (St. Louis: Concordia, 1992); Darr, *Character Building*, 108-10; M. Gourgues, "Le père prodige (Lc 15,11-32): De l'exégèse à l'actualisation," *NRT* 114 (1992) 3-20; S. Durber, "The Female Reader of the Parables of the Lost," *JSNT* 45 (1992) 59-78; J. V. Kozar, "Absent Joy: An Investigation of the Narrative Pattern of Repetition and Variation in the Parables of Luke 15," *Toronto Journal of Theology* 8 (1992) 85-94; W. Pöhlmann, *Der verlorene Sohn und das Haus: Studien zu Lukas 15,11-32 im Horizont der antiken Lehre von Haus, Erziehung und Ackerbau* (WUNT 68; Tübingen: Mohr-Siebeck, 1993); Just, *Ongoing Feast*, 180-84; T. J. Geddert, "The Parable of the Prodigal: Priorities (Luke 15:11-32)," *Direction* 24 (1995) 28-36; E. Borghi, "Lc 15,11-32: Linee esegetiche globali," *RivB* 44 (1996) 279-308; du Plessis, "Applying the Results," 352-55; J. A. Harrill, "The Indentured Labor of the Prodigal Son (Luke 15:15)," *JBL* 115 (1996) 714-17; M. C. Parsons, "The Prodigal's Elder Brother: The History and Ethics of Reading Luke 15:25-32," *Perspectives in Religious Studies* 23 (1996) 147-74; E. R. Wendland, "Finding Some Lost Aspects of Meaning in Christ's Parables of the Lost--and Found (Luke 15)," *Trinity Journal* 17 (1996) 19-65; A. Batten, "Dishonour, Gender and the Parable of the Prodigal Son," *Toronto Journal of Theology* 13 (1997) 187-200.

[3] See chapter 2 on 5:27-32.

collectors and sinners (5:30), now they complain that Jesus himself acts as host as he even welcomes sinners with an offer of hospitality (προσδέχεται) and shares meal fellowship with them.[4]

At Levi's banquet Jesus answered their complaint by declaring that he has not come to invite the righteous but sinners to repentance (5:32). This not only explained that he is eating and drinking with tax collectors and sinners in order to invite and celebrate their repentance, but also provocatively prods the Pharisees and the scribes to recognize themselves as sinners, whom Jesus likewise invites to repent. The audience knows that the Pharisees and the scribes lack repentance. In contrast to the tax collectors who were baptized with John's baptism of repentance (7:29; 3:3), the Pharisees and the lawyers rejected God's plan for themselves by not receiving John's baptism of repentance (7:30). Instead of repenting they are among those who call Jesus a "glutton and drunkard, a friend of tax collectors and sinners" (7:34), who is now hosting the meals he is sharing with these outcasts (15:2).

Parable celebrating the finding of a lost sheep (15:3-7)

Jesus then addressed to them this "parable" (15:3), a metaphorical comparison to confront them in a dramatically unusual, provocative way. The parable is addressed not only to the tax collectors and sinners who were coming near to hear him (15:1), but also, and most especially, it serves as Jesus' reply to the complaint of the grumbling, unrepentant Pharisees and scribes: "This man welcomes sinners and eats with them" (15:2).

Jesus' introductory question, "Which one of you?," draws the Pharisees and scribes into the parable, inviting them to empathize with a shepherd. This is somewhat shocking, since observant Jews avoided tending sheep.[5] But if any one of them had a hundred sheep and lost one of them, they would surely, like this shepherd, who characterizes Jesus, leave the ninety-nine in the wilderness and go after the lost one until they found it (15:4). Still having ninety-nine sheep does not deter the shepherd from leaving them and going after a mere one that is lost. The audience knows from Ezekiel 34:11-12, 16 that God himself promises to seek out and bring back like a shepherd the lost among the people of Israel.[6] The parable then calls for the Pharisees and

---

[4] A. Palzkill, "προσδέχομαι," *EDNT* 3.162; Donahue, *Gospel in Parable*, 147.

[5] Donahue, *Gospel in Parable*, 148.

[6] On the prominent contribution of Ezekiel 34 to the NT shepherd metaphor, see J. P. Heil, "Ezekiel 34 and the Narrative Strategy of the Shepherd and Sheep Metaphor in Matthew," *CBQ* 55 (1993) 698-708.

scribes to identify with the rejoicing of the shepherd, who is so overcome with joy when he finds the lost sheep that he sets it upon his shoulders (15:5) to carry it home himself.[7] This characterizes Jesus' "welcome" of tax collectors and sinners (15:2).

That the shepherd comes into the house, the place of household hospitality, calls together friends and neighbors, and invites them to rejoice with him because he has found his sheep that was lost (15:6) implies the celebration of a festive meal. That the shepherd "calls together" (συγκαλεῖ) friends and neighbors to "rejoice with" (συγχάρητέ) him explains why Jesus "eats with" (συνεσθίει) tax collectors and sinners (15:2). His meal with them is a celebration of joy over their repentance. Like the shepherd, Jesus is inviting the Pharisees and scribes to share in the celebration of his joy in "finding" the tax collectors and sinners who were "lost" in their sinfulness. He has "found" them who were "lost" because they answered his call to repent (5:27-32; 7:29).

The joy of the shepherd (15:5) that he shares with his friends and neighbors (15:6) extends to God in the heavenly realm. Jesus' statement that there will be more joy in heaven over one sinner who repents than over ninety-nine righteous who have no need of repentance (15:7) further applies the parable to the Pharisees and scribes. They are to see themselves in the ninety-nine righteous who think they have no need of repentance. Jesus invites them not only to share in his joy as the shepherd, but to cause even greater joy in heaven by recognizing and repenting of their own sinfulness.

Parable celebrating the finding of a lost coin (15:8-10)

Jesus draws the Pharisees and scribes into another parable, inviting them this time to empathize with a woman who has ten silver coins, literally, ten drachmas, which were not of particularly great economic value.[8] A parable about a female figure thus balances, complements, and reinforces the parable about a male shepherd.[9] The woman who loses one of her ten silver coins is not content that she still has nine, but exercises great effort in finding the one she lost. She lights a lamp, sweeps the house, and searches carefully until she finds it (15:8). When she finds the coin she lost, the woman "calls together"

---

[7] The participle "rejoicing" (χαίρων) is placed in an emphatic position at the end of the sentence in 15:5.

[8] W. Pesch, "δραχμή," EDNT 1.354; Fitzmyer, Luke X-XXIV, 1081.

[9] For a list of other passages in Luke paralleling men and women, see Bailey, Finding the Lost, 97-99.

(συγκαλεῖ) friends and neighbors to "rejoice with" (συγχάρητέ) her (15:9), implying a celebration of a festive meal.[10] This reinforces that Jesus "eats with" (συνεσθίει) tax collectors and sinners (15:2) to celebrate the joy of their repentance with a meal. Like the shepherd and the woman, Jesus is inviting the Pharisees and scribes to share in the celebration of his joy in finding the lost tax collectors and sinners.

The joy of the woman also has its correspondence in heaven, as Jesus concludes: "In just the same way, I tell you, there is joy among the angels of God over one sinner who repents" (15:10). This time there is no comparison with the nine who have no need of repentance (cf. 15:7), so that the focus is exclusively and climactically on the one sinner who repents. Jesus thus reinforces his invitation for the Pharisees and scribes as well as the Lukan audience not only to share his and God's joy at the repentance of tax collectors and sinners, but to cause joy among the angels of God by repenting themselves.

Parable celebrating the finding of a lost son and brother (15:11-32)

The parables about a man having a hundred sheep (15:4) and about a woman having ten drachmas (15:8) are followed by a parable about a certain man who had two sons (15:11). As both the shepherd and the woman characterized Jesus as God's agent in search of repentant sinners, the audience expects the man with two sons likewise to portray Jesus as God's agent and to explain further to the Pharisees and scribes why he welcomes and eats with sinners (15:2).

The younger son repents after leaving his father and family (15:11-19)

The audience is shocked to hear the younger son brazenly ask his father to give him now the share of the family property that will come to him as an inheritance after his father dies. This rude request is most disrespectful, the equivalent of wishing that his father was already dead. Contrary to the sage advice of Sirach 33:20-24 not to dishonor oneself by distributing one's inheritance before death, the father surprisingly divided his estate between both of his sons (15:12). This further stuns the audience, as it goes against the

---

[10] Bailey (*Finding the Lost*, 103) sees an increase in personal responsiblity in the second parable, as the woman admits finding the coin *she had lost* (15:9), while the shepherd states his finding of the sheep *that was lost* (15:6).

household ethos of first century Palestine, which was based on preserving and maintaining the familial property intact rather than dividing and distributing it.[11]

The younger son continues his rebellious separation from his father and family as he soon gathered everything he had and emigrated to a distant country, leaving not only his home but his homeland. There he squandered his inherited property in dissolute living (15:13). After he had spent everything, the theme of eating and drinking emerges as a severe famine took place throughout that country, and he began to be in need of food (15:14). Having separated himself from his own father and family, the younger son is now forced to attach himself to a foreigner, one of the citizens of that distant country.[12] It becomes evident that the younger son has attached himself to a Gentile, because he sends him to feed pigs, something abhorrent for Jews, who consider pigs to be unclean animals (15:15).[13] Pathetically and ironically, the one feeding the pigs longed to satisfy his own hunger with the pods the pigs were eating, but no one gave him anything to eat (15:16). With no human being to offer him even the food of animals, the son finds himself in a situation worse than the unclean animals he is feeding.

Dire hunger motivates the younger son's repentance. Unable to obtain food to save his life, the son comes to his senses, realizing that while he is dying of hunger where he is, his father's hired workers have more than enough food (15:17). The expression of his repentance continues as he resolves to get up and go to his father. He rehearses his confession, acknowledging that he has sinned both against God and his father (15:18). He knows that he has completely forfeited his former status as a son in the household of his father, so he begs merely to be treated as one of his father's hired workers in order to have enough food to live on (15:19).

---

[11] Pöhlmann, *Verlorene Sohn*, 186.

[12] Harrill ("Prodigal Son," 717) suggests the more specific translation, "he was indentured to one of the citizens of that country," and notes: "The parable thus portrays the economic position of the son as extremely low in order to heighten the drama of the acceptance by the father. Read in this way, the parable becomes intelligible as one important part of Luke's larger theological theme of hospitality to the poor, outcast, and marginal, expressed in the language of ancient economics."

[13] Fitzmyer, *Luke X-XXIV*, 1088; Donahue, *Gospel in Parable*, 153: "The son, however, does not turn to his own but 'joined himself' to a Gentile, and his degradation is highlighted by his work as a swineherd, an occupation no Jew would assume. He has lost his familial, ethnic, and religious identity."

The father celebrates with a feast the return of his repentant son (15:20-24)

The younger son began to carry out his resolve (15:18) as he got up and went to his father. But while the son was still a long way off, his father saw him and, rather than being angry with his sinful son as the audience might expect, he was filled with compassion (15:20). When the neighborly Samaritan saw the half-dead man who had been attacked by robbers, he was moved to compassion (ἐσπλαγχνίσθη) for him (10:33). When Jesus saw the widow whose son had died, he was moved to compassion (ἐσπλαγχνίσθη) for her (7:13). Similarly, when the father saw his son dying of hunger (15:17), he was moved to compassion (ἐσπλαγχνίσθη) for him. Rather than waiting for his son to come to him, the father shocks the oriental sensibilities of the audience by running to his son.[14] He demonstrated his compassion as he threw his arms around his son's neck, literally "fell upon his neck," and kissed him affectionately (15:20).[15] The father running, embracing, and kissing his son corresponds to the shepherd going after his lost sheep and placing it upon his shoulders in joy when he finds it in the first parable (15:4-5), and to the woman lighting a lamp, sweeping the house, and searching carefully until she finds her lost silver coin in the second parable (15:8). But the lost sheep and coin that were found now progress to a person, the prodigal son, who repents and returns to his father.

The repentant son began to repeat the confession he had rehearsed (15:18-19), as he told his father, "Father, I have sinned against heaven and before you, I am no longer worthy to be called your son" (15:21). But he is not allowed to utter the concluding plea of his rehearsed confession, "treat me as one of your hired workers" (cf. 15:19). Rather than treat him as one of his hired workers, the father not only restores him to his status as son in the family, but eagerly and excitedly welcomes him to the household's hospitality as a special guest of honor. The father commanded the household servants to quickly bring out the finest, literally "first," robe and honor the son by putting it on him, to give him a ring for his hand, restoring his authority as son over the household servants (cf. Gen 41:42), and sandals for his feet, treating him as a son, not a slave or hired worker, who went barefoot (15:22).[16]

---

[14] Donhaue, *Gospel in Parable*, 154-55.

[15] The expression "fell upon his neck" imitates the LXX of Gen 33:4 (reunion of Esau and Jacob) and Gen 45:14 (reunion of Joseph and Benjamin).

[16] Donahue, *Gospel in Parable*, 155; Scott, *Hear Then the Parable*, 118; Marshall, *Luke*, 610-11.

When the excited father then ordered the household servants to bring the fatted calf, the one reserved for a special occasion, and slaughter it, he joyfully called for a grand household feast of abundant food, "Let us eat and celebrate" (15:23).[17] The feast of the fatted calf serves not only as a meal of sumptuous and abundant nourishment, restoring the life of the son who is dying of hunger (15:17), but also as a communal meal of joy, celebrating the return and restoration of the son to the father and his household.[18] With great emphasis on the son's relationship as son, "this *son of mine*," the father announces the reason for the joyful feast. *His son* was as good as dead, not only because he was dying of hunger, but because he was "dead" to his father, separated from him and not living in relation to him as his son. But through his own repentance and the nourishing meal of celebration the son "has come back to life" with his father. Just as the finding of the lost sheep and the finding of the lost coin called for communal celebrations of joy implying a meal, "Rejoice with me" (15:6, 9), so the father calls for a communal meal of joyful celebration, "Let us eat and celebrate" (15:23), for *his son* "was lost but has been found." And then they began their meal of celebration (15:24), which further explains Jesus' eating with tax collectors and sinners (15:1-2) as a joyful celebration of their repentance and restoration to the community.

The father appeals for the older son to repent and celebrate the feast (15:25-32)

The older son was not part of the celebration as he was in the field. That he heard "music and dancing" as he approached the house underlines the joyful and festive character of the communal meal (15:25). He called to one of the servant boys and asked what the celebration was all about (15:26). The servant boy answered in terms of the older son's familial relationship to both the younger son, "Your brother has come," and to the father, "Your father has slaughtered the fatted calf, because he has got him back safe and sound" (15:27). Rather than rejoicing upon the return of his own brother and sharing the joy of his father upon the return of his younger son, the older son became

---

[17] Bailey, *Finding the Lost*, 155: "The amount of meat butchered is an important clue to the size of the banquet. It would take perhaps two hundred people to eat a fatted calf. A grand occasion is anticipated."

[18] Scott, *Hear Then the Parable*, 118: "The killing of the fatted calf and the feast correlate with the theme of nourishment. The son has been starving, now he will be feasted. The two sets of symbols are not contrasted but woven together into the full theme of restoration."

angry and refused to participate in the communal meal of celebration. That the father left the great feast he was hosting and pleaded with rather than reprimanded his rebellious older son surprises the audience (15:28).[19]

In contrast to the younger son, who began his confession of sin with the respectful address, "Father" (15:18, 21), the older son neither addresses nor relates to his father as a father. Whereas the younger son acknowledged that he is no longer worthy to be called a son and wanted to be treated as a hired worker (15:19), the older son has for "all these years" related to his father as a faithful slave rather than as a son, "serving" him strictly, never disobeying his command (15:29). Both sons, therefore, have failed to relate properly to their father as true sons.

The parable's focus on the celebratory nature of eating and drinking continues in the older son's reproach of his father. He resents the fact that his father has never given him even a young goat so that "I might celebrate with my friends" (15:29). Rather than relating to his father as a son and asking for a young goat to celebrate with his friends, the older son expected the father to reward him as a servant for his many years of faithful service. His objection betrays his failure to relate not only as a son to his father but as a brother to his brother. The father, the younger son, and the whole household began to celebrate ($\varepsilon\dot{\upsilon}\phi\rho\alpha\acute{\iota}\nu\varepsilon\sigma\theta\alpha\iota$) in joy (15:24) after the father called for a communal meal of celebration by dining on the fatted calf, "Let us eat and celebrate ($\varepsilon\dot{\upsilon}\phi\rho\alpha\nu\theta\hat{\omega}\mu\varepsilon\nu$)" (15:23). But the older son is more concerned that he could not celebrate ($\varepsilon\dot{\upsilon}\phi\rho\alpha\nu\theta\hat{\omega}$) a communal meal of a young goat with his friends (15:29) than he is about celebrating this great feast of a fatted calf with his own father and brother.[20]

Although the servant boy told the older son that "your brother" has come (15:27), the older son completely disowns him. To his father he refuses to even acknowledge him as his brother, referring to him derogatively as "this son of yours" (15:30). The audience experiences the irony that the reason for the father's grand meal of celebration is precisely because the younger son has come back to life and been found as "this son of mine" (15:24). In contrasting himself to the younger son as "this son of yours," the older son ironically underscores how he himself relates to his father not as a "son of yours" but as

---

[19] Donahue, *Gospel in Parable*, 156: "The image of the father, leaving a celebration at which he is host to cajole an angry son, upsets the cultural expectations of the audience no less than his earlier running."

[20] S. Pedersen, "$\varepsilon\dot{\upsilon}\phi\rho\alpha\acute{\iota}\nu\omega$," *EDNT* 2.86: "The vb. is used in contexts of relationship. Jubilant joy presupposes the experience of the realization of community."

a faithful slave. Employing an eating metaphor, the older son accuses his younger brother of having "devoured" (καταφαγών) his father's estate with prostitutes (15:30), embellishing what the narrator reported (cf. 15:13-16). He resents that his father never gave "me" (ἐμοὶ), the one who faithfully served, even a young goat (15:29), but he slaughtered for "him" (αὐτῷ), this "devouring" son of his, the fatted calf (15:30).

Although the older son did not respectfully address the father as his father (15:29) like the younger son (15:18, 21), the father addresses him affectionately as his "child" (15:31). After eight occurrences of the word υἱός in the parable to refer to the father's sons, the father himself, at the climactic conclusion of the parable, addresses his older son with the more familiar and tender term τέκνον.[21] By addressing his older son as his beloved "child," the father is calling him to repent, to change his way of relating to his father only as a faithful servant and realize that he is also his father's son, indeed his cherished "child."

In contrast to the younger son, who had abandoned his father, was lost, and as good as dead (15:24), "you," the father tells the older son with an emphatic use of the pronoun σὺ, "are always with me" (15:31). The father thus affirms the older son's years of faithful and obedient service (15:29). But he calls him to repent from relating to his father as merely a faithful servant and to relate to him as his beloved son and companion who has always been and still is with him.

The father's assurance to his older son that "everything that is mine is yours" (15:31) continues his appeal for him to repent and change the way he relates to his father. He does not need to relate to his father as a servant who expects to be rewarded with a young goat to celebrate with his friends (15:29). All he has to do is ask his father as his son for what belongs to him. He should not resent that the fatted calf has been slaughtered for his younger brother (15:30), since it and everything the father owns belongs to him as the older son as well.

The continuation of the father's pleading (15:28) with his older son adds an explicit note of joy to the meal of celebration. That "it was necessary to celebrate and rejoice (χαρῆναι)" (15:32) assimilates the joy of this grand feast with the communal celebrations of joy in the first two parables. The shepherd was rejoicing (χαίρων) when he found his lost sheep (15:5) and called others to rejoice with (συγχάρητέ) him (15:6). Jesus compared this to the joy (χαρὰ) in heaven over one repentant sinner (15:7). The woman who

---

[21] BAGD, 808; Scott, *Hear Then the Parable*, 121-22; Bailey, *Finding the Lost*, 183; Fitzmyer, *Luke X-XXIV*, 1091; Marshall, *Luke*, 612.

found her lost coin likewise called for others to rejoice with (συγχάρητέ) her (15:9), and Jesus likewise compared this with the joy (χαρὰ) before God over one repentant sinner (15:10).

When the father called for the communal meal of celebration, he gave as the reason: "*This son of mine* was dead but has come back to life, he was lost but has been found" (15:24). Now, as he urges his older son to join the celebration, he gives as the reason: "*This brother of yours* was dead but has come to life, and he was lost but has been found" (15:32).[22] Although the servant boy told the older son that "your brother" has come (15:27), the older son disdained his brother before his father, referring to him derogatively as "this son of yours" (15:30). Now the father appeals for the older son to repent not only by relating to him as his father (15:31), but by relating to the younger son as "this brother of yours." As the finding of the lost sheep (15:3-7) and the finding of the lost coin (15:8-10) called for communal celebrations of joy, so the father urges his older son that "it was necessary" (ἔδει, 15:32) for the whole household community, including the older son, to celebrate and rejoice, since not only "this son of mine" but "this brother of yours" was lost but has been found.

This third parable remains provocatively open-ended. Does the older son repent and join in the communal meal of joyful celebration? The Pharisees and the scribes are to answer that question by seeing themselves in the older son. Like the older son who became angry and refused to join in the communal meal of celebration (15:28), the Pharisees and the scribes grumbled because Jesus welcomes and eats with sinners (15:2). The three parables indicate that Jesus' meals with sinners are communal celebrations of joy over their repentance. Jesus is thus prodding the Pharisees and the scribes, as well as the audience of Luke, to conclude the final parable by their own repentance. He calls them to relate to God not just as faithful servants (15:29) but as cherished sons of a loving and compassionate father (15:31), and to relate to other sinners who repent as brothers of that same father (15:32). By repenting themselves and experiencing what it means to come back to life and be found as lost sons of God, their compassionate father (15:24, 32), the Pharisees and the scribes can join Jesus' meals that celebrate God's joy over any sinner who repents (15:7, 10).

---

[22] On the characterization of the lost son and brother as "dead" in 15:24, 32, see Roth, *The Blind*, 183-86.

Summary of the Theme of Eating and Drinking in Luke 15:1-32

The theme of eating and drinking pervades the sequence of scenes in Luke 15:1-32. After the Pharisees and the scribes grumbled about Jesus eating with sinners (15:2), the joyful communal celebrations following the finding of the lost sheep and of the lost coin, with their implicit meals (15:6, 9), began to indicate that Jesus eats with sinners in order to communally celebrate the joy of their being found by repenting. The acute hunger of the younger son, who longed to eat the food he was feeding to pigs (15:14-16), motivated his decision to repent and return to his father, whose hired workers have more than enough food (15:17-19). That the father calls for a special household feast of fatted calf when his younger son repented and returned continued to interpret Jesus' meals with sinners as communal celebrations of joy over their repentance (15:23-24). After the older son angrily contrasted the fatted calf slaughtered for the younger son, who "devoured" the father's property with prostitutes, to the goat he did not receive from his father for a meal of celebration with his friends (15:29-30), the father urged him to repent and join the feast of the fatted calf celebrating the joy of the return of the son and brother who came back to life and was found by repenting (15:31-32).

Relation of Luke 15:1-32 to Previous Meal Scenes

1) The parabolic festive meals of Luke 15:1-32 develop the *theme of calling for and celebrating the repentance of sinners at communal meals*. After the Pharisees and the scribes grumbled at Levi's great banquet that Jesus and his disciples share meal fellowship with tax collectors and sinners, Jesus explained that he eats with sinners to call for and celebrate their repentance (5:27-32). Now, after the Pharisees and the scribes grumbled more intensely that Jesus even welcomes as a host and eats with sinners (15:2), he explains with three parables how his meals with sinners are communal celebrations of great joy over the finding and coming to life of lost sinners (15:5-6, 9, 23-24, 32), celebrations of great joy that have their correspondence with God in heaven (15:7, 10).

2) Implicitly at Levi's banquet and explicitly at his three meals with Pharisees (7:36-50; 11:37-54; 14:1-24) Jesus called for *the Pharisees and the scribes to repent of their own sinfulness*. He now prods them to see themselves in the parable's older son, who refused to join in the joyful feast celebrating the repentance and return of the younger son (15:28). Like the older son, they are urged to repent by relating to God not merely as faithful and obedient servants but as cherished sons of a compassionate and loving father (15:29, 31). Like the older son, they are further urged to repent by relating to those

sinners who have repented as their fellow brothers. Having thus repented themselves, they can then appreciate and share in, rather than grumble against (5:30; 15:2), Jesus' meals celebrating God's great joy over the repentance of any sinner (15:6-7, 9-10, 23-24, 32).

3) The festive meals of Luke 15:1-32 develop the *theme of the joy, nourishment, and abundance of the eschatological banquet that is making its appearance with Jesus*. Levi's great banquet celebrating the joy of repentance prefigured the great eschatological banquet that Jesus is bringing about (5:27-32). That was followed by the disciples' festive eating and drinking rather than fasting because of the presence of Jesus as the "bridegroom" of the end-time wedding banquet (5:33-39). Jesus then allowed his disciples to satisfy their hunger on the sabbath as an anticipation of the final time of salvific refreshment he has inaugurated (6:1-5). Jesus and his apostles nourished a great crowd of people with a miraculously overabundant meal that anticipates the abundance of the messianic banquet (9:10-17).

Now, Jesus' meals with repentant sinners (15:1-2), which anticipate God's great end-time banquet, are characterized as grand feasts celebrating the tremendous joy of God himself over any sinner who repents (15:7, 10). The grand feast of the fatted calf adds to the rich flavor of the eschatological banquet arriving with Jesus. It abundantly satisfies and nourishes the dire hunger of the younger son, who acknowledged that even the hired workers of his father have more than enough food (15:17). Greatly surpassing the older son's desired meal of a young goat to celebrate with his friends (15:29), the father's (God's) feast of fatted calf provides a sumptuously and abundantly nourishing celebration for the entire household of family and servants (15:22-24, 31-32).

Pragmatics of the Meal Scenes in Luke 15:1-32

1) With three parables Jesus invites the Pharisees and the scribes, as well as the audience of Luke, to empathize with the shepherd (15:3-7), the woman (15:8-10), and the father (15:11-32), who celebrate most appropriately with communal and festive meals the great joy of finding a lost sheep, a lost coin, and a lost son. Then they can not only appreciate his meals with sinners (15:1-2) as communal celebrations of finding what was lost, but also participate in his and God's (15:7, 10) *compassionate celebration of great joy over any sinner who repents*. They will then be compassionate as their Father is compassionate (6:36).

2) By identifying with the younger son, who represents the repentant tax collectors and sinners who eat with Jesus (15:1-2), the audience realizes the possibility and necessity of their own repentance from sin, which can render

them "lost" and "dying" of hunger in their relationship to God. When they repent of their sinfulness, the audience can expect to be received with the *overwhelming forgiveness, abundantly satisfying nourishment, and tremendous joy of God as their loving and merciful Father*. Their repentance is worthy of being celebrated with communal and festive meals of great joy (15:6-7, 9-10, 11-24).

3) The older son provides a provocative model and mirror in which the Pharisees and the scribes and thus the audience can see themselves. Jesus prods them to complete the final parable by answering the father's plea for the older son to repent from relating to him as merely a faithful and obedient servant and *relate to him as a cherished child of a lovingly compassionate father*. By further repenting and relating to any sinner who repents as their fellow brothers and sisters, they can share in the grand end-time banquet communally celebrating God's immense joy over the repentance of any and all sinners (15:25-32).

CHAPTER 9

THE MEALS OF A RICH MAN AND LAZARUS
LUKE 16:19-31

The next meal scenes also occur within the fifth section of the travel narrative (14:25-17:10) in the parable that contrasts a rich, well-fed man with a poor, hungry man named Lazarus (16:19-31). The parable climaxes Jesus' address to the Pharisees as lovers of money (16:14-18).

Jesus Addresses the Pharisees as Lovers of Money (16:14-18)

Jesus concluded his parable to the disciples about the dishonest steward (16:1-13) with the warning that you cannot serve God and "mammon," that is, property or wealth (16:13).[1] The Pharisees overheard this and, being lovers of money, sneered at Jesus (16:14). Just as he told the Pharisees and scribes who grumbled against him for welcoming and eating with sinners (15:2) parables aimed at their repentance (15:3-32), so now he challenges the sneering Pharisees to repent.[2]

Jesus accuses the Pharisees of "justifying" themselves before human beings (16:15) by loving money (16:14) and serving mammon (16:13). This recalls and develops for the audience how they have rejected God's plan for themselves (7:30) and have not "justified" God by being baptized with John's baptism of repentance (7:29; 3:3). That God knows their hearts (16:15) means that God knows that in their hearts they are serving mammon and loving money rather than serving and loving God (16:13; cf. 11:39-44; 12:29). The service of mammon and love of money that exalts them among human beings is an abomination ($\beta\delta\acute{\epsilon}\lambda\upsilon\gamma\mu\alpha$), that is, idolatry, before God (16:15).[3] Jesus is thus warning the Pharisees of their need to repent from their worship of money as a false god.[4]

That "the law and the prophets (were) until John" (16:16) means that John's preaching of a baptism of repentance for the forgiveness of sins (3:3) is in continuity with the call for repentance in the law and the prophets. The audience has already heard the angel of the Lord before the birth of John tell his father Zechariah that John would continue the prophet Elijah's call for the

---

[1] BAGD, 490; H. Balz, "$\mu\alpha\mu\omega\nu\hat{\alpha}\varsigma$," *EDNT* 2.382.

[2] J. J. Kilgallen, "The Purpose of Luke's Divorce Text (16,18)," *Bib* 76 (1995) 229-38.

[3] J. Zmijewski, "$\beta\delta\acute{\epsilon}\lambda\upsilon\gamma\mu\alpha$," *EDNT* 1.210; Moxnes, *Economy*, 148; Ireland, *Stewardship*, 127.

[4] J. J. Kilgallen, "Luke 15 and 16: A Connection," *Bib* 78 (1997) 375.

people to repent and reform. He "will turn" or convert many in Israel to the Lord their God. He will go before the Lord in the spirit and power of Elijah to "turn" the disobedient to the understanding of the righteous, to make ready for the Lord a people prepared by their repentance (1:16-17; cf. 1:76-77; 7:26).[5] John is the one whom the law and the prophets (cf. Exod 23:20; Mal 3:1) wrote about as the messenger sent by God before Jesus to prepare his way before him (7:27) by calling for repentance (cf. 3:3-4, 8; 7:29).

But "from then on," that is, in continuity with the time of the preaching of John and of the law and the prophets, the kingdom of God "is being proclaimed as good news" (16:16). The proclaiming of the good news of the kingdom of God by Jesus (4:18, 43; 7:22; 8:1) and his apostles (9:6) continues John's proclaiming of good news to the people (3:18). Just as John's preaching and evangelizing called for repentance, so the proclamation of the good news of the kingdom of God means "everyone is forcing himself into it" ($\pi\hat{\alpha}\varsigma$ $\varepsilon\grave{\iota}\varsigma$ $\alpha\grave{\upsilon}\tau\grave{\eta}\nu$ $\beta\iota\acute{\alpha}\zeta\varepsilon\tau\alpha\iota$) (16:16), that is, everyone entering it is exerting the personal force or effort, the repentance, called for.[6] Shortly after warning the crowds (12:54; 13:1) that they will all perish if they do not repent (13:3, 5), Jesus answered the question of how many will be saved with the exhortation: "Struggle ($\dot{\alpha}\gamma\omega\nu\acute{\iota}\zeta\varepsilon\sigma\theta\varepsilon$) to enter through the narrow gate" (13:24). Jesus is thus challenging the Pharisees to hear the good news of the arrival of the kingdom of God and to join all those who are exerting the force and struggling to enter it by repenting.

Jesus then greatly bolsters the law and the prophets as the enduring foundation of the good news and its corresponding new demands for entering the kingdom of God by asserting that it would be easier for heaven and earth to pass away than for a stroke of a letter of the law to become invalid (16:17). His next statement, "everyone who divorces his wife and marries another commits adultery, and whoever marries a woman divorced from her husband commits adultery" (16:18), exemplifies both the enduring validity of the law as well as one of the new demands for entering the kingdom of God. Since divorce was previously permitted by the law (Deut 24:1-4), eliminating it

---

[5] Fitzmyer, *Luke I-IX*, 327: "John's role will be a continuation of the reform effort of the famous prophet of old."

[6] For a discussion of the many problems involved with translating and interpreting this clause, see Marshall, *Luke*, 629-30; Fitzmyer, *Luke X-XXIV*, 1117-18; Ireland, *Stewardship*, 130-32; W. Stenger, "$\beta\iota\acute{\alpha}\zeta o\mu\alpha\iota$," *EDNT* 1.216-17.

represents a new demand of the kingdom.[7] Rather than undermining the law, this new demand for avoiding divorce sharpens it by extending the law against adultery (Exod 20:13; Lev 20:10; Deut 5:17; 22:22) to include divorce.[8] The repentance to which Jesus calls the Pharisees and Luke's audience includes avoiding divorce as an example of what it means to struggle to enter the kingdom by force.[9]

The Reversed Meals of a Rich Man and Poor Lazarus (16:19-31)

19 "There was a certain man who was rich, and he used to dress in purple and fine linen, feasting sumptuously every day. 20 At his gate was lying a certain poor man named Lazarus covered with sores 21 and longing to satisfy his hunger from what fell from the table of the rich man. But rather, dogs were coming and licking his sores.

22 The poor man died and he was carried away by angels to the bosom of Abraham. The rich man also died and was buried. 23 Lifting up his eyes in Hades, being in torture, he saw Abraham from afar and Lazarus at his bosom. 24 And calling out he said, 'Father Abraham, have mercy on me and send Lazarus to dip the tip of his finger in water and cool my tongue, for I am suffering torment in these flames.' 25 But Abraham said, 'Child, remember that you received your good things during your life, and Lazarus likewise bad

---

[7] The saying in 16:18, then, is not merely a figurative, parabolic lesson to be learned from the irrevocability of marriage, as suggested by Kilgallen ("Luke's Divorce Text," 229-38), but an actual teaching about avoiding divorce.

[8] Marshall, *Luke*, 631: "...the saying is included by Luke at this point in order to illustrate the continuing validity of the law but in the new form given to it by Jesus."

[9] Note the progressive parallelism in 16:16-18, in which statements upholding the validity of the law (a) alternate with statements asserting the new demands of the kingdom of God which are in continuity with the law (b):

(a) The *law* and the prophets (were) until John,

(b) from then on the kingdom of God is proclaimed as good news and *everyone* ($\pi\hat{\alpha}\varsigma$) is forcing his way into it.

(a) It is easier for heaven and earth to pass away than for one stroke of a letter of the *law* to become invalid.

(b) *Everyone* ($\pi\hat{\alpha}\varsigma$) who divorces his wife and marries another commits adultery, and whoever marries a woman divorced from her husband commits adultery.

things; but now he is comforted here, whereas you are suffering torment. 26 Besides all this, between us and you a great chasm has been fixed, so that those wishing to cross from here to you cannot do so, and no one can cross over from there to us.'

27 He said, 'I beg you then, father, to send him to the house of my father, 28 for I have five brothers, so that he may warn them, lest they too come to this place of torture.' 29 But Abraham said, 'They have Moses and the prophets; let them listen to them.' 30 He said, 'No, father Abraham, but if someone from the dead goes to them, they will repent.' 31 He said to him, 'If they do not listen to Moses and the prophets, not even if one were to rise from the dead will they be convinced.'"[10]

The rich man feasts while poor Lazarus suffers in hunger (16:19-21)

That the parable begins by introducing "a certain man who was *rich*" (16:19) recalls for the audience Luke's previous negative associations with

---

[10] There has been much interest in various extra biblical backgrounds and parallels to 16:19-31: R. F. Hock, "Lazarus and Micyllus: Greco-Roman Backgrounds to Luke 16:19-31," *JBL* 106 (1987) 447-63; E. Reinmuth, "Ps.-Philo, *Liber Antiquitatum Biblicarum* 33,1-5 und die Auslegung der Parabel Lk 16:19-31," *NovT* 31 (1989) 16-38; L. Kreitzer, "Luke 16:19-31 and 1 Enoch 22," *ExpTim* 103 (1992) 139-42; J. G. Griffiths, "Cross-Cultural Eschatology with Dives and Lazarus," *ExpTim* 105 (1993) 7-12.

For a balanced assessment of many of the parallels that have been proposed, see R. Bauckham, "The Rich Man and Lazarus: The Parable and the Parallels," *NTS* 37 (1991) 225-46.

Recent additional treatments of 16:19-31 include Pilgrim, *Good News to the Poor*, 113-19; Seccombe, *Possessions*, 173-81; Donahue, *Gospel in Parable*, 169-76; Scott, *Hear Then the Parable*, 141-59; W. Vogels, "Having or Longing: A Semiotic Analysis of Luke 16:19-31," *Église et Théologie* 20 (1989) 27-46; Gowler, *Host*, 257-63; Heininger, *Sondergutgleichnissen*, 177-91; York, *Last Shall Be First*, 62-71; Ireland, *Stewardship*, 134-38; R. A. Piper, "Social Background and Thematic Structure in Luke 16," *The Four Gospels 1992: Festschrift Frans Neirynck* (BETL 100; ed. F. Van Segbroeck, et al; Leuven: Leuven University Press, 1992) 1637-62; W. R. Herzog, *Parables as Subversive Speech: Jesus as Pedagogue of the Oppressed* (Louisville: Westminster/Knox, 1994) 114-30; Böhlemann, *Jesus und der Täufer*, 138-40; Roth, *The Blind*, 186-93; M. L. Rigato, "'Mosè e i profeti' in chiave cristiana: un pronunciamento e un midrash (Lc 16,16-18 + 19-31)," *RivB* 45 (1997) 143-77.

riches: Jesus' "Woe to you *rich*" (6:24); the wealth of a *rich man* made him foolish (12:16-21); and Jesus warned his Pharisee host not to invite to meals *rich* neighbors, who can reciprocate (14:12).[11] It also links the parable directly to his audience of Pharisees, who have just been described as "lovers of money" (16:14). They are invited possibly to see something of themselves in the parable's rich man.

The excessively wealthy lifestyle of the rich man is emphasized: He customarily dressed in expensive "purple and fine linen, feasting sumptuously every day" (16:19).[12] Whereas in a previous parable a foolish rich man looked forward, because of his accumulated wealth, to the many years in which he could relax, eat, drink, and "feast" (12:19), and whereas the parable of the lost sons mentioned special occasions for "feasting" (15:23, 24, 29, 32), the rich man of this parable was "feasting" not occasionally but every day "sumptuously," "splendidly," or "ostentatiously" ($\lambda\alpha\mu\pi\rho\hat{\omega}\varsigma$).[13] The rich man's festive meals, his enjoyment of the pleasures of food and drink with others, appear to be extravagant in their frequency, quantity, and quality.

At the very "gate" of the rich man, that is, at the entrance of his home, and thus in a position of close vicinity and visibility to the rich man and those participating in his daily luxuriant feasts, was lying a certain poor man named Lazarus covered with sores (16:20). Although Lazarus was one of the "*poor*," the rich man has not invited him to his banquet, thus failing to heed Jesus' injunction to the money-loving Pharisees to invite to their banquets the *poor*, the crippled, the lame, the blind (14:13), who will be included by God in the eschatological banquet (14:21). In contrast to the anonymous rich man the poor man has a name that associates him with God, since "Lazarus," an abbreviation of "Eliezar," means "he whom God helps."[14] Whereas the rich

---

[11] On riches in Luke, see H. Merklein, "$\pi\lambda o\acute{u}\sigma\iota o\varsigma$," *EDNT* 3.115-16.

[12] Fitzmyer, *Luke X-XXIV*, 1130: "His garments, described in OT terms (Prov 31:22), insinuate that he lived like a king." Scott, *Hear Then the Parable*, 148: "Purple and fine linen place the man among the elite, possibly an urban elite." Herzog, *Parables*, 117: "In short, the rich man dresses with imported luxury items to display his great wealth as a form of conspicuous consumption."

[13] On $\lambda\alpha\mu\pi\rho\hat{\omega}\varsigma$ here Scott (*Hear Then the Parable*, 149 n. 26) remarks: "The root sense of the term is 'bright, shining, radiant.' Perhaps 'ostentatious' is a more accurate translation."

[14] Fitzmyer, *Luke X-XXIV*, 1131; Marshall, *Luke*, 635; York, *Last Shall Be First*, 67; Herzog, *Parables*, 120; Scott, *Hear Then the Parable*, 149: "The name Lazarus contrasts the two characters: one is full of possessions, and the other is empty except for a name, but the meaning of the name may well hold out a promise."

man was luxuriously dressed in purple and fine linen, the poor Lazarus was covered with sores. That Lazarus "was lying" (ἐβέβλητο) at the gate of the rich man connotes that he "was thrown down" or "confined" there, bedridden as a result of his poverty and sickness.[15]

Whereas the rich man was feasting sumptuously every day (16:19), the poor Lazarus was "longing to satisfy his hunger" (ἐπιθυμῶν χορτασθῆναι) from the excess food that fell from the table of the rich man (16:21).[16] But unfortunately the hungry Lazarus received no food from the table of the feasting rich man. The predicament of Lazarus reminds the audience of the prodigal son who likewise "longed to satisfy his hunger (ἐπεθύμει χορτασθῆναι) from the pods the pigs were eating, but no one gave him anything" (15:16). Rather than being fed, Lazarus's situation only worsened as he became a food-like object for the dogs, often viewed as wild, ravaging, unclean animals, who were coming and licking his sores (16:21).[17] Instead of enjoying the hospitality of meal fellowship in the company of human beings, Lazarus was ignored by the rich man to starve as a victim of savage animals. The stark contrast between the rich man merrily feasting in uncompassionate bliss and the pathetic plight of the poor, afflicted, and hungry Lazarus should evoke the thorough disgust of the audience.

Lazarus is carried to Abraham while the rich man thirsts in Hades (16:22-26)

When the poor man Lazarus died, he received the divine assistance promised by the meaning of his name. Apparently left unburied by human beings, he became the recipient of God's special care, as "he was carried away by angels to the bosom of Abraham" (16:22). In a dramatic reversal to his exclusion from the rich man's luxurious feast, Lazarus was lavishly transported by God's own angels to the very bosom of Abraham. He was given the position of an honored guest with the great patriarch (cf. 13:28-29) at the

---

[15] BAGD, 131; O. Hofius, "βάλλω," *EDNT* 1.191; Fitzmyer, *Luke X-XXIV*, 1131; York, *Last Shall Be First*, 66 n. 3; Herzog, *Parables*, 118.

[16] For the view that what fell from the table refers to loaves of bread used as napkins, see Herzog, *Parables*, 118. Marshall (*Luke*, 636) discounts this interpretation.

[17] S. Pedersen, "κύων," *EDNT* 2.332; Marshall, *Luke*, 636; Hock, "Lazarus and Micyllus," 458 n. 41; York, *Last Shall Be First*, 66 n. 6; Scott, *Hear Then the Parable*, 151; Herzog, *Parables*, 118-19.

eschatological banquet in God's kingdom.[18] Like Lazarus the rich man died and in accord with his wealthy status, but unlike the poor Lazarus, was blessed with a proper burial (16:22). That the rich man was simply "buried," however, sharply contrasts with the poor man's swift transferal by angels to a place in the heavenly banquet with Abraham.

It is surely shocking for the "lovers of money" (16:14) in Jesus' audience to hear that the rich man has not been admitted to the heavenly banquet like Lazarus. Instead he finds himself being tormented in Hades, the realm of the dead.[19] A most dramatic reversal involving positions at meals has occurred. Whereas the rich man had been feasting *above* Lazarus, so that he was longing for what fell down from the table of the rich man (16:21), now Lazarus is enjoying table fellowship at the very bosom of Abraham *above* the rich man, so that he must "lift up" his eyes to see them. Ironically, the rich man, who apparently never looked down to see Lazarus in need when he was nearby, "at his gate" (16:20), now lifts up his eyes and sees Lazarus at the bosom of Abraham "from afar" (16:23).[20] The rich man who is being tormented in Hades now finally sees from afar the Lazarus whose torment he overlooked when he was at his very gate.

The exclusion of the rich man from the eschatological banquet confirms for the audience Jesus' previous warning to those who fail to enter God's kingdom through the narrow gate (13:24) by repenting (13:3, 5). The unrepentant rich man experiences now the anguish they will experience when they see Abraham with the other patriarchs and all the prophets reclining at table in the kingdom of God while they are cast outside (13:28-29). Despite John's previous warning that those who fail to produce fruit worthy of repentance cannot rely upon their descent from "father" Abraham (3:8), the unrepentant rich man presumptuously pleads for "father Abraham," renowned for his hospitality, to have mercy on him by sending "Lazarus to dip the tip of

---

[18] Marshall, *Luke*, 636; York, *Last Shall Be First*, 67. On his position in the bosom (κόλπον) of Abraham, Fitzmyer (*Luke X-XXIV*, 1132) notes: "...it may suggest either a place of honor for a guest at a banquet at the right hand of the host (see John 13:23) or an association of intimacy (see John 1:18)." Herzog, *Parables*, 121: "The image of Lazarus as honored guest at the banquet of the patriarchs would seem most appropriate to the context. The great banquet of Abraham would then contrast with the sumptuous feasts of the first scene of the parable."

[19] O. Böcher, "ᾅδης," *EDNT* 1.30-31.

[20] On the spatial contrasts in the story, see Vogels, "Having or Longing," 39-41; Herzog, *Parables*, 122.

his finger in water and cool my tongue, for I am suffering torment in these flames" (16:24).[21]

That the rich man recognizes Lazarus betrays his neglect of the poor man with whom he was familiar during their lives. He callously demonstrates his continuing unrepentance in his relationship with Lazarus, whom he selfishly regards as a mere servant to be sent for his comfort.[22] The irony of the reversal is delectable. Whereas Lazarus in his extreme hunger longed to be filled from the mere morsels of food falling from the rich man's table (16:21), the rich man burning in thirst now longs for his tongue to be cooled by a mere drop of water falling from the tip of Lazarus's finger (16:24).[23] Whereas the rich man allowed the sores of Lazarus to be disgustingly licked by the tongues of ravaging dogs (16:21), he now wants Lazarus to refresh his own scorching tongue, the previously pampered tongue with which he had selfishly enjoyed the sumptuous food and drink he failed to share with the poor, hungry and thirsty Lazarus. As it reinforces the note of his being in torture (16:23), the rich man's acknowledgment that "I am suffering torment in these flames" (16:24) sharpens the surprising shock that serves as a warning to the "lovers of money" (16:14) in the audience.

In response to his address of Abraham as "father" (16:24), Abraham addresses the rich man with the affectionate term "child" (τέκνον, 16:25). The audience recalls how the father of the prodigal son addressed his elder son as "child" (τέκνον, 15:31) when he urged him to repent by acknowledging the

---

[21] For the Jewish tradition of relying upon descent from Abraham as a guarantee of salvation, see O. Betz, "'Αβραάμ," *EDNT* 1.2; Fitzmyer, *Luke I-IX*, 468; D. L. Bock, *Luke 1:1-9:50* (BECNT 3A; Grand Rapids: Baker Books, 1994) 305-6. On Abraham as a model of hospitality in Jewish tradition, see Scott, *Hear Then the Parable*, 153-54; Herzog, *Parables*, 122-23.

[22] Herzog, *Parables*, 123: The rich man "is still an elite, accustomed to issuing orders and having them obeyed...To the rich man, Lazarus is self-evidently a servant, a domestic, an errand boy to do Abraham's bidding...The rich man's recognition of Lazarus exposes his hardness of heart. Lazarus was not just a nameless, anonymous beggar at his gate; the rich man knew his name...But he has not yet perceived that Abraham is both his father and Lazarus's father."

[23] Scott, *Hear Then the Parable*, 154: "...the rich man's request for Lazarus to dip the very tip of his finger in water draws a contrast between the drop of water he so earnestly desires and his sumptuous banquets during his life."

prodigal son as "this brother of yours" (15:32). Now, similarly, father Abraham is urging the rich man, as his child, to repent by acknowledging Lazarus as a fellow child of Abraham and therefore as his brother, whom he failed to assist during their lives. Abraham reminds the rich man that he received his good things during his life, while Lazarus likewise received bad things. Now, Lazarus, whom the rich man failed to comfort as his fellow child of Abraham with the good things he had received, is comforted by God (divine passive) here, as he receives the place of an honored guest in the heavenly banquet at the bosom of Abraham. But now their contrasting positions have been reversed, as the rich man, "you" (emphatic σύ), is the one suffering torment (16:25). Abraham's acknowledgment that the rich man is now suffering torment reinforces both the rich man's own and the narrator's (Jesus') statement of this torment (16:24) and torture (16:23) to add to the shock that warns the rich man as well as the "lovers of money" (16:14) in the audience to repent.

That the hungry Lazarus, who longed to be satisfied with the food that fell from the table of the rich man (16:21), now has a place with Abraham at the heavenly banquet, while the rich man, who feasted sumptuously every day (16:19) on the "good things" he received (16:25), is now excluded from that banquet provides the audience with another example of Mary's programmatic proclamation in her Magnificat that God "has filled the hungry with good things, but the rich he has sent away empty" (1:53). That the hungry *poor man* Lazarus, who longed *to be satisfied* with the food that fell from the table of the rich man (16:20-21), is now comforted at the banquet of the kingdom of God with Abraham (16:25) confirms for the audience Jesus' previous beatitudes: "Blessed are you who are *poor*, for the kingdom of God is yours; blessed are you who hunger now, for *you will be satisfied*; blessed are you who are weeping now, for you will laugh" (6:20-21). While the *rich man*, who feasted sumptuously every day and was *comforted* with the good things he received, but is now suffering torment in thirst outside of the banquet (16:23, 24, 25), confirms for the audience Jesus' previous warnings: "Woe to you *rich*, for you have received your *comfort*; woe to you, who are filled now, for you will be hungry; woe to you who laugh now, for you will grieve and weep" (6:24-25).

Abraham then broadens the predicament of the unrepentant rich man. With the concentrated use of the singular pronoun for "you"--"your (σου) good things during your (σου) life...whereas you (σύ) are suffering torment" (16:25)--the focus has been on the fortune of this one particular rich man. But when Abraham says "between us and you a great chasm has been fixed" (16:26), he uses the plural pronoun for "you" (ὑμῶν), so that the audience learns that the rich man is not alone in his predicament. This adds to the shocking warning for the "lovers of money" (16:14) in the audience. They could find themselves with the rich man. The story is not just about one particular rich man and one particular poor man. It is about the social injustice between the rich and the poor in general, about all those who, like this generic, anonymous rich man and possibly like the "lovers of money," neglect all the poor among them represented by Lazarus.

Whereas during his life Lazarus was lying at the very gate of the rich man (16:20), so that he could have easily approached and assisted him, he kept his distance from the poor man. Now that their positions have been reversed that distance has become a great chasm fixed by God (divine passive), over which no one can cross. Even if Lazarus or any of those with him and Abraham would wish to cross from here to "you" (ὑμᾶς), the rich man and those with him (plural pronoun), in order to help, they cannot. Neither can the rich man or any of those with him help themselves by crossing "from there to us" (16:26). Now, during their lives and while they are able, is the time for the rich and the "lovers of money" (16:14) in the audience to cross over to, reach down toward, and compassionately help, especially by feeding, those who are poor and hungry among them.[24]

Abraham refuses to send Lazarus to the rich man's brothers (16:27-31)

Although the rich man turns his attention from his own predicament, realizing it is now too late for him, to his still living five brothers, he continues to display his remarkably callous and arrogant unrepentance with regard to the poor man Lazarus. He again addresses Abraham as "father," but displays more concern and compassion for his five brothers in the house of "my father" (16:27) than for the poor Lazarus, his fellow brother as a child of Abraham.[25] He continues to regard Lazarus as a mere servant to be sent (cf. 16:24), as he begs Abraham to send Lazarus this time to his brothers, "so that he may warn them, lest they too come to this place of torture" (16:28). This further broadens the social and communal dimension of the story. Not only the rich man but his five brothers have neglected the poor man, whom they would recognize if he was sent to them. But the rich man seems more concerned that his brothers avoid "this place of torture" than that they have compassion for

---

[24] Scott, *Hear Then the Parable*, 155: "...the parable maintains that the divisions in the afterlife replicate those on earth: those divisions are the result not of divine will but of human insensitivity."

[25] Fitzmyer, *Luke X-XXIV*, 1134: "Note the subtle play on 'father' in this verse; the rich man's natural father is contrasted with 'Father Abraham.'"

the poor.[26] This fourth reference to the "torment" or "torture" (cf. 16:23, 24, 25, 28) of the rich man adds to the shock for the "lovers of money" (16:14) in the audience, who are invited to see themselves in the rich man's brothers.[27]

Abraham again refuses the rich man's request. Instead of sending Lazarus to warn his five brothers, he tells the rich man, "They have Moses and the prophets; let them listen to them" (16:29). Abraham thus further bolsters Jesus' previous address to the Pharisees as "lovers of money" (16:14), emphasizing that the law (Moses) and the prophets contain the enduring foundational call for repentance that stands in continuity with the call for repentance issued by John and demanded for entering the kingdom of God (see above on 16:16-18). Throughout the law (Moses) and the prophets, the Jewish scriptures proclaimed in the synagogues frequented by the five brothers (and the Pharisees), there are numerous warnings for the children of Abraham to take care of and feed the poor and hungry among them.

For the third time (cf. 16:24, 27) the rich man addresses Abraham as "father" as he disagrees: "No, father Abraham, but if someone from the dead goes to them, they will repent" (16:30). The rich man thinks that if Lazarus or some other poor person, whom his brothers have neglected, goes to them from the dead, then they will repent and share their abundant food with the hungry poor still among them. The irony is that the rich man, although he is the one who has experienced the reversal of meals between the poor man and himself, and although he himself has the vision of Lazarus he wishes for his brothers, still has not repented. Even now he still regards the poor man as a servant to be sent rather than as a fellow brother and child of Abraham deserving of his compassion!

Abraham issues the final word of warning addressed to the rich man but meant for his five brothers, the Pharisees, and whomever would be "lovers of money" in the audience (16:14): "If they do not listen to Moses and the prophets, not even if one were to rise from the dead will they be convinced"

---

[26] Herzog, *Parables*, 124: "But the man's concern is confined to his father and brothers; he wants them warned lest they share his fate. His failure to recognize Lazarus as a brother at least implies that he does not intend the desired warning to change their attitudes or behavior toward the poor."

[27] Note the chiastic sequence in the two Greek terms used for the "torture" and "torment" of the rich man, the only one who uses both terms:

(a) Narrator (Jesus): "...being in torture ($\beta\alpha\sigma\acute{\alpha}\nu o\iota\varsigma$)..." (16:23)
(b) Rich man: "...I am suffering torment ($\acute{o}\delta\upsilon\nu\tilde{\omega}\mu\alpha\iota$)..." (16:24)
(b) Abraham: "...you are suffering torment ($\acute{o}\delta\upsilon\nu\tilde{\alpha}\sigma\alpha\iota$)..." (16:25)
(a) Rich man: "...to this place of torture ($\beta\alpha\sigma\acute{\alpha}\nu o\upsilon$)..." (16:28)

(16:31). This ultimate affirmation of the law (Moses) and the prophets (cf. 16:16-18) underlines their foundational authority as a most potent call for repentance with regard to the poor and hungry. The rich and "lovers of money" in the world need only listen to Moses and the prophets powerfully calling them to repent by recognizing the hungry poor among them as their brothers and sisters deserving of their compassionate care. They are to utilize their wealth to feed the hungry poor, if they wish not just to avoid the torture and torment of the rich man but to become true children at the eschatological banquet in the kingdom of God with their father Abraham.

That the rich man still has not repented, although he has the heavenly vision in the realm of the dead of the divinely comforted poor man he failed to feed, confirms Abraham's warning that not even if one were to rise from the dead will the rich be persuaded to repent with regard to the hungry poor. This warning bodes even more poignantly and provocatively for the audience, who knows that Jesus himself will rise from the dead (9:22, 26, 28-36) after being put to death with the help of the unrepentant scribes and Pharisees (11:47-54; 13:31-35) he is now calling to conversion.

Relation of Luke 16:19-31 to Previous Meal Scenes

1) The meals in Luke 16:19-31 develop the *theme of the meal scenes as calls of conversion to the hospitable and compassionate satisfying of physical hunger as an anticipation of the complete satisfaction of all hunger in the eschatological banquet.* Jesus called the Pharisees and scribes to convert by recognizing the propriety for the disciples to feast rather than fast in anticipation of the eschatological wedding banquet whose bridegroom is already present in the person of Jesus (5:33-39). As lord of the sabbath, Jesus also called the Pharisees to convert by realizing the aptness for the disciples to satisfy their hunger even on the sabbath in anticipation of the eschatological refreshment the sabbath prefigures (6:1-5).

Jesus called his disciples to convert from their proposal to send the crowd away hungry, as he enabled them to hospitably and compassionately satisfy the hunger of the large crowd with an overabundance that anticipates the eschatological banquet (9:10-17). Jesus called the Pharisees to convert from their practice of inviting to their banquets those who can reciprocate and invite rather the poor, the crippled, the lame, the blind (14:13) in anticipation of the eschatological banquet (14:21). The father of the prodigal younger son called his elder son to convert by joining the feast of the fatted calf, an anticipation of the eschatological banquet, and sharing in the father's hospitable and compassionate feeding of the younger son, who had longed to satisfy his hunger from the pods the pigs were eating, but no one gave him anything (15:11-32).

Now Jesus calls the Pharisees to convert from a self-absorbing love of money (16:14) to a compassionate and hospitable feeding of the poor, who, like Lazarus, long for their hunger to be satisfied. If they, like the rich man, feast while the poor starve, they, even though they are Abraham's children, risk exclusion from the eschatological banquet (16:19-31).

2) The meals in Luke 16:19-31 advance the *theme of the meal scenes as calls of conversion to welcome social outcasts into the hospitality of meal fellowship as an anticipation of their inclusion in the eschatological banquet.* Jesus called the Pharisees and scribes to convert by recognizing the appropriateness of sharing meal fellowship with repentant tax collectors and sinners at Levi's banquet (5:27-32), of welcoming and forgiving a publicly known woman sinner at a meal with Pharisees (7:36-50), and of compassionately curing a man with dropsy at a sabbath meal with leading Pharisees (14:1-6). He called the Pharisee who invited him to the sabbath meal to convert by inviting to his meals not his friends, brothers, relatives, and wealthy neighbors, who may repay him, but social outcasts--the poor, crippled, lame, blind, who cannot repay him (14:12-14). Such social outcasts (14:21) will be included in the banquet of God's kingdom (14:15), while the self-absorbed rich (14:18-20) will be excluded (14:24).

Jesus then called the Pharisees and scribes who grumbled over his welcoming and eating with sinners (15:2) to convert from the position of the elder son, who refused not only to welcome and eat with the younger, prodigal son but to recognize and accept him as his brother. They are invited to emulate the father, who joyfully welcomed with a feast of fatted calf his returning and repentant son, as his own son and not as a hired servant (15:11-32). Now Jesus calls the Pharisees as lovers of money (16:14) to convert by recognizing the hungry poor among them as their brothers and sisters in need, their fellow children of Abraham, and extending meal fellowship to them. Only then can they expect to be included in the meal fellowship with their father Abraham and the hungry poor at the eschatological banquet (16:19-31).

3) The meals in Luke 16:19-31 develop the *theme of the meal scenes as calls to repentance of personal sinfulness in order to participate in the eschatological banquet in the kingdom of God.* With his powerful pronouncement, "I have not come to call the righteous but sinners to repentance," concluding the meal scene of Levi's great banquet, which points to the eschatological banquet (5:27-32), Jesus called the scribes and Pharisees to realize their need to repent of their self-righteousness.

At his first meal with a Pharisee Jesus implicitly called Simon to repent of his not loving Jesus even a little in contrast to the great love demonstrated by the repentant woman sinner (7:36-50). At his second meal with Pharisees Jesus vehemently urged the Pharisees and lawyers to repent of their sinfulness as religious leaders of the people (11:37-54). At his third meal with Pharisees Jesus exhorted the invited guests to repent of their self-seeking of honor by taking the first places at banquets. They should rather humble themselves at banquets in order to be exalted by God to the eschatological banquet (14:7-11), along with the lowly and poor social outcasts, who will also be exalted to the banquet in God's kingdom (14:15-24).

Jesus challenged the Pharisees and scribes who grumbled at his welcoming and eating with sinners (15:2) to recognize their own sinfulness and repent from relating to God as merely faithful and obedient servants, like the elder son, and relate to him as children of a loving father, like the younger, prodigal son. They were invited, like both sinful sons, to join in the meal fellowship that festively celebrates God's compassionate love and forgiveness for sinners who repent and return to him. Such sharing of the meal fellowship that celebrates God's forgiveness of repentant sinners anticipates the joyful final feast of the fatted calf in God's kingdom (15:3-32).

With the meal scenes in Luke 16:19-31 Jesus warns the Pharisees to repent of their sinful love of money (16:14). It may lead them, like the rich man, to be so self-absorbed in their own feasting that they neglect to feed the hungry poor, who are their fellow children of Abraham. They need to heed Moses and the prophets calling them to compassionately share their food to satisfy the hunger of the poor among them. Only then will they, as children of Abraham, be able to share and have their hunger completely satisfied by God in the eschatological banquet of God's kingdom.

Pragmatics of the Meal Scenes in Luke 16:19-31

1) The shocking reversal of fortunes of the rich man who feasted sumptuously every day yet was excluded from the heavenly eschatological feast, even though he was a child of Abraham, warns the audience, who may be inclined to be "lovers of money" like the Pharisees (16:14), not to emulate the rich man. By identifying with the plight of the rich man the audience arrives at a deeper appreciation of Jesus' previous teaching that one's life does not consist in an abundance of possessions (12:15) and one may not expect to feast sumptuously and blissfully for years to come like the foolish rich man (12:16-21). Rather than seeking to satisfy their hunger by the frequency, quality, and quantity of their meals, the audience must *rely upon God as the only one who can and will completely satisfy all their hungers in the eschatological banquet.*

2) The rich man was so self-absorbed in his extravagant, daily feasting that he failed to heed Moses and the prophets warning him against ignoring the dire hunger of those who are poor and in pain like Lazarus, his fellow human

being and fellow child of Abraham. As a result he was excluded from the heavenly banquet of God's kingdom. The audience is challenged to heed Moses and the prophets and satisfy the hunger of the poor among them by *compassionately and hospitably sharing the food they have to rectify the social injustice of their fellow human beings in need*. They will thereby anticipate the meal fellowship they may look forward to sharing with the hungry poor at the eschatological banquet.

3) The rich man never did change his attitude or relationship toward the hungry poor man Lazarus. Although he was familiar with Lazarus suffering in hunger and pain at his gate, he ignored him. Even after Lazarus was carried by angels to a position of an honored guest at Abraham's bosom, the rich man did not regard him as a brother, a fellow child of Abraham. Rather, he arrogantly expected Abraham to send Lazarus as a mere servant to refresh his thirsting tongue and to warn his five brothers still at home from arriving in the same place of torture and torment (16:23-28). This persuades the audience not only to satisfy the hunger of the poor among them, but *to regard and relate to the poor as fellow human beings*, fellow children of Abraham, fellow brothers and sisters of the God who "has filled the hungry with good things, but the rich he has sent away empty" (1:53). Indeed, the story encourages the audience not only to humanely feed the hungry, suffering poor among them. It also provokes the audience to relate to the hungry poor so compassionately and hospitably that they themselves have the courageous faith to become not as the comfortable rich, the satisfied, and the laughing, who will ultimately go hungry and grieve (6:24-25), but as the poor, the hungry, and the weeping, whom Jesus promised that God will fully satisfy and make happy at the eschatological banquet in the kingdom of God (6:20-21).

CHAPTER 10

JESUS' MEAL WITH ZACCHAEUS
LUKE 19:1-10

References to eating and drinking conclude the fifth section of the travel narrative (14:25-17:10), as Jesus compares the disciples to table servants who must perform their duty of preparing the meal for their master before they themselves eat and drink (17:7-10).[1] In the sixth section of the travel narrative (17:11-18:30) Jesus uses references to eating and drinking to instruct his disciples about his final coming as the Son of Man (17:26-30). The next actual meal scene, Jesus' meal with a chief tax collector and rich man named Zacchaeus (19:1-10), occurs in the seventh and concluding section of the travel narrative (18:31-19:48).[2]

Jesus Bids His Disciples To Be Like Servants Who Prepare Their Master's Meal (17:7-10)

After Jesus warned the disciples about their duty to avoid scandal (17:1-2) and to forgive one who sins against them but repents even seven times in one day (17:3-4), the apostles asked him to increase their faith (17:5). But Jesus exhorted them to be content with faith the size of a mustard seed, for it has the power to uproot a mulberry tree and plant it in the sea (17:6). They must also be content with the humble, thankless service they are called to perform as servants who must first prepare the dinner for their master before they themselves can eat and drink (17:7-10).[3]

Jesus induced his apostles to agree that if any of them had a servant who came in from the field after plowing or tending sheep, he would not say to that servant, "Come here immediately and recline at table" (17:7). Rather he would say to him, "Prepare something for my dinner; gird yourself and serve me while I eat and drink, and afterwards you yourself will eat and drink" (17:8). He would not be grateful to that servant simply for doing what was commanded (17:9). The apostles should adopt the same humble and unpresumptuous attitude as servants of their master, the Lord Jesus, and say,

---

[1] Although a meal is the focus of this narrative unit, it does not qualify as an actual "meal scene," since it refers to a hypothetical meal that does not actually take place in the narrative. For the definition of a "meal scene," see chapter 1.

[2] For descriptions of these structural sections of the travel narrative, see O'Fearghail, *Introduction to Luke-Acts*, 57-59.

[3] P. Houzet, "Les Serviteurs de l'Évangile (Luc 17,5-10) sont-ils inutiles? Ou un contresens traditionnel," *RB* 99 (1992) 335-72.

"We are unprofitable servants; we have done what we were obliged to do" (17:10).[4]

Luke has once again used the motif of table service as a symbol for discipleship (cf. 4:38-39; 7:36-50; 10:38-42). If they "gird themselves and serve" (περιζωσάμενος διακόνει, 17:8) Jesus, their master, in the manner of humble table servants, the apostles (and audience) can look forward to eating and drinking at the eschatological banquet ("afterwards you yourself will eat and drink," 17:8). Indeed, Jesus previously promised his disciples (and audience) that if they are ready for his return at the end of time, he, although their Lord, will serve them, the servants, dinner at the eschatological banquet: "Blessed are those servants whom the Lord will find watching when he comes. Amen I say to you, he will gird himself (περιζώσεται), make them recline, and come and serve (διακονήσει) them" (12:37).

Jesus Warns against the Distractions of Eating and Drinking (17:26-30)

In his warning to the disciples (and audience) to be alert and prepared for his final coming as the Son of Man to complete the arrival of the kingdom of God (17:20-37), Jesus employed a comparison involving eating and drinking during the days of Noah and Lot.[5] As it was in the days of Noah (Gen 6-8), thus it will be in the days of the Son of Man (17:26). People were going about their normal, everyday lives nonchalantly and complacently, "eating, drinking, marrying, and giving in marriage, until the day Noah entered the ark, and the flood came and destroyed them all" (17:27). Similarly, in the days of Lot (Gen 18-19), people were heedlessly going about their business, "eating, drinking, buying, selling, planting, building" (17:28). On the day Lot went out of Sodom, fire and brimstone rained down from heaven and destroyed them all (17:29). So it will be on the day the Son of Man is revealed (17:30), so that the disciples (and audience) must not allow their everyday activities, including *eating and drinking*, to distract them from being ready for the final coming of Jesus as the Son of Man.

---

[4] In light of the literary structure of Luke 17:7-10 and of the etymology of ἀχρεῖος the phrase δοῦλοι ἀχρεῖοι ἐσμεν (17:10) is translated, "We are servants to whom no favor is owed," by J. J. Kilgallen, "What Kind of Servants Are We? (Luke 17,10)," *Bib* 63 (1982) 549-51.

[5] For a discussion of the admonitory function of 17:20-37 from a reader or audience oriented perspective, see L. Hartman, "Reading Luke 17,20-37," *The Four Gospels 1992: Festschrift Frans Neirynck* (BETL 100; ed. F. Van Segbroeck, et al; Leuven: Leuven University Press, 1992) 1663-75.

These warnings to the audience about the possible distractions of a heedless preoccupation with eating and drinking reinforce previous warnings. The foolish rich man thought he could "rest, eat, drink, be merry" for many years to come, but his life was taken from him that very night (12:19-20). Jesus exhorted his disciples (and audience) that they are not anxiously to seek what to eat and what to drink, for the Father knows they need these things. They are rather to seek God's kingdom and these things will be given to them as well (12:29-31). If the audience abuses food by "eating and drinking and getting drunk," they will not be ready and thus lose their eschatological reward by being placed with the unfaithful (12:45-46).

Zacchaeus Shares the Meal Hospitality of His Home with Jesus (19:1-10)

1 Having entered Jericho, he was passing through it. 2 Now a man was there called Zacchaeus by name; he was a chief tax collector and he was a rich man. 3 He was seeking to see who Jesus was, but because of the crowd he could not, for he was short in stature. 4 Running ahead to the front, he climbed a sycamore tree in order to see him, for he was about to pass that way.

5 When he came to the place, Jesus looked up and said to him, "Zacchaeus, hurry and come down, for today I must stay at your house." 6 So he hurried and came down and welcomed him joyfully.

7 But all who saw this kept grumbling, saying, "With a man who is a sinner he has gone in to lodge." 8 Stopping, however, Zacchaeus said to the Lord, "Behold, half of my possessions, Lord, I am going to give to the poor, and if I have extorted anything from anyone I am going to repay it fourfold."

9 Jesus then said to him, "Today salvation has arrived in this house, because he too is a son of Abraham. 10 For the Son of Man has come to seek and to save what was lost."[6]

---

[6] Recent discussions of 19:1-10 include J. O'Hanlon, "The Story of Zacchaeus and the Lukan Ethic," *JSNT* 12 (1981) 2-26; Seccombe, *Possessions*, 130-32; A. J. Kerr, "Zacchaeus's Decision to Make Fourfold Restitution," *ExpTim* 98 (1986) 68-71; Tannehill, *Narrative Unity*, 1.107-8, 122-25; idem, "The Story of Zacchaeus as Rhetoric: Luke 19:1-10," *The Rhetoric of Pronouncement* (*Semeia* 64; ed. V. K. Robbins; Atlanta: Scholars Press, 1994) 201-11; F. Contreras Molina, "El Relato de Zaqueo en el Evangelio de Lucas," *Communio* 21 (1988) 3-47; D. Hamm, "Luke 19:8 Once Again: Does Zacchaeus Defend or Resolve?" *JBL* 107 (1988) 431-37; idem, "Zacchaeus Revisited Once More: A Story of Vindication or Conversion?" *Bib* 72 (1991) 249-52; A. C. Mitchell, "Zacchaeus Revisited: Luke 19,8 as a Defense," *Bib* 71 (1990) 153-76; Neale, *None But the Sinners*, 179-90; R. F.

The rich, chief tax collector Zacchaeus seeks to see who Jesus is (19:1-4)

Jesus entered the town of Jericho, which he had drawn near (18:35) when he healed a blind beggar (18:35-43). He was passing through Jericho (19:1) on his way up to Jerusalem in accord with his recent announcement to the twelve, "Behold we are going up to Jerusalem" (18:31).[7] That Jesus was passing through Jericho means that his predicted suffering, death and resurrection in Jerusalem (9:22, 31, 44, 51; 17:25; 18:31-33) is now quite imminent.[8]

In contrast to the anonymous blind beggar (18:35) there was in Jericho a man called Zacchaeus by name, who was both a chief tax collector and a rich man (19:2).[9] Although this Jewish man possesses a name that in Hebrew means "clean, innocent,"[10] that he is a chief tax collector associates him with the gentile Roman occupation and renders him ironically anything but clean or innocent in Jewish, especially Pharisaic, eyes. The audience remembers,

---

O'Toole, "The Literary Form of Luke 19:1-10," *JBL* 110 (1991) 107-16; D. A. S. Ravens, "Zacchaeus: The Final Part of a Lucan Triptych?" *JSNT* 41 (1991) 19-32; York, *Last Shall Be First*, 158-60; Ireland, *Stewardship*, 189-92; Just, *Ongoing Feast*, 184-93; J.-P. Gérard, "Les riches dans la communauté lucanienne," *ETL* 71 (1995) 71-106; M. J. Hassold, "Eyes to See: Reflections on Luke 19:1-10," *Lutheran Theological Journal* 29 (1995) 68-73; Matson, *Household Conversion*, 70-76.

[7] Jericho was a turning point for pilgrims journeying from Galilee up to Jerusalem. As Fitzmyer (*Luke X-XXIV*, 886) notes: "It is not the Jericho of OT times, but the town founded by Herod the Great about a mile and a half to the south on the western edge of the Jordan plain, where the Wadi Qelt opens on to it."

[8] O'Fearghail, *Introduction to Luke-Acts*, 58: "Jesus' words to the twelve in 18,31-34 mark a new stage on the journey to Jerusalem. Up to now Jesus has been journeying towards the city, but without making much progress. The statement ἰδοὺ ἀναβαίνομεν εἰς Ἰερουσαλήμ of 18,31 gives his journey a new urgency and an immediate goal, initiating the final ascent to the theatre of Jesus' passion, death and resurrection."

[9] The pleonastic Greek phrase, "by name (ὀνόματι) called (καλούμενος) Zacchaeus," draws the audience's attention to the name; see Marshall, *Luke*, 696; O'Hanlon, "Zacchaeus," 12.

[10] Fitzmyer, *Luke X-XXIV*, 1223. Ravens's ("Zacchaeus," 19-32) attempt to link Zacchaeus to Simon (7:36-50) and Lazarus (16:19-31) in a triptych of symbolically significant names fails to convince.

however, that, in sharp contrast to the Pharisees, tax collectors have proved to be paragons of the humble repentance that justifies them before God (3:12; 5:27-32; 7:29-30, 34-35; 15:1; 18:10-14). That Zacchaeus is not just a tax collector but a *chief* tax collector adds to his significance, suggesting a certain climactic character to his encounter with Jesus about to enter Jerusalem.[11] But that Zacchaeus is also a rich man ($\pi\lambda o \acute{v} \sigma \iota o \varsigma$) links him with the previous references to rich people, all of which are negative in some way (6:24; 12:16; 14:12; 16:1, 19-22; 18:23-25), and even associates him with the "money-loving" Pharisees (16:14). For the audience Zacchaeus appears as a rather ambiguous figure at this point, having both favorable (as chief tax collector) and unfavorable (as rich man) connections to the previous narrative.

That Zacchaeus "was seeking to see" ($\dot{\varepsilon}\zeta\acute{\eta}\tau\varepsilon\iota\ \dot{\iota}\delta\varepsilon\hat{\iota}\nu$) Jesus, "who he is" ($\tau\acute{\iota}\varsigma\ \dot{\varepsilon}\sigma\tau\iota\nu$) (19:3), adds to his ambiguous associations for the audience. On the negative side, it possibly will align him with Herod the tetrarch who likewise "was seeking to see" ($\dot{\varepsilon}\zeta\acute{\eta}\tau\varepsilon\iota\ \dot{\iota}\delta\varepsilon\hat{\iota}\nu$) Jesus, "who he is" ($\tau\acute{\iota}\varsigma\ \delta\acute{\varepsilon}\ \dot{\varepsilon}\sigma\tau\iota\nu$), about whom he had heard such things (9:9), including that Jesus was John raised from the dead, or Elijah, or one of the ancient prophets (9:7-8). But Herod was the one who had beheaded John (9:9) and now wanted to kill Jesus (13:31). Or will the rich, chief tax collector ($\dot{\alpha}\rho\chi\iota\tau\varepsilon\lambda\acute{\omega}\nu\eta\varsigma$, 19:2) prove to be like the extremely rich official ($\ddot{\alpha}\rho\chi\omega\nu$, 18:18), who sought out and asked Jesus to teach him how to inherit eternal life, but was unable to leave behind his wealth and follow Jesus (18:18-23)?

On the positive side, that Zacchaeus was seeking to see who Jesus was, but because of the crowd could not, for he was short in stature (19:3) possibly will join him to the blind beggar, who eventually not only saw and experienced who Jesus was but followed him on his way to suffering, death and resurrection in Jerusalem (18:43). Just as the crowd's rebuke presented an obstacle for the blind beggar to overcome in his encounter with Jesus (18:36-39), so the crowd prevents Zacchaeus from seeing Jesus. As the beggar was physically unable to see (18:41), so Zacchaeus's short physical stature hindered his view of Jesus. Both Zacchaeus and the beggar are in some way

---

[11] Neale, *None But the Sinners*, 182-83: "Where our 'sinner' material began with the toll collector Levi in ch. 5, Luke now climaxes Jesus' ministry with a similar encounter. But this time it is the $\dot{\alpha}\rho\chi\iota$-toll collector and he represents, in a dramatic and culminative sense, all of his kind who have gone before him in the story...The call of the outcast is now symbolized and epitomized in the archetypal figure of Zacchaeus and his encounter with Jesus."

blind to Jesus' true and more profound identity. Will Jesus enable Zacchaeus, like the blind beggar, to see and experience who he is?[12]

The "blindness" of both the beggar and Zacchaeus metaphorically characterizes the mental blindness of the twelve. After Jesus again told them of his imminent passion, death and resurrection in Jerusalem (18:31-33), they were emphatically "blinded" from understanding it: "But they understood nothing of these things; this saying remained hidden from them and they did not comprehend what was being said" (18:34).[13]

The blind beggar overcame the rebuke of the crowd by calling out all the more, "Son of David, have mercy on me!" (18:39). The blinded Zacchaeus overcomes the obstacle of the crowd and his short stature by eagerly running ahead to the front and climbing a sycamore tree in order to see Jesus. The beggar not only saw but followed Jesus on his way to Jerusalem (18:43). Zacchaeus, however, remains a mere spectator of Jesus' final and fateful journey to Jerusalem. He is perched in a sycamore tree, trying to gain a glimpse of Jesus, who was about to pass that way (19:4).[14]

Jesus invites himself and Zacchaeus welcomes him to meal hospitality in his home (19:5-6)

When Jesus came to the place where Zacchaeus was perched in the sycamore tree, he looked up and caught sight of the rich, chief tax collector who was seeking to see him. The Jesus who enabled the blind beggar to "see again" ($\dot{\alpha}\nu\alpha\beta\lambda\acute{\epsilon}\pi\omega$ in 18:41, 42, 43) so that he followed Jesus on his way to Jerusalem (18:43) now himself "looked up" ($\dot{\alpha}\nu\alpha\beta\lambda\acute{\epsilon}\psi\alpha\varsigma$) at Zacchaeus and provocatively invited himself to be a guest in the home of the rich, chief tax collector: "Zacchaeus, hurry and come down, for today I must stay at your house" (19:5). By urging Zacchaeus to "hurry and come down" from the tree, Jesus bids him to become a specially chosen participant rather than a mere spectator of his divinely ordained journey to Jerusalem. The emphatic personal pronouns, "I ($\mu\epsilon$) must stay in your ($\sigma o\nu$) house," underline Jesus' surprising choice to stay in the home of the rich, chief tax collector. That Jesus "must"

---

[12] D. Hamm, "Sight to the Blind: Vision as Metaphor in Luke," *Bib* 67 (1986) 457-77, esp. 462-65.

[13] B. C. Frein, "The Literary and Theological Significance of Misunderstanding in the Gospel of Luke," *Bib* 74 (1993) 328-48.

[14] Note how the verb for "passing through" ($\delta\acute{\iota}\eta\rho\chi\epsilon\tau o$ in 19:1 and $\delta\iota\acute{\epsilon}\rho\chi\epsilon\sigma\theta\alpha\iota$ in 19:4), which reminds the audience that Jesus is on his way to Jerusalem (18:31), frames this introductory unit (19:1-4).

(δεῖ) stay at the house of Zacchaeus "today" indicates to the audience the necessity in accord with God's plan for Jesus to stay with Zacchaeus "*today*," at this important point on his journey to Jerusalem.[15] Jesus is thus giving Zacchaeus an opportunity to play an important role in God's salvific plan by extending to Jesus on his way to suffering, death and resurrection in Jerusalem the hospitality to "stay" (μεῖναι) at his home, which would include the sharing of a meal.[16]

By offering Jesus the hospitality to "stay" (μεῖναι) at his home, Zacchaeus can play his role in demonstrating with regard to Jesus himself Jesus' previous missionary instructions to the twelve (9:1-6) and to the seventy-two (10:1-12). He told the twelve to take nothing for their journey, not even food (9:3), but rather to accept the hospitality of staying in the homes of those who receive them: "Whatever house you enter, stay (μένετε) there and leave from there" (9:4). He told the seventy-two: "Stay (μένετε) in the same house, eating and drinking what is offered by them" (10:7) and "whatever town you enter and they welcome you, eat what is set before you" (10:8). These missionary instructions of Jesus to his disciples indicate to the audience how his "staying" at the house of Zacchaeus implies the inclusion of a meal as part of the hospitality Jesus relies upon as he travels to Jerusalem.

Zacchaeus's immediate obedience of Jesus' command to "hurry and come down" (19:5) is noteworthy, as he precisely "hurried and came down" (19:6) from the tree. He not only graciously accepted Jesus' self-invitation to stay as a guest in his house, as he "welcomed him," but he did so "joyfully," literally, "rejoicing" (19:6). That Zacchaeus welcomed him (ὑπεδέξατο αὐτὸν) as he finally nears Jerusalem reminds the audience how Martha likewise

---

[15] Note the occurrences of δεῖ, "it is necessary," in Jesus' previous passion predictions in 9:22 and 17:25. See also C. H. Cosgrove, "The Divine *Dei* in Luke-Acts: Investigations into the Lukan Understanding of God's Providence," *NovT* 26 (1984) 168-90, esp. 175; O'Hanlon, "Zacchaeus," 15. On Luke's use of σήμερον, "today," at important moments in his story of God's salvation that has now arrived with Jesus, see M. Völkel, "σήμερον," *EDNT* 3.241; Fitzmyer, *Luke I-IX*, 234; O'Hanlon, "Zacchaeus," 14-15; Just, *Ongoing Feast*, 189-90.

[16] Just, *Ongoing Feast*, 188: "Although the story of Zacchaeus makes no explicit references to a meal or to the act of eating, Luke's use of 'to stay' (μεῖναι) and 'to be a guest' (καταλῦσαι) strongly suggest that Jesus has eaten a meal with Zacchaeus at his home. To spend the night at someone's house necessarily implies that a meal would be eaten." See also Matson, *Household Conversion*, 71-72, 75.

welcomed him (ὑπεδέξατο αὐτόν, 10:38) earlier on this same wandering trip to Jerusalem. Just as the welcome of the journeying Jesus by Martha and her sister Mary into the hospitality of their home involved the preparation of a meal for their guest (10:38-42), so also Zacchaeus's welcome of Jesus into his home implies the hospitality of a meal.

That Zacchaeus welcomed Jesus "rejoicing" (χαίρων) reminds the audience how the shepherd in the parable told by Jesus (15:3-7) placed his lost sheep upon his shoulders "rejoicing" (χαίρων, 15:5). The shepherd was rejoicing because he had finally found the lost sheep he was searching for. Zacchaeus is now similarly rejoicing because he has not only finally seen the Jesus he was seeking to see (19:3), but is privileged to welcome him as a guest into his home (19:6). Such "rejoicing" is appropriately celebrated in the context of a communal meal (cf. 15:6, 9, 22-24, 32).

Zacchaeus repents by giving to the poor and repaying those he extorted (19:7-8)

When Jesus attended the great banquet in the home of the tax collector named Levi, the Pharisees and their scribes were grumbling (ἐγόγγυζον) to his disciples, saying, "Why do you *eat and drink* with tax collectors and sinners?" (5:30). Jesus later pointed out to the Pharisees and lawyers (7:30) that "the Son of Man came *eating and drinking*, and you said, 'Behold a glutton and a drunkard, a friend of tax collectors and sinners'" (7:34). When all the tax collectors and the sinners were coming near to Jesus to hear him, the Pharisees and the scribes kept grumbling (διεγόγγυζον), saying, "This man welcomes sinners and *eats* with them" (15:1-2). Now, not only the Pharisees and scribes but "all" (πάντες) who saw Jesus welcomed as a guest into the home of the chief tax collector Zacchaeus kept grumbling (διεγόγγυζον), saying, "With a man who is a sinner he has gone in to lodge" (19:7). They are all grumbling that Jesus has gone in to lodge (καταλῦσαι) with one they consider to be a sinner and social outcast because to lodge with Zacchaeus involves eating and drinking, the sharing of meal fellowship, with him.[17]

---

[17] H. Hübner, "καταλύω," *EDNT* 2.264: "Only in Luke (9:12; 19:7) does καταλύω mean *rest, lodge* (literally 'unharness* the pack animals')." The close association of food with lodging has been indicated earlier in the narrative, when the twelve told Jesus: "Dismiss the crowd, so that they may go into the surrounding villages and farms to lodge (καταλύσωσιν) and find provisions" (9:12). The vocabulary of a traveling guest "remaining in the home" (19:5), being "welcomed" into the home (19:6), and "lodging" in the home (19:7), as well as the continual "grumbling" (19:7), which earlier was always directed toward Jesus' meal fellowship with sinners (5:30; 7:34, 39;

Jesus abruptly stopped (σταθεὶς δὲ ὁ Ἰησοῦς, 18:40) when he heard the blind beggar continuing to cry out to him (18:39) and immediately addressed the situation. Similarly, Zacchaeus abruptly stopped (σταθεὶς δὲ Ζακχαῖος, 19:8) when he heard everyone grumbling (19:7) and immediately addressed the Lord: "Behold, half of my possessions, Lord, I am going to give to the poor, and if I have extorted anything from anyone I am going to repay it fourfold" (19:8).[18] The rich, chief tax collector, who "was seeking to see Jesus, who he is" (19:3), is now on his way to seeing and recognizing Jesus' true identity since he addresses him as "Lord." With future-referring present tenses of the verbs, "I am going to give" (δίδωμι) and "I am going to repay" (ἀποδίδωμι), which emphasize the immediacy and the strong determination of his resolve, Zacchaeus boldly and dramatically announces the repentance of his sinfulness as a rich, chief tax collector, who apparently gained his wealth by disregarding the needs of the poor and by defrauding those from whom he collected.[19]

Zacchaeus's public profession of determined repentance makes even clearer to the audience why Jesus shares meal fellowship with tax collectors and sinners. It is not to condone, overlook, or sanction their sinfulness, as the continual grumbling of the Pharisees and scribes (5:30; 7:34, 39; 15:2) and now "all" (19:7) might seem to suggest. Rather, as Jesus pronounced at Levi's great banquet in which he ate and drank with tax collectors and sinners (5:29),

---

15:2), indicate to the audience that an implicit meal shared by Jesus with Zacchaeus is a dominant concern of this scene, which justifies our treatment of it as a "meal scene," even though no meal is explicitly narrated. See the definition of a "meal scene" in chapter 1; Hamm, "Zacchaeus Revisited," 250; Just, *Ongoing Feast*, 188.

[18] Johnson, *Luke*, 285: "The verb σταθεὶς is literally 'stood,' suggesting that Zacchaeus halted in their progress toward the house to deliver this statement publicly." See also Marshall, *Luke*, 697; Fitzmyer, *Luke X-XXIV*, 1224-25.

[19] On the future-referring present tense in Greek, see Porter, *Verbal Aspect*, 230-32. Some interpret the present tenses here as expressions of Zacchaeus's customary behavior, so that he is stating his defense and vindication rather than his repentance and resolve; see, e.g., Fitzmyer, *Luke X-XXIV*, 1225; Mitchell, "Zacchaeus Revisited," 153-76; idem, "Luke 19:8," 546-47; Ravens, "Zacchaeus," 19-32; Gérard, "Les riches," 98-101. But the many reasons marshalled by the majority of interpreters that Zacchaeus is expressing his determined repentance remain quite convincing; see esp. Hamm, "Zacchaeus Revisited," 249-52; idem, "Luke 19:8 Once Again," 431-37; Neale, *None But the Sinners*, 185-88; Tannehill, "Zacchaeus," 203-4; Hassold, "Eyes to See," 68-73; Matson, *Household Conversion*, 72-74.

he has not come to invite the righteous but sinners to repentance (5:32). The "Lord" Jesus' offer to stay in the house of the rich, chief tax collector and share meal fellowship with him has motivated him to repent of his sinfulness (19:8).

As the audience recalls, the very rich official (ἄρχων, 18:18) went away from Jesus sad (18:23), unable to obey his command to sell all that he had and distribute it to the poor (πτωχοῖς), in order to have treasure in heaven and be able to follow Jesus (18:22) to inherit eternal life (18:18). In contrast, the rich, chief tax collector (ἀρχιτελώνης, 19:2) now gladly promises to give half of his possessions to the poor (πτωχοῖς) (19:8).[20] In generously giving away half of his possessions (ὑπαρχόντων) Zacchaeus admirably follows Jesus' previous admonition for the audience to guard against all greed, for though one may have an abundance, one's life does not consist of possessions (ὑπαρχόντων) (12:15).

The audience has heard Jesus' parable contrasting the temple prayers of a self-righteous Pharisee with a humble tax collector (18:9-14). The Pharisee thanked God that he was not like the sinful tax collector (18:11). But the tax collector humbly begged God to have mercy on him, a sinner (ἁμαρτωλῷ) (18:13). The tax collector, in contrast to the Pharisee, went home justified and exalted by God (18:14). Now, the chief tax collector Zacchaeus, accused of being a sinner (ἁμαρτωλῷ) by self-righteous grumblers (19:7), repents of his sinfulness (19:8) and receives in his home the salvation of God that Jesus brings (19:9).[21] Like the humble tax collector praying in the temple (18:13) but unlike the very rich official (18:22-23, 25), the rich, chief tax collector Zacchaeus demonstrates by his humble repentance the childlike humility needed to enter the kingdom of God (18:15-17).

When tax collectors came to be baptized by John, they asked him what they must do (3:12) to "produce the fruits worthy of repentance" (3:8), that is,

---

[20] O'Hanlon, "Zacchaeus," 16, 20. Tannehill ("Zacchaeus," 203) points out that "the reference to 'half' is not meant as a limit on the distribution of wealth, permitting Zacchaeus to keep the rest, but simply recognizes that he must also compensate those from whom he has extorted wealth."

[21] Neale, *None But the Sinners*, 181: "The events of Lk. 19:1-10 are a real-life demonstration of the attitudes set out in parable form in Lk. 18.9-14. We cannot read the one incident without reflecting on the other and thus forming a fuller understanding of Luke's conception of what the 'sinner' must do." See also F. G. Downing, "The Ambiguity of 'The Pharisee and the Toll-Collector' (Luke 18:9-14) in the Greco-Roman World of Late Antiquity," *CBQ* 54 (1992) 80-99.

to demonstrate the sincerity of their repentance. He told them not to collect more than what is prescribed (3:13). Then John told the soldiers who likewise asked what they must do to demonstrate their true repentance not to rob anyone by violence or extort (συκοφαντήσητε) money from them, and to be satisfied with their wages (3:14). Now the chief tax collector Zacchaeus, who undoubtedly acquired much of his wealth by exacting more than was prescribed and perhaps with the help of soldiers, resolves to demonstrate his sincere repentance by repaying whomever he has extorted (ἐσυκοφάντησα) a more than generous fourfold (19:8).[22]

Jesus pronounces that Zacchaeus has been saved as a son of Abraham (19:9-10)

In response to Zacchaeus's remarkable resolve to repent Jesus utters the public pronouncement that climaxes and concludes this meal scene: "Today salvation has arrived in this house, because he too is a son of Abraham. For the Son of Man has come to seek and to save what was lost" (19:9-10). That "today salvation has arrived in this house" (19:9) develops directly from Jesus' previous statement to Zacchaeus that "today I must stay in your house" (19:5). *Today* salvation has arrived, or more literally "happened" (ἐγένετο, 19:9), in the household of Zacchaeus not only because *today* Jesus, the Lord and savior (2:11), had to stay in Zacchaeus's house on the way to his divinely ordained salvific death and resurrection, but also because Zacchaeus accepted Jesus' invitation and joyfully welcomed him into his home (19:6) as a repentant sinner (19:8). It is because the rich, chief tax collector repented of his sinfulness after Jesus offered to share with him the hospitality that includes

---

[22] On the construction "if I have extorted anything from anyone" (εἴ τινός τι ἐσυκοφάντησα, 19:8), Plummer (*Luke*, 435) notes: "The indic. shows that he is not in doubt about past malpractices: 'if, as I know is the case, I have,' etc." Marshall (*Luke*, 698) remarks: "The conditional clause is to be translated 'From whomsoever I have wrongfully exacted anything,' and thus does not put the fact of extortion in doubt, but rather its extent." See also Hamm, "Luke 19:8," 434; idem, "Zacchaeus Revisited," 252. On the fourfold restitution, Fitzmyer (*Luke X-XXIV*, 1225) points out that "Zacchaeus willingly restores the damage according to such regulations in the Pentateuch as Exod 21:37 (22:1E), 'four sheep for a (stolen) sheep' (cf. 2 Sam 12:6)." See also Spicq, *Theological Lexicon*, 3.377-78; "τετραπλοῦς," *EDNT* 3.353: "Luke 19:8 refers to Zacchaeus's *fourfold* restitution, a quantity considered generous enough in every respect."

meal fellowship that salvation has "happened" in the household of Zacchaeus.[23]

Jesus pointed out to those objecting (13:14) how it was necessary for the crippled woman, who was a daughter of Abraham, to be freed from her bondage on the day of the sabbath (13:16). Similarly, it is now necessary for Jesus to stay at the house of Zacchaeus so that he, like the crippled woman, can personally experience the salvation Jesus brings, "because he too is a son of Abraham" (19:9). Through the parable of the rich man and the poor Lazarus (16:19-31) Jesus called the Pharisees, as lovers of money (16:14), represented by the parable's rich man, to have compassion on the poor among them, represented by Lazarus, as their fellow children of Abraham (16:22-30).[24] Now Jesus is calling all of those grumbling because he has gone to lodge with the Zacchaeus they consider a sinner (19:7) to recognize that Zacchaeus, although he is a tax collector, remains, like them and any other Jew, a son of Abraham entitled to the salvation promised to Abraham and his descendants (1:55, 73) and now available with Jesus. But the audience recalls John's warning to the crowds that they cannot consider themselves to be truly children of Abraham unless they produce the fruits worthy of repentance (3:8). They thus experience the irony that the tax collector Zacchaeus, who repented of his extortion (19:8), just as John urged the soldiers to repent of their extortion (3:14), proves to be indeed a true son of Abraham in contrast to the unrepentant Pharisees and lawyers (7:30).

When the Pharisees and scribes grumbled that Jesus was eating and drinking with tax collectors and sinners at Levi's great banquet (5:30), he uttered the climactic pronouncement, "I have not come to invite the righteous but sinners to repentance" (5:32). It not only explained why he ate and drank with tax collectors and sinners but challenged the Pharisees and scribes to recognize their own need to repent of their sinfulness in order to partake of the messianic banquet now arriving with Jesus.[25] Similarly, Jesus' climactic pronouncement that "the Son of Man has come to seek and to save what was

---

[23] Fitzmyer, *Luke X-XXIV*, 1225-26; Johnson, *Luke*, 286; Tannehill, "Zacchaeus," 205 n. 8; O'Toole, "Luke 19:1-10," 110: "To have Jesus as one's guest is to be host to salvation." Matson, *Household Conversion*, 74: "The story of Zacchaeus recounts not only a conversion but a particular kind of conversion--the bestowal of salvation to the personified οἶκος by the Lukan Jesus. Jesus' declaration to Zacchaeus highlights the sphere of the house as the place for the restoration and cleansing of 'sinners'."

[24] See chapter 9.

[25] See chapter 2.

lost" (19:10) not only explains why he has gone to lodge, and thus to eat and drink, with the rich, chief tax collector. It also challenges all those grumbling because he has gone to lodge in the household of a sinner (19:7) to recognize their own need to repent as lost sinners in order to experience the salvation that Jesus is bringing about as the Son of Man on his way to suffering, death and resurrection in Jerusalem.

Jesus' reference to himself as the "Son of Man" here recalls for the audience the most recent passion prediction in which Jesus likewise refers to himself as the Son of Man (18:31-33).[26] Indeed, Jesus has referred to himself as the Son of Man in all of his previous passion predictions (9:22, 44; 17:24-25). It is part of his divine mission as the Son of Man that Jesus must go to suffering, death and resurrection in Jerusalem. That "salvation" has happened in the household of Zacchaeus because Jesus has come as the Son of Man to seek and "to save" what was lost (19:9-10) helps the audience to realize that the goal of Jesus' suffering, death and resurrection as the Son of Man is to bring about God's salvation for his people (cf. 1:77).

Salvation can "happen" for people when they, like Zacchaeus, repent of their sinfulness. Zacchaeus's reception of salvation after repenting as a rich person answers for the audience the question of "Who can be *saved?*" (18:26), after Jesus proclaimed the extreme difficulty for a rich person to enter the kingdom of God (18:25). It was the faith of the blind beggar that restored his sight and brought him salvation, as Jesus announced: "Your faith has *saved* you!" (18:42). Now it is the repentance of the rich, chief tax collector that brings him *salvation* from the Jesus who came as the Son of Man to seek and *to save* what was lost (19:9-10).

That Jesus has come as the Son of Man to seek and to save what was lost clarifies for the audience why he came as the Son of Man "eating and drinking" with tax collectors and sinners (7:34). It was to call not only the tax collectors and sinners but all who grumble against Jesus' eating and drinking with them (5:30; 7:34; 15:2; 19:7) to repent of their own sinfulness in order to experience the salvation Jesus is bringing as the Son of Man.

At the beginning of this meal scene Zacchaeus was on a quest. He "was seeking (ἐζήτει) to see Jesus, who he is" (19:3). But the seeker has also become the one sought, as Jesus was also on a quest. By inviting himself to meal fellowship with Zacchaeus, Jesus succeeded in his quest as the Son of Man to seek (ζητῆσαι) and to save the Zacchaeus who was lost in his sinfulness as a rich, chief tax collector (19:9). Zacchaeus has also succeeded in

---

[26] On the background of the "Son of Man" as a christological title and its use in Luke, see above on Luke 6:5 in chapter 2.

his quest "to see Jesus, who he is" (19:3). In welcoming Jesus to the hospitality that includes the sharing of a meal, he has seen and experienced Jesus as the Lord (19:8) and savior who sought out and saved him as a lost sinner, restoring him to his dignity as a true son of Abraham (19:9-10).[27]

That Jesus has come as the Son of Man to seek and to save what was lost reminds the audience of the parables of repentance in Luke 15:1-32. Jesus sought (ἐζήτει) and saved, and thus found, the Zacchaeus who was lost (ἀπολωλός) as a sinful tax collector (19:10). Similarly, the shepherd goes after the one lost (ἀπολωλός) sheep until he finds it (15:4, 6), the woman seeks (ζητεῖ) the one silver coin she lost (ἀπώλεσα) until she finds it (15:8-9), and the father welcomed back his repentant prodigal son, who was lost (ἀπολωλὼς) but has been found (15:24, 32). The joyful, communal celebrations that followed each of these findings of what was lost (15:6-7, 9-10, 23-24, 32) characterized Jesus' eating with sinners (15:2) as meals of communal joy celebrating the repentance of sinners who were lost but have been found. Similarly, the meal hospitality that Zacchaeus joyfully (19:6) shares with Jesus not only motivates but celebrates his repentance from a lost sinner to a found and saved son of Abraham (19:9-10).

Jesus' divine mission as the Son of Man who has come to seek (ζητῆσαι) and to save (σῶσαι) what was lost (τὸ ἀπολωλός) (19:10) extends beyond the lost sinner Zacchaeus to the entire people of Israel. From their knowledge of the OT the audience recognizes that Jesus is fulfilling God's promise to be the true shepherd of his people, the lost and scattered sheep. Through the prophet Jeremiah God said: "My people have become lost (ἀπολωλότα) sheep" (LXX Jer 27:6). But through the prophet Ezekiel God promised: "I will seek (ζητήσω) what was lost (τὸ ἀπολωλὸς)...and I will save (σώσω) my sheep" (LXX Ezek 34:16, 22). The climactic pronouncement that Jesus as the Son of Man has come to seek and to save what was lost (19:10) explains why he shares the hospitality that includes a meal with the repentant sinner Zacchaeus. But it also invites all the people of Israel, the rest of the "lost sheep," especially all those grumbling (19:7) like the Pharisees and scribes (5:30; 7:34; 15:2) about his meal fellowship with public sinners, to repent of their own sinfulness in order to experience the salvation Jesus is bringing about as the Son of Man on his way to suffering, death and resurrection in Jerusalem.

---

[27] O'Toole, "Luke 19:1-10," 114; Tannehill, "Zacchaeus," 205: "Zacchaeus's successful quest is placed within the context of Jesus' quest for the lost."

Relation of Luke 19:1-10 to Previous Meal Scenes

1) The meal scene of Luke 19:1-10 brings to a climax the *theme of Jesus' meals as calls to conversion for those objecting to his meal fellowship with social outcasts and public sinners*. At the beginning of Jesus' ministry the tax collector Levi, who repented by abandoning his sinful profession and following Jesus, gave a great banquet at which Jesus shared meal fellowship with a large crowd of tax collectors and sinners. Jesus' pronouncement that "I have not come to call the righteous but sinners to repentance" (5:32) not only explained why he eats and drinks with tax collectors and sinners but provocatively challenged the objecting Pharisees and scribes to recognize their own need to repent of their sinfulness in order to participate in the eschatological banquet (5:27-32). Now at the end of his ministry, as Jesus was approaching his suffering, death and resurrection in Jerusalem, the rich, chief tax collector Zacchaeus, who repented by promising to give half of his possessions to the poor and to repay those he extorted fourfold, welcomed Jesus into the hospitality of his home to share meal fellowship with him. Jesus' pronouncement that "the Son of Man has come to seek and to save what was lost" (19:10) not only explained why he has gone to lodge with a public sinner but summoned all those objecting, who are part of the lost sheep of Israel, to repent of their own sinfulness in order to experience the salvation Jesus brings as the Son of Man (19:1-10).

As a call to conversion, Jesus' meal with Zacchaeus climaxes all of his other meals that involve the objection to or avoidance of social outcasts or public sinners. Jesus called those objecting to the sinful woman he forgave at the meal with Simon the Pharisee (7:36-50) to likewise repent of their sinfulness in order to be forgiven more so they can love more (7:47). At his sabbath meal with leading Pharisees (14:1-24) Jesus called them to repent by approving his healing of the man with dropsy (14:1-6) and by inviting to their banquets such social outcasts as the poor, crippled, lame, and blind (14:13, 21). Through his parables of repentance (15:1-32) Jesus called the Pharisees and scribes objecting to his meal fellowship with sinners (15:2) to repent by relating to God as his beloved rather than servile children, so they can joyfully welcome to meal fellowship other repentant sinners as their fellow brothers and sisters (15:31-32). They are to realize that Jesus eats with sinners and tax collectors not only to invite but to celebrate their repentance as those who were lost but have been found (15:6-7, 9-10, 24, 32; 19:6, 10).

2) The meal scene of Luke 19:1-10 advances the *theme of Jesus' meals as models of hospitality that anticipate the great eschatological banquet*. After his conversion the tax collector Levi extended to Jesus and his disciples the hospitality of a great banquet foreshadowing the eschatological banquet

(5:27-32). As the messianic bridegroom Jesus permitted his disciples the hospitality of feasting rather than fasting (5:34). As the Lord of the sabbath Jesus allowed his disciples the hospitality of satisfying their hunger by work on the sabbath (6:1-5). Jesus empowered his disciples to extend to the large crowd the hospitality of an overabundant meal rather than sending them away to procure food for themselves (9:10-17). Martha with her sister Mary welcomed Jesus into the hospitality of their home while he was on his way to Jerusalem, and thus anticipated the choice of the "best portion" at the eschatological banquet (10:38-42). And now the rich, chief tax collector Zacchaeus welcomed Jesus into the hospitality of his home and anticipated the salvation (19:9-10) of the eschatological meal fellowship Jesus will bring about by his suffering, death and resurrection in Jerusalem.

3) The meal scene of Luke 19:1-10 develops the *theme of the meal scenes as calls for the rich to convert by sharing their wealth with the poor*. In his second meal with a Pharisee (11:37-54) Jesus exhorted the Pharisees as religious leaders to cleanse and purify the greed and wickedness that is within them by giving alms to the poor (11:39-41). Jesus' parable about the luxuriantly feasting rich man who neglected to share his food with the poor and hungry Lazarus (16:19-31) warned the Pharisees, who loved money (16:14), to repent by welcoming and hospitably sharing their wealth and food with the poor and hungry as their fellow children of Abraham. After being invited by Jesus to share the meal hospitality of his home with him (19:5), Zacchaeus the rich man repented by promising to give half of his possessions to the poor and to repay those he extorted fourfold (19:8).

Pragmatics of the Meal Scene in Luke 19:1-10

1) Jesus exhorted his disciples and thus the audience *to rely upon the hospitality of those to whom they proclaim the good news of the kingdom of God* (9:1-6; 10:1-12). He exhorted the disciples and the audience not to worry about what they are to eat and drink (12:22, 29) but to seek the kingdom of God and these things will be provided them (12:31). Jesus himself now models for the audience these exhortations as he relies upon the hospitality of Zacchaeus for his food and drink while on his way to Jerusalem, enabling Zacchaeus to anticipate the salvation of God's kingdom that Jesus will bring about by his suffering, death and resurrection.

2) All of those who grumbled that Jesus went to lodge with a sinner (19:7) provide the audience with a negative model. Unlike them the audience must *not exclude social outcasts and public sinners from their meal fellowship*. They are rather to imitate Jesus, whose invitation to meal fellowship with Zacchaeus motivated his repentance. Meals the audience shares with social

outcasts and public sinners can serve not only as invitations but as joyful celebrations of their repentance.

3) The rich, chief tax collector Zacchaeus provides the audience with a stunning *model of genuine repentance*. His firm determination to give half of his possessions to the poor and to repay those he has extorted fourfold (19:8) dramatically demonstrates how it is possible for a rich person to enter the kingdom of God and be saved (18:25-26). The Zacchaeus who sought to see Jesus was sought by Jesus so that he truly saw who Jesus was. He saw and experienced Jesus as the Lord whose invitation to meal fellowship enabled the repentant Zacchaeus, as a true son of Abraham, to anticipate the salvation Jesus will complete by his suffering, death and resurrection. Like Zacchaeus the audience is called to repent of their sinfulness, especially their neglect of the poor and wrongdoing toward others, in order to see and experience Jesus as the Son of Man who came to seek and to save what was lost.

CHAPTER 11

JESUS' LAST SUPPER
LUKE 22:7-38

After Jesus finally arrived in Jerusalem and taught the people and his disciples in the temple (20:1-21:38), one of the twelve apostles, Judas, as the feast of Passover was approaching, conspired with the Jewish leaders on how to put Jesus to death (22:1-6). The audience then encounters the next meal scene, Jesus' last Passover supper with his disciples before his death (22:7-38). This major meal scene begins with the preparation for the Passover meal (22:7-13) followed by the actual meal with its predictions and instructions for the disciples (22:14-38).

Jesus' Last Passover Supper with His Disciples before His Death (22:7-38)

7 Then came the day of Unleavened Bread, on which it was necessary that the Passover lamb be sacrificed. 8 So he sent Peter and John, saying, "Go prepare for us to eat the Passover meal." 9 They said to him, "Where do you want us to prepare it?" 10 He said to them, "Behold, when you are entering into the city, a man carrying a jar of water will meet you. Follow him into the house into which he enters. 11 Then you shall say to the householder of the house, 'The teacher says to you, "Where is the guest room where I may eat the Passover meal with my disciples?"' 12 That man will show you a large upper room spread with couches. Prepare the meal there." 13 They went out and found it just as he had told them, and they prepared the Passover meal.

14 When the hour arrived, he reclined and the apostles with him. 15 He said to them, "How eagerly I have desired to eat this Passover meal with you before I suffer! 16 For I say to you that I will never eat it again until it is fulfilled in the kingdom of God." 17 Then taking a cup and giving thanks he said, "Take this and share it among yourselves. 18 For I say to you that from now on I will never drink from the fruit of the vine until the kingdom of God comes."

19 Then taking bread and giving thanks he broke it and gave it to them saying, "This is my body which is being given for you. Keep doing this in remembrance of me." 20 And likewise the cup after supper, saying, "This cup is the new covenant in my blood which is being poured out for you.

21 "But behold! The hand of the one betraying me is with me at the table. 22 For the Son of Man indeed goes as it has been determined, but woe to that man by whom he is being betrayed!" 23 Then they began to question among themselves which one of them it could be who was going to do this.

24 A quarrel even arose among them as to which one of them seemed to be greatest. 25 He said to them, "The kings of the Gentiles rule over them and those in authority over them are called benefactors. 26 But not so with you!

165

Rather, the greatest among you must become as the youngest, and the leader as the one who serves. 27 For who is greater, the one who reclines or the one who serves? Is it not the one who reclines? Yet I am in your midst as the one who serves.

28 "But you are in fact those who have been remaining with me throughout my trials. 29 And so I confer on you, just as my Father has conferred on me, kingship, 30 that you may eat and drink at my table in my kingdom, and you will sit on thrones ruling the twelve tribes of Israel.

31 "Simon, Simon, behold Satan has demanded to sift all of you like wheat. 32 But I have prayed for you that your own faith may not fail. And you, once you have turned back, strengthen your brothers." 33 But he said to him, "Lord, I am ready to go with you to prison and to death!" 34 He replied, "I say to you, Peter, the cock will not crow today until you have three times denied that you know me."

35 He said to them, "When I sent you out without a purse or bag or sandals, did you lack anything?" They said, "Nothing." 36 He said to them, "But now the one having a purse must take it, and likewise a bag. And the one not having a sword must sell his cloak and buy one. 37 For I say to you that it is necessary that this scripture be completed in me, 'And he was reckoned with the lawless' (Isa 53:12). For indeed what concerns me is having its completion." 38 They said, "Lord, behold here are two swords!" He said to them, "It is enough."[1]

---

[1] On Luke 22:7-38 as a whole, in addition to the commentaries, see H. Schürmann, "Der Abendmahlsbericht Lk 22,7-38 als Gottesdienstordnung, Gemeindeordnung, Lebensordnung," *Ursprung und Gestalt: Erörterungen und Besinnungen zum Neuen Testament* (Düsseldorf: Patmos, 1970) 108-50; I. H. Marshall, *Last Supper and Lord's Supper* (Grand Rapids: Eerdmans, 1980) 101-6; Q. Quesnell, "The Women at Luke's Supper," *Political Issues in Luke-Acts* (eds. R. J. Cassidy and P. J. Scharper; Maryknoll: Orbis, 1983) 59-79; D. M. Sweetland, "The Lord's Supper and the Lukan Community," *BTB* 13 (1983) 23-27; W. S. Kurz, "Luke 22:14-38 and Greco-Roman and Biblical Farewell Addresses," *JBL* 104 (1985) 251-68; F. J. Matera, *Passion Narratives and Gospel Theologies: Interpreting the Synoptics Through Their Passion Stories* (Mahwah: Paulist, 1986) 159-66; X. Léon-Dufour, *Sharing the Eucharistic Bread: The Witness of the New Testament* (New York: Paulist, 1987) 230-47; P. Sellew, "The Last Supper Discourse in Luke 22:21-38," *Forum* 3 (1987) 70-95; D. Senior, *The Passion of Jesus in the Gospel of Luke* (Collegeville: Liturgical Press, 1989) 51-83; J. S. Kloppenborg, "*Exitus Clari Viri*: The Death of Jesus in Luke," *Toronto Journal of Theology* 8 (1992) 106-20; Just, *Ongoing Feast*, 227-53.

Jesus provides for the preparation of the Passover meal with his disciples (22:7-13)

Before the narration of the conspiracy to kill Jesus (22:2-6) the audience heard that "the feast of Unleavened Bread called Passover was approaching" (22:1). That feast has now arrived with the notice that "then came the day of Unleavened Bread, on which it was necessary that the Passover lamb be sacrificed" (22:7).[2] This places the events of Jesus' suffering, death, and resurrection within not only the temporal but also the interpretive context of this great Jewish pilgrimage feast that centers upon a ceremonial meal in Jerusalem as a ritual remembrance of God's saving events in the exodus from Egypt. The feast began with the eating and drinking of the Passover supper, including the eating of the Passover lamb, and continued with the eating of only unleavened bread for the seven days of the festival. By this ritual eating and drinking the Jewish people not only relived and made present their past salvific exodus from Egypt, in which God liberated them from slavery and death by "passing over" their houses sprinkled with the blood of the Passover lamb (Exod 12:1-30; Deut 16:1-8), but also anticipated their share in God's future and final salvation.[3] Jesus' transfiguration into a heavenly figure (9:28-36), which anticipated his salvific passage from death to heavenly glory, already alerted the audience to the Passover character of his death and resurrection. Moses and Elijah in heavenly glory spoke to him of "his exodus (ἔξοδον), which he was going to accomplish in Jerusalem" (9:31).

The notice that on the day of Unleavened Bread it was necessary (ἔδει) that the Passover lamb be sacrificed (22:7) places the death of the Passover lamb within the framework of the divine necessity of God's plan of salvation as prescribed in scripture (Exod 12:6, 21; Deut 16:2, 5-6). This associates the death of the Passover lamb with the death of Jesus. As the audience recalls, the suffering, death, and resurrection of Jesus in Jerusalem is also necessary (δεῖ, 9:22; 17:25) according to God's scriptural plan (18:31). That it was necessary for the Passover lamb to be sacrificed (θύεσθαι) reminds the audience that the death of the Passover lamb was the sacrificial death that saved Israel from

---

[2] Depending on the context, πάσχα can refer to the Passover festival (22:1), the Passover lamb (22:7), or the Passover meal (22:8, 11, 15). See BAGD, 633; J. Nolland, *Luke 18:35-24:53* (WBC 35C; Dallas: Word Books, 1993) 1033.

[3] Marshall, *Last Supper*, 21-23; H. Patsch, "πάσχα," *EDNT* 3.50.

death in the original Passover event before their exodus from Egypt.[4] It implies that the necessary death of Jesus, plotted within the context of the Passover feast (22:1, 7), is also a sacrificial death with salvific effects.[5]

Earlier Jesus "sent" two anonymous disciples (19:29) to procure the colt on which he was to make his triumphal entrance into Jerusalem (19:30-39). Now he "sent" two named disciples, Peter and John, to prepare for them to eat the Passover meal (22:8). When Jesus raised Jairus's daughter from death, he allowed no one to enter the house with him except Peter, John, and James and the child's parents (8:51). Peter, John, and James were the disciples who accompanied Jesus to witness his transfiguration into a heavenly figure (9:28). Only Peter (8:45; 9:20, 33; 12:41; 18:28) and John (9:49), however, have previously distinguished themselves as spokesmen for the whole group of disciples.[6] That he sent two of the most important of his twelve apostles (6:14) indicates to the audience the great significance of this particular Passover meal.

Judas, "the one called Iscariot, who was of the number of the twelve" (22:3; cf. 6:16), was directed by Satan, who had entered into him, to betray Jesus to death (22:2-6). In contrast, two other named members of the twelve, Peter and John (6:14), are now directed by Jesus to prepare the Passover meal (22:8). They are to prepare "for us," that is, for Jesus together with the whole group of his disciples, to eat the Passover meal which includes the Passover lamb which had to be sacrificed (22:7).[7] Hence, the Passover meal was a sacrificial meal, in which the eating of the Passover lamb that had been

---

[4] Moses instructed the elders of Israel to sacrifice ($\theta\acute{u}\sigma\alpha\tau\varepsilon$) the Passover lamb (LXX Exod 12:21) and to tell their children that "this is the Passover sacrifice ($\theta\upsilon\sigma\acute{\iota}\alpha$) of the Lord, as he passed over the houses of the Israelites in Egypt; when he struck down the Egyptians, he saved our houses" (LXX Exod 12:27). See also LXX Deut 16:2, 4-6; Marshall, *Luke*, 791; Fitzmyer, *Luke X-XXIV*, 1382.

[5] Note how the references to the approach (22:1) and arrival (22:7) of the Passover feast form a literary inclusion which envelopes the narration of the plot to put Jesus to death (22:2-6).

[6] Fitzmyer, *Luke X-XXIV*, 1382; H. Schürmann, "Der Dienst des Petrus und Johannes (Lk 22,8)," *Ursprung und Gestalt: Erörterungen und Besinnungen zum Neuen Testament* (Düsseldorf: Patmos, 1970) 274-76.

[7] Fitzmyer, *Luke I-IX*, 440: "The celebration of Passover included the ritual slaying of the lamb in the Temple area, a festal meal at sundown in a family circle of at least ten people, and the consumption of the entire animal." See also Marshall, *Last Supper*, 21.

sacrificed to God in the Temple united the participants in a close spiritual communion with the God who saved Israel in the exodus event.[8]

In obedient response to Jesus' authoritative initiative Peter and John ask where he wants them to prepare the Passover meal (22:9). Within the suspense aroused in the audience by the focus on "how" (τὸ πῶς) the chief priests and the scribes are going to kill Jesus (22:2), and on "how" (τὸ πῶς) Judas is going to betray him (22:4), the focus now becomes "where" (ποῦ) Jesus and his disciples are to gather for this last Passover meal before his death. The audience has just heard of the dramatic and emphatically expressed "entrance" (εἰσῆλθεν) of Satan "into" (εἰς) Judas (22:3), indicating Satan's diabolical control of the plot to betray Jesus to death. But, with authoritative directions involving two other emphatically expressed entrances (22:10), Jesus demonstrates his own prophetic control of the place to eat his last Passover meal. With an authoritative "behold" (ἰδού), Jesus directs the "entrance" (εἰσελθόντων) of Peter and John "into" (εἰς) the city (Jerusalem), where a man carrying a jar of water will meet them; they are to follow him "into" (εἰς) the house "into" (εἰς) which he "enters" (εἰσπορεύεται).[9]

That Peter and John are to address "the householder of the house" (τῷ οἰκοδεσπότῃ τῆς οἰκίας, 22:11), a pleonastic expression emphasizing the "house,"[10] after they have followed the man with the water jar into the house (οἰκίαν, 22:10), underlines for the audience that this Passover meal will take place in the private, familial, and intimately hospitable setting of a household as prescribed by scripture (Exod 12:3-4). Jesus empowered the two anonymous disciples with his authority as "the lord" (ὁ κύριος), when he instructed them to tell anyone who asks about their taking the colt, "The lord has need of it"

---

[8] J. J. Castelot and A. Cody, "Religious Institutions of Israel," *NJBC*, 1272-73: "The sacrifice, then, served as a gift expressing the Israelite sense of dependence on God, but it also indicated the *desire for union with God*...When God had received his share of the victim, the ones who had presented it ate the remainder in a sacrificial meal. The fact that the one victim had both been offered to God and eaten by the worshipers brought the two parties together in a spiritual communion, establishing and consolidating the covenant bond between the two." See also Marshall, *Last Supper*, 18-19.

[9] They are apparently on the Mount of Olives, where Jesus has been staying; see 21:37.

[10] This pleonasm is noted by Plummer (*Luke*, 493), Fitzmyer (*Luke X-XXIV*, 1383), and Nolland (*Luke 18:35-24:53*, 1033-34). But none of them recognizes how it serves to emphasize the household setting of the Passover meal. For Fitzmyer it is merely "an unneeded pleonasm."

(19:31). Now he empowers Peter and John with his authority as "the teacher" (ὁ διδάσκαλος) to tell the householder of the house, "The teacher says to you, 'Where is the guest room where I may eat the Passover meal with my disciples?'" (22:11). Jesus' reference to himself as "the teacher" who will eat the Passover meal with "my disciples" indicates that the special fellowship to be shared at this Passover meal will strengthen his close teacher-disciple bond with them (cf. 6:40).[11] It will enable Jesus, as his death is being plotted, to impart final, farewell instructions to his disciples as "the" authoritative teacher.

The question of "where" (ποῦ) is the guest room "where" (ὅπου) Jesus may eat the Passover meal with his disciples (22:11) continues the focus on "where" (ποῦ) the Passover meal is to be prepared (22:9), in suspenseful contrast to "the how" (τὸ πῶς, 22:2, 4) of his betrayal to death. The focus on the "house" narrows to a "guest room" within the house, further underlining the intimacy of this Passover meal. As the audience recalls, the hospitality of a place in the guest room (ἐν τῷ καταλύματι), was not available for the parents of Jesus at his birth (2:7). But now Jesus, with his death imminent, receives that hospitality from the householder who grants him the guest room (τὸ κατάλυμα) in his house for a final Passover meal (2:11).[12]

Jesus continues to demonstrate his prophetic foreknowledge and authoritative control of the situation as he predicts to Peter and John, "That man will show you a large upper room spread with couches" (22:12). The focus on the place for preparing the Passover meal has now reached its specific goal. The focus has progressed from "the house" (22:10-11) to "the guest room" (22:11) to a "large upper room spread with couches." It is a specially secluded and private upstairs room large enough for the whole group of Jesus and his disciples, hospitably spread with couches or cushions for their reclining at the meal. With an emphatic "there" (ἐκεῖ) Jesus finally answers the question of where (22:9) they are to prepare the Passover meal (22:12).

That "they went out and found it just as he had told them" (22:13) echoes the previous situation of finding the colt for Jesus' triumphal entrance into Jerusalem, when "those sent went out and found it just as he told them" (19:32). This further assures the audience of Jesus' prophetic foreknowledge

---

[11] Although usually celebrated as a family feast with a lamb for each household (Exod 12:3), the Passover meal was also shared by teachers with the group of their disciples; see Johnson, *Luke*, 333.

[12] On τὸ κατάλυμα in 22:11 Fitzmyer (*Luke X-XXIV*, 1383) notes that "the reader of the Greek text would catch it as an echo," having heard it in 2:7.

and authoritative control not only of the preparation for his last Passover meal but also of everything else he has predicted regarding his suffering, death, and resurrection (9:22, 44; 17:25; 18:31-33). Peter and John then "prepared the Passover meal" (22:13) in obedience to Jesus' authoritative instructions and in contrast to Judas, who is seeking to betray Jesus to death (22:3-6). That they finally "prepared" the Passover meal concludes the concern for its careful "preparation" (22:8, 9, 12, 13), thus preparing the audience for the special significance of this particular Passover meal.[13]

Jesus hosts, serves, and interprets the meal for his disciples (22:14-38)

This Passover meal anticipates the final meal in God's kingdom (22:14-18)

The progression from the approaching "feast" of Unleavened Bread called Passover (22:1) to the coming of the "day" of Unleavened Bread (22:7) has now reached the arrival of the "hour" for the Passover meal (22:14). The arrival of "the hour" not only marks the time for the meal (cf. 14:17), but also connotes a critical moment in Luke's story of salvation, as the audience has repeatedly heard of "the hour" at which significant events take place (1:10; 2:38; 7:21; 10:21; 12:12, 39, 40, 46; 13:31; 20:19). When the hour for the meal arrived Jesus "reclined and the apostles with him" (22:14). Included among the disciples with whom Jesus, as "the teacher," intended to share the fellowship of the Passover meal (22:11) are the twelve disciples he specially chose and called apostles (6:13).[14] This subtly and ominously indicates the presence of the betrayer, Judas, "being of the number of the twelve" (22:3). That the apostles reclined "with him" complements Jesus' expressed desire to eat the Passover meal "with my disciples" (22:11) and points to the centrality of Jesus as the teacher and host of the meal.[15]

---

[13] Johnson, *Luke*, 333: "With the concluding remark, 'they prepared the Passover (meal),' Luke has repeated an allusion to the feast six times in thirteen verses. The symbolic importance of this meal is unmistakably being underscored."

[14] As Quesnell ("Women at Luke's Supper," 65-66) observes, the mention of the apostles does not necessarily exclude the presence of other disciples but highlights the presence of the twelve.

[15] Johnson, *Luke*, 337: Luke "has the apostles recline 'with him' rather than he 'with them,' emphasizing the central role of Jesus as teacher and host." Marshall, *Luke*, 795: "The wording tends to stress the initiative and dominant position of Jesus."

Jesus expressed his wish to share the Passover meal with his disciples when he instructed Peter and John to ask the householder, "Where is the guest room where I may eat the Passover meal with my disciples?" (22:11). Now, with a grammatically intensified expression, "how eagerly I have desired," literally, "with desire I have desired" (ἐπιθυμίᾳ ἐπεθύμησα; cf. LXX Gen 31:30),[16] Jesus expresses to the group of his disciples his deep desire to eat "this" (emphatic τοῦτο) particular Passover meal with them before he suffers (22:15).[17] After stating his wish to eat the Passover meal "with my disciples" (22:11), complemented by the apostles reclining "with him" (22:14), Jesus discloses directly to his disciples his deep desire to eat *this* Passover meal "with you." That he greatly desires to eat it with them before he *suffers* recalls the divine necessity that he *suffer* much on his way to death and resurrection (9:22; 17:25). His deep desire to share the special meal fellowship of this Passover with his disciples continues to impress upon the audience the great importance of this final Passover meal as a means of closely uniting the disciples with Jesus before he suffers a necessary sacrificial death like that of the Passover lamb (22:7).[18]

With a solemn introduction, "For I say to you," Jesus utters a prophetic pronouncement predicting that he will never (οὐ μὴ, emphatic negative) eat "it," that is, the Passover meal, again "until it is fulfilled in the kingdom of God" (22:16). He indicates that this particular Passover meal is not only the last that he will share with his disciples before his death, but also the one that

---

[16] Some interpret this as Jesus' unfulfilled wish or intention to abstain from actually eating at the meal. For a discussion of the various opinions, see Marshall, *Luke*, 796; Fitzmyer, *Luke X-XXIV*, 1395-96. But the implication is surely that Jesus does eat (and drink) at this Passover meal, as indicated by his previous question, "Where *may I eat* the Passover meal with my disciples?" (22:11).

[17] Fitzmyer (*Luke X-XXIV*, 1396) notes the emphasis on "this" particular Passover meal, adding that "it is not a merely generic reference to the celebration of the Passover that year." Although τοῦτο τὸ πάσχα here could be translated more specifically as "this Passover lamb" (cf. 22:7), it is probably best to translate it more generally as "this Passover meal," which centered on the eating of the sacrificial Passover lamb together with unleavened bread and bitter herbs (Exod 12:8; Num 9:11).

[18] Johnson, *Luke*, 337; Fitzmyer, *Luke X-XXIV*, 1396: "The Lucan Jesus relates the eating of the Passover meal (or lamb) to his own suffering...there is not only a hint of the death of Jesus, but also of its

anticipates the great eschatological banquet in the kingdom of God (cf. 13:29; 14:15).[19] This accords with the future, prophetic orientation of the Passover meal, which looked forward to the fulfillment in God's kingdom of the great salvific deeds of the past celebrated and made present during the Passover meal.

Complementing the eating of the elements of the Passover meal (lamb, unleavened bread, bitter herbs, see Exod 12:8; Num 9:11) was the drinking of wine, underlining the festive character of the meal.[20] In his role as host of this special Passover meal Jesus takes a cup of wine, gives thanks to God for it, and tells his disciples, "Take this and share it among yourselves" (22:17). That they all drink from the cup Jesus gives them rather than from their own individual cups intensifies their meal fellowship with one another, as it unites them all to Jesus on his way to death.[21] As he explains, repeating the solemn introduction, "For I say to you" (cf. 22:16), from now on he will never (οὐ μή, emphatic negative) again drink from the fruit of the vine with them until the kingdom of God comes (22:18).[22] This is their last opportunity not only to eat the Passover meal but to drink its festive wine with Jesus before his death. But by doing so, they anticipate their future sharing of festive meal fellowship with Jesus when he will again eat and drink wine with them at the final banquet in God's kingdom.

The bread and cup Jesus serves join the disciples to his sacrificial death (22:19-20)

After referring to the eating (22:15-16) and drinking (22:17-18) that comprise his last Passover meal with his disciples, Jesus, building upon the

---

significance."

[19] Nolland, *Luke 18:35-24:53*, 1050: "This is no vow of abstinence but a prophetic anticipation." Senior, *Passion of Jesus*, 57: "...the 'no more' of death is tempered by the 'until' of hope."

[20] Schürmann, "Abendmahlsbericht," 115: "Bei einer gewöhnlichen Mahlzeit pflegte man zur Zeit Jesu in Palästina wohl nicht Wein zu trinken, sondern Wasser. Der Wein charakterisiert das festliche Gastmahl."

[21] Fitzmyer, *Luke X-XXIV*, 1398; Schürmann, "Abendmahlsbericht," 114; Marshall, *Luke*, 799: "...the act of drinking together unites the participants into a table fellowship with one another. And the significance of the action is that this is the last occasion on which they can do so with Jesus."

[22] "Fruit of the vine" as an expression for wine made from grapes occurs in LXX Deut 22:9; Isa 32:12 as well as in the blessing over the cup at the Passover meal; see Johnson, *Luke*, 338; Marshall, *Luke*, 799; Fitzmyer,

highly symbolic character of the meal and its elements, adds a new symbolic significance to the bread and wine of the Passover meal.[23] First he took bread, that is, some of the unleavened bread eaten during the Passover meal and festival (22:1, 7).[24] As the audience knows, it was eaten with the sacrificed Passover lamb and was symbolically interpreted as the "bread of oppression (ἄρτον κακώσεως), because in haste you came out of Egypt, so that you may remember the day of your exodus from the land of Egypt all the days of your life" (LXX Deut 16:2-3). That he then gave thanks to God for the bread and broke it in pieces, so that they could all share from the same loaf, assimilates this eating of bread into the meal fellowship indicated by the drinking of the wine from the same cup, for which Jesus likewise gave thanks to God before they shared it among themselves (22:17).[25] He then gave the bread to them with a new symbolic interpretation: "This is my body which is being given for you. Keep doing this in remembrance of me" (22:19).

In identifying the bread as his "body" (σῶμά), that is, his whole person, his entire self, Jesus further associates his imminent death with the sacrificial death of the Passover lamb, whose entire body was eaten roasted whole and without a bone broken, together with the unleavened bread and bitter herbs (Exod 12:8-9, 46; Num 9:11-12; Deut 16:2-3). Just as eating the unleavened bread and the roasted body of the Passover lamb enabled them to experience in the communion of meal fellowship the salvation God effected by the sacrificial death of the Passover lamb, so now eating the bread identified as

---

Luke X-XXIV, 1398.

[23] For the text-critical reasons for accepting the longer (22:19-20) rather than the shorter reading (omitting vv. 19b-20: "which is being given for you. Keep doing this in remembrance of me."), see Metzger, *Textual Commentary*, 173-77; Marshall, *Luke*, 799-800; Fitzmyer, *Luke X-XXIV*, 1387-88; Senior, *Passion of Jesus*, 59; K. Petzer, "Style and Text in the Lucan Narrative of the Institution of the Lord's Supper (Luke 22.19b-20)," *NTS* 37 (1991) 113-29.

[24] The term ἄρτος (bread) is used several times in the LXX to refer to unleavened bread; see Fitzmyer, *Luke X-XXIV*, 1399; Nolland, *Luke 18:35-24:53*, 1052.

[25] On the significance of "breaking" the bread for sharing, see Marshall, *Luke*, 802; Fitzmyer, *Luke X-XXIV*, 1399: "the one loaf is divided in order to be shared." As Nolland (*Luke 18:35-24:53*, 1052) notes: "there is no reason to suspect any symbolism here of the breaking of the body of Jesus." And Schürmann ("Abendmahlsbericht," 118) remarks: "Nicht das zerstückelte

the very body of Jesus (22:19) unites the disciples closely with him in an anticipation of the salvation God will effect by his sacrificial death.

That Jesus' body now "is being given" for them underscores the sacrificial character of his death. Since the plot to kill him is underway (22:2-6), Jesus' body is already in the process of being given for their sake in death. It is being given for them by Jesus himself, as the audience recalls, in accord with the necessity of God's plan (9:22; 17:25), just as it was necessary for the Passover lamb to be sacrificed (22:7). By eating the bread that is his body, they are partaking in the sacrificial meal that he "gave" (ἔδωκεν) to them to unite them already to his body that is being and will be "given" (διδόμενον) for them in a sacrificial death (22:19).[26] That Jesus' body is being given "for you" (ὑπὲρ ὑμῶν) indicates the vicarious nature of Jesus' death as a sacrifice given to effect God's salvation for the benefit of the disciples, just as the sacrificial death of the Passover lamb brought God's salvation to the Israelites in their exodus from Egypt.[27]

Jesus then instructs the disciples to "keep doing this" (τοῦτο ποιεῖτε, present imperative expressing continued practice), to continue as a regularly repeated ritual the sharing of bread designated as the sacrificial body of Jesus, just as the Passover meal was to be continually celebrated as a perpetual institution (Exod 12:17, 24; 13:10). They are to keep doing this in remembrance (ἀνάμνησιν) of the Jesus who is giving himself in sacrificial death for their salvation, just as the Israelites were to keep eating the Passover meal as a continual "memorial" (μνημόσυνον, LXX Exod 12:14; 13:9) of their salvation: "so that you may remember (μνησθῆτε) the day of your exodus from the land of Egypt all the days of your life" (LXX Deut 16:3; see also LXX

Brot soll sein Lebensschicksal erklären, sondern das dargereichte Brot wird als hingegebener Leib erklärt."

[26] The present participle διδόμενον is a future-referring present, expressing that the future "giving" of Jesus' body in his sacrificial death is as good as present; see Porter, *Verbal Aspect*, 230; Fitzmyer, *Luke X-XXIV*, 1400.

[27] On the vicarious and soteriological significance of the preposition ὑπέρ here, see H. Patsch, "ὑπέρ," *EDNT* 3.397; Fitzmyer, *Luke X-XXIV*, 1401: "The vicarious gift of himself is the Lucan Jesus' intention in

Exod 13:3).[28] For the Israelites to "remember" the exodus event by eating the Passover meal meant not simply recalling it as a past event but actually reliving it, making it present for them again, and experiencing its salvific effects in the communion with God and one another created by the fellowship of the sacrificial Passover meal. Likewise, for the disciples to "keep doing this in remembrance of me" (22:19) means that, by repeatedly sharing the bread designated as Jesus' body, they not only recall the significance of Jesus' sacrificial death for them, but also continue to share in its salvific effects.[29]

The gestures Jesus performs in serving the bread as host of the meal-- taking (λαβὼν) bread (ἄρτον), giving thanks (εὐχαριστήσας) for it, breaking (ἔκλασεν) it, and giving (ἔδωκεν) it to his disciples (22:19)--reminds the audience of the overabundant meal Jesus shared earlier with his disciples and the crowd (9:10-17). Similarly taking (λαβὼν) the five loaves (ἄρτους) and the two fish, and looking up to heaven, he blessed (εὐλόγησεν) them, broke (κατέκλασεν) them, and kept giving (ἐδίδου) them to the disciples to set before the crowd (9:16). That Jesus has already empowered his disciples to feed the hungry crowd with the abundant bread he kept giving them, as well as his command for ritual repetition (22:19), indicate that they are not only to keep sharing among themselves the bread that he gave them as his sacrificial body

---

reinterpreting the Passover offering of old; it implies the soteriological aspect of his life and death."

[28] Fitzmyer, *Luke X-XXIV*, 1401; Just, *Ongoing Feast*, 240-41; Nolland, *Luke 18:35-24:53*, 1048: "...both the Passover practice that, according to Exod 12, reiterated the experience of the night in which the Israelites left Egypt and the Lord's Supper practice that developed out of this Last Supper experience share the same pattern: the originating occasion anticipated the saving event, while the ongoing celebration looked back to the saving event."

[29] On the word for "remembrance" here H. Patsch ("ἀνάμνησις," *EDNT* 1.85) notes: "In regard to its meaning one must be sensitive to the OT and Jewish content of the semantic field represented by the root *zkr* in the sense of re-presentation, making present the past which can never remain merely past but becomes effective in the present." And Johnson (*Luke*, 338) adds that it "means 'to bring to mind' in something more than a mechanical way; it is a form of presence...It is therefore easily transferred to the language of sacrifice as something that makes God 'remember' the people as well as the people 'remember' the Lord." For sacrificial offerings described as memorials or remembrances, see LXX Lev 24:7; Num 5:15; 10:9-10; Ps 19:4. See also

but also to feed others with it continually for the rest of time. The audience realizes the necessity for Jesus to give his body in sacrificial death in order to bring about the eschatological banquet in the kingdom of God, the banquet which has already been foreshadowed by his miraculously overabundant meal and anticipated by his last Passover meal before his death (22:15-18).

That Jesus took the cup "likewise after supper," that is, that he took the cup, like he took the bread--after the Passover supper, indicates that the sharing not only of the bread that is his sacrificial body but also of this after-dinner cup (22:19-20) occurs after the Passover supper as a separate, additional, and new ritual to be repeated in remembrance of Jesus' death.[30] The "cup" that Jesus took likewise after supper recalls the "cup" he took during the Passover supper, which he shared with his disciples (22:17). They are likewise to share this additional cup, Jesus' own personal cup, among themselves.[31] They are to share it, like the bread, in remembrance of him (22:19). As he did with the bread, Jesus gave this additional cup to them with a new symbolic interpretation: "This cup is the new covenant in my blood which is being poured out for you" (22:20).

In identifying the cup of wine taken after the Passover supper as the new covenant "in my blood" ($\dot{\epsilon}\nu \ \tau\hat{\omega} \ \alpha\H{\iota}\mu\alpha\tau\acute{\iota} \ \mu o\nu$), Jesus exploits the ability of wine, often described as the blood ($\alpha\H{\iota}\mu\alpha$) of grapes (LXX Gen 49:11; Deut 32:14; Sir 39:26; 50:15), to symbolize his own blood, that is, his actual life.[32] He thus further interprets his imminent death as a sacrificial offering to God of his total person, symbolized both by the bread that is his own body (self) and the wine that is his own blood (life). Both the body and blood of the sacrificed Passover lamb were instrumental in effecting God's salvation of the Israelites in the exodus event--its blood was placed on the door posts and lintels of every house in which its body was eaten, enabling every Israelite

---

M. Macina, "Fonction liturgique et eschatologique de l'anamnèse eucharistique (Lc 22,19; 1 Co 11,24.25): Réexamen de la question à la lumière des Ecritures et des sources juives," *Ephemerides Liturgicae* 102 (1988) 3-25.

[30] Marshall (*Luke*, 805) misconstrues this when he states: "The phrase $\mu\epsilon\tau\grave{\alpha} \ \tau\grave{o} \ \delta\epsilon\iota\pi\nu\hat{\eta}\sigma\alpha\iota$ separates the two parts of the new ritual from each other by the Passover meal." Senior (*Passion of Jesus*, 63) points out how the "likewise" ($\dot{\omega}\sigma\alpha\acute{\nu}\tau\omega\varsigma$) in 22:20 helps extend Jesus' command "to keep doing this in remembrance of me" (22:19) to the sharing of the cup as well as of the bread.

[31] Nolland, *Luke 18:35-24:53*, 1054: "Jesus is actually sharing his own personal cup with the disciples present, rather than having them drink from their individual cups."

household to be "passed over" and thus escape destruction (Exod 12:7, 13, 22-23). Knowing this, the audience realizes that, similarly, both the sacrificial body and blood of Jesus are now instrumental in making his death a new event of God's salvation for his people.

Going beyond an allusion to the important sacrificial blood of the Passover lamb, Jesus relates his blood to the blood of the sacrifice, the "sacrifice of salvation" (θυσίαν σωτηρίου, LXX Exod 24:5), that sealed the covenant, the special bond between God and Israel, in which God pledged to be their God and they pledged to be his people.[33] Moses took half of the blood of sacrificed bulls and poured it forth before the altar (θυσιαστήριον) of Israel's God, representative of God himself.[34] After the people listened to the words of the Lord in "the book of the covenant" and agreed to uphold their half of the covenant, Moses took the other half of the sacrificial blood and sprinkled the people with it. He then said: "Behold the blood of the covenant (τὸ αἷμα τῆς διαθήκης), which the Lord established with you concerning all these words" (LXX Exod 24:6-8). The sacrificial blood not only united the people with their God in a mutual covenantal relationship, but also implied atonement for their sins, as sacrificial blood always implied some notion of expiation.[35] This sacrificial sealing of the covenant concluded with a communal meal. After the leaders had seen the place where the God of Israel stood, "they both ate and drank" (LXX Exod 24:11).

But the people continued to sin against God, failing to uphold their part of this covenant, so that the hope arose for a new covenant. The cup of wine Jesus designated as "the new covenant" (ἡ καινὴ διαθήκη) in his blood (22:20) reminds the audience of this hope for a new covenant, as it is expressed in LXX Jer 38:31-34:

> Behold days are coming, says the Lord, when I will establish for the house of Israel and the house of Judah a new covenant (διαθήκην καινήν), not like the covenant which I established for their fathers on the day of my taking their hand to lead them out of the land of Egypt, for they did not remain in my covenant, and I neglected them, says the

---

[33] Fitzmyer, *Luke X-XXIV*, 1402. On the concept of covenant, see H. Hegermann, "διαθήκη," *EDNT* 1.299-301.

[34] Castelot and Cody, "Religious Institutions," 1267-68; J. Roloff, "θυσιαστήριον," *EDNT* 2.163-64.

[35] Castelot and Cody, "Religious Institutions," 1273: "The use of blood gave all animal sacrifices expiatory overtones (Lev 17:11)." On the atonement implied by "the blood of the covenant" in Exod 24:8, see Hegermann, "διαθήκη," 300.

Lord. But this is the covenant which I will establish for the house of Israel after those days, says the Lord. I will place my laws into their mind and I will write them upon their hearts. And I will be for them as God, and they will be to me as people...For I will be merciful of their iniquities and their sins I will remember no longer.

Thus, the sacrificial blood of the death of Jesus now fulfills this hope by establishing "the new covenant" by which God promises his new, definitive, eschatological forgiveness of sins.

That the cup of wine designated as the covenantal blood of Jesus "is being poured out" (22:20) not only expresses Jesus' death by violent murder (cf. 18:32-33), but also underscores the sacrificial character of his death as an atonement for sins. "To pour out the blood" of someone means to murder him (Gen 9:6; Isa 59:7; Ezek 18:10). And since the plot to murder Jesus is underway (22:2), his blood is already in the process of being poured out. But Jesus' blood is also being poured out as the sacrificial blood that establishes the new covenant. That the covenantal blood of Jesus is being "poured out" (ἐκχυννόμενον) reminds the audience of how Moses poured (ἐνέχεεν) half of the sacrificial blood of the covenant into bowls, and the other half he poured forth (προσέχεεν) before the altar of God (LXX Exod 24:6). As the priest "pours out" (ἐκχεεῖ) the blood of sacrificed animals on the altar as a sin offering to atone for the sins of the people (LXX Lev 4:7, 18, 25, 30, 34), so the sacrificial blood of Jesus is being "poured out" in death to establish the new covenant that definitively unites God to his people through his forgiveness of their sins.[36]

By submitting himself to the necessity of God's plan of salvation (9:22; 17:25), Jesus is allowing his blood to be poured out vicariously "for you" (22:20), that is, for the salvific benefit of his disciples. By drinking from his personal cup of wine that he has "poured out" for them after the Passover supper, the disciples are already being united into the new covenantal relationship with God that will be established by the blood of Jesus that is being and will be "poured out" for them in his sacrificial death.[37] The cup of wine that is the new covenant in Jesus' blood "which is being poured out for you" (22:20) parallels and complements the bread that is his body "which is

---

[36] On Jesus' blood being poured out as expressive of both his murderous and his sacrificial death, see F. G. Untergassmair, "ἐκχέω," *EDNT*, 1.424; Johnson, *Luke*, 339.

[37] Like διδόμενον (22:19), ἐκχυννόμενον is a future-referring present participle expressing that the future "pouring out" of the blood of Jesus in his sacrificial death is as good as present; see Porter, *Verbal Aspect*, 230.

being given for you" (22:19). By eating the bread that unites them to the sacrificial body of Jesus and drinking the wine that unites them to the sacrificial blood of Jesus, the disciples already begin to receive the salvific benefits of the death of Jesus in their sharing with him of the close fellowship of the sacrificial and covenantal meal he has provided for them before his death. This new and unique addition to the Passover meal, which they are to keep doing in remembrance of him (22:19), will not only keep them and their successors (the audience) always in union with his salvific, sacrificial, and covenantal death, but also anticipates their reunion with him in the meal fellowship of the final banquet in God's kingdom (22:16-18).[38]

Jesus predicts Judas's betrayal of him (22:21-23)

With a startling transition, "But behold!," the emphatic adversative conjunction "but" ($\pi\lambda\dot{\eta}\nu$) followed by the exclamation "behold" ($i\delta o\dot{\upsilon}$), Jesus shocks the audience by introducing a dramatic contrast to the intimate meal fellowship he is sharing with his disciples. He then pronounces that "the hand of the one betraying me is with me at the table" (22:21). The repetitive stress on "*me*" highlights the treacherous incongruity of the one betraying *me* also sharing fellowship *with me* "at the table" or at the meal (cf. Ps 41[LXX 40]:10).[39] The focus on the "hand," often expressive of hostile power, of the one betraying Jesus also being with him at the table sharply contrasts with the audience's mental image of the disciples taking with their "hands" the cup and bread that Jesus shared with them in meal fellowship (22:17-20).[40]

Jesus' dramatic pronouncement about the one "betraying" him (22:21) continues to demonstrate his authoritative knowledge of the events of his

---

[38] On the salvific significance of Jesus' death in 22:19-20, see A. Büchele, *Der Tod Jesu im Lukasevangelium: Eine redaktionsgeschichtliche Untersuchung zu Lk 23* (Frankfurter Theologische Studien 26; Frankfurt: Knecht, 1978) 167-69; B. D. Ehrman, "The Cup, The Bread, and the Salvific Effect of Jesus' Death in Luke-Acts," *SBLASP* 30 (1991) 576-91; I. J. du Plessis, "The Saving Significance of Jesus and His Death on the Cross in Luke's Gospel--Focusing on Luke 22:19b-20," *Neot* 28 (1994) 523-40.

[39] The word "table" ($\tau\rho\dot{\alpha}\pi\epsilon\zeta\alpha$) often refers to the meal itself and here emphasizes the table fellowship involved; see *EDNT* 3.367; BAGD, 824; Just, *Ongoing Feast*, 245.

[40] On "hand" ($\chi\epsilon\dot{\iota}\rho$) as expressive of hostile power, see 1:71 where "from the hand ($\chi\epsilon\iota\rho\dot{o}\varsigma$) of all those who hate us" parallels "from our enemies." See also 1:74; 9:44; 20:19; 21:12; 22:53; 24:7 and BAGD, 880; W. Radl, "$\chi\epsilon\dot{\iota}\rho$," *EDNT* 3.463.

suffering, death, and resurrection in accord with the necessity of God's plan of salvation. He continues his prediction by declaring that as the Son of Man he indeed goes "as it has been determined" by God (divine passive), but to that man by whom he "is being betrayed" he pronounces a prophetic woe (22:22).[41] Jesus' prediction assures the audience not only that he already knows that Judas is seeking an opportunity "to betray" him (22:6), after having discussed with the Jewish leaders how he might "betray" him to them (22:4), but that his betrayal is encompassed by God's prophetic plan of salvation. It recalls how he already predicted that, in accord with everything written through the prophets about him as the Son of Man (18:31), he "will be betrayed" (18:32). Indeed, through Luke's intriguing word play the audience experiences the sad irony that it is by "the *hand*" of Judas as "that *man*" by whom Jesus is being betrayed as "the Son of *Man*" (22:21-22) that Jesus as "the Son of *Man*" is going "to be betrayed into the *hands* of *men*" (9:44).

Since the "one betraying ($\pi\alpha\rho\alpha\delta\iota\delta\acute{o}\nu\tau\sigma\varsigma$) me" (22:21) can be more literally translated as the "one giving ($\delta\iota\delta\acute{o}\nu\tau\sigma\varsigma$) me over ($\pi\alpha\rho\alpha$)," the audience realizes that Judas's "betraying" is ironically advancing the "giving" ($\delta\iota\delta\acute{o}\mu\epsilon\nu\sigma\nu$) of Jesus' body (22:19) in his self-sacrificial death in accord with the necessity of God's plan of salvation.[42] The "betraying" or "giving over" of Jesus completes a triplet of future-referring present participles--"is being given" (22:19), "is being poured out" (22:20), and "is giving over" or "is betraying" (22:21), which express the future destiny of Jesus as already in the process of being made present. This underscores how Jesus knows that Judas is already in the process of betraying or giving him over (22:3-6) to a sacrificial death (22:19-20). Whereas the "one giving me over" is a present active participle, accenting Judas's activity, in Jesus' pronouncement of woe to that man by whom the Son of Man "is being betrayed" or "is being given over" (22:22), the verb $\pi\alpha\rho\alpha\delta\acute{\iota}\delta\sigma\tau\alpha\iota$ is a present passive indicative, expressing the double meaning that Jesus is both being betrayed by Judas and being given over by God.[43]

That God is ultimately the one "giving over" Jesus to a sacrificial death recalls for the audience how Jesus' death is fulfilling what was written in the

---

[41] On "as it has been determined" ($\kappa\alpha\tau\grave{\alpha}$ $\tau\grave{o}$ $\acute{\omega}\rho\iota\sigma\mu\acute{e}\nu\sigma\nu$) as expressive of the divine necessity of the plan of salvation, see Fitzmyer, *Luke X-XXIV*, 1420; G. Schneider, "$\acute{o}\rho\acute{\iota}\zeta\omega$," *EDNT* 2.532.

[42] W. Popkes, "$\pi\alpha\rho\alpha\delta\acute{\iota}\delta\omega\mu\iota$," *EDNT* 3.18; BAGD, 614-15.

[43] Nolland (*Luke 18:35-24:53*, 1060) suggests that the prepositional phrase, "by whom," before the verb $\pi\alpha\rho\alpha\delta\acute{\iota}\delta\sigma\tau\alpha\iota$ in 22:22 "may point to the ambivalent nature of the delivering up of Jesus: Jesus is delivered up by God, by means of Judas."

prophet Isaiah (cf. 18:31) about the servant of God: "The Lord gave him over (παρέδωκεν) for our sins" (LXX Isa 53:6) and "his life was given over (παρεδόθη) to death, and he was reckoned with the lawless; he bore the sins of many and for the sake of their sins he was given over (παρεδόθη)" (LXX Isa 53:12). For the audience Judas's betrayal of Jesus (22:21-23) is ultimately God's giving him over to a sacrificial death that atones for sins and that effects the new covenant by which God will forgive sins (22:19-20).

Although the one betraying Jesus is ultimately fulfilling God's plan of salvation, he is nevertheless fully responsible for his egregious deed. Paralleling his introductory interjection, "but behold!" (πλὴν ἰδοὺ, 22:21), Jesus continues with a "but woe!" (πλὴν οὐαὶ), issuing to the one "by whom" (δι' οὗ) he is being betrayed (22:22) a stern warning of misfortune, threatening his exclusion from eschatological salvation. Jesus' lamentful warning here recalls for the audience his previous very similar warning to the disciples that it is inevitable for scandals to come, "but woe by whom" (πλὴν οὐαὶ δι' οὗ) they come (17:1).[44] It triggers in the disciples a questioning (συζητεῖν) among themselves as to which one of them it could be who was going to do this (22:23).[45] So uncertain are they of their own faithfulness that they readily accept Jesus' prediction. The only question is which one of them will betray him. Their uncertainty chillingly reminds the audience that any one of them could betray Jesus.[46]

Jesus exhorts his disciples to a leadership that imitates his service (22:24-27)

The questioning (συζητεῖν) among the disciples as to which one of them it could be who was going to betray Jesus (22:23) develops into a quarrel (φιλονεικία) within them as to which one of them seemed to be greatest

---

[44] For the other previous warnings of "woe" in the narrative, see 6:24-26; 10:13; 11:42-44, 46-47, 52; 21:23.

[45] E. Larsson, "συζητέω," *EDNT* 3.284: "The sense of Luke 22:23 is ambivalent: Though the disciples' response to Jesus' prediction that one of them will betray him could be simple 'questioning,' the context suggests a *dispute* or *argument*." See also Nelson, *Leadership and Discipleship*, 140.

[46] As Matera (*Passion Narratives*, 163) remarks: "Luke warns his community that everyone who partakes of the Eucharist is capable of betraying the Lord. Mere presence at the Eucharist is no assurance of perseverance. Indeed, only Jesus' intimates can betray him!"

(22:24).[47] It reminds the audience of the previous argument (διαλογισμὸς) that arose within the disciples as to which of them might be greatest (9:46). Occurring immediately after Jesus' prediction that he was going to be betrayed/given into the hands of men (9:44), an argument about their individual greatness appeared rather incongruous to the audience. It demonstrated the disciples' emphatic, fearful lack of understanding regarding Jesus' prediction: "But they did not understand this saying and it was concealed from them so that they did not grasp it, and they were afraid to ask him about this saying" (9:45). Now a quarrel about their greatness similarly appears rather incongruous after Jesus' pronouncement that he is being betrayed/given over by one of them (22:21-23).[48] It continues to demonstrate the disciples' total non-understanding of Jesus' prediction of his passion, death, and resurrection (18:31-33): "They comprehended nothing of these things and this saying was hidden from them and they did not understand what was being said" (18:34).

The disciples are quarreling about which of them "seemed" to be greatest (22:24), that is, about which of them not only would not betray him (22:23), but which of them appeared to be greatest in their eyes and in the eyes of others in a culture that placed a high value on social honor and status. In response Jesus points to those who appear to be great in society: "The kings of the Gentiles rule over them and those in authority over them are called benefactors" (22:25). In the normal experience of Greco-Roman society the greatness of their kings lies in their status as "lords," those who "lord or rule over" people (not necessarily in an oppressive or overbearing way). And those who are in positions of authority over people strive for the greatness that comes from being called and publicly acclaimed as "benefactors" (εὐεργέται), a prestigious and honorific title recognizing the good that those of high status

---

[47] On 22:24-27, see Just, *Ongoing Feast*, 246-49; D. J. Lull, "The Servant-Benefactor as a Model of Greatness (Luke 22:24-30)," *NovT* 28 (1986) 289-305; P. K. Nelson, "The Flow of Thought in Luke 22.24-27," *JSNT* 43 (1991) 113-23; idem, *Leadership and Discipleship*, 123-72; I. Sloan, "The Greatest and the Youngest: Greco-Roman Reciprocity in the Farewell Address, Luke 22:24-30," *SR* 22 (1993) 63-73.

[48] After pointing out the various connections between the dispute about betrayal in 22:23 and the quarrel about greatness in 22:24, Nelson (*Leadership and Discipleship*, 141) adds: "These connections imply that for the apostles to prize greatness is not unlike betrayal."

do for society.[49] Jesus is not describing anything unusual but simply the kind of greatness that kings and authorities ordinarily seek.[50]

With a quick interjection, "But not so with you!" (22:26), Jesus introduces a stern injunction for the disciples not to strive for the kind of greatness normally sought after and prized by kings and authorities.[51] Rather, seizing upon their individual desires to be the greatest (22:24), Jesus enjoins the greatest among them to become as the youngest (22:26). Instead of eliminating their quest for individual greatness, Jesus transforms it, calling for a reversal of the normal ideas of social greatness. Rather than compare themselves with kings and authorities who are called benefactors, the disciples are to become "as" (ὡς) the youngest, that is, those of low social status and esteem, those who perform for people the simple, humble, menial tasks that go unrecognized by society. They are thus to renounce high estimations of their social importance as individuals. The paradoxical greatness that consists in becoming as the youngest reminds the audience of the earlier argument about the disciples' individual greatness (9:46), in which Jesus proclaimed that the one who is least among all of them, the one who is like a lowly child (9:47), is the one who is truly great (9:48).

---

[49] On καλοῦνται in 22:25 as having a passive (called by others) rather than reflexive (call themselves) sense, see Nelson, *Leadership and Discipleship*, 153-54. On the highly prized and sought after title of "benefactor," see F. W. Danker, *Benefactor: Epigraphic Study of a Graeco-Roman and New Testament Semantic Field* (St. Louis: Clayton, 1982); G. Schneider, "εὐεργετέω," *EDNT* 2.76-77; Fitzmyer, *Luke X-XXIV*, 1417; Nelson, *Leadership and Discipleship*, 150-52.

[50] As Nelson (*Leadership and Discipleship*, 154) points out: "To say that kings rule and authorities are called benefactors is not *in and of itself* a negative portrayal. It is only in light of the progression of thought in context (i.e., vv 23-24, 26-27) that the picture of kings and rulers takes on a negative hue. It is probable, then, that Luke wishes to pinpoint something negative about *ordinary* patterns of ruling (not just oppressive rule) and *usual* concerns for public honor (not just the improper acquistion of titles)." On the sense of "benefactors" in 22:25, see also F. W. Danker, *Jesus and the New Age: A Commentary on St. Luke's Gospel* (Philadelphia: Fortress, 1988) 348.

[51] For a convincing refutation of Lull's ("Servant-Benefactor," 289-305) interpretation that v 26a is descriptive rather than proscriptive, so that Jesus is rebuking the disciples for failing to achieve the greatness of kings and authorities who are benefactors, see Nelson, *Leadership and Discipleship*, 132-36.

Appropriately alluding at this Passover supper to the menial service involved in a meal, Jesus challenges any disciple who would aspire to be a leader to become "as" (ὡς) the one who serves at a meal (22:26; cf. 4:39; 10:40; 12:37; 17:8).[52] He then responds to their question (22:24), "who" of them seems to be "greatest," by asking "who is greater," the one who reclines at the meal or the one who serves? After forcing them to agree that it is surely the one who reclines, he continues his paradoxical reversal and transformation of the audience's normal thinking about the greatness of leadership, as he shockingly states that he, however, is among them as the one who serves (22:27).

Even though Jesus, and the apostles with him, "reclined" for this Passover supper (22:14), and even though he presided as host over the meal (22:15-20), he nevertheless is among them as the one who serves.[53] Jesus "served" them at the meal itself by giving them the bread and wine designated as his body and blood, which anticipated his more profound humble and lowly service for them in his sacrificial death (22:19-20). But that "I am in your midst as the one who serves" (22:27) encompasses Jesus' entire life of child-like humility and lowly service, as it recalls his proclamation that "whoever receives this child in my name, receives me, and whoever receives me, receives the One who sent me" (9:48). As the one who *serves* others, Jesus anticipates the eschatological banquet at which he himself will make recline and *will serve* those servants he finds watching for his coming at the end of time (12:37). Jesus has thus indicated to his disciples and the audience that the new Passover meal he has given them to be continually celebrated in remembrance of him (22:19-20) should issue in a leadership that imitates his humble life and sacrificial death, a leadership concerned not with the greatness of public acclaim but with the paradoxical greatness of lowly, selfless service of others (22:24-27).

---

[52] The present participle ὁ ἡγούμενος refers to someone in any leading position; it is not necessarily a technical term for a specific office of leadership in the church. See BAGD, 343; T. Schramm, "ἡγέομαι," *EDNT* 2.113; Nelson, *Leadership and Discipleship*, 157-58.

[53] The verb ἀνέπεσεν in 22:14 (see also 11:37; 14:10; 17:7) and the participle ἀνακείμενος in 22:27 (only here in Luke) are synonymous expressions for the position of reclining at a meal. See also Nelson, *Leadership and Discipleship*, 166.

Jesus promises his disciples that they will eat and drink in his kingdom (22:28-30)

With an emphatic "you" (ὑμεῖς δὲ), Jesus rebuked the disciples for desiring the greatness of gentile kings and authorities: "But not so with *you!*" (22:26). Now with a similarly emphatic "you" (ὑμεῖς δέ), he commends them for persevering with him: "But *you* are in fact those who have been remaining with me throughout my trials" (22:28).[54] That the disciples have been and still are remaining (διαμεμενηκότες, perfect passive) with Jesus means that they have been and still are in close union with him in the trials involved in his ministry of humble service. He points out that whereas "*I* am in *your midst* as the one who serves" (22:27), "*you* are those who have been remaining *with me* in *my* trials" (22:28).[55] That the disciples have persevered in solidarity "with me" throughout "my" trials intensifies for the audience the tragedy of the rupture of that close union during the intimacy of table fellowship by the one disciple who is betraying "me," whose hand is "with me" at the table (22:21).

There is usually the implication of a diabolical origin for "trials" (cf. 4:2, 13), and Satan has already entered Judas (22:3).[56] But the trials of Jesus here (22:28) refer not to the diabolical trials he experienced before calling his disciples (4:1-13), nor to any trials alluded to since Satan entered Judas, but to all the trials he encountered while his disciples were *with him*.[57] The disciples were implicitly present (cf. 11:1-13), for example, when some of Jesus' opponents, "testing" him, sought from him a sign from heaven (11:16).

The trials Jesus experienced while the disciples were in close union with him (22:28), however, remind the audience particularly of the disciples' controversial eating and drinking while with Jesus. At Levi's great banquet the

---

[54] For a helpful, detailed discussion of 22:28, see Nelson, *Leadership and Discipleship*, 179-97.

[55] On the close connection between vv 27 and 28 Nelson (*Leadership and Discipleship*, 181-82) notes that "what Jesus is aligns with what the apostles have been." See also idem, "The Unitary Character of Luke 22.24-30," *NTS* 40 (1994) 609-19.

[56] W. Popkes, "πειράζω," *EDNT* 3.67.

[57] Nelson (*Leadership and Discipleship*, 188) notes "that the Lukan Passion Narrative contains no reference to an adverse experience endured by Jesus *with the apostles* (22:28) between the time of Satan's new initiative (22:3) and the time Jesus is portrayed as delivering the saying at hand. None of the incidents described in 22:3-27 which could be construed as 'trials' for Jesus are experienced by Jesus with the apostles."

Pharisees and their scribes directed their grumbling to the disciples who were with Jesus: "Why do you eat and drink with tax collectors and sinners?" (5:30). When Jesus' opponents complained to him that the disciples of John and of the Pharisees fast but "yours eat and drink," Jesus explained that they cannot make the wedding guests (disciples) fast while the bridegroom (Jesus) is "with them" (5:33-34). After some of the Pharisees objected that his disciples were picking and eating ears of grain on the sabbath, Jesus defended their eating as lawful because, like those who were "with" David, the disciples are "with" Jesus as the Son of Man who is lord of the sabbath (6:1-5).[58] Thus, the disciples persevered in their solidarity with Jesus especially during the controversial attacks on the close union of the meal fellowship they shared with him.[59]

As a reward for persevering with him throughout the many trials he encountered (22:28) while in their midst as "the one who serves" (22:27), Jesus confers on his disciples, just as his Father has conferred on him, kingship (22:29).[60] That the Father has conferred kingship on Jesus reminds the audience of Jesus' favored relationship as the Father's beloved Son (2:49; 3:22; 9:35), to whom the Father has handed over "everything" (10:21-22). The Father's conferral of a kingship or a kingdom on Jesus explicitly reinforces previous allusions to Jesus as a king (19:38), who possesses his own kingdom from God (1:33; 19:11-12, 15), that is, a special share in the very

---

[58] On the controversial meals of the disciples with Jesus in 5:27-6:5, see chapter 2.

[59] As Nelson (*Leadership and Discipleship*, 197) concludes: "V 28 needs to be seen against the backdrop of a strand of thought in Luke-Acts highlighting the importance of solidarity with Jesus. The reference to Jesus' trials hearkens back to pre-Passion experiences of Jesus with the apostles in which he endured resistance, disbelief, opposition and demonic activity."

[60] Here βασιλείαν (kingdom) is best translated as "kingship" or "royal rule;" see Fitzmyer, *Luke X-XXIV*, 1419; Nelson, *Leadership and Discipleship*, 208-12. Although διατίθεμαι can have a testamentary sense, "to will, bequeath," or a covenantal sense, "to covenant, make a covenant," it should be translated here as "to assign, confer," because of the comparison between Jesus and the Father; see "διατίθεμαι," *EDNT* 1.314 and Nelson (ibid., 198-205), who concludes that "Jesus' action is best understood simply as a *conferral*, a bestowing upon or giving to the apostles. The action of the Father in conferring on Jesus is the pattern upon which Jesus' deed is based, and this comparison weighs against testamentary and covenantal understandings of v 29" (p. 205).

kingdom of God, his Father. By giving his disciples, whom Jesus exhorted to seek the kingdom of God (12:31), a share in the kingship/kingdom the Father has given him, Jesus fulfills the promise he made to his disciples "that it has pleased your Father to give you the kingdom" (12:32). The Jesus whom the Father rewarded with the kingdom for his humble service in turn rewards his disciples with that same kingdom for remaining with him during the trials of his humble service.[61]

With an emphatic repetition of the pronoun "my," Jesus explains that the disciples' share in the kingship that the Father has conferred on "me" (22:29) includes the intimate union of meal fellowship with Jesus himself at his own table in his own kingdom. The disciples, who have remained "with me" throughout "my" trials (22:28), are assured "that you may eat and drink at *my* table in *my* kingdom" (22:30).[62] Despite the tragic violation of table fellowship with Jesus at this Passover meal by the disciple betraying "me" whose hand is "with me" *at the table* (22:21), the disciples who have remained with Jesus throughout his trials will share table fellowship with him by eating and drinking "*at my table*" at the eschatological banquet in "my kingdom" (22:30). The table fellowship that unites them to the sacrificial death of Jesus not only in this present meal but in its future commemoration (22:19-20) will reach its fulfillment in the table fellowship that will reunite the persevering disciples with the risen Jesus triumphantly exalted in his eschatological kingdom.

This means that the disciples will take their places at Jesus' table along with all the others who will come from the east and the west and from the north and the south and will recline at the eschatological banquet in the kingdom of God (13:29). Their position at the table with Jesus is not one of exclusivistic privilege that might correspond to their desire for the greatness of kings and authorities called benefactors (22:24-25). Rather, as those who have persevered with Jesus throughout the trials of his humble, lowly service (22:27-28), they will be blessed to eat bread in the kingdom of God (14:15) along with all the others, such as the poor and crippled and blind and lame,

---

[61] Note the alliterative word play linking the disciples' remaining (δια-μεμενηκότες) with Jesus and Jesus' conferring (δια-τίθεμαι) on them the kingdom the Father conferred (διέ-θετό) on him.

[62] Nelson (*Leadership and Discipleship*, 213-14) points out that "the nature of the banquet of v 30a is clarified by the fact that it is in Jesus' kingdom and at Jesus' table; the apostles will dine *with Jesus* in his kingdom in reward for their faithful perseverance *with Jesus* during his trials" (his emphasis).

who will be included despite their lowly social status (14:21).[63] Jesus' promise that his disciples will "eat and drink" at his table in his kingdom (22:30) assures them of meal fellowship with him at the eschatological banquet, as it complements his previous promises at this Passover meal that he will never "eat" it again until it is fulfilled in the kingdom of God (22:16) and that he will never "drink" from the fruit of the vine until the kingdom of God comes (22:18).

The disciples' share in the kingship of Jesus (22:29) means not only that they will join him at the eschatological banquet, but also that, as he further assures them, "you will sit on thrones ruling the twelve tribes of Israel" (22:30). That the disciples will sit "on thrones" places them in a position of kingly authority associating them with the royal rule of Jesus, to whom God promised to give the "throne" of king David his father (1:32). The God who brought down the mighty "from thrones" but exalted the lowly (1:52) will exalt the lowly disciples to positions of power, as they will sit "on thrones" in Jesus' kingdom.[64] From their thrones the disciples, specifically the twelve called apostles (cf. 22:14; 6:13), will be "ruling," "governing," or "judging" (κρίνοντες) the twelve tribes of Israel, that is, the people of Israel reunited as the people of God into their traditional twelve tribes in the eschatological kingdom of God.[65]

Rather than judging in the sense of condemning or ruling in the manner of gentile kings and authorities seeking public acclaim (22:25), the disciples will be ruling the twelve tribes of Israel (22:30) as servant-leaders concerned with their people's welfare in imitation of the servant-leader Jesus (22:27-28). The disciples' eating and drinking at the table of Jesus is closely related to their ruling, indicating that one of the predominant ways they can rule the

---

[63] Senior, *Passion of Jesus*, 74: "In Luke's Gospel, dining in the kingdom is a metaphor of inclusion, not of privilege."

[64] D. Sanger, "θρόνος," *EDNT* 2.156-58.

[65] On the sense of κρίνοντες here, M. Rissi ("κρίνω," *EDNT* 2.319) explains that "the disciples will sit on twelve thrones in order to *judge* the tribes of Israel, i.e., to *rule* them." And Nelson (*Leadership and Discipleship*, 221) points out that "it does not seem necessary to choose ruling or judging to the exclusion of the other, even though the prevalence of βασιλεία in the context of v 30b (vv 29, 30a; cf. vv 16, 18) may tilt the balance toward the kingly model with its predominant broad idea of ruling." On the eschatological significance of the "twelve tribes" of Israel, see Holtz, "δώδεκα," 1.362-63; Nelson, ibid., 221-23; Fitzmyer, *Luke X-XXIV*, 1419.

people of God is by serving them the eschatological meal.[66] By miraculously multiplying five loaves and two fish, Jesus, as an anticipation of the eschatological banquet, not only served the overabundant food to his twelve apostles but empowered them in turn to serve it to the crowd. Indeed, Jesus provided his twelve apostles with twelve baskets of leftover food, symbolic of the capacity he gave them to serve food not only to the present crowd but to the future, renewed twelve tribes of the people of Israel (9:10-17).[67] Jesus, the one serving in their midst (22:27), promised that he himself would serve the eschatological meal to his persevering, vigilant disciples (12:37). By promising that the disciples will eat and drink the meal he will serve them at his table in his kingdom, Jesus indicates that one of the ways they will be ruling the twelve tribes of Israel is by serving them from the same eschatological meal they were served by Jesus.[68]

Jesus predicts Peter's denial of him (22:31-34)

With a repetition of Peter's original name, "Simon, Simon" (22:31), Jesus addresses Peter, who along with John prepared this final Passover meal (22:8), in an affectionate yet reproachful way reminiscent of his double address of "Martha, Martha" (10:41) in an earlier meal scene.[69] Jesus'

---

[66] On the dining and ruling of the disciples taking place only at the eschaton rather than at the time of the church, see P. K. Nelson, "Luke 22:29-30 and the Time Frame for Dining and Ruling," *TynBul* 44 (1993) 351-61; idem, *Leadership and Discipleship*, 224-30.

[67] For a full discussion of 9:10-17, see chapter 4.

[68] On the disciples imitating and sharing in the royal ruling authority of Jesus as a servant-leader, see also 12:42-46; 19:11-27; and Nelson, *Leadership and Discipleship*, 239-43. In summary of 22:29-30, Nelson (ibid., 230) states that "the conferral of kingship upon the apostles (v 29) is grounded in their faithful perseverance in Jesus' trials (v 28). This 'kingship' or 'royal authority' enables them, in the age to come, to rule over the people of God, reconstituted Israel (v 30b). But this reward and responsibility is to be accompanied by a banquet with Jesus at his table in his kingdom (v 30a). In this way the apostles are to experience the ultimate fulfillment of the Last Supper they presently share with Jesus, and the Lord's Supper they would yet share with each other."

[69] On 22:31-34, in addition to the commentaries, see Schürmann, "Abendmahlsbericht," 128-31; Feldkämper, *Der betende Jesus*, 206-23; Senior, *Passion of Jesus*, 75-79; D. Crump, *Jesus the Intercessor: Prayer and Christology in Luke-Acts* (WUNT 2; Tübingen: Mohr, 1992) 154-62.

address of Peter as Simon reminds the audience of the emergence of Simon Peter as leader and spokesman of the disciples (4:38; 5:3-10; 6:14; 8:45, 51; 9:20, 28, 32-33; 12:41; 18:28). At the quarrel that arose among the disciples at this meal as to which one of them seemed to be greatest (22:24), Simon Peter would seem to have in the eyes of the audience the best claim to that distinction.

With an attention grabbing "behold" (ἰδοὺ), Jesus warns Simon Peter that Satan, who entered into Judas (22:3) as the demonic instigation for his betrayal of Jesus (22:4-6, 21), also demanded to sift "you," that is, all of the disciples (plural ὑμᾶς'), like wheat (22:31).[70] Satan, the chief demon, whom God permits to test certain people's faithfulness to God (cf. Job 1:6-12; 2:1-7), arrogantly and aggressively "demanded" God, the implied addressee, for the opportunity to test the faithfulness of the disciples, as he had previously tested Jesus' faithfulness (4:1-13). He wants to "sift" the disciples "like wheat," that is, to shake violently and separate them, as sifted wheat is separated from chaff, from their persevering loyalty to Jesus throughout his trials (22:28).

In contrast to Satan's arrogant and aggressive "demanding" of God to test the fidelity of the whole group of disciples (22:31), Jesus assures Simon Peter that "I" (emphatic ἐγὼ) in proper and humble subordination, have "prayed" to God in intercession for "you," that is, Peter alone (singular σοῦ) as the leader of the apostles, so that his own faith may not fail (22:32) during Satan's testing. With an emphatic "you" (σύ) in correspondence to his emphatic "I" and in further contrast to Satan, Jesus commands Simon Peter that "you," once you have turned back from your temporary fall but not total failure of faith, are to strengthen your brothers (22:32). Jesus' intercessory prayer will empower Simon Peter not only to turn back after his own personal setback in faithfulness but also to continue Jesus' servant leadership (22:24-27) by strengthening his brothers, his fellow apostles and disciples, after the testing of their faithfulness by Satan.[71]

---

[70] For the role of Satan, synonymous with "the devil," in the previous narrative, see 4:1-13; 8:12; 10:18; 11:18; 13:16. On the Jewish apocalyptic background on Satan or the devil as the chief demonic power and heavenly adversary, see O. Böcher, "διάβολος," EDNT 1.297-98; idem, "σατανᾶς," EDNT 3.234.

[71] Feldkämper, Der betende Jesus, 213: "Wie die endgültige Treue Petrus zu Jesus, so ist aber auch die Stärkung der Brüder Folge des Betens Jesu." Crump (Jesus the Intercessor, 161-62) undermines both the power of Jesus' intercessory prayer and the special leadership role of Peter here when he strains the text for an implication that Jesus actually prayed for all the disciples.

In contrast to Jesus' praying "for you," for Simon Peter, that his faithfulness to Jesus may not fail (22:32), Peter insists that he is ready to go "with you," with the Jesus he addresses as "Lord," to *prison* and to *death* (22:33). This indicates to the audience that Peter thinks he is capable of persevering with Jesus in accord with what Jesus warned as a possible fate for his followers: "They will lay their hands on you and persecute you, handing you over to synagogues and *prisons*, leading you before kings and governors for the sake of my name...and they will put some of you to *death*" (21:12, 16). Peter indeed thinks he is ready to fulfill in their most literal sense Jesus' challenging demands of being his disciple: "If anyone wishes to come after me, let him deny his very self and take up his cross daily and follow me...whoever loses his life for my sake will save it" (9:23-24).

But Simon Peter is the one who earlier exclaimed to Jesus: "Depart from me, for I am a sinful man, Lord" (5:8). Although Peter thinks he is ready to go with Jesus, Jesus explains to the weak and sinful Peter why he had to pray for him. Before the cock crows today Peter will, a quick and definitive three times, deny that he even knows Jesus (22:34). That Jesus now addresses him as "Peter" (22:34) after the initial double address of "Simon, Simon" (22:31) underlines for the audience the tragedy of Peter's triple denial as the leader of the apostles, whom Jesus himself gave the name of "Peter" (6:14). The Peter who would go "with you" to prison and death (22:33) will thrice deny not himself (cf. 9:23) but that he even knows "me," the Lord Jesus. Because of Jesus' intercessory prayer for him, however, Peter will turn back from this triple denial instigated by Satan (22:31) and be able, as a true servant leader (22:24-27), to strengthen his brothers (22:32).

The audience realizes that before Peter and the rest of the disciples will be able to eat and drink at the table of Jesus in his kingdom (22:30), they will have to undergo a temporary setback in their persevering loyalty to Jesus (22:28) because of Satan's violent sifting of them. But the power of Jesus' prayer of intercession for their leader, Simon Peter, will enable all of them to withstand Satan's arrogant and aggressive testing, so that Satan will not be able finally to separate them from union with Jesus in the meal fellowship of the eschatological banquet in the kingdom of God.

Jesus exhorts his disciples to be equipped for their share in his death (22:35-38)

Jesus then prompts the whole group of disciples to recall that when he sent them out to preach the good news of the arrival of the kingdom of God, both as the twelve (9:1-6) and as the seventy-two (10:1-12), "without a purse or bag or sandals" (cf. 10:4; 9:3) they lacked nothing (22:35).[72] As the audience remembers, the missionary apostles and disciples were provided the hospitality that totally satisfied their needs by those who received their message favorably and welcomed them.

With an emphatic "but now" (ἀλλὰ νῦν), Jesus prepares the disciples for a dramatic change from that situation, now that Satan has entered Judas, who will betray him to death (22:2-6, 21-22), and now that Satan has demanded to sift the whole group of disciples like wheat (22:31). Now they must not expect a favorable and hospitable welcome from others, so that "the one having a purse must take it, and likewise a bag" (22:36). They must indeed be ready for a violent assault so serious that the one not having a sword for protection should go so far as to sell even his cloak, his most essential garment, in order to buy a sword (22:36).[73] The urgent need to acquire a sword, a metaphor to be as prepared as possible for self defense, warns the disciples and the audience to be ready for the violent hostility they can expect from those plotting the death of Jesus (6:11; 11:53-54; 19:47; 20:19; 22:2-6) which is now imminent.

The disciples must be as ready as possible for the death of Jesus because they will be drawn into it as part of the lawless with whom Jesus is associated

---

[72] On 22:35-38, in addition to the commentaries, see Schürmann, "Abendmahlsbericht," 131-36; J. Gillman, "A Temptation to Violence: The Two Swords in Lk 22:35-38," *LS* 9 (1982) 142-53; D. J. Moo, *The Old Testament in the Gospel Passion Narratives* (Sheffield: Almond, 1983) 132-38; G. W. H. Lampe, "The Two Swords (Luke 22:35-38)," *Jesus and the Politics of His Day* (eds. E. Bammel and C. F. D. Moule; Cambridge: Cambridge University Press, 1984) 335-51; Tannehill, *Narrative Unity*, 1.265-68; D. L. Bock, *Proclamation from Prophecy and Pattern: Lucan Old Testament Christology* (JSNTSup 12; Sheffield: JSOT, 1987) 137-39; J. B. Green, *The Death of Jesus: Tradition and Interpretation in the Passion Narrative* (WUNT 2; Tübingen: Mohr-Siebeck, 1988) 50-52; Senior, *Passion of Jesus*, 79-83; R. Heiligenthal, "Wehrlosigkeit oder Selbstschutz?: Aspekte zum Verständnis des lukanischen Schwertwortes," *NTS* 41 (1995) 39-58.

[73] On the sword as a weapon of deadly violence in Luke, see 21:24. Lampe, "Two Swords," 337: "...the cloak (ἱμάτιον) which served the peasant as a kind of sleeping-bag is the most necessary garment of all, which a man would be most reluctant to surrender (cp. Exod. 22:26-7, LXX)...In 22:36, however, the need to buy a sword is so pressing as to demand even the sacrifice of the cloak itself--as though this were the last thing that anyone would want to sell."

by the Jewish leaders seeking his death. As Jesus explains in a very carefully worded, progressively parallel statement that emphasizes his death in accord with God's scriptural plan: "For I say to you that it is necessary that this scripture be completed in me, 'And he was reckoned with the lawless' (Isa 53:12). For indeed what concerns me is having its completion" (22:37). That Jesus "was reckoned with the lawless" by those putting him to death accords with what is written about the servant of God in Isa 53:12, which is divinely necessary to be prophetically, finally fulfilled or completed ($\tau\epsilon\lambda\epsilon\sigma\theta\hat{\eta}\nu\alpha\iota$) in the person of Jesus.[74] And this scripture will be completed by the death of Jesus, "for indeed," as Jesus explains, "what concerns me is having its completion," that is, "my life is coming to its end." But "what ($\tau\grave{o}$) concerns me" also refers to "what ($\tau\grave{o}$) is written" in Isa 53:12 ($\tau\grave{o}$ K$\alpha\grave{\iota}$...) with which it is linguistically parallel. In other words, what originally concerned the servant of God in Isa 53:12 now concerns Jesus and is reaching its final goal, its eschatological completion ($\tau\acute{\epsilon}\lambda o\varsigma$) in his death.[75]

Particularly during the disciples' controversial eating and drinking while Jesus was with them, the Jewish leaders have already "reckoned" Jesus with the disciples as the "lawless" (5:30, 33-34; 6:1-5). But that Jesus "was reckoned with the lawless" (22:37) has another, more profound meaning for the audience. The "giving over" or betraying of Jesus by Judas (22:21-23) was ultimately God's giving him over to a sacrificial death that atones for sins and that effects the new covenant by which God will forgive sins (22:19-20). So also, the reckoning of Jesus with the lawless is ultimately God's reckoning ($\grave{\epsilon}\lambda o\gamma\acute{\iota}\sigma\theta\eta$ as divine passive) of him with the lawless so that by his being given over to death he can take away their sins, their lawlessness. This is clearly seen in the fuller quotation and context of LXX Isa 53:12, of which the "reckoning" is a part and which was alluded to by the "giving over" or betraying of Jesus earlier (22:21-23): "The Lord gave him over for our sins" (LXX Isa 53:6) and "his life was given over to death, and he was reckoned with the lawless; he bore the sins of many and for the sake of their sins he was given over" (LXX Isa 53:12). That "he was reckoned with the lawless" is paralleled and further explained by "he bore the sins of many and for the sake of their sins he was given over" to death. That Jesus was reckoned with the

---

[74] On the meaning of $\tau\epsilon\lambda\epsilon\sigma\theta\hat{\eta}\nu\alpha\iota$ here as prophetic fulfillment or completion, see H. Hübner, "$\tau\epsilon\lambda\acute{\epsilon}\omega$," *EDNT* 3.346-47.

[75] On $\tau\acute{\epsilon}\lambda o\varsigma$ as an eschatological term here, see H. Hübner, "$\tau\acute{\epsilon}\lambda o\varsigma$," *EDNT* 3.347-48.

lawless means that his sacrificial death which fulfills God's scriptural plan atones for the sins of the lawless, especially his "lawless" disciples.[76]

Jesus' reckoning "*with* the lawless" (22:37) reinforces the intimate union that he shares with his disciples in this final Passover meal with them in which he joins them closely to his salvific, sacrificial death on their behalf. Before the meal Jesus expressed his wish to eat the Passover *with* his disciples (22:11). After the apostles reclined *with* him for the meal (22:14), Jesus uttered his deep desire to eat the Passover "*with you*," his disciples, before he suffers death (22:15). That the disciples are those who have remained "*with me*," Jesus, throughout his trials (22:28) is climactically complemented by Jesus' being reckoned *with* them as the lawless in his death for them, which will ultimately enable them to eat and drink the eschatological banquet with him at his table in his kingdom (22:30).

The disciples' reply, "Lord, behold here are two swords!" (22:38), indicates to the audience that they have misunderstood by taking literally Jesus' metaphor about acquiring a sword to be ready for his death. It continues the disciples' utter non-understanding and total blindness to the divine necessity and significance of his death (9:44-45; 18:31-34). Jesus' rejoinder, "It is enough ($\grave{\iota}\kappa\alpha\nu\acute{o}\nu$)" (22:38), has an ironic double meaning for the audience. On the surface level it cuts off and dismisses the disciples' misunderstanding in the sense of "Enough of that."[77] But on the deeper level it expresses that their presentation of two swords, weapons with a potential for lawlessness, is "enough" to confirm that they are numbered among the lawless, the sinful, with whom Jesus is to be reckoned. With the words, "It is enough," Jesus brings this scene of his last Passover meal with the disciples before his death to its climactic close. They have now done enough to fulfill their roles in God's scriptural plan that Jesus be "reckoned with the lawless" (22:37) to a sacrificial death on their behalf.

---

[76] In his remarks on the prophecy of Isa 53:12 in Luke 22:37 Lampe ("Two Swords," 346) notes: "Indeed, that prophecy, according to the LXX, went on to say that it was because of their sins that the Servant was 'handed over' to death ($\pi\alpha\rho\epsilon\delta\acute{o}\theta\eta$), the word used of the betrayal of Jesus by Luke (22:48, cp. 22:4, 6, 21, 22) as also by the other evangelists. It may well have been the appearance of the key-word $\pi\alpha\rho\epsilon\delta\acute{o}\theta\eta$ which led Luke to apply the Isaianic prophecy to the 'reckoning' of Jesus with the 'lawless' disciples."

[77] P. Trummer, "$\grave{\iota}\kappa\alpha\nu\acute{o}\varsigma$," *EDNT* 2.185; Fitzmyer, *Luke X-XXIV*, 1434.

Relation of Luke 22:7-38 to Previous Meal Scenes

1) Jesus' last supper advances the *theme of Jesus' meals as anticipations of the great eschatological banquet*. Jesus and his disciples shared meal fellowship with repentant tax collectors and public sinners (5:27-32; 15:1-2) as an anticipation of the eschatological banquet which will joyfully celebrate the inclusion of repentant sinners (7:36-50; 15:3-32; 19:1-10), the hungry (9:10-17), the sick (14:1-6), the poor (16:19-31), and those of lowly social status (14:7-24). The disciples' feasting while they are, with Jesus as their "bridegroom" anticipated the joyful feasting and ultimate sabbath refreshment of the eschatological banquet (5:33-39; 6:1-5). The overabundant feeding of the hungry crowd by Jesus and his disciples anticipated the overabundance of the eschatological banquet (9:10-17). The meals of hospitality that Martha and Mary and later Zacchaeus offered to Jesus on his way to death in Jerusalem anticipated the choice of the "best portion" and the "salvation" of meal fellowship with the risen Jesus at the eschatological banquet (10:38-42; 19:1-10). Now Jesus' final Passover meal in which he joins his disciples to his salvific death by giving them his body and blood to eat and drink (22:19-20) anticipates his eating and drinking with them at the eschatological banquet in the kingdom of God (22:16, 18, 30).

2) As his farewell meal with the disciples, Jesus' last supper develops the *theme of Jesus' meals as preparations for the time after his death*. Although Jesus permitted his disciples to feast rather that fast while he was with them as their "bridegroom" (5:33-34), he pointed to the time that he would be taken away from them as a time for them to practice fasting (5:35). The abundance of food left over, "twelve baskets," after Jesus empowered his disciples to feed the hungry crowd indicates their ability to feed the hungry people of God in the future after the death of Jesus (9:10-17). Now, as *the* authoritative teacher (22:11), Jesus prepares his disciples to keep celebrating in memory of him this final Passover meal in which they are to keep giving to others his body and blood that he gave them to unite them to his sacrificial death (22:19-20). He challenges his disciples to imitate the greatness of his servant leadership after his death (22:24-27). His intercessory prayer empowers Simon Peter as the leader of the apostles to strengthen his fellow disciples after the death of Jesus once he has turned back from thrice denying Jesus (22:31-34). He warns the disciples to expect not just hospitality but also hostility as the "lawless" with whom he is reckoned by those putting him to death (22:35-38). But he promises them that for persevering with him throughout his trials they will eat and drink with him at the eschatological banquet at his table in his kingdom as they sit on thrones ruling the restored twelve tribes of Israel (22:28-30).

3) Jesus' last supper continues the *theme of Jesus' meals as challenges to the proper leadership to be displayed by disciples in contrast to the leadership of others.* Jesus' meals with repentant sinners challenged the Pharisees and scribes not only to celebrate in meal fellowship the repentance of those they lead but to repent of their own sinfulness in order to participate in the eschatological banquet (5:27-32; 7:36-50; 15:1-32; 19:1-10). Jesus' meals with Pharisees challenged them not only to allow others, like the sinful woman, to repent but to imitate her great faith and love as a repentant sinner (7:36-50). At a second meal he challenged Pharisees and lawyers to a compassionate leadership that gives alms to the poor and hungry (11:39-41), is concerned with social justice and the love of God (11:42), is unconcerned with the honor of their status (11:43-44), helps people to carry the burdens they lay upon them (11:46), heeds God's prophets (11:47-51), and uses their knowledge to lead themselves and others into the kingdom of God (11:52). At a third meal he challenged these leaders to allow people to be healed on the sabbath (14:1-6), to humble themselves by taking the lowest places at banquets (14:7-11), to invite the poor, the disabled, and the socially non-elite to their banquets (14:13, 21, 23), and to a complete social conversion by turning away from the wealthy and toward the poor (14:12-13, 18-23).

After challenging his disciples to feed the hungry crowd, Jesus enabled them to nourish the people they are to lead with the overabundance he provided (9:10-17). Now, in contrast to Judas, who will betray Jesus (22:3-6, 21-22), Peter and John illustrate how disciple leaders are to obey the authoritative instructions of Jesus, *the* teacher, as he directs them to prepare his final Passover meal with them (22:7-13). At this farewell meal Jesus challenges those disciples who will not betray him (22:23) to be leaders who seek the greatness not of social honors but of selflessly serving the needs of others in imitation of Jesus himself, who is in their midst as the leader who serves (22:24-27). Because they are those who have persevered with Jesus throughout his trials, the disciples are the leaders who will rule the people of God, serving them the eschatological meal they will be served by Jesus himself (22:28-30; 12:37). Simon Peter illustrates how a servant leader depends upon the power of Jesus' intercessory prayer to ensure that his own faithfulness, weakened by his triple denial of Jesus at the instigation of Satan, will not completely fail. When he then turns back to Jesus, he will be able to strengthen the faithfulness of his fellow disciples, who will likewise be "sifted" by Satan (22:31-34).

Pragmatics of the Meal Scene in Luke 22:7-38

1) By obediently following Jesus' authoritative instructions to prepare his final Passover meal which will closely join his disciples with him on his

way to betrayal and death, Peter and John model how the audience can be *united to Jesus' salvific death by obeying him as their authoritative teacher* (22:7-13).

2) As successors to the disciples, the audience is to fulfill Jesus' command, "Keep doing this in remembrance of me" (22:19). That is, they are *to continue to share* the new Passover bread that is his sacrificial body given for their salvation and the new Passover cup of wine that is his sacrificial blood which establishes the new covenant that atones for and forgives sins (22:19-20).

3) Jesus' prediction of his betrayal by Judas warns the audience that any one of them, despite partaking of Jesus' sacrificial body and blood, *could also betray him* (22:21-23).

4) Rather than seeking the greatness of social honors, the audience is to imitate the greatness of Jesus' servant leadership by humbly and selflessly *serving the needs of one another* (22:24-27).

5) By persevering with Jesus on his way to death, the audience gains the hope that they *will eat and drink with Jesus in the eschatological banquet* at his table in his kingdom (22:14-18). As servant leaders they will be able to serve others the eschatological meal they will be served by Jesus (22:28-30).

6) The audience depends upon the power of Jesus' intercessory prayer to ensure that their faithfulness to him does not fail completely. Like Simon Peter, who will thrice deny Jesus, they may fail in faithfully following Jesus on his way to suffering and death. But Jesus' prayer empowers them to become true servant leaders not only by returning to Jesus after their failure but also by *strengthening the faithfulness of others who will likewise fail* (22:31-34).

7) The audience can expect *to encounter hostility as they follow Jesus on his way to suffering and death.* But as part of the "lawless" with whom Jesus is "reckoned," they will be saved and their sins will be forgiven by the sacrificial death of Jesus on their behalf in completion of God's plan of salvation (22:35-38).

CHAPTER 12

THE RISEN JESUS' MEAL AT EMMAUS
LUKE 24:28-35

After Jesus' suffering, death, and burial in Jerusalem the disciples encounter him as the risen Lord. The message of the resurrection of Jesus is revealed by angels to the women at his empty tomb (24:1-12). Then the risen Jesus himself appears unrecognized to two disciples going away from Jerusalem to the village of Emmaus (24:13-27) and is recognized when he shares a meal with them (24:28-35).[1]

The Risen Jesus Travels with and Teaches Two Disciples
Going to Emmaus (24:13-27)

---

[1] On the Emmaus narrative in 24:13-35, in addition to the commentaries, see J. Wanke, *Die Emmauserzählung: Eine redaktionsgeschichtliche Untersuchung zu Lk 24,13-35* (ETS 31; Leipzig: St. Benno, 1973); idem, "'...wie sie ihn beim Brotbrechen erkannten': Zur Auslegung der Emmauserzählung Lk 24,13-35," *BZ* 18 (1974) 180-92; R. J. Dillon, *From Eye-Witnesses to Ministers of the Word* (AnBib 82; Rome: Biblical Institute, 1978) 69-155; G. R. Osborne, *The Resurrection Narratives: A Redactional Study* (Grand Rapids: Baker, 1984) 115-26; B. P. Robinson, "The Place of the Emmaus Story in Luke-Acts," *NTS* 30 (1984) 481-97; A. Delzant, "Les disciples d'Emmaüs (Luc 24,13-35)," *RSR* 73 (1985) 177-85; P. Fiedler, "Die Gegenwart als österliche Zeit--erfahrbar im Gottesdienst: Die 'Emmausgeschichte' Lk 24,13-35," *Auferstehung Jesu--Auferstehung der Christen: Deutungen des Osterglaubens* (QD 105; ed. L. Oberlinner; Freiburg: Herder, 1986) 124-44; Tannehill, *Narrative Unity*, 1.279-93; J.-N. Aletti, "Luc 24,13-33: Signes, accomplissement et temps," *RSR* 75 (1987) 305-20; L. Dussaut, "Le triptyque des apparitions en Luc 24 (Analyse structurelle)," *RB* 94 (1987) 161-213; U. Borse, "Der Evangelist als Verfasser der Emmauserzählung," *SNT(SU)* 12 (1987) 35-67; J. Kremer, "Die Bezeugung der Auferstehung Christi in Form von Geschichten: Zu Schwierigkeiten und Chancen heutigen Verstehens von Lk 24,13-53," *Geist und Leben* 61 (1988) 172-87; F. Rousseau, "Un phénomène particulier d'inclusions dans Luc 24.13-35," *SR* 18 (1989) 67-79; C. Combet-Galland and F. Smyth-Florentin, "Le pain qui fait lever les Écritures: Emmaüs, Luc 24/13-35," *ETR* 68 (1993) 323-32; Just, *Ongoing Feast*; G. J. Goldberg, "The Coincidences of the Emmaus Narrative of Luke and the Testimonium of Josephus," *JSP* 13 (1995) 59-77; J. D. M. Derrett, "The Walk to Emmaus (Lk 24,13-35): The Lost Dimension," *EstBib* 54 (1996) 183-93; Matson, *Household Conversion*, 76-80.

The two disciples do not recognize the risen Jesus (24:13-16)

The two disciples traveling away from Jerusalem to the obscure village of Emmaus were not only talking but questioning (συζητεῖν, 24:15), reminding the audience of the disciples' questioning (συζητεῖν, 22:23) among themselves in the previous meal scene as to which one of them it could be who was going to betray Jesus.[2] As the disciples' questioning among themselves at Jesus' last Passover supper indicated their non-understanding of Jesus' prediction of his betrayal, so the questioning of the two travelers to Emmaus indicates their non-understanding of "all these things that had occurred" (24:14).

With an emphatic expression of his personal name, "Jesus himself" (καὶ αὐτὸς Ἰησοῦς) makes his first, dramatically subtle appearance in the narrative as the Risen One. He himself came near the two who were "going" to Emmaus (24:13) and he was "going with" them (24:15). This brief journey of the risen Jesus with only two disciples recapitulates for the audience the narrative's main journey of Jesus with all his disciples (9:51-19:48), but with one significant and suspenseful difference--they are going away from rather than toward Jerusalem, the city of prophetic destiny and fulfillment (13:33-35).[3]

As the audience recalls, shortly before the main journey to Jerusalem, the disciples' non-understanding of Jesus' passion predictions (9:22, 44) was emphatically expressed: "But they did not understand this saying and it was concealed from them so that they did not grasp it, and they were afraid to ask him about this saying" (9:45). Toward the end of the journey the disciples' continuing failure to understand Jesus' prediction of his passion, death, and resurrection (18:31-33) is emphatically reiterated: They comprehended nothing of these things and this saying was hidden from them and they did not understand what was being said" (18:34). As the divine passives, "was concealed" and "was hidden," indicate, the disciples' complete non-understanding was ultimately caused by God himself. And now, that the "eyes" of the two traveling disciples "were held" by God (divine passive) from recognizing the risen Jesus traveling with them (24:16) adds to the

---

[2] On the problem of locating Emmaus, see Fitzmyer, *Luke X-XXIV*, 1561-62.

[3] On the Emmaus journey as a recapitulation of the main journey to Jerusalem, see Dillon, *From Eye-Witnesses*, 145.

dramatic suspense of this total non-understanding on the part of Jesus' disciples.[4]

At this point the audience experiences a triple tension: The two disciples and the risen Jesus are going away from the main group of disciples in Jerusalem (24:13), the city of the prophetic fulfillment of Jesus' death and resurrection (13:33-35); the two departing disciples continue the total non-understanding of all the disciples regarding "all these things that had occurred" (24:14-15), namely, Jesus' suffering, death, and resurrection in Jerusalem; and the two Emmaus disciples fail to recognize the risen Jesus traveling with them (24:16).

The two disciples recount events regarding Jesus (24:17-24)

The risen Jesus' question about "these words" dramatically interrupts their journey, as "they stopped, looking dejected" (24:17).[5] Their gloomy appearance indicates an unexplained sadness adding new suspense for the audience and suggesting a possible motivation for their journey away from Jerusalem. One of the two disciples with the name Cleopas, thus not one of "the eleven" (24:9; 6:14-16), responds to Jesus' question with his own question, "Are you the only visitor to Jerusalem who does not know the things that happened in it in these days?" (24:18). His question contributes to the story's triple tension. First, it advances the dramatic tension regarding their departure in sadness from Jerusalem. Although Cleopas keeps the focus upon Jerusalem and the momentous things that happened "in it," he and his companion, with gloomy faces, are traveling away from this city of prophetic destiny and fulfillment.[6]

Secondly, Cleopas's question continues to remind the audience of the disciples' non-understanding of the things that happened. It implies the

---

[4] Fitzmyer, *Luke X-XXIV*, 1563; Dillon, *From Eye-Witnesses*, 146-47. Regarding the "eyes" (ὀφθαλμοὶ) of the two disciples being held from recognizing Jesus, Völkel ("ὀφθαλμός," 552) notes: "Perception in the sense of recognizing or understanding, characteristic of most of the vbs. of seeing in the NT, is present in ὀφθαλμός as well."

[5] For an alternative translation and interpretation based on the variant reading καὶ ἔστε over καὶ ἐστάθησαν, which would eliminate the journey's interruption and have Jesus rather than the narrator state the disciples' sadness, see L. Ramaroson, "La première question posée aux disciples d'Emmaüs en Lc 24,17," *ScEs* 47 (1995) 299-303.

[6] Johnson, *Luke*, 393: "Notice the repetitive reminder of 'Jerusalem' as the place where the events took place, stressed again by the phrase 'in it'."

widespread knowledge of the significant events that happened in Jerusalem in these days so that even a visitor should know of them, yet ironically he and his companion are still discussing and questioning them, not yet knowing their meaning. Indeed, his suggestion, as one of those whose "eyes (ὀφθαλμοὶ) were held from recognizing him" (24:16), that this "visitor" does not know (ἔγνως) the things that happened in Jerusalem (24:18) ironically reminds the audience of the non-understanding of these crucial events even by the resident citizens of Jerusalem. When Jesus drew near to Jerusalem and wept over it, he said: "Would that even this day you knew (ἔγνως) the things that make for peace! But now they are hidden from your eyes (ὀφθαλμῶν)!" (19:42).[7]

Thirdly, Cleopas's question reinforces the suspense of the disciples' failure to recognize the identity of Jesus as the Risen One. His designation of Jesus as merely a "visitor" (πάροικεῖς) of Jerusalem in these days, that is, one of the many pilgrims to visit the city for the days of the Passover festival, functions as an ironic understatement for the audience who remembers Jesus' triumphal entry into Jerusalem as no ordinary visitor. Indeed, he was acclaimed as the "king" who comes in the name of the Lord (19:38).[8] The audience enjoys the rich irony of the intimation of what this "visitor" does "not know" (24:18) about the important events centered around Jesus by one of those who "do not recognize" (24:16) this "visitor" as the risen Jesus himself.[9]

The apparently dashed hope of the two disciples that Jesus was the one who was going to redeem Israel (24:21) explains why they are leaving Jerusalem (24:13) in dejection (24:17). They recount how some women of "our group" astounded "us," that is, the whole group of disciples (24:22).[10]

---

[7] On the parallel between 24:18 and 19:41-42, see Just, *Ongoing Feast*, 44-45.

[8] On the meaning of πάροικεῖς here, see H. Balz, "παροικέω," *EDNT* 3.42.

[9] Tannehill, *Narrative Unity*, 1.282: "The disciples do not recognize that they are trying to inform Jesus about Jesus. Irony is strong as they rebuke Jesus for ignorance (v. 18), when they themselves are the ones who do not understand." Nolland, *Luke 18:35-24:53*, 1202: "There is a nice irony in the disciples accusing Jesus of being one who *does not know* when it is they who *do not know* who is talking with them or that the resurrection has taken place" (emphasis Nolland).

[10] On the disciples being "astounded" (ἐξέστησαν) by the women, Johnson (*Luke*, 395) states: "The sense is that they were both surprised and confused."

"Not finding his body" in the tomb, the women claimed "that they had indeed seen a vision of angels, who say he is alive" (24:23; cf. 24:5-6). Although "some of those who were with us went to the tomb" (cf. 24:12) and discovered the negative evidence that it was empty, "just as the women had said," they still disbelieved the women (24:11), lacking the positive evidence that "he is alive" (24:23)--"but *him* they did not see" (24:24; cf. 24:10-12). That "*him* (emphatic αὐτὸν) they did not see" deepens for the audience the ironic suspense of the inability not only of the Emmaus disciples to see the risen Jesus with whom they are speaking, but of all the disciples, despite all the evidence they have, of believing in Jesus' resurrection.[11] They still lack the final piece of the puzzle, a vision of the risen Jesus himself.[12]

From the scriptures Jesus explains the necessity for his suffering as the Messiah (24:25-27)

Having played the role of curious questioner (24:19), the risen Jesus becomes the chastising teacher: "Oh, how foolish you are and how slow of heart to believe in all that the prophets have spoken!" (24:25).[13] Their foolishness and slowness of heart further explains for the audience the disciples' incapacity to understand and believe (9:45; 18:34) not only what Jesus, "a prophet powerful in deed and word" (24:19), spoke in his passion and resurrection predictions (9:22, 44; 17:25; 18:31-33; 24:6-7), but also "*all* that the prophets have spoken" (cf. 18:31).[14] It further explains why they are

---

[11] According to Dillon (*From Eye-Witnesses*, 111), "the *totality of facts* is developed in ironic counterpoint to their *total incomprehension* by those who experience and recount them" (emphasis Dillon).

[12] Tannehill (*Narrative Unity*, 1.281) notes that "the negative statement, 'But him they did not see' (24:24)...suggests that seeing the risen Jesus would make a crucial difference."

[13] Dillon, *From Eye-Witnesses*, 111; Just (*Ongoing Feast*, 202) remarks that "Jesus, now the speaker in the dialogue, is introduced by the emphatic 'and he (καὶ αὐτὸς) said to them'" and notes that "the intensive use of καὶ αὐτὸς is Luke's favorite expression for Jesus in the Emmaus story, 24:15, 25, 28, and 31" (202 n. 15).

[14] Just, *Ongoing Feast*, 202: "Whereas the women remembered Jesus' own prophecies in Galilee, the Emmaus disciples are to remember *both* the Old Testament prophecies as well as the prophecies of Jesus. In either case the question is one of *faith*--faith to believe all that the prophets have spoken, *including the prophet Jesus* who on three occasions predicted his passion and resurrection" (emphasis Just).

leaving Jerusalem dejected (24:17), with disillusioned hope (24:21). Although they are able accurately to recount all the evidence needed to believe in Jesus' resurrection (24:19-24), they are not yet able to believe in it, because they have not believed the prophets who predicted it.[15] The audience realizes that the disciples *did not believe* the women who relayed the heavenly revelation of the resurrection (24:11), because they are foolish and slow of heart *to believe* in all that the prophets have spoken (24:25).

With a persuasive rhetorical question introduced by οὐχὶ, demanding an affirmative answer, the risen Jesus himself begins to convince his non-understanding, unbelieving disciples: "Was it not necessary that the Messiah should suffer these things and then enter into his glory?" (24:26). As the audience recalls, as soon as Peter finally identified Jesus as the Messiah (Χριστὸν) of God (9:20), Jesus rebuked the disciples and instructed them not to tell this to anyone (9:21). Then, when Jesus predicted the divine necessity of his suffering, death, and resurrection, he referred to himself not as the Messiah but as the mysterious Son of Man (9:22, 44; 17:24-25; 18:31-33; 22:22; 24:7) or as the rejected prophet (13:33). Now that those predictions have proved true, the risen Jesus himself indicates to the disciples (and audience) that he is indeed the Messiah (Χριστὸν) whose identity embraces the divine necessity of his suffering and death before entering into his heavenly glory (24:26).[16]

By inducing the Emmaus disciples to realize that it was "necessary that the Messiah should suffer these things" (24:26), the risen Jesus not only restores but transforms their hope in him as the Messiah. Rather than dashing their hope in him as the one "who was going to redeem Israel" (24:21), that is, the Messiah (cf. 1:68; 2:26, 38), Jesus' condemnation and crucifixion by the chief priests and leaders of Israel (24:20) is encompassed by the divine necessity that as the Messiah he should suffer these things. The Emmaus disciples and the audience may continue to place their hope in Jesus as the

---

[15] Just (*Ongoing Feast*, 206) points out that Jesus here "is not merely referring to prophetic passages in the Old Testament but is also pointing to the prophets themselves who embody in their lives (teaching, miracles, rejection) proleptic manifestations of Jesus' teaching, miracles, and crucifixion that bring to completion the prophetic tradition of the Old Testament."

[16] Dillon, *From Eye-Witnesses*, 39-41, 140-41. He states that "the necessity of the messiah's passion could simply not be known before he himself could make it the matter of *Easter revelation*" (pp. 40-41); and that "Jesus could not be known as *messiah* until his path *through suffering to glory* was complete" (p. 140; emphasis Dillon).

Messiah, but they must transform and deepen it into a hope based on the understanding that as the Messiah he had to suffer and die before being raised to heavenly glory.[17]

In the previous meal scene of his last supper Jesus stated that "what concerns me" is having its eschatological completion in fulfillment of "this scripture" (22:37), the prophetic text of Isaiah 53:12. Now, continuing as teacher, he interprets for the Emmaus disciples "the things concerning himself" in fulfillment of what was prophesied "in *all* the scriptures" (24:27). The audience is overwhelmed by the totality of the prophetic scriptural witness that predicted the prophetic fate of Jesus--"all" (24:25) that "all" the prophets have spoken in "all" the scriptures (24:27). All of this underlines for the audience how the suffering, death, resurrection, and exaltation of Jesus as the messianic, rejected prophet (24:19, 21, 26) fulfills all that was predicted by both the prophetic scriptural words and lives of all the prophets who preceded him in all the scriptures.[18]

The Risen Jesus' Meal with Two Disciples at Emmaus (24:28-35)

28 Then they came near to the village where they were going, but he gave the impression of going on farther. 29 But they urged him, saying, "Stay with us, for it is towards evening and the day has already declined." So he went in to stay with them. 30 When he reclined at table with them, taking bread, he blessed it and breaking it, he was giving it over to them. 31 Then their eyes were opened and they recognized him, but he disappeared from them. 32 Then they said to one another, "Were not our hearts burning within

---

[17] Tannehill (*Narrative Unity*, 1.284 n. 13) notes that "'enter into his glory' seems to embrace both resurrection and exaltation, with the emphasis on the new status of Jesus which results." See also A. W. Zwiep, *The Ascension of the Messiah in Lukan Christology* (NovTSup 87; Leiden: Brill, 1997) 151-53.

[18] Bock (*Proclamation from Prophecy*, 274) suggests that we "call Luke's use of the OT for christology, 'proclamation from prophecy and pattern'. By this phrase it is meant that Luke sees the Scripture fulfilled in Jesus in terms of fulfilment of OT prophecy and in terms of the reintroduction and fulfilment of the OT patterns that point to the presence of God's saving work." On Luke's use of the OT here, see also Just, *Ongoing Feast*, 208-18. For some of the relevant OT texts already cited or alluded to in the previous narrative, see R. C. Tannehill, *Luke* (Abingdon New Testament Commentaries; Nashville: Abingdon, 1996) 355.

us while he was speaking to us on the way, while he was opening to us the scriptures?"

33 Rising that same hour, they returned to Jerusalem, and they found gathered together the eleven and those with them, 34 saying, "The Lord has indeed been raised and has appeared to Simon!" 35 Then they recounted what happened on the way and how he was made known to them in the breaking of the bread.

The two disciples recognize Jesus during his meal with them (24:28-32)

The journey motif continues as the two disciples came near to the village (Emmaus) where they were *"going"* (cf. 24:13), while he gave the impression of *"going"* on farther (24:28). This adds to the dramatic suspense for the audience, as it threatens to terminate the disciples' traveling fellowship with Jesus, who was *"going with"* them (24:15). It thus threatens to deprive these disciples of the opportunity to respond to Jesus' instruction (24:25-27) and to recognize him (24:16). But it also sets up a hospitality dynamic, as it gives them the opportunity to invite their fellow traveler to a meal that will transform their traveling fellowship into table fellowship.[19]

Rather than allow the traveling stranger to continue his journey, the Emmaus disciples strongly urged him to stop for the night, inviting him to share their hospitality: "Stay with us, for it is towards evening and the day has already declined" (24:29).[20] The audience remembers how Jesus, traveling to Jerusalem out of the divine necessity of God's salvific plan, invited himself to share the hospitality of a chief tax collector: "Zacchaeus, hurry and come down, for today I must (δεῖ) stay (μεῖναι) at your house" (19:5). Now the Emmaus disciples sense the necessity for the traveling Jesus to interrupt his journey and continue his fellowship with them, as they "strongly urged," "forced," or "prevailed upon" (παρεβιάσαντο) him to "stay (μεῖνον) with

---

[19] On Jesus' pretense of going on farther, Marshall (*Luke*, 897) explains that "he is merely giving them the opportunity to invite him in, and will not force his presence on them." Fitzmyer (*Luke X-XXIV*, 1567) adds: "The pretense is a literary foil for the disciples to urge him to stay with them; they so react out of a motive of hospitality for a stranger."

[20] Nolland, *Luke 18:35-24:53*, 1205: "In the ancient world, hospitality to strangers ranked high as a religious virtue. Both the Jewish and Greco-Roman worlds affirmed this virtue with stories about hospitality extended to incognito gods or angels."

us."[21] Their strong urging that he stay "with us" counters his pretense of leaving them by going on farther, as it indicates their deep desire to prolong their encounter with the stranger traveling with them.[22]

They try to persuade the traveling stranger to accept their offer of hospitality by noting that it is almost evening and "the day has already *declined*" (24:29). This reminds the audience of the same temporal motive for Jesus and the disciples to provide meal hospitality for the crowd rather than send them on their way: "the day began *to decline*" (9:12).[23] For the audience the tension of the disciples' continuing failure to recognize the risen Jesus intensifies. The "day" that has already declined is "that same day" (24:13), "the third day since these things happened" (24:21), the day of Jesus' predicted resurrection, and they still have not recognized the risen Jesus (24:16) with whom they have traveled and talked. But they still have the opportunity to do so. The risen Jesus resolves the suspense of his pretension of going on farther by accepting the disciples' invitation of hospitality. The Jesus who earlier "*went in*" to lodge with the sinner Zacchaeus (19:7), bringing salvation to his house (19:9), now "*went in*" to stay with the Emmaus disciples as the Risen One whom they do not yet recognize (24:29).[24]

---

[21] On the strong and forceful sense of παρεβιάσαντο here, see BAGD, 612; *EDNT* 3.15. On the comparison with Zacchaeus, Just (*Ongoing Feast*, 222) remarks: "The meal with Zacchaeus reveals the *abiding presence* of God's salvation in the forgiveness of sins because of *the presence of Jesus* at the table with Zacchaeus. Just as it was necessary that Jesus stay with Zacchaeus, so it is necessary that Jesus now stay with the Emmaus disciples" (emphasis Just).

[22] The impact of their strong urging and invitation is enhanced by alliteration. It begins with a repetition of smooth "por/pro" sounds: "they were going (ἐπορεύοντο), but he gave the impression of going on farther (προσεποιήσατο πορρώτερον πορεύεσθαι)" (24:28). But this sonorous combination is countered by a slightly more strident combination of "par" and "bia" sounds in their strong urging (παρεβιάσαντο) followed by the "m" and "n" sounds of their alliterative invitation, "stay with us (μεῖνον μεθ᾿ ἡμῶν)" (24:29).

[23] Just (*Ongoing Feast*, 221) points out that the time reference in Luke 24:29 "reminds the reader that other meals in Luke's table fellowship matrix occurred when the day was drawing to a close, particularly the feeding of the five thousand in 9:12-17 and the Last Supper in 22:14-38."

[24] On this and other connections with the Zacchaeus meal scene, see Just, *Ongoing Feast*, 222.

The beginning of the actual meal with the notice that "he reclined with them" (24:30) climaxes the transformation of the traveling fellowship into table fellowship. The audience has experienced a dramatic progression in this fellowship theme. The Jesus who was "going with" (συνεπορεύετο) them (24:15) was invited by them to stay "with us" (μεθ᾽ ἡμῶν), and so he went to be "with them" (σὺν αὐτοις) in their house (24:29). Now he has reclined at table "with them" (μετ᾽ αὐτῶν) for the meal (24:29).[25]

The traveling stranger who was invited to be the guest of the Emmaus disciples takes on the role of the host of the meal when "taking bread, he blessed it and breaking it, he was giving it over to them" (24:30).[26] This explicitly stated sequence of meal gestures recalls for the audience two noteworthy meals that Jesus shared with his disciples. Jesus similarly performed the role of host at the miraculously overabundant feeding of the crowds when "taking the five loaves and the two fish, and looking up to heaven, he blessed them, broke them, and kept giving them to the disciples to set before the crowd" (9:16). And at his last supper with his disciples Jesus acted as the host when "taking bread and giving thanks he broke it and gave it to them saying, 'This is my body which is being given for you. Keep doing this in remembrance of me'" (22:19).[27] The risen Jesus' restoration of meal fellowship with his disciples, which was interrupted by his death, strengthens the audience's anticipation of him sharing the eschatological banquet with his

---

[25] The use of both prepositions to express the "with" of fellowship, σύν and μετά, is noteworthy here in light of W. Grundmann's ("σύν-μετά," *TDNT* 7.796) conclusion that "σύν and μετά are particularly important in connection with meals, for the meal creates fellowship." And Just (*Ongoing Feast*, 222) notes that "these two words belong to the vocabulary of the table fellowship matrix (Luke 7:36; 15:2, 29f.; 22:15, 21; and 24:29f.)."

[26] Just, *Ongoing Feast*, 225: "Jesus has moved from being an ignorant stranger, to teacher, to guest, to host, whereas the disciples have moved from being hosts, to guests, to catechumens."

[27] On the sequence of meal gestures in 24:29 Tannehill (*Narrative Unity*, 1.290) remarks: "The careful repetition of this sequence of actions would not be necessary if it were not significant. It suggests an intention to recall previous occasions on which this occurred." See also Johnson, *Luke*, 396.

disciples and the audience when the kingdom of God finally comes (22:16-18, 29-30).[28]

The dramatic tension aroused for the audience by the failure of the two Emmaus disciples to recognize the risen Jesus traveling with them is now resolved. Whereas the two disciples' "eyes" had been held from "recognizing" him (24:16), now their "eyes" were opened and they finally "recognized" him as the risen Jesus (24:31). Just as their eyes "were held" by God (divine passive), so now their eyes "were opened" by God so that they recognized him. That they recognized the risen Jesus precisely in his action of breaking the bread and giving it over to them as the host of the meal develops for the audience the theme of the special meal fellowship formed by Jesus breaking and distributing bread to his disciples.[29]

It was by breaking and giving to his disciples the bread designated at his own body given in death for them (22:19) that Jesus united himself to his disciples in a meal fellowship that made them recipients of the salvific benefits of his sacrificial death. Whenever the disciples and the audience "keep doing this in remembrance" of Jesus (22:19), that is, celebrate Jesus' last supper, they are united in meal fellowship not only to the Jesus who gave himself in death for their salvation but to the Jesus who empowered them to feed the hungry people, when he broke the loaves and kept giving them to the disciples to set before the crowd (9:16). The overabundance of that miraculous meal

---

[28] Tannehill, *Narrative Unity*, 1.290: "The memory of Jesus presiding at the meal and breaking the bread turns such meals into symbols of continuity in fellowship with Jesus. In particular, the Emmaus meal becomes a symbol of restoration of a fellowship broken by death." *Contra* Robinson ("Emmaus Story," 486) the Emmaus disciples are not "now feasting at his table in his Kingdom." And *contra* Just (*Ongoing Feast*, 233) the meal at Emmaus is not "the first meal after Jesus comes in the kingdom." Rather, the Emmaus meal anticipates that final banquet that is still to come in the kingdom of God that has not yet finally and completely arrived (cf. Acts 1:3, 6-7).

[29] The imperfect tense to express ongoing action, "was giving over" (ἐπεδίδου, 24:30), enhances the simultaneity of them recognizing him precisely while he was in the process of breaking and giving over to them the bread. Marshall (*Luke*, 898) states that "their eyes are opened by God to see the significance of the action and thus to recognise Jesus." As Just (*Ongoing Feast*, 223) points out: "The breaking of the bread in Luke 24:30 cannot be separated from the opening of the eyes, the recognition, and the disappearance in 24:31, for these two verses are linked grammatically as one complete thought."

(9:17) not only indicated that through their meal fellowship with Jesus the disciples and the audience will be able to continue to feed the hungry, but also anticipated the overabundance of the messianic banquet. Now whenever the disciples and the audience break and give bread in remembrance of Jesus' last supper, they are also united in meal fellowship with the risen Jesus who broke bread and gave it over to his disciples after his death (24:31), the Prophet and Messiah who had to suffer death before entering into his glory (24:19, 26).

But as soon as the Emmaus disciples recognized the risen Jesus as he was breaking and giving over the bread to them, he disappeared from them (24:31).[30] This fleeting visibility of the risen Jesus enhances the audience's expectation of an enduring vision of the risen Jesus in the permanent meal fellowship they will share with him at the eschatological banquet in God's kingdom (22:16-18, 29-30). It reminds the audience that it is now as the invisible one that the risen Jesus unites himself to them in meal fellowship, whenever, in remembrance of him at his last supper, they break and give to one another the bread he gave as his body for them in sacrificial death (22:19).[31]

When the two disciples began their journey to Emmaus, they were talking with one another ($\pi\rho\dot{o}\varsigma$ $\dot{\alpha}\lambda\lambda\dot{\eta}\lambda o\upsilon\varsigma$) "about all these things that had occurred" (24:14), the things concerning the death of Jesus which they did not understand. After the risen Jesus, whom they did not recognize, joined their journey (24:15-16), he introduced the expression of their non-understanding of the passion facts (24:19-24) with the question: "What are these words that you are exchanging with one another ($\pi\rho\dot{o}\varsigma$ $\dot{\alpha}\lambda\lambda\dot{\eta}\lambda o\upsilon\varsigma$) as you walk along?" (24:17). Now the dramatic tension of their failure to understand begins to be resolved for the audience, as the two disciples voiced to one another ($\pi\rho\dot{o}\varsigma$ $\dot{\alpha}\lambda\lambda\dot{\eta}\lambda o\upsilon\varsigma$) the exclamatory, rhetorical question: "Were not our hearts burning within us while he was speaking to us on the way, while he was opening to us the scriptures?" (24:32).[32]

Their burning "heart" begins to reverse Jesus' rebuke of them as "foolish and slow of heart" (24:25). Their hearts were no longer "slow" but "burning" to believe in all that the prophets "have spoken," while Jesus, a prophet powerful in deed and word (24:19), "was speaking" to them on the

---

[30] For diagrams of the chiastic structure of 24:31, see Just, *Ongoing Feast*, 254-57.

[31] On this significance for the disappearance of the risen Jesus in 24:31, see Just, *Ongoing Feast*, 260-61.

[32] On the relation between 24:14, 17 and 32, see Just, *Ongoing Feast*, 57-58.

way (24:32). Their coming to understand and believe while he was speaking to them "on the way" to Emmaus finally shatters for the audience the suspense of the disciples' total non-understanding (9:45; 18:34) of Jesus' prophetic predictions of the divine necessity of his suffering, death, and resurrection (9:22, 44; 17:25; 18:31-33) while they were going with him and listening to his teaching "on the way" to Jerusalem (9:57; 19:36).[33] Before their eyes "were opened" and they recognized the risen Jesus in the breaking of the bread (24:31), he "was opening" to them on the way the scriptures concerning himself (24:32, 27). The audience realizes that before the disciples' eyes could be opened to recognize the risen Jesus, he had to open for them the scriptures, which contain all the prophecies that confirm his predictions that it was divinely necessary for him as the Messiah to suffer death before entering into his glory (24:25-27).[34]

That the hearts of the Emmaus disciples were burning within them while the risen Jesus was speaking to them on the way and opening for them the scriptures (24:32) further contributes to the theme of the special meal fellowship formed by Jesus breaking and giving bread to his disciples. Whenever the audience celebrates Jesus' last supper in remembrance of him (22:19), they will be united in meal fellowship with the risen Jesus when they listen to the scriptural teaching that explains Jesus' prophetic predictions of the divine necessity of his death and resurrection, so that they can recognize his invisible presence with them when they break and give to one another the bread designated as his sacrificial body. The Emmaus disciples' experience of the risen Jesus in both his scriptural teaching and breaking of the bread is paradigmatic for the audience's experience of the invisible risen Jesus in both their scriptural teaching and breaking of the bread whenever they celebrate his last supper.

---

[33] Note how the phrase "on the way" serves as a literary inclusion for Jesus' fateful journey to Jerusalem (9:51-19:48), occurring towards the beginning (9:57) and conclusion (19:36) of the journey. With regard to "on the way" in 24:32 Just (*Ongoing Feast*, 58) affirms that "the reader is reminded of the teaching of Jesus to his disciples on the road to Jerusalem."

[34] Tannehill, *Luke*, 358: "The whole Emmaus narrative is a revelatory process, for the disciples needed to understand how death and resurrection befits the Messiah before they could recognize the risen Lord." Johnson, *Luke*, 397: "As they perceived the true, messianic meaning of the Scripture, they were also able to 'see' Jesus in the breaking of the bread."

The two disciples report how Jesus was made known to them during the meal (24:33-35)

The rising of the Emmaus disciples "that same hour" (24:33) "that same day" (24:13) on which they had left Jerusalem reminds the audience of a similar progression of temporal focus from the "day" of Unleavened Bread (22:7) to the arrival of the momentous "hour" for Jesus' last Passover meal (22:14).[35] "That same hour" refers to the evening (24:29) of "that same day" (24:13), "the third day since these things happened" (24:21), the day of Jesus' predicted resurrection. It was that same momentous hour in which their eyes were finally opened to recognize the risen Jesus in the breaking of the bread (24:30-31), after he had opened the scriptures for them finally to understand and believe his passion and resurrection predictions (24:32). So momentous was "that same hour" that, despite its lateness as the motive for Jesus to stay with the Emmaus disciples rather than continue his journey (24:28-29), they urgently arose during it and began to return the sixty stades back to Jerusalem (24:33; cf. 24:13).[36]

Their return to Jerusalem begins to resolve for the audience the suspense aroused by their going away from the main group of disciples in Jerusalem, the city of the prophetic fulfillment of Jesus' death and resurrection. They had left Jerusalem dejected (24:17), their hope that Jesus would be the one to redeem Israel dashed by his death at the hand of their leaders (24:20-21), because they were foolish and slow of heart to believe in all that the prophets, especially the prophet Jesus (24:19), have spoken (24:25). But now their encounter with the risen Jesus has promptly propelled them back to the city of prophetic destiny with eyes opened to understand and

---

[35] On the movement from the "day" to the "hour" in both these meal scenes, Just (*Ongoing Feast*, 48) states: "In both Luke 22 and Luke 24, this movement conveys an urgency of the moment and a focus on a particular event." See also Dillon, *From Eye-Witnesses*, 92.

[36] Fitzmyer (*Luke X-XXIV*, 1568) translates the phrase as "even at that late hour" and explains that "after having dissuaded Christ from going farther because it was evening, and the day was already spent, they themselves decide to go back to Jerusalem."

hearts burning to believe (24:31-32), their dejection dissolved and their hope revived.[37]

The tension of the Emmaus disciples' separation from the main group of disciples in Jerusalem is resolved for the audience upon their return, as "they found gathered together the eleven and those with them" (24:33). The Emmaus disciples were included with "the eleven and all the rest" (24:9), who did not believe the women's report of Jesus' resurrection (24:9-11), some of whom "went to the tomb and found it just as the women had said, but him they did not see" (24:24). When the two wandering disciples rejoined their associates in Jerusalem, they found that "the eleven and those with them" were now definitively gathered together (ἠθροισμένους, perfect tense) as a newly and permanently assembled Jerusalem community (24:33).[38]

Before they can relate their own encounter with the risen Jesus, the returning disciples are met by the Jerusalem assembly's exclamatory confession, whose content was the impetus that gathered them together: "The Lord has indeed been raised and has appeared to Simon!" (24:34).[39] The audience felt the tension of the Jerusalem disciples' disbelief of the women's report of the angelic revelation at the empty tomb (24:9-11, 22-24): "He is not here, but has been raised!" (24:6). Now that tension is resolved as the disbelievers confirm: "The Lord has *indeed* been raised!" (24:34). The

---

[37] Dillon, *From Eye-Witnesses*, 93: "The travelers left Jerusalem in confusion and disappointment; they now return there aglow with the revelation of the risen Lord. There is thus the closest relationship between the 'journey' motif, with its contrasting moments of *concealment* and *revelation*, and the return to Jerusalem, presented almost as a homecoming" (emphasis Dillon).

[38] On the prominent position and pregnant sense of the perfect passive participle (ἠθροισμένους) Dillon (*From Eye-Witnesses*, 96) points out that "this is the very first mention of an actual *gathering together* of 'the Eleven' and their fellows; the two groups were mentioned in 24,9ff., but their 'togetherness' remained unspecific there (emphasis Dillon)..." After referring to the frequent association of this verb with gatherings of the religious and cultic community of Israel, Dillon adds: "Considering both this traditional (LXX) flavoring of the verb and the tense of the participle, we are entitled to suggest the Emmaus disciples 'found,' on their return to Jerusalem, the risen Lord's definitive reconstitution of his assembly of followers" (p. 97).

[39] Dillon (*From Eye-Witnesses*, 97) points out "the close conceptual relationship between the two participles, '*gathered*' and '*saying*': the content of the disciples' confession (λέγοντας) is the event which was the basis of their regrouping (ἠθροισμένους) as the 'church-to-be.'"

centurion, who witnessed the crucified Jesus entrust his spirit into God's hands as he died (23:46), affirmed him to be an innocently suffering just one: "*Indeed* (ὄντως) this man was just!" (23:47). With the confession that Jesus has *indeed* (ὄντως) been raised by God (divine passive) from death, the audience experiences Jesus' climactic vindication as God's innocently suffering just one.[40]

The report that the risen Lord "*has appeared*" to Simon (24:34), one of those who "went to the tomb and found it just as the women had said, but him they *did not see*" (24:24; cf. 24:12), supplies the lack of a vision of the risen Jesus for witnesses of the empty tomb, which complements the women's "*seeing*" at the empty tomb "a *vision* of angels, who say he is alive" (24:23). The use of the name "Simon" after that of "Peter" (24:12) alludes to his call to be a disciple (5:1-11) and his renaming as the leader of the twelve apostles (6:14). It recalls for the audience Jesus' double address of the Peter who would deny him three times (22:34) as "Simon, Simon" (22:31) at his last supper.[41] That the appearance of the risen Lord to "Simon" has gathered together the disciples at Jerusalem to exclaim their faith in Jesus' resurrection and has thus revived their hope that he would be the one to redeem Israel (24:21) indicates to the audience the beginning of the fulfillment of Jesus' promise that after "Simon" has turned back from his triple denial of Jesus, he would strengthen his brothers (22:32).[42]

---

[40] On the connection between the confessions in 23:47 and 24:34, see Dillon, *From Eye-Witnesses*, 100-103; Just, *Ongoing Feast*, 218.

[41] On the references to "Simon" in 22:31 and 24:34, Tannehill (*Narrative Unity*, 1.292-93) states: "The connection between these two passages is reinforced by the fact that they are the only places in Luke where Peter is called Simon after the formal indication in 6:14 that Jesus gave Simon a new name."

[42] Dillon, *From Eye-Witnesses*, 100: "The wayward disciple, who both denied the Master on trial (Lk 22,34.54ff.) and could only wonder at the sight of the empty tomb, has presumably 'turned' and can now 'strengthen' his brothers." On the references to "Peter" (24:12) and "Simon" (24:34) that frame the Emmaus meal, Just (*Ongoing Feast*, 251) asserts: "Taken together, these two references form Peter's rehabilitation to his status as leader of the Church in fulfillment of Luke 22. *The risen Christ* has restored Peter, bringing about his repentance, conversion, and forgiveness. Thus, Luke 22:31-34 prepares the reader for the restoration of Peter in Luke 24" (emphasis Just). Tannehill (*Narrative Unity*, 293) adds: "Simon is warned and charged with responsibility in 22:31-32, and he begins to fulfill that responsibility by bearing witness to the risen Jesus before Jesus' other followers."

The Emmaus disciples then recounted "what happened on the way" (24:35), that is, that their hearts were burning within them as he spoke and opened the scriptures for them to understand the divine necessity of his death "on the way" (24:32). And they recounted how he was "made known" by God (divine passive) "to them in the breaking of the bread" (24:35). Thus, the "opening" of the scriptures by the risen Jesus was climactically complemented by the "opening" of their eyes by God to recognize the risen Jesus as he broke and gave them the bread, restoring meal fellowship with them (24:30-31). To the unique "appearance" of the risen Lord to Simon, the leader of the disciples, who witnessed the empty tomb (24:34), is added the unique "recognition" by and "making known" to the Emmaus disciples the presence of the risen Lord in his breaking the bread of meal fellowship with them. That the presence of the risen Jesus was uniquely recognized and made known to the Emmaus disciples "in the breaking of the bread" before he disappeared (24:31) reinforces the suggestion that whenever the audience breaks and distributes the bread of Jesus' last supper in remembrance of him (22:19), the invisible presence of the risen Lord is recognized and made known to them.[43]

Relation of Luke 24:28-35 to Previous Meal Scenes

1) The Emmaus meal scene adds to the *theme of the special meal fellowship formed by Jesus breaking and distributing bread to his disciples.* When Jesus took, blessed, broke, and kept giving loaves to his disciples to set before the crowd (9:16), he united himself to his disciples in a meal fellowship that empowered them to feed the hungry people with an overabundance (9:17). By taking, giving thanks, breaking, and distributing to his disciples the bread he designated as his own body given in death for them (22:19), Jesus united himself to his disciples in a meal fellowship that made them recipients of the salvific benefits of his sacrificial death. Now by taking, blessing, breaking, and giving over bread to the two disciples at Emmaus (24:30), Jesus unites himself to his disciples in a meal fellowship in which they recognize his presence, divinely made known to them in the eucharistic breaking of the bread (24:35), as the risen Lord (24:31), the Prophet and Messiah who had to suffer death before entering into his glory (24:19, 26).

---

[43] Fitzmyer, *Luke X-XXIV*, 1569: "What is above all important is that the disciples report that they knew him 'in the breaking of the bread' (v. 35) and not by seeing him." On 24:33-35, see also L. M. Maloney, *"All That God Had Done with Them": The Narration of the Works of God in the Early Christian Community as Described in the Acts of the Apostles* (American University Studies VII/91; New York: Lang, 1991) 37-41.

2) The meal with the risen Jesus at Emmaus develops the *theme of meal hospitality offered to traveling missionaries*. When Jesus sent out the twelve apostles to proclaim the kingdom of God and heal, he instructed them not to take food, but to stay in whatever house that offers them hospitality (9:1-4). The seventy-two are to accept the meal hospitality they are offered by eating and drinking in whatever house accepts their greeting of peace (10:6-7). In whatever town they enter that welcomes them, they are to eat what is set before them (10:7-8). While Jesus was traveling on his fateful journey to Jerusalem, Martha and Mary offered him meal hospitality in their home (10:38-42). Approaching Jerusalem, the traveling Jesus invited himself to stay in the home of Zacchaeus, who joyfully welcomed him with the hospitality that implied a meal (19:1-10). After the unrecognized Jesus accepts his fellow travelers' offer of hospitality, he becomes the host of their meal by breaking and giving them the bread, so that they recognize his presence as the risen Lord (24:28-35).

3) The meal at Emmaus continues the *dual role of Jesus as both the guest and the host* of previous meal scenes. Invited by Levi as a guest of his great banquet, Jesus revealed himself as the bridegroom hosting the great messianic wedding feast (5:27-6:5). Invited by Simon the Pharisee to be the chief guest of his symposium banquet, Jesus relates to the sinful woman he forgives as host to uninvited guest (7:36-50). Welcomed by Martha as a guest for a meal, Jesus relates to Mary as the host who provides the best portion, the one necessary dish of the meal (10:38-42). Jesus invited himself to be the guest of Zacchaeus, but brought salvation to his house in anticipation of the eschatological banquet Jesus will host as a result of his death and resurrection (19:1-10). Now the Emmaus disciples invite the unrecognized risen Jesus to be their guest, but he becomes their host by breaking and giving them the bread that restores the meal fellowship he shared with them before his death, so they can recognize him as the risen Lord.

4) The Emmaus meal advances the *theme of Jesus bringing about the eschatological banquet of God's kingdom by his death and resurrection*. As the bridegroom (5:33-34) and the host of the overabundant meal which prefigures the final messianic meal (9:10-17), Jesus offered Mary the one necessary dish, the best portion of the meal (10:42), namely, his word about the necessity of his suffering, death, and resurrection in Jerusalem (9:22, 35, 44). By welcoming Jesus to his home, Zacchaeus anticipated the salvation of the eschatological meal Jesus is bringing about on his way to death and resurrection in Jerusalem (19:1-10). By giving his disciples the bread and wine designated as his body and blood at his last supper, Jesus united them to the sacrificial death (22:19-20) necessary for him to undergo before he celebrates with them the eschatological banquet in the kingdom of God (22:16-18, 29-

30). Now the risen Jesus finally convinces the Emmaus disciples of the divine necessity for him as the Messiah to suffer death before entering into his glory (24:26) in prophetic fulfillment of all the scriptures (24:27, 32). Only then do they recognize him as the risen Lord made known in his breaking the bread that restores meal fellowship with them after his death (24:30-31, 35). His sudden disappearance once they recognize him as the risen Lord (24:31) awakens the expectation of his permanent presence with them in the meal fellowship of the future banquet he promised to share with them in the kingdom of God (22:16-18, 29-30).

Pragmatics of the Meal Scene in Luke 24:28-35

1) The audience is invited to share along with the assembled community in Jerusalem their faith in the angelic revelation to the women at the tomb (24:4-7, 22-23) that *"the Lord has indeed been raised!"* (24:34), because he has appeared to Simon Peter (24:34), who also witnessed his empty tomb (24:12, 24), and was made known to the two Emmaus disciples in the breaking of the bread (24:31, 35).

2) Like Simon Peter, who "turned back" from the unfaithfulness of his triple denial of Jesus and strengthened his fellow disciples (22:32) with the message that Jesus has been raised from the dead, so the audience can *strengthen the faithfulness of themselves and others* by proclaiming their faith that the Jesus who was recognized and made known in his breaking of bread with the Emmaus disciples (24:28-33) has indeed been raised (24:34).

3) By accepting the hospitality of the Emmaus disciples (24:28-29), the risen Jesus models for the audience his own exhortations of how they are not to worry about what they are to eat and drink (12:22, 29), but to rely upon the hospitality of those to whom they proclaim the good news of the kingdom of God (9:1-6; 10:1-12). Like the risen Jesus they are *to offer those who welcome them the scriptural teaching that illuminates the divine necessity for Jesus' death and resurrection as well as the breaking of the bread that unites them in meal fellowship with the invisible presence of the risen Lord.*

4) Like the Emmaus disciples, whose hearts were burning within them when the risen Jesus opened the scriptures for them (24:32), the audience is *to deepen and share with others (24:35) their hope* that the mighty prophet Jesus (24:19) will indeed be the one to redeem God's people (24:21), precisely because of the prophetic and scriptural divine necessity that as the Messiah he had to suffer death before entering into his glory (24:26).

5) The Emmaus disciples' heart-felt experience of the risen Jesus in his scriptural teaching (24:32) and their recognition of him made known in the breaking of the bread (24:30-31, 35) presents the audience with a *paradigm for*

celebrating Jesus' last supper in remembrance of him (22:19). Whenever they celebrate the last supper in the eucharist, they will be united in meal fellowship with the risen Jesus by remembering the scriptural teaching that explains Jesus' prophetic predictions of the divine necessity of his death and resurrection, so that they can recognize and experience his invisible presence with them when they give to one another the bread and wine that have become his sacrificial body and blood.

6) Whenever the audience celebrates Jesus' last Passover supper in remembrance of him (22:19) by sharing the bread and wine he gave them as his body and blood, they are united in meal fellowship with the invisibly present risen Lord (24:30-35), the Jesus who empowers them to feed the hungry with an overabundance that anticipates the eschatological banquet (9:10-17). The audience's experience of the risen Lord in the breaking of the bread of the eucharist *reinforces their hope of being united with him in the meal fellowship of the final banquet* in the kingdom of God (22:16-18, 29-30).

CHAPTER 13

THE RISEN JESUS' MEAL IN JERUSALEM
LUKE 24:41-43

The appearance of the risen Lord to Simon Peter caused the disciples in Jerusalem to gather together as a community assembled around their faith that the Lord has indeed been raised (24:33-34). The recognition and making known of the risen Lord in the breaking of the bread with the two disciples going to Emmaus (24:28-32) brought them back to share their encounter with the gathered assembly in Jerusalem (24:35). When the risen Jesus then appears to the whole group of disciples in Jerusalem (24:36-40), he eats a piece of baked fish in their presence (24:41-43).

The Risen Jesus Appears to the Disciples in Jerusalem (24:36-40)

When the risen Jesus, who appeared to Simon Peter alone (24:34) and who was made known and recognized by the Emmaus pair in the breaking of the bread (24:31, 35), finally appears suddenly to the entire assembly of disciples in Jerusalem, he greets them with "Peace be with you!" (24:36). The risen Jesus himself thus begins to model for the audience his missionary instructions to the disciples. When Jesus sent out the seventy-two, he instructed them first to greet whatever house they entered with "Peace to this house!" (10:5). Then they are to accept the hospitality of whatever house or city welcomes them, eating whatever food they are offered before proclaiming to their hosts the arrival of the kingdom of God (10:7-9; cf. 9:1-4).[1]

In the epiphany genre there are often reactions of fear by the witnesses who cannot properly identify the epiphanic being.[2] Accordingly, the disciples became terrified and frightened (cf. 24:5), as they thought they saw a spirit (24:37) or ghost, that is, the ephemeral appearance of a dead person rather

---

[1] On this missionary "protocol for the household," Dillon (*From Eye-Witnesses*, 187) states that it "bids Jesus' emissary bestow the greeting of *peace* on the household he enters and make his dwelling therein, partaking of the *food* of the household" (emphasis Dillon). See also Johnson, *Luke*, 401. That this greeting of peace occurs for the audience only in 10:5 and 24:36 secures the connection, despite Nolland's (*Luke 18:35-24:53*, 1212) objection that it is a standard Jewish greeting.

[2] For a description of these elements of the epiphany genre, see J. P. Heil, *Jesus Walking on the Sea: Meaning and Gospel Functions of Matt 14:22-33, Mark 6:45-52 and John 6:15b-21* (AnBib 87; Rome: Biblical Institute, 1981) 11-12.

than the risen Jesus.[3] Reminding the audience of his rebuke of the Emmaus disciples for being slow of "heart" to believe (24:25; see also v 32), the epiphanic Jesus begins to reassure his startled disciples by asking why they are troubled and why doubts are arising in their "heart" (24:38). He then begins to dispel their disbelief by inviting them to see his hands and his feet, which identify him as "I myself."[4] They can touch him themselves and see that he is not a bodiless, shadowy spirit of a dead person, but has the flesh and bones of a living human being.[5] That he showed them his hands and feet (24:39-40), then, not only identifies him as the same Jesus they knew before his death, but also indicates that he is no longer in the realm of the dead but has been raised as a living person.

The Risen Jesus Eats before the Disciples in Jerusalem (24:41-43)

41 While they were still disbelieving for joy and wondering, he said to them, "Have you anything here to eat?" 42 They gave over to him a piece of baked fish. 43 Then taking it, he ate it before them.[6]

---

[3] Nolland, *Luke 18:35-24:53*, 1213: "Probably we need to go to the world of mediums and the consulting of the dead to understand the role of 'spirit' here (cf. 1 Sam 28:3-19; Isa 8:19; 19:3; 29:4). Though the dead were essentially tied to their graves, it was considered possible at times to call up the dead in the form of ghostly apparitions. One ought, however, not to think of these apparitions as being in any proper sense the person: it was more like some sort of residue of what had been the life of the person."

[4] As Johnson (*Luke*, 401) points out, for Luke, unlike John 20:20, 25, 27, "the hands and feet" of Jesus are not necessarily the marks of crucifixion but the evidence for his identity and living reality. See also Nolland, *Luke 18:35-24:53*, 1213.

[5] Johnson, *Luke*, 401: "The biblical idiom derives from 'bone of my bone and flesh of my flesh' in LXX Gen 2:23, so that 'flesh and bones' suggests not only being human, but the sharing of a common humanity..."

[6] On the meal scene in 24:41-43, in addition to the commentaries, see Dillon, *From Eye Witnesses*, 184-203; Osborne, *Resurrection Narratives*, 126-29; G. D. Kilpatrick, "Luke 24:42-43," *NovT* 28 (1986) 306-8; Tannehill, *Narrative Unity*, 1.291-93; G. O'Collins, "Did Jesus Eat the Fish (Luke 24:42-43)?" *Greg* 69 (1988) 65-76.

The risen Jesus asks his joyful but disbelieving disciples for something to eat (24:41)

Although their terror and fright (24:37) has been transformed into "joy," the disciples are still "disbelieving" like the Emmaus pair previously, who were slow of heart to believe (24:25) before their recognition of the risen Jesus in the breaking of the bread. And like Peter, who was "wondering" at the empty tomb (24:12) before the risen Lord appeared to him, they are still "wondering" whether it is really the risen Jesus (24:41).[7] Jesus' question, "Have you anything here to eat?" (24:41), initiates a focus on food that addresses both parts--the joy and the wondering disbelief--of the disciples' ambivalent response.

By asking his disciples for something to eat (24:41), the risen Jesus first of all continues to demonstrate that he is not the spirit or ghost of a dead person (24:37), but has been raised from the dead as a living person capable of eating (cf. 8:55). The risen Jesus' presentation of his hands and feet to his disciples indicated that he has flesh and bones, which therefore distinguish him from the bodiless spirit of a dead person (24:39-40). By now showing that he is capable of eating as a living person, the risen Jesus will further dispel the disciples' disbelief and wonderment whether he has really been raised from the dead.

The risen Jesus' request for something to eat (24:41) also responds to the disciples' "joy" at recognizing that what they thought was a spirit is actually the Jesus they knew, "I myself" (24:39). By asking *his disciples* to give him something to eat, the risen Jesus demonstrates for the audience that he is capable of resuming the meal fellowship he enjoyed with his disciples before his death. As the audience recalls, many of the meals involving Jesus and his disciples were celebrations of joy with repentant sinners whose ruptured relationships with God were being restored (5:27-32; 7:34, 36-50; 15:1-32; 19:1-10). Most noteworthy for the appropriateness of the risen Jesus to continue the "joy" of the disciples by sharing the meal fellowship that restores him to them as a living person after his death are the statements of the father in the parable of the two lost sons: "Let us eat and celebrate, for this

---

[7] On the ambivalent response of 24:41 as typical of the epiphany genre, see Heil, *Jesus Walking on the Sea*, 15. In an attempt to explain how "joy" can be the cause of "unbelief" Johnson (*Luke*, 402) suggests that "Luke is portraying a purely *emotional* response which is so powerful that they are too overwhelmed to really 'believe' it in the sense of committing themselves to its reality" (emphasis Johnson).

son of mine was dead but has come back to life" (15:23-24) and "it was necessary to celebrate and rejoice, for this brother of yours was dead but has come to life" (15:32).

By asking his disciples for something to eat (24:41) after his greeting of peace for them (24:36), the risen Jesus himself continues to model for the audience his missionary instructions. He had instructed the seventy-two to accept the meal hospitality they are offered by eating and drinking what the household has (10:7): "Eat what is set before you" (10:8). The risen Jesus is thus showing his willingness to eat what the disciples have, what they will set before him, giving them the opportunity to play their role as his receptive host.[8] After the Emmaus disciples invited him to stay with them as their guest, the risen Jesus restored table fellowship with them by performing as the host of the meal, breaking and distributing the bread to them (24:29-30). Now, by asking, "Have you anything here to eat?" (24:41), the risen Jesus gives his disciples the opportunity to be the host of the meal that restores him to table fellowship with the entire assembled community at Jerusalem.[9]

The risen Jesus' question whether the disciples have "anything to eat" ($\beta\rho\omega\sigma\iota\mu\rho\nu$) here (24:41) reminds the audience of the exchange between Jesus and his disciples in the earlier meal scene of their overabundant feeding of the crowds (9:10-17). After Jesus told his disciples to give the crowds something to eat, they objected: "We have no more than five loaves and two fish, unless we ourselves are to go and buy food ($\beta\rho\omega\mu\alpha\tau\alpha$) for all this people" (9:13).[10] Jesus then miraculously empowered them to feed the crowd with an overabundance from the meager food they had. The twelve baskets of fragments left over implied their ability to continue to offer meal hospitality to the people (9:16-17). That Jesus gave the disciples the multiplied loaves and fish "to set before" ($\pi\alpha\rho\alpha\theta\epsilon\hat{\iota}\nu\alpha\iota$) the crowd (9:16) indicated their ability to invite missionary guests to eat what is "set before" ($\pi\alpha\rho\alpha\tau\iota\theta\epsilon\mu\epsilon\nu\alpha$) them

---

[8] For the connection between the risen Jesus as "proto-missionary" and his instructions to the seventy-two, see Dillon, *From Eye-Witnesses*, 187-88, 228-40.

[9] As Nolland (*Luke 18:35-24:53*, 1214) points out: "There is a certain (inverse) correspondence between the request for food here and the offer of hospitality (including food) in v 29." See also Dillon, *From Eye-Witnesses*, 189.

[10] Nolland (*Luke 18:35-24:53*, 1214) notes the linguistic connection: "$\beta\rho\omega\sigma\iota\mu\rho\nu$ is cognate with the word used for 'food' at 9:13 ($\beta\rho\omega\mu\alpha\tau\alpha$)."

(10:8).[11] When the risen Jesus asks if they have anything to eat, anything to set before him, they cannot possibly refuse, for he has already empowered them to feed people overabundantly. He now gives the assembly of his disciples the opportunity to demonstrate the ability he gave them to feed others by setting whatever they have to eat before their missionary guest, the risen Jesus himself.

The disciples give the risen Jesus a piece of baked fish (24:42)

When Jesus assumed the role of host in meals he shared with his disciples, he empowered, authorized, and facilitated them in turn to perform as the hosts of the future meals they are to celebrate in remembrance of him. Jesus empowered his disciples to become hosts when he kept giving ($\dot{\epsilon}\delta\dot{\iota}\delta ou$) them the blessed and broken loaves and fish to set before the crowd (9:16). When Jesus gave ($\ddot{\epsilon}\delta\omega\kappa\epsilon\nu$) his disciples the broken bread he designated as his sacrificial body, he authorized them to become the future hosts of the celebration of his last Passover supper, instructing them to "keep doing this in remembrance of me" (22:19), to keep giving themselves and others the bread he gave them. Although the risen Jesus was invited to be the guest of the Emmaus meal (24:29), he took on the role of host, as he "was giving over" ($\dot{\epsilon}\pi\epsilon\delta\dot{\iota}\delta ou$) to them the broken bread (24:30). But his sudden disappearance (24:31) facilitated their return to the role of hosts especially in the future celebrations of the breaking of the bread of his last Passover supper in his memory. Now, for the climactic first time, the gathered assembly of disciples in Jerusalem perform as the host of the meal that restores their table fellowship with Jesus, as they "gave over" ($\dot{\epsilon}\pi\dot{\epsilon}\delta\omega\kappa\alpha\nu$) to the risen Jesus a piece of baked fish (24:42).[12]

That the disciples gave over to the risen Jesus a piece ($\mu\dot{\epsilon}\rho o\varsigma$) of "fish" (24:42) reminds the audience of the left over pieces or fragments ($\kappa\lambda\alpha\sigma\mu\dot{\alpha}\tau\omega\nu$,

---

[11] On the "setting before" of food as an expression of meal hospitality, see also Luke 11:6: "For a friend of mine has come to me from a journey and I do not have anything to set before ($\pi\alpha\rho\alpha\theta\dot{\eta}\sigma\omega$) him." Trummer ("$\pi\alpha\rho\alpha\tau\dot{\iota}\theta\eta\mu\iota$," 22) remarks: "The vb., which occurs 19 times in the NT, designates the serving of food as a sign of hospitality (Luke 10:8; 11:6; Acts 16:34; 1 Cor 10:27), which Jesus himself affirmed by providing food in abundance (Mark 6:41; 8:6 bis, 7; Luke 9:16)."

[12] Nolland (*Luke 18:35-24:53*, 1214) notes how the disciples' "giving over" of fish to Jesus recalls his "giving over" of fish and bread to them in his previous meals with them.

9:17) of broken bread and "fish" (9:13, 16) that Jesus kept giving his disciples to set before the crowd, empowering them to offer meal hospitality also to others, especially future missionary guests, represented here by the risen Jesus.[13] The piece of fish served by the disciples at Jerusalem complements the broken bread served by Jesus at Emmaus (24:30), so that together these two meals recall the miraculously overabundant feeding of the crowd with the broken pieces of bread and fish (9:16-17).[14] Whereas at his last Passover supper Jesus shared with his disciples the pieces of broken bread he designated as his body, thus uniting them with his sacrificial death for them (22:19), the disciples now share with Jesus a piece of (broken) fish that unites them in meal fellowship with the risen Lord. That the piece of fish was "baked" further underlines the meal fellowship, implying that the disciples are sharing with their guest a piece of the fish they have prepared for their own meal.[15]

The risen Jesus takes the fish and eats it before his disciples (24:43)

When Jesus was the host of meals with his disciples, he "took" ($\lambda\alpha\beta\grave{\omega}\nu$) the five loaves and the two fish before giving them to his disciples (9:16), so that all ate ($\check{\epsilon}\phi\alpha\gamma o\nu$) and were satisfied (9:17). And he "took" ($\lambda\alpha\beta\grave{\omega}\nu$) the bread of his last Passover supper and of the Emmaus meal (22:19; 24:30) before giving it to his disciples for them to eat. That he now "takes" ($\lambda\alpha\beta\grave{\omega}\nu$)

---

[13] On the recall of the feeding of the crowd with the loaves and "fishes," see O'Collins, "Did Jesus Eat the Fish," 70-71. As Nolland (*Luke 18:35-24:53*, 1214) points out, "$\mu\acute{\epsilon}\rho o\varsigma$ is found only here in the NT with the sense 'piece'; though the Greek word is quite different, in light of the other links, an echo of $\kappa\lambda\alpha\sigma\mu\acute{\alpha}\tau\omega\nu$, 'fragments/pieces,' in 9:17 may be intended."

[14] Johnson, *Luke*, 402. Nolland (*Luke 18:35-24:53*, 1214) states "that 'fish' here has its counterpart in the 'bread' of v 30, and so together they correspond to the bread and fish of 9:13, 16."

[15] Kilpatrick ("Luke 24:42-43," 306-8) suggests that the phrase $\kappa\alpha\grave{\iota}$ $\dot{\alpha}\pi\grave{o}$ $\mu\epsilon\lambda\iota\sigma\sigma\acute{\iota}ov$ $\kappa\eta\rho\acute{\iota}ov$ ("and from a honeycomb") after $\mu\acute{\epsilon}\rho o\varsigma$ in manuscripts of Luke 24:42 may have been original. He claims honeycomb was the food of immortality, suggesting a connection to the resurrection of Jesus. But according to Metzger (*Textual Commentary*, 187-88) these words "are an obvious interpolation, for it is not likely that they would have fallen out of so many of the best representatives of the earlier text-types. Since in parts of the ancient church honey was used in the celebration of the Eucharist and in the baptismal liturgy, copyists may have added the reference here in order to provide scriptural sanction for liturgical practice."

the piece of baked fish and eats (ἔφαγεν) it himself before the disciples (24:43) indicates to the audience that his transition from host to guest of the disciples has been completed.[16] By actually eating the piece of baked fish the disciples have set before him as their guest, the risen Jesus continues to represent itinerant missionaries, modeling for the audience his missionary instruction to "eat what is set before you" (10:8).

That the risen Jesus ate the piece of baked fish "before" or "in the presence of" (ἐνώπιόν) his disciples (24:43) completes the demonstration that he is a living person capable of eating rather than a bodiless "spirit" of the dead (24:37-40). But it also continues to restore him to meal fellowship with his disciples after his death.[17] The audience has heard those who declare to Jesus, "We ate before (ἐνώπιόν) you and drank, and you taught in our streets" (13:26; see also 2 Kgdms 11:13; 3 Kgdms 1:25), in which eating "before" Jesus expresses meal fellowship with him during his earthly life. Now this meal fellowship is climactically complemented on the part of the risen Jesus himself, who ate "before" his disciples.[18]

Although it was certainly implied that Jesus himself ate during the meals he shared with his disciples and others (cf. 5:30; 7:34, 36; 11:37; 14:1; 15:2; 19:5-7; 22:15), his own actual eating was never the primary focus and the audience never heard it explicitly narrated in the meal scenes. That the

----

[16] As Nolland (*Luke 18:35-24:53*, 1214) points out, "λαβών (lit. 'having taken') and ἔφαγεν, 'he ate,' are likely here to echo Luke 9:16-17." These echoes are *contra* Marshall (*Luke*, 903), who claims that in 24:43 Luke "has not developed allusions to the feeding of the multitude or the Last Supper."

[17] According to Tannehill (*Luke*, 360), "in eating the fish, Jesus is not only demonstrating his physical reality but also sharing food with his disciples."

[18] On the preposition ἐνώπιόν here Dillon (*From Eye-Witnesses*, 200-201) notes that it "is a septuagintal idiom for 'in the presence of,' or 'with,' especially in situations of meals taken by guests '*before*' their host...the parallel texts and the range of the preposition's idiomatic usage in Lk both urge the sense: 'he ate it *at their table*,' or '*in their company*,' '*as their guest*,' in Lk 24,43" (emphasis Dillon). Tannehill (*Narrative Unity*, 1.291) adds: "References to eating 'before (ἐνώπιον)' someone (24:43) occur elsewhere in contexts which clearly imply a meal shared with those 'before' whom one eats. This is the case in Luke 13:26, where the point of saying 'we ate and drank before you' is not that they rudely ate while Jesus simply watched but that they shared meals with Jesus." See also H. Krämer, "ἐνώπιον," *EDNT* 1.462.

risen Jesus now actually ate the piece of baked fish before his disciples (24:43), then, represents the climactic first time that his eating is explicitly expressed as the primary focus of a meal scene. The risen Jesus' eating as a guest of the entire assembly of disciples in Jerusalem complements the meal fellowship he shared with the Emmaus disciples as their host (24:30).

The actual eating of the risen Jesus with his disciples is particularly noteworthy for the audience, who heard him solemnly declare to his disciples at his last Passover supper before his death: "How eagerly I have desired to eat (φαγεῖν) this Passover meal with you before I suffer! For I say to you that I will never eat (φάγω) it again until it is fulfilled in the kingdom of God" (22:15-16). That Jesus actually ate (ἔφαγεν) with his disciples after his death, restoring meal fellowship with them both as their host (24:30) and as their guest (24:41-43), greatly bolsters the audience's hope of sharing meal fellowship with him at the final banquet in the future kingdom of God (14:15; 22:16-18, 29-30). The audience nourishes this hope whenever they celebrate Jesus' last Passover supper in remembrance of him, which unites them in meal fellowship with the risen Lord who ate with his disciples after giving them his sacrificial body and blood to eat and drink before his death (22:19-20).

The Risen Jesus Teaches the Disciples in Jerusalem (24:44-49)

Although the eating of the risen Jesus before his disciples has demonstrated that he is not a dead, bodiless spirit but the same living Jesus with whom they previously shared meal fellowship, there is still no indication to the audience that the disciples' disbelief and wonderment (24:41) have been resolved. It was not the meal alone but the combination of scriptural teaching and meal that brought the Emmaus disciples to recognize the risen Jesus (24:25-32, 35). Similarly, the risen Jesus now adds to his meal with the entire assembly of disciples in Jerusalem his words of scriptural instruction (24:44-49).[19]

Just as the eating of the risen Jesus before his disciples verified his identity--that these are "my hands and my feet" (24:39)--and recalled his previous sharing of meal fellowship with them before his death, so now Jesus begins his teaching with the reminder: "These are my words which I spoke to

---

[19] On 24:44-49, in addition to the commentaries, see Dillon, *From Eye-Witnesses*, 203-20; Osborne, *Resurrection Narratives*, 129-36; Tannehill, *Narrative Unity*, 1.293-98; T. S. Moore, "The Lucan Great Commission and the Isaianic Servant," *BSac* 154 (1997) 47-60.

you while I was still with you" (24:44).[20] The risen Jesus explained the meaning of his previously non-understood passion predictions to the Emmaus disciples (24:25-27) by opening the scriptures for them (24:32). So now to the Jerusalem assembly of disciples he explains the divine necessity of his death and resurrection as the Christ in prophetic fulfillment of all that was written about him in the Law of Moses, in the Prophets, and in the Psalms (24:44-46) by opening their mind to understand the scriptures (24:45).[21]

But now the risen Jesus extends this scriptural fulfillment to include the necessity that "repentance for the forgiveness of sins be preached in his name to all the nations, beginning from Jerusalem" (24:47).[22] He then appoints the assembly of disciples gathered together in Jerusalem to carry out this preaching mission: "You are witnesses (μάρτυρες) of these things" (24:48).[23] They will be equipped for this universal mission by the divine assistance Jesus promises will come upon them as they stay in Jerusalem (24:49).

The audience realizes that it was especially the various meals of Jesus that have helped to prepare the disciples (and the audience) to be the witnesses

---

[20] Dillon (*From Eye-Witnesses*, 204) remarks that "the words are no less a 'demonstrative sign' of his identity, still unrecognized, than the physical traits were."

[21] Fitzmyer, *Luke X-XXIV*, 1582: "It is not so much the words themselves that Christ recalls for them as their meaning, which the following statements (vv. 44b,45,46) make clear." See also Johnson, *Luke*, 402.

[22] With Dillon (*From Eye-Witnesses*, 214), *contra* Johnson (*Luke*, 400, 403) and Tannehill (*Luke*, 361), we take the phrase "beginning from Jerusalem" with v 47 rather than with v 48. As Dillon explains: "No less than the death and resurrection of Christ and the universal preaching in his name, the mission's starting point at Jerusalem is understood by Lk to be part of the provisions of OT prophecy."

[23] J. Beutler, "μάρτυς," *EDNT* 2.394: "Luke develops a usage according to which the apostles are 'witnesses' not only to the outward events of Jesus' life, death, and resurrection, but also to their salvific meaning according to Scripture....Μάρτυς...expresses not only the element of valuation but also that of personal engagement." Dillon, *From Eye-Witnesses*, 217: "Rescued from the dullness of their human senses by the divine word, and experiencing thus the *gift* of Easter faith, the 'eye-witnesses' *became* 'ministers of the word' (Lk 1,2). Luke's Easter story is, in fact, the story of that 'becoming'" (emphasis Dillon). See also Spicq, *Theological Lexicon*, 2.447-52; M. Coleridge, "'You Are Witnesses' (Luke 24:48): Who Sees What in Luke," *AusBR* 45 (1997) 1-19.

who preach *repentance* for the forgiveness of sins (24:47). Indeed, Jesus demonstrated his own preaching of repentance in and through his meals. When the disciples were with Jesus at Levi's banquet, they heard him proclaim why he and his disciples share meal fellowship with repentant tax collectors and sinners: "I have not come to invite the righteous but sinners to *repentance!*" (5:32). By this meal Jesus not only celebrated the repentance of sinners but implicitly called the Pharisees and scribes (5:30) to likewise repent.[24]

Jesus' first meal with a Pharisee (7:36-50) prepared the audience for their mission of preaching repentance "for the forgiveness of sins" (24:47) by demonstrating that forgiveness is one of the salvific benefits of meal fellowship with Jesus. To Simon, the host of the meal, Jesus explained that the many sins of the sinful woman, whose hospitable gestures toward Jesus indicated her repentance, "have been forgiven, for she has loved greatly" (7:47). He then called the Pharisee to a repentance that recognizes his own need for greater love and forgiveness: "The one to whom little is forgiven, loves little" (7:47). After Jesus declared to the sinful woman, "Your sins are forgiven" (7:48), the fellow guests of the meal began to question among themselves, "Who is this man who even forgives sins?" (7:49).[25] This and Jesus' other meals with (11:37-54; 14:1-24) and about (15:1-32; 16:19-31) the scribes and Pharisees have shown the audience that they can proclaim repentance for the forgiveness of sins in and through the sharing of meals.

Jesus' meal with the chief tax collector and rich man Zacchaeus (19:1-10) indicated to the audience how the mere invitation to the hospitality that includes meal fellowship can bring about repentance for the forgiveness of sins (24:47). After Jesus invited himself to lodge and thus share meal fellowship in Zacchaeus's house, Zacchaeus welcomed him joyfully (19:5-6) and promptly pronounced his repentance (19:8). Jesus then announced the arrival in his house of the salvation that implies his forgiveness (19:9). Like Jesus who "has come to seek and to save what was lost" (19:10) by sharing a meal with Zacchaeus, the audience can invite others to repentance for the forgiveness of sins by sharing meal fellowship with them.[26]

When Jesus gave the cup of wine to his disciples at his last Passover supper with them, he declared, "This cup is the new covenant in my blood which is being poured out for you" (22:20). The new covenant established by the pouring out of the sacrificial blood of Jesus indicates the fulfillment of God's promise for the eschatological forgiveness of sins (LXX Jer 38:31-34).

---

[24] On the meal scene in 5:27-32, see chapter 2.

[25] On the meal scene in 7:36-50, see chapter 3.

[26] On the meal scene in 19:1-10, see chapter 10.

Whenever the disciples celebrate Jesus' last supper in remembrance of him (22:19), they are beneficiaries of his sacrificial death, which establishes the new covenant that definitively unites God to his people through his forgiveness of their sins.[27]

It was during his last Passover supper that Jesus indicated Simon Peter's need for repentance. He instructed him to strengthen his fellow disciples, "once you have turned back (ἐπιστρέψας)" (22:32), that is, converted or repented of his triple denial of Jesus (22:34).[28] The appearance of the risen Lord to Simon (24:34) began to strengthen his fellow disciples, as it "gathered together the eleven and those with them" (24:33) in Jerusalem. The risen Jesus then restored meal fellowship with the entire assembly of disciples (24:41-43), after it was interrupted by the "sifting" of the now strengthened disciples and the triple denial of the now repentant and forgiven Peter (22:31-34). For the audience, then, it is most appropriate that the risen Jesus commissions the disciples in the context of his restored meal fellowship with them to preach repentance for the forgiveness of sins (24:47). It was in and through meals, after all, that Jesus himself brought about and celebrated repentance for the forgiveness of sins.

After Jesus Ascends to Heaven the Disciples Return to Jerusalem with Joy (24:50-53)

After the risen Jesus led the disciples as far as Bethany, and while he was blessing them, he departed from them and was taken up into heaven (24:50-51).[29] That the risen Jesus, who suddenly stood (ἔστη) in their midst before his meal with them (24:36), now departed (διέστη) from them (24:51) after the meal (24:41-43) reminds the audience how he suddenly disappeared from the Emmaus disciples as soon as they recognized him in the breaking of

---

[27] On Jesus' last Passover supper, see chapter 11.

[28] S. Légasse, "ἐπιστρέφω," *EDNT* 2.40: "'Ἐπιστρέφω in a 'moral' sense designates primarily the fulfillment of religious 'conversion'...the vocabulary of conversion is often represented by μετανοέω and μετάνοια, although in Lukan material ἐπιστρέφω predominates over μετανοέω.

[29] On 24:50-53, in addition to the commentaries, see Dillon, *From Eye-Witnesses*, 220-25; Osborne, *Resurrection Narratives*, 136-44; Tannehill, *Narrative Unity*, 1.298-301; M. C. Parsons, *The Departure of Jesus in Luke-Acts: The Ascension Narratives in Context* (JSNTSup 21; Sheffield: JSOT, 1987); A. W. Zwiep, "The Text of the Ascension Narratives (Luke 24.50-3; Acts 1.1-2, 9-11)," *NTS* 42 (1996) 219-44; idem, *Ascension*, 86-94.

the bread (24:31).[30] But that he was now taken up into heaven means that whenever the audience celebrates the breaking of the bread of Jesus' last Passover supper in remembrance of him (22:19), they are united in meal fellowship with the invisibly present risen Lord now ascended to a position of heavenly exaltation.

The dramatic suspense aroused for the audience by the disciples, who "were still disbelieving *for joy* and wondering" (24:41) before the meal, is now finally resolved. They worshiped him and returned to Jerusalem *with great joy*, and were continually in the temple praising God (24:52-53).[31] As the two Emmaus disciples "returned to Jerusalem" (24:33) so the entire group of disciples "returned to Jerusalem" (24:52) in obedience to Jesus' instruction to stay in the city until they are clothed with power from on high (24:49). Their meal with the risen Jesus propelled the two traveling disciples to *return to Jerusalem* (24:28-35) where they shared in the meal of the risen Jesus with the entire assembly of disciples (24:41-43), who were gathered in and have now *returned to Jerusalem*. This climactic meal scene, in which the risen Jesus renewed meal fellowship with the entire community of disciples *in Jerusalem*, has qualified and prepared the disciples and the audience to be witnesses (24:48) for the mission of preaching repentance for the forgiveness of sins to all nations, *beginning from Jerusalem* (24:47).[32]

---

[30] On Jesus' sudden departure in 24:51, Zwiep (*Ascension*, 92) notes: "Διέστη ἀπ᾽ αὐτῶν is to be understood on the analogy of the earlier withdrawal and appearance (v.31 καί αὐτὸς ἄφαντος ἐγένετο ἀπ᾽ αὐτῶν; cf. v.36 αὐτὸς ἔστη ἐν μέσῳ αὐτῶν): Jesus departed from them suddenly vanishing from the scene."

[31] Dillon, *From Eye-Witnesses*, 224: "When we hear of their *great joy* at this point, we can hardly fail to recall the *disbelief from joy* which still afflicted them as they observed the risen One take food at their table. The veil of mystery which prevented their recognition of the Visitor has been drawn aside--progressively, indeed--through the totality of his gestures, his revealing word, his bequest, and his final blessing. Recognition thus came about in much the same delayed and tantalizing fashion as held the reader's rapt attention during the Emmaus story" (emphasis Dillon).

[32] For the significance of "beginning from Jerusalem" here, see Dillon, *From Eye-Witnesses*, 214-15.

Relation of Luke 24:41-43 to Previous Meal Scenes

1) The Jerusalem meal of the risen Jesus adds to the *theme of Jesus' meals as celebrations of joy*. Many of the meals of Jesus were joyful celebrations with repentant sinners whose relationships with God were being restored (5:27-32; 7:34, 36-50; 15:1-32; 19:1-10). The statements of the father in the parable of the two lost sons indicate how a meal appropriately celebrates the joy of being restored to one who was thought to be dead: "Let us eat and celebrate, for this son of mine was dead but has come back to life" (15:23-24) and "it was necessary to celebrate and rejoice, for this brother of yours was dead but has come to life" (15:32). Now, the risen Jesus invites his disciples to celebrate the "joy" (24:41; cf. 24:52) of recognizing as a living person him whom they thought was a dead spirit (24:37-40) with a meal that restores them to the meal fellowship he shared with them before his death (24:41-43).

2) The risen Jesus' Jerusalem meal advances the *theme of his empowerment of the disciples to be the hosts of his special meals*. When Jesus kept giving broken loaves and broken pieces of fish to his disciples to set before the crowd (9:16), he united himself to his disciples in a special meal fellowship that empowered them to be the hosts who feed the hungry people with an overabundance of broken pieces, which enabled them to feed still others (9:17). Jesus now gives his disciples the opportunity to demonstrate their empowerment as hosts who can feed the hungry by feeding him with a piece of baked fish, uniting them in a special meal fellowship with the risen Lord (24:41-43).

That the risen Jesus now actually "ate" the piece of baked fish "before" his disciples (24:43) represents the climactic first time that his eating is explicitly expressed as the primary focus of a meal scene. Others declared to Jesus, "We ate before you and drank, and you taught in our streets" (13:26), in which "eating before" Jesus expresses meal fellowship with him. Now, this meal fellowship is climactically complemented on the part of the risen Jesus himself, who "ate before" the entire assembly of disciples in Jerusalem as their guest.

Jesus empowered his disciples to become the future hosts of the celebration of his last Passover supper, instructing them to "keep doing this in remembrance of me" (22:19), to keep giving themselves and others the bread and wine he gave them as his sacrificial body and blood. Although the risen Jesus was invited to be the guest of the Emmaus meal (24:29), he took on the role of host (24:30). But his sudden disappearance (24:31) facilitated their return to the role of hosts, especially in the future celebrations of his last Passover supper in his memory. Now, the entire gathered assembly of disciples in Jerusalem anticipate their role as hosts of future celebrations of the Lord's last supper by performing, for the climactic first time, as the hosts of the meal that restores them to meal fellowship with the risen Jesus (24:41-43).

3) The meal with the risen Jesus at Jerusalem develops the *theme of meal hospitality offered to traveling missionaries*. Jesus instructed the twelve apostles not to take food for their missionary journey, but to stay in whatever house that offers them hospitality (9:1-4). The seventy-two are to accept the meal hospitality they are offered by eating and drinking in whatever house accepts their greeting of peace (10:6-7). In whatever town they enter that welcomes them, they are to eat what is set before them (10:7-8). Jesus himself modeled these instructions when he accepted meal hospitality at the beginning of his journey to Jerusalem from Martha and Mary (10:38-42) and at its conclusion from Zacchaeus (19:1-10). Now, the risen Jesus, who greeted his disciples with "Peace be with you!" (24:36; cf. 10:5), models his missionary instructions by accepting meal hospitality from his disciples, eating the piece of baked fish they set before him (24:41-43).

That Jesus gave the disciples the multiplied broken loaves and broken pieces of fish "to set before" the crowd (9:16) indicated their ability to invite missionary guests to eat what is "set before" them (10:8). The piece of fish the disciples set before Jesus at Jerusalem (24:42) complements the broken bread served by Jesus at Emmaus (24:30), so that together these two meals recall the miraculously overabundant feeding of the crowd with the broken pieces of bread and fish (9:16-17). Now, when the risen Jesus asks if they have anything to eat, anything to set before him, he gives the assembly of his disciples the opportunity to demonstrate the ability he gave them to offer meal hospitality to others by setting before their missionary guest, the risen Jesus himself, a piece of baked fish (24:41-43).

4) The risen Jesus' eating of a meal with his disciples reinforces the *theme of his meals as anticipations of the eschatological banquet*. At his last Passover supper before his death Jesus solemnly declared to his disciples: "How eagerly I have desired to eat this Passover meal with you before I suffer! For I say to you that I will never eat it again until it is fulfilled in the kingdom of God" (22:15-16). That Jesus now actually "ate" with his disciples after his death, restoring meal fellowship with them both as their host (24:30) and as their guest (24:41-43), bolsters his promise of sharing meal fellowship with his disciples at the eschatological banquet in the kingdom of God (14:15; 22:16-18, 29-30).

5) The previous meal scenes in which Jesus celebrated the forgiveness of sinners and called others to repent (5:27-32; 7:36-50; 11:37-54; 14:1-24; 15:1-32; 16:19-31; 19:1-10; 22:7-38) have prepared the disciples for their *mission of preaching repentance for the forgiveness of sins to all nations*

beginning from Jerusalem (24:47), where the entire assembly of disciples received this mission at a meal with the risen Jesus (24:41-43).

Pragmatics of the Meal Scene in Luke 24:41-43

1) The risen Jesus, who greeted the disciples at Jerusalem with "peace" (24:36), brought them "joy" (24:41), and accepted their meal hospitality (24:42-43), models how the audience is *to depend upon the meal hospitality of those to whom they bring peace and joy* by proclaiming to them the good news of the kingdom of God (9:1-6; 10:1-12).

2) The assembly of disciples at Jerusalem, who extended meal hospitality to the risen Jesus by offering him a piece of baked fish (24:41-43), model how the audience is *to extend meal hospitality to others*, especially traveling missionaries, who represent Jesus himself (10:16).

3) That the risen Jesus for the climactic first time actually "ate before" the assembly of disciples at Jerusalem as their *guest* (24:43), enabling them for the climactic first time to perform as hosts, and then again departed from them (24:51), complemented how he was the *host* of the Emmaus meal before suddenly disappearing (24:30-31). This empowers the audience *to be the hosts and guests of the future celebrations of Jesus' last Passover supper*, to "keep doing this in remembrance of me" (22:19). As hosts and guests of the eucharist in which they share with one another the bread and wine Jesus gave them as his sacrificial body and blood (22:19-20), they unite themselves in meal fellowship with their invisibly present host and guest, the risen and heavenly exalted Lord.

4) That the assembly of disciples in Jerusalem gave the risen Jesus a *piece* of baked *fish* (24:43) reminds the audience how Jesus empowered his disciples to feed others from the overabundance of pieces of broken bread and fish that he gave them to give to the hungry people (9:16-17). The piece of fish at the Jerusalem meal complemented the broken bread at the Emmaus meal (24:30, 35) to recall both the miraculous feeding (9:10-17) and the last supper (22:19-20). Whenever the audience celebrates the eucharist, then, they are united in meal fellowship with the risen and exalted Lord who empowers them *to feed others from the overabundance with which he feeds them* in the bread and wine of his sacrificial body and blood.

5) That Jesus actually *ate before* his disciples after his death, restoring meal fellowship with them both as their host (24:30) and as their guest (24:41-43), reinforces the audience's *hope of sharing meal fellowship with him in the future kingdom of God* (14:15; 22:16-18, 29-30). The audience nourishes this hope whenever they celebrate the eucharist, which unites them in meal fellowship with the risen and exalted Lord who ate again with his disciples

after giving them his sacrificial body and blood to eat and drink in anticipation of the eschatological banquet in the kingdom of God.

6) As the climax of his previous meals, in which Jesus celebrated the forgiveness of sinners and called others to repent (5:27-32; 7:36-50; 11:37-54; 14:1-24; 15:1-32; 16:19-31; 19:1-10; 22:7-38), the meal of the risen Jesus with the entire assembly of his disciples gathered together in Jerusalem (24:41-43), where they are to await being clothed with power from on high (24:49), *qualifies and prepares the audience to be witnesses* (24:48) for the mission of proclaiming repentance for the forgiveness of sins to all nations beginning from Jerusalem (24:47).

CHAPTER 14

COMMUNAL MEALS OF NEW BELIEVERS IN JERUSALEM
ACTS 2:42-47

In the prologue of Luke's second volume, the Acts of the Apostles, the audience hears a recapitulation of the meal the risen Jesus shared with his disciples gathered together in Jerusalem (Acts 1:4; cf. Luke 24:41-43).[1] In the section of Acts focusing upon Jerusalem (2:1-8:3) the audience encounters the next meal scene in the summary account of the communal meals shared by the believers in Jerusalem (2:42-47). Later in this same Jerusalem section the audience hears of the Twelve's concern about the service at table that includes the distribution of food to widows (6:1-3).

Recapitulation of the Risen Jesus' Meal with the Disciples in Jerusalem (1:4)

The prologue (1:1-26), which serves as a transition between the Gospel of Luke and the Acts of the Apostles, recapitulates and further elaborates for the audience how Jesus, after suffering death, presented himself alive to the apostles by many proofs, appearing to them during forty days and speaking about the kingdom of God (1:3).[2] While the risen Jesus was eating with them, he commanded them not to leave Jerusalem but to wait for the promise of the Father, baptism with the holy Spirit (1:4-5). That the risen Jesus was sharing table fellowship or literally "eating salt with" ($\sigma\upsilon\nu\alpha\lambda\iota\zeta\acute{o}\mu\varepsilon\nu o\varsigma$) them (1:4) refers the audience again to his taking the piece of baked (and salted?) fish the disciples gave over to him and eating it in their presence (Luke 24:42-43). This final meal of the risen Jesus with the entire assembly of disciples in Jerusalem not only served as proof that he was alive (1:3), but also provided the appropriate meal setting for issuing the promise that the Father would clothe them with power from on high to equip them for their mission of being his witnesses. Since it was especially at his meals with them that the apostles witnessed Jesus' mission of proclaiming repentance for the forgiveness of sins, it was most fitting that at his final meal with them the risen Jesus bestowed

---

[1] For a discussion of the structural outline of the Acts of the Apostles that we are following, see O'Fearghail, *Introduction to Luke-Acts*, 67-84.

[2] On the preface to Acts, see L. Alexander, "The Preface to Acts and the Historians," *History, Literature, and Society in the Book of Acts* (ed. B. Witherington; Cambridge: Cambrdige University Press, 1996) 73-103.

upon them the mission of continuing and expanding this proclamation to all peoples (Luke 24:47-49).[3]

The Communal Meals of the Jerusalem Believers (2:42-47)

42 They were devoting themselves to the teaching of the apostles and to the fellowship, to the breaking of the bread and to the prayers. 43 Awe came upon every person, and many wonders and signs were being done through the apostles. 44 All who believed were together and had all things in common. 45 They were selling their property and possessions, and were distributing them to all, as any had need. 46 Daily, devoting themselves to meeting together in the temple, and breaking bread in their houses, they were sharing food with gladness and generosity of heart, 47 praising God and having favor before all

---

[3] Although the meaning of συναλιζόμενος has been disputed and textual variants proposed, there seems to be a consensus among recent interpreters that it means literally "eating salt with" and refers to table fellowship. After pointing to the possibility that it means "spending the night with" or "staying with," Zwiep (*Ascension*, 100-101) states that "a more plausible meaning of the verb is 'eating salt together with' (from συν- and ἁλίζω), hence: 'eating together' (*convescens*)...As in Lk 24:43, the mealtime scenario may serve to underline the reality of the (physical) resurrection of Jesus (cf. also IgnSm 3:3), although a more dominant concern seems be (sic) to stress the apostles' intimate fellowship with the risen Lord in view of their future mission." D. L. McConaughy ("An Old Syriac Reading of Acts 1:4 and More Light on Jesus' Last Meal before His Ascension," *Oriens Christianus* 72 [1988] 63-67) notes that from the second to the seventh centuries the Syrians understood συναλιζόμενος here to mean "salted together with" or "eat" and suggests that the reference to salt (see Num 18:19; 2 Chr 13:5; Ezra 4:14) indicates that the risen Jesus' final meal with the apostles was one of great solemnity. See also BAGD, 783-84; Green, *Luke*, 760 n. 55; *EDNT* 3.297: "in ancient custom salt and table fellowship were associated"; R. Pesch, *Die Apostelgeschichte (Apg 1-12)* (EKK V/1; Zürich: Benziger, 1986) 65-66; J. B. Polhill, *Acts* (NAC 26; Nashville: Broadman, 1992) 82; L. T. Johnson, *The Acts of the Apostles* (SacPag 5; Collegeville: Liturgical Press, 1992) 25; C. K. Barrett, *The Acts of the Apostles: Volume I: Preliminary Introduction and Commentary on Acts I-XIV* (ICC; Edinburgh: Clark, 1994) 71-72.

the people. And daily the Lord was adding those who were being saved to the community.[4]

They were devoting themselves to the breaking of the bread (2:42)

Those who were baptized and received the gift of the holy Spirit after repenting at the preaching of Peter (2:37-38, 41) were devoting themselves not only to the teaching of the apostles, the fellowship, and the prayers, but also to "the breaking of the bread" (2:42). The audience's previous encounters with Jesus' distinctive breaking of bread at meals with his disciples indicates that more is meant here than just an ordinary meal or the rite of blessing before a meal.[5] The reference to the communal meals of the Jerusalem believers as "the breaking of the bread" means that they are continuing the special meal fellowship Jesus modeled for them by his own breaking of the bread.

Jesus' deliberate gesture of "the breaking of the bread" was a noteworthy and memorable feature of his meals with the disciples. Jesus "broke into pieces" ($\kappa\alpha\tau\acute{\epsilon}\kappa\lambda\alpha\sigma\epsilon\nu$) the bread and fish that he gave to his disciples, empowering them to share the food he broke for them in meal

---

[4] On 2:42-47, in addition to the commentaries, see P. H. Menoud, "The Acts of the Apostles and the Eucharist," *Jesus Christ and the Faith* (PTMS 18; Pittsburgh: Pickwick, 1978) 86-89; T. D. Andersen, "The Meaning of EXONTES CHARIN PROS in Acts 2.47," *NTS* 34 (1988) 604-10; F. Montagnini, "La communità primitiva come luogo cultuale: Nota da *At* 2,42-46," *RivB* 35 (1988) 477-84; Tannehill, *Narrative Unity*, 2.43-47; M. A. Co, "The Major Summaries in Acts: Acts 2,42-47; 4,32-35; 5,12-16: Linguistic and Literary Relationship," *ETL* 68 (1992) 49-85; A. C. Mitchell, "The Social Function of Friendship in Acts 2:44-47 and 4:32-37," *JBL* 111 (1992) 255-72; G. E. Sterling, "'Athletes of Virtue': An Analysis of the Summaries in Acts (2:41-47; 4:32-35; 5:12-16)," *JBL* 113 (1994) 679-96; J. Rius-Camps, "Las variantes de la Recensión Occidental de los Hechos de los Apóstoles (VI) (Hch 2,41-47)," *Filologia Neotestamentaria* 8 (1995) 199-208.

[5] Wanke, "$\kappa\lambda\acute{\alpha}\omega$," 295-96: "'Breaking of bread' refers to a firmly fixed rite at the opening of the Jewish meal...The phrase...was used only of the beginning of the meal, not of the entire meal." E. Haenchen, *The Acts of the Apostles: A Commentary* (Philadelphia: Westminster, 1971) 191: "the $\kappa\lambda\acute{\alpha}\sigma\iota\varsigma$ $\tauο\hat{υ}$ $\acute{\alpha}\rho\tauου$ is the name for the Christians' communal meal...Considering the simplicity of the ritual meal, consisting essentially of bread (and wine), it is not hard to imagine that its opening action might come to stand for the whole."

fellowship with the hungry crowd (Luke 9:16). So abundant was the food Jesus broke that twelve baskets of "broken pieces" (κλασμάτων) were taken up (9:17). At his last supper Jesus "broke" (ἔκλασεν) the bread he gave to his disciples as "my body which is being given for you" (Luke 22:19), enabling them to share in the salvific benefits of his sacrificial death. He then instructed them to "keep doing this in remembrance of me" (Luke 22:19), that is, to keep breaking the bread that is his body and sharing it with one another as a memorial of his sacrificial death. When the risen Jesus "broke" (κλάσας) the bread and gave it to the Emmaus disciples, they immediately recognized him (Luke 24:30). They recounted to the disciples in Jerusalem how he was made known to them in "the breaking of the bread" (τῇ κλάσει τοῦ ἄρτου, 24:35). The devotion of the Jerusalem believers to "the breaking of the bread" (τῇ κλάσει τοῦ ἄρτου, 2:42), then, indicates to the audience that their communal meal fellowship included the eucharistic breaking of the bread that Jesus instructed them to do in remembrance of him as a way of uniting them to his death and resurrection.[6]

They were sharing food with gladness and generosity of heart (2:43-47)

The fellowship (κοινωνία, 2:42) of the Jerusalem believers who were together and had all things in common (κοινά, 2:44) was a publicly and privately manifested communal unity. The daily devotion of the believers to meeting together publicly "in the temple" was paralleled and complemented by their breaking (κλῶντές) of bread (ἄρτον) privately "in their houses" or "in the house" (2:46), further specifying their general devotion to "the breaking of the bread" (2:42).[7] Not only were they continually breaking bread in their

---

[6] H. Conzelmann, *Acts of the Apostles* (Hermeneia; Philadelphia: Fortress, 1987) 23: "When Luke speaks of the breaking of bread he does not mean only the rite at the beginning of the meal, but rather the meal itself...Luke is thinking of the ordinary daily meal here, but he does not make a distinction between it and the Eucharist. The unity of the two is part of the ideal picture of the earliest church." See also Johnson, *Acts*, 58; Barrett, *Acts*, 164-65; J. Kodell, *The Eucharist in the New Testament* (Collegeville: Liturgical Press, 1988) 111-12; E. LaVerdiere, *The Eucharist in the New Testament and the Early Church* (Collegeville: Liturgical Press, 1996) 104.

[7] According to Matson (*Household Conversion*, 131 n. 192): "Translating κατ' οἶκον in its non-distributive sense at Acts 2.46 ('in the house'), a usage found elsewhere in the New Testament (1 Cor. 16.19; Col. 4.15; Phlm 2), heightens the rhetorical contrast between house and temple as respective spheres of religious activity."

houses, following the model and instructions of Jesus to keep celebrating his eucharistic last supper in remembrance of him (Luke 22:19), but they were also practicing an ideal communal table fellowship, "sharing food with gladness and generosity of heart" (2:46).

That they were "sharing food" expands the description of their communal fellowship and how they "had all things in common" (2:44). Not only were they sharing their property and possessions with one another, "as any had need" (2:45), but they were even sharing their food with one another. Their sharing of food that accompanies their breaking of the bread models for the audience what Jesus taught and empowered his disciples to do when he broke the bread and fish and gave them to the disciples to share with the hungry crowd, so that "all"--the crowd and the disciples--ate and were satisfied (Luke 9:16-17). Jesus taught his disciples to pray that God keep giving them "*daily*" their necessary bread (Luke 11:3). Now, the Jerusalem community of believers is "*daily*" (2:46) sharing the food God gives them with one another, unlike the rich man who, as the audience recalls, "*daily*" feasted sumptuously without sharing his food with the hungry Lazarus (Luke 16:19-21).

That the believers were sharing food "with gladness" (2:46) expresses the joyful celebration of their repentance for the forgiveness of their sins (2:38). As the audience recalls, Jesus illustrated the appropriateness of celebrating the joy of repentance with festive meals in his parables about the finding of lost sinners (Luke 15:6-7, 9-10, 23-24, 32).[8] The repentant sinner Zacchaeus joyfully welcomed Jesus to meal hospitality in his house (19:5-6). The audience heard how the unborn John the Baptist leapt "with gladness" (Luke 1:44) when his mother heard Mary's greeting heralding the salvation coming with the birth of Jesus. Now the community of believers is sharing food "with gladness" because of their reception of the gift of the holy Spirit (2:38) from the risen and exalted Jesus (2:33).[9] The "gladness" of their meals echoes in the ears of the audience the "gladness" (2:26; LXX Ps 15:9) with which David rejoiced in anticipation of Jesus' resurrection (2:30-31), as

---

[8] Although these parables employ the term "joy" (χαρά) rather than "gladness" (ἀγαλλιάσις), these terms are closely associated. See, for example, Luke 1:14 and A. Weiser, "ἀγαλλιάω," *EDNT* 1.7-8.

[9] Johnson, *Acts*, 59: "The term 'gladness' (ἀγαλλίασις) is one that suggests eschatological joy in the presence of the Lord (see Luke 1:14, 44, 47; 10:21)."

quoted by Peter in the speech that aroused the repentance of these Jerusalem believers (2:38).[10]

When those in Jerusalem heard Peter's speech to the effect that God made the Jesus they crucified Lord and Messiah (2:36), they were cut "to the heart" (2:37). But now that they have repented and been baptized for the forgiveness of their sins (2:38), they were sharing food with gladness and "generosity of heart" (2:46). Their gladness and generosity of heart, which occurs in the context of their praising of God (2:47), further reminds the audience how they are imitating the "jubilant heart" (2:26; LXX Ps 15:9) of David who rejoiced in anticipation at God's salvation in Jesus.[11]

The "generosity," "sincerity," or "simplicity" (ἀφελότητι) of heart (2:46) with which the Jerusalem believers shared their food corresponds to the generosity of their fellowship.[12] They were together and had all things in common, selling their property and possessions, and generously distributing them to all, as any had need (2:44-45). Their sharing of food with gladness and sincerity or simplicity of heart stands in sharp contrast to the quarrel that arose among the disciples at Jesus' last supper about which one of them seemed to be greatest, rather than being concerned with serving one another (Luke 22:24-27). It presents the audience with an ideal of meal fellowship that accords with Jesus' teaching against the kind of meal fellowship that serves oneself by promoting individualistic honors and social reciprocity (Luke 14:7-

---

[10] For an analysis and interpretation of the quotation of Psalm 15 in Peter's speech here, see M. L. Soards, *The Speeches in Acts: Their Content, Context, and Concerns* (Louisville: Knox, 1994) 35; G. J. Steyn, *Septuagint Quotations in the Context of the Petrine and Pauline Speeches of the Acta Apostolorum* (CBET 12; Kampen: Pharos, 1995) 100-113.

[11] As Pedersen ("εὐφραίνω," 87) notes: "In Acts 2:26 the vb. expresses a jubilant, joyous confession that God's redeeming presence is connected with Jesus *sui generis*. This was the case not only in his earthly activity (v. 22), but also in his death on the cross (vv. 23ff.). Jesus' death and resurrection become a testimony to the totality and universality of the joy in relationship, manifested...by the unity of the eucharistic community (2:46)."

[12] The word ἀφελότης, which occurs only here in the NT and not at all in the LXX, is usually translated as "simplicity" or "sincerity" (BAGD, 124; *EDNT* 1.180), but in view of the context seems to connote "generosity." As Johnson (*Acts*, 59) states: "It appears related to ἁπλότης, which has the sense of simplicity and generosity, as opposed to double-mindedness and grudging envy." See also Conzelmann, *Acts*, 24; Barrett, *Acts*, 171.

14).[13] That they are generously sharing their possessions and food with one another, rather than being preoccupied with acquiring wealth and status in society, qualifies them for the blessing of dining at the great eschatological banquet in the kingdom of God (Luke 14:18-20, 24).

The ideal table fellowship of the Jerusalem believers contributed to the constant and continual growth of the community, as they gained the favor of all the people. In correspondence to their "*daily*" breaking of the bread and sharing of food with gladness and generosity of heart (2:46), "*daily*" the Lord was adding those who were being saved to the community (2:47). In correspondence to Peter's exhortation that those in Jerusalem "*be saved* from this crooked generation" (2:40) by repenting and being baptized for the forgiveness of their sins (2:38), the Lord was adding those who were *being saved* to the community (2:47). Thus the community of those being saved experienced, celebrated, and demonstrated their salvation by sharing meal fellowship with one another.

As the audience later learns, the Hellenists among the Jerusalem believers complained against the Hebrews, because their widows were being neglected in the daily distribution or service (τῇ διακονίᾳ τῇ καθημερινῇ) of food (6:1). This prompted the Twelve to call together the community of disciples and declare, "It is not acceptable for us to abandon the word of God to serve at tables (διακονεῖν τραπέζαις)" (6:2). This reminds the audience of Mary's choice of leaving her sister Martha alone to do the serving (διακονεῖν, Luke 10:40) of the meal in order to listen to the word of Jesus (Luke 10:38-42).[14] But so important was this daily distribution of food for the widows that the Twelve directed the community to choose reputable members to be appointed for this particular "need" (6:3).[15]

Relation of Acts 2:42-47 to Previous Meal Scenes

1) The meal fellowship of the Jerusalem believers, which includes the breaking of the bread, serves as a notable transition from Jesus' breaking of

---

[13] For the meal fellowship in Acts 2:44-47 as a challenge to the reciprocity ethic that was part of the Greco-Roman notion of friendship, see Mitchell, "Social Function of Friendship," 266-68.

[14] Seim (*Double Message*, 108) states that "the story of Martha and Mary in Lk 10.38-42 represents the normative regulation, explicitly backed by Jesus' authority, which then is further applied in Acts 6."

[15] For recent discussions of the role of widows in Acts 6:1-7 see F. S. Spencer, "Neglected Widows in Acts 6:1-7," *CBQ* 56 (1994) 715-33; Price, *Widow Traditions*, 210-16.

the bread with his disciples to *the believing community's eucharistic breaking of the bread*. As the Jerusalem believers continue to break the bread of Jesus' last Passover supper in remembrance of him, their sharing of the broken bread designated as Jesus' body and the wine designated as his blood unites them to the salvific benefits of his sacrificial death (Luke 22:19-20), especially the forgiveness of sins (Acts 2:38). Although Jesus is no longer visibly present with them, in their eucharistic breaking of the bread they experience the invisible presence of the risen and ascended Jesus (Luke 24:30-35, 41-43; Acts 1:4). Their breaking of the bread and sharing of food with one another (Acts 2:42, 46) and with the needy widows in Jerusalem (Acts 6:1-3) continues Jesus' empowerment of the disciples to feed the hungry crowd with the bread and fish he broke for them (Luke 9:16-17). Unlike the rich man, who daily feasted sumptuously without sharing his food with the hungry Lazarus (Luke 16:19-21), the Jerusalem community of believers daily shared their God-given food with one another.

2) The table fellowship of the Jerusalem believers continues the *theme of meals as celebrations of joy*. In the previous narrative meals were appropriate occasions for celebrating the joy of repentance for the forgiveness of sins (Luke 15:6-7, 9-10, 23-24, 32; 19:5-6). Now the Jerusalem believers, who have experienced repentance for the forgiveness of their sins (Acts 2:38), "were sharing food *with gladness* and generosity of heart" (Acts 2:46).

The risen Jesus invited his disciples to celebrate the "joy" (Luke 24:41; cf. 24:52) of recognizing as a living person him whom they thought was dead (Luke 24:37-40) with a meal that restores them to the table fellowship he shared with them before his death (Luke 24:41-43). Now the Jerusalem believers "were sharing food *with gladness* and generosity of heart" (Acts 2:46) because of their reception of the gift of the holy Spirit (Acts 2:38) from the risen and exalted Jesus (Acts 2:33).

3) The "generosity," "sincerity," or "simplicity" of heart with which the Jerusalem believers gladly shared their food (Acts 2:46) demonstrates the *ideals of meal fellowship that Jesus taught*. Their sharing of food with gladness and generosity of heart illustrates the kind of harmony and selfless service Jesus taught his disciples at his last supper to practice instead of quarreling about which one of them seemed to be greatest (Luke 22:24-27). Their ideal table fellowship accords with Jesus' teaching against the kind of meal fellowship that serves oneself by promoting individualistic honors and social reciprocity (Luke 14:7-14).

4) The ideal table fellowship of the Jerusalem believers advances the *theme of the meals as anticipations of the eschatological banquet*. Their generous and selfless sharing of possessions and food with one another, including the poor and needy widows among them (Acts 6:1-3), qualifies them

for the eschatological blessing of dining in the great banquet of God's kingdom (Luke 14:15-24). Their celebration of the joy of their repentance for the forgiveness of their sins (Acts 2:38) by gladly and generously sharing food anticipates the eschatological banquet as God's joyful celebration of the repentance of sinners (Luke 15:6-7, 9-10, 23-24, 32). Their eucharistic breaking of the bread, which unites them in meal fellowship with the invisibly present Jesus, anticipates their presence with him at the eschatological banquet (Luke 22:16-18, 29-30). Their ideal table fellowship will also lead others to the eschatological banquet, as it attracted the favor of the people, so that "daily the Lord was adding those who were being saved to the community" (Acts 2:47).

Pragmatics of the Meal Scene in Acts 2:42-47

1) The ideal table fellowship of the Jerusalem believers serves as a *model for the eucharistic celebrations of the audience*. Now that the risen Jesus has ascended to heavenly exaltation and is no longer visibly present, their eucharistic breaking of the bread is a way of uniting them to the salvific benefits of his sacrificial death and invisible presence as the risen and ascended Lord (Luke 24:30-35, 41-43; Acts 1:4) in anticipation of being with him at the eschatological banquet (Luke 22:16-18, 29-30). Their eucharistic table fellowship should result in a glad and generous sharing of their food and possessions with one another (Acts 2:42-46), especially those who are most needy among them (Acts 6:1-3). By practicing and promoting eucharistic celebrations that lead them to selflessly serve one another in imitation of Jesus himself (Luke 22:24-27), rather than seek individualistic honors and social repayment (Luke 14:7-14), the audience assures their inclusion in the eschatological banquet of the kingdom of God (Luke 14:15-24).

2) The ideal table fellowship of the Jerusalem believers demonstrated one of the ways in which they were witnesses for the mission of proclaiming repentance for the forgiveness of sins to all nations beginning from Jerusalem (Luke 24:47-48; Acts 1:8). Their glad and generous eucharistic meal fellowship, in which they celebrated the joy of their own repentance for the forgiveness of their sins (Acts 2:38), attracted the favor of the people, so that "*daily* the Lord was adding those who were being saved to the community" (Acts 2:47) in correspondence to their *daily* meal fellowship (Acts 2:46). Likewise, through the eucharistic meal fellowship by which they celebrate their own repentance for the forgiveness of sins, the audience can be *witnesses who attract others to repent and be forgiven*, and so share in the joy and generosity of their communal meal fellowship.

CHAPTER 15

PETER'S MEAL FELLOWSHIP WITH CORNELIUS
ACTS 10:1-11:18

In the section of Acts focusing on missionary preaching (8:4-21:17), the first subsection (8:4-11:18) recounts the missionary movement from the Samaritans to the Gentiles.[1] The audience hears that Saul, who did not eat or drink for three days after his dramatic encounter with the risen Jesus (9:9), took food and was strengthened (9:19) after his baptism. Later the audience meets the next major meal scene, Peter's meal fellowship with the gentile Cornelius and those in his household (10:1-11:18).

Saul's Meal after His Conversion and Baptism (9:19)

After the Jerusalem addressees of Peter repented, were baptized, and received the gift of the holy Spirit (2:37-38, 41), they were sharing food ($\mu\epsilon\tau\epsilon\lambda\acute{\alpha}\mu\beta\alpha\nu o\nu$ $\tau\rho o\phi\hat{\eta}\varsigma$) with gladness and generosity of heart (2:46), while devoting themselves to the communal fellowship of the eucharistic breaking of the bread in their houses (2:42, 46).[2] Now, Saul, converted from his mission of persecuting the believers at Damascus and informed by Ananias that he is to be filled with the holy Spirit (9:17), is baptized (9:18) and, taking food ($\lambda\alpha\beta\grave{\omega}\nu$ $\tau\rho o\phi\grave{\eta}\nu$), was strengthened (9:19).[3] Just as their sharing of food in meal hospitality "in their houses" (2:46) was part of what united the newly baptized Jerusalem believers with all other believers (2:44), so the newly baptized Saul's taking of food in meal hospitality "in the house of Judas" (9:11) is part of what unites him to the believing community at Damascus. Saul's taking ($\lambda\alpha\beta\grave{\omega}\nu$) of food reminds the audience of the risen Jesus' taking ($\lambda\alpha\beta\grave{\omega}\nu$) of the piece of baked fish the disciples offered him and eating it before them in meal fellowship (Luke 24:42-43).[4] Saul not only took the food he was offered in meal fellowship in the house of Judas, but continued to accept the meal hospitality of the disciples in Damascus as he stayed with them "for some days" (9:19).

Since Saul neither ate nor drank for three days after his encounter with the risen Jesus (9:9), his taking of food halts his fast and restores his physical

---

[1] O'Fearghail, *Introduction to Luke-Acts*, 79-80: "Thus 8,4-11,18 acts as an introduction to the whole missionary section which sees the word being preached especially among the Gentiles."

[2] On Acts 2:42-47, see chapter 14.

[3] That this is the first reference in Acts to the taking of "food" ($\tau\rho o\phi\acute{\eta}$) after 2:46 enhances the connection.

[4] On this meal of the risen Jesus with his disciples, see chapter 13.

245

strength. That Saul was strengthened (ἐνίσχυσεν) after taking food (9:19) also reminds the audience of how an angel from heaven appeared in answer to the prayer of Jesus, strengthening (ἐνισχύων) him to accept his approaching death as his Father's will (Luke 22:43).[5] This recall of the heavenly, spiritual "strengthening" of the praying Jesus, as well as the fact that Saul's "strengthening" not only accompanied his baptism (9:18) but occurred after the indication that he would be filled with the holy Spirit (9:17), suggests to the audience that his also was not only a physical but a heavenly, spiritual strengthening resulting from his meal fellowship with the believing community. That Saul's taking of food spiritually strengthened him to carry out God's will for him is confirmed as he begins to fulfill his missionary commission (9:15). When Saul immediately began to proclaim in the synagogues that Jesus was the Son of God (9:20), he was all the more strengthened (μᾶλλον ἐνεδυναμοῦτο) and confounded the Jews living in Damascus, proving that this is the Messiah (9:22).[6]

Saul's sharing of meal hospitality in the house of Judas with Ananias and the other disciples at Damascus suggests eucharistic connotations to the audience. Not that Saul's "taking of food" in itself necessarily indicates a eucharistic meal. But it occurs in the context of the meal fellowship he shared with the disciples at Damascus "for some days" (9:19). Since the audience knows that the meal fellowship of an ideal believing community includes regular devotion to the eucharistic breaking of the bread (2:42, 46), Saul's meal fellowship with the Damascus disciples for some days implies his sharing in their eucharistic meals. Saul's sharing of meal hospitality with the disciples at Damascus prompted his immediate preaching of Jesus in the synagogues (9:20) and contributed to the spiritual strength he needed to persevere in that

---

[5] These are the only two occurrences of ἐνισχύω in Luke-Acts, if Luke 22:43-44 can be considered part of the Gospel's text. For a discussion of the uncertain text-critical situation, see Metzger, *Textual Commentary*, 177; Marshall, *Luke*, 831-32; Fitzmyer, *Luke X-XXIV*, 1443-44; Feldkämper, *Der betende Jesus*, 241-43.

[6] Matson, *Household Conversion*, 99 n. 58: "That Paul engages in such preaching immediately after taking food suggests that more than physical strength is in view. The verb used at 9:22 to describe Paul's strengthening (ἐνδυναμόω) is used primarily of religious and spiritual strength." See also H. Paulsen, "ἐνδυναμόω," *EDNT* 1.451.

preaching (9:22).[7] This suggests to the audience that eucharistic meal fellowship is a source of spiritual strength for the apostolic mission.

Peter's Meal Fellowship with Gentiles (10:1-11:18)

Cornelius's vision and Peter's hospitality with a tanner (10:1-8)

The communal dimension and household context of the story of Peter's meal fellowship with Gentiles (10:1-11:18) is evident to the audience from the beginning.[8] Cornelius, a gentile centurion in Caesarea, is introduced as devout

---

[7] With regard to Saul's "taking food" (9:19) in itself and as an individual, isolated expression, Barrett (*Acts*, 458) may be correct in stating: "There is nothing here to suggest a reference to the eucharist." But a consideration of the total narrative context supports Matson (*Household Conversion*, 99), who states: "An allusion to the Eucharist is perhaps present here."

[8] On 10:1-11:18, in addition to the commentaries, see C. House, "Defilement by Association: Some Insights from the Usage of κοινός/κοινόω in Acts 10 and 11," *AUSS* 21 (1983) 143-53; B. R. Gaventa, *From Darkness to Light: Aspects of Conversion in the New Testament* (OBT 20; Philadelphia: Fortress, 1986) 107-25; Esler, *Community and Gospel*, 93-97; R. W. Wall, "Peter, 'Son' of Jonah: The Conversion of Cornelius in the Context of Canon," *JSNT* 29 (1987) 79-90; J. D. M. Derrett, "Clean and Unclean Animals (Acts 10:15, 11:9): Peter's Pronouncing Power Observed," *HeyJ* 29 (1988) 205-21; Tannehill, *Narrative Unity*, 2.128-45; J. H. Elliott, "Household and Meals Vs. Temple Purity: Replication Patterns in Luke-Acts," *BTB* 21 (1991) 102-8; J. J. Scott, "The Cornelius Incident in the Light of Its Jewish Setting," *JETS* 34 (1991) 475-84; C. Lukasz, *Evangelizzazione e conflitto: Indagine sulla coerenza letteraria e tematica della pericope di Cornelio (Atti 10,1-11,18)* (Europäische Hochschulschriften 23; Frankfurt: Lang, 1993); R. D. Witherup, "Cornelius Over and Over and Over Again: 'Functional Redundancy' in the Acts of the Apostles," *JSNT* 49 (1993) 45-66; Shepherd, *Holy Spirit*, 197-205; E. M. Humphrey, "Collision of Modes?--Vision and Determining Argument in Acts 10:1-11:18," *Textual Determinacy Volume II* (*Semeia* 71; eds. R. B. Robinson and R. C. Culley; Atlanta: Scholars Press, 1995) 65-84; J. B. Green, "Internal Repetition in Luke-Acts: Contemporary Narratology and Lucan Historiography," *History, Literature, and Society in the Book of Acts* (ed. B. Witherington; Cambridge: Cambridge University Press, 1996) 293-95; Matson, *Household Conversion*, 86-134; Böhlemann, *Jesus und der Täufer*, 311-12; W. S. Kurz, "Effects of Variant Narrators in Acts 10-11," *NTS* 43 (1997) 570-86.

and God-fearing "with all his household" (10:2).[9] After he saw in a vision an angel of God enter into his house and instruct him to summon a certain Simon called Peter (10:3-5), he sent two of his "household servants" and a devout soldier to Joppa (10:7-8).[10] The audience has already been informed that Peter "was staying a considerable number of days in Joppa with a certain Simon, a tanner" (9:43).[11] But now the hospitality, implying the sharing of meals, that Peter is enjoying as a guest in the household of Simon the tanner is underscored for the audience as the angel identifies Simon Peter as the one who "is receiving hospitality ($\xi\varepsilon\nu i\zeta\varepsilon\tau\alpha\iota$) from another Simon, a tanner, who has a house by the sea" (10:6).[12] From the *house* of a Jewish tanner in Joppa, where he is lodging as a guest, Peter is to be summoned by *household* servants to the *house* of a gentile centurion in Caesarea.[13]

Peter's vision commanding him to eat what God has cleansed (10:9-16)

The household context of the story continues as Peter went up to the housetop ($\delta\hat{\omega}\mu\alpha$) of the tanner's house to pray around noon (10:9).[14] The meal hospitality implied in Peter's lodging with the tanner becomes explicit for the

---

[9] On Cornelius and his household as "God-fearers," that is, those Gentiles who had close relations with Jews and frequented their synagogues, see I. Levinskaya, *The Book of Acts in Its Diaspora Setting* (The Book of Acts in Its First Century Setting 5; Grand Rapids: Eerdmans, 1996) 121.

[10] Polhill, *Acts*, 253 n. 77: "The word for servant ($oi\kappa\acute{\varepsilon}\tau\eta\varsigma$) refers to household servants who were considered part of the family, as opposed to mere slaves ($\delta o\hat{\upsilon}\lambda o\iota$)."

[11] That being a tanner may have been considered an unclean occupation in Jewish eyes does not seem to play an explicit role in the story. That Simon was a tanner distinguishes him from Simon called Peter. The point is that Simon Peter is lodging in the household of a fellow Jew, also named Simon but a tanner, when he is summoned to the household of a Gentile. See Johnson, *Acts*, 178-79; Barrett, *Acts*, 486-87.

[12] On $\xi\varepsilon\nu i\zeta\varepsilon\tau\alpha\iota$ meaning "received as a guest" here, see BAGD, 547; J. H. Friedrich, "$\xi\varepsilon\nu i\zeta\omega$," *EDNT* 2.485.

[13] Matson, *Household Conversion*, 103: "The story of Cornelius is striking for the way it makes the spatial setting of the house a central component of its plot." See also Humphrey, "Collison of Modes," 77.

[14] "$\delta\hat{\omega}\mu\alpha$," *EDNT* 1.363: "The word appears in the NT in common phrases which presuppose the oriental flat roof as a living space in the open air."

audience with the notice that Peter became hungry and wanted to eat (γεύσασθαι, 10:10).[15] While "they," presumably the members of the tanner's household, were preparing the meal, a trance fell upon Peter (10:10). Whereas Cornelius had a vision of an angel while praying in his house at three in the afternoon (10:2-3), the next day around noon Peter on the tanner's housetop has a vision while praying in a hunger-induced trance.

After Peter saw in his vision a vessel like a large sheet, which contained all the four-legged animals and reptiles of the earth and the birds of the sky, descending from heaven to the earth by its four corners (10:11-12), a voice told him, "Rise, Peter; slaughter and eat" (10:13). That Peter is to eat from "all" (10:12) the animals and birds contradicts the audience's knowledge that the Jewish people avoid foods that God has declared unclean (Lev 11:1-47; Deut 14:3-21) for them as God's sacred people. Since God has chosen and set them apart from all the other nations to be peculiarly God's own, they must set apart the clean animals from the unclean, so that they may not be contaminated with their uncleanness (Lev 20:24-26; Deut 14:2). And so Peter replied, "Not at all, Lord, for never have I eaten anything profane (κοινὸν) and unclean (ἀκάθαρτον)" (10:14; cf. LXX Ezek 4:14).[16] But a voice spoke to him again, a second time, "What God has declared clean (ἐκαθάρισεν), you must not treat as profane (κοίνου)" (10:15). This happened a definitive three times and immediately the vessel was taken up into heaven (10:16).

In the house of the tanner Peter shares meal hospitality with Cornelius's men (10:17-23a)

The story's focus on the hospitality Peter is receiving by lodging as a *guest* in the *house* of the tanner (10:6) continues as the men sent by Cornelius asked for the *house* of Simon (10:17) and inquired whether Simon called Peter

---

[15] Barrett, *Acts*, 505: "γεύσασθαι here must mean *to eat, to have a meal*, though more usually in means *to taste*." It is used in Luke 14:24 for the tasting of the great dinner that points to the eschatological banquet. See also H.-J. van der Minde, "γεύομαι," *EDNT* 1.245-46.

[16] On "profane and unclean," Johnson (*Acts*, 184) notes that the phrase "is strictly redundant, although Luke may have felt the need for both terms since he had previously used κοινός only in its meaning of 'shared' (Acts 2:44; 4:32), and ἀκάθαρτος only with reference to 'unclean spirits'." Although ἀκάθαρτος is the word used for food considered ritually unclean in the LXX of Lev 11:1-47; 20:24-26 and Deut 14:3-21, κοινός is the word used in 1 Macc 1:47, 62. See also Barrett, *Acts*, 508; Polhill, *Acts*, 255.

was lodging as a *guest* there (10:18). Still perplexed as to the meaning of his vision (10:17, 19), Peter is directed by the Spirit to go without hesitating with the three men, who have been sent not only by Cornelius (10:8) but by the Spirit himself (10:20). That Peter is to go "without hesitating" (μηδὲν διακρινόμενος), with its nuance of "without discriminating," begins to interpret for Peter and the audience the meaning of his vision. Just as Peter is not to discriminate between clean and unclean animals (10:15), so he as a Jew is not to hesitate to go to the house of a Gentile, not to discriminate himself as a Jew from a Gentile.[17]

Peter begins to obey the instructions of the Spirit, who told him to descend and go with the men he sent (10:20), as he descended, identified himself to the men as the one they are seeking, and asked them to explain their presence (10:21) at the house of the Jewish tanner. The men then develop the narrator's previous description of Cornelius (10:1-2) for the audience. The gentile centurion Cornelius, who gives many alms to "the people," that is, the Jews as God's chosen people (10:2), is attested moreover "by the whole nation" of the Jews (10:22; cf. Luke 7:5).[18] The devout centurion, who "together with all his household" fears God (10:2), is the upright and God-fearing man who received a revelation from a holy angel to summon Peter "to his household" and to hear words from him (10:22). This broadens the issue of sharing meal hospitality beyond Peter and Cornelius as important individuals. Cornelius's men are inviting Peter as a representative of the Jewish *people* (10:2), the *whole nation* of the Jews (10:22), to be a guest in the *household* (10:22) of the Cornelius who represents *all his household* (10:2) of God-fearing Gentiles.[19]

---

[17] On the double nuance of διακρινόμενος here Johnson (*Acts*, 185) states: "Peter in effect is told not to be filled with doubts about the course of events which will eventually lead him to understand how he is not to discriminate between people (see 11:2, 12; 15:9)." See also G. Dautzenberg, "διακρίνω," *EDNT* 1.305; Matson, *Household Conversion*, 105.

[18] On the translation "attested moreover" (μαρτυρούμενος τε), Johnson (*Acts*, 185) states: "The particle τε in this case seems to give a special emphasis which the translation 'moreover' seeks to capture."

[19] After suggesting some thematic interplay here in the use of the words ἔθνος (nation) and οἶκος (household), Witherup ("Cornelius," 55-56) states: "Since the pericope is a major story on conversion in Acts, it is easy to discern here its largely symbolic proportions. The conversion of Cornelius and his household really represents the conversion of a people ('nation'). The final effect is to make Cornelius and his house symbolic of the Gentile church (or house-church)."

Before Peter goes as a guest to the household of the gentile centurion Cornelius, he invites Cornelius's men into the house of the Jewish tanner. The Peter who is himself receiving the hospitality that implies meal fellowship in the house of Simon the tanner (10:6, 18) extended that hospitality to these members of Cornelius's household (10:23). Before becoming a guest in the household of the Gentile, Peter serves as the host of Gentiles in the household of a Jew. This indicates to the audience how Peter is already beginning to understand the meaning of his vision, that he is not to separate himself as a Jew from Gentiles.[20]

Peter is allowed to share meal fellowship with Cornelius and his household (10:23b-33)

The communal dimension of Peter's association with Cornelius develops for the audience as Peter, rising on the next day, went out of the Jewish house of the tanner *with them*, the men sent by the gentile Cornelius, while some of the brothers from Joppa went *with him* as well (10:23b). Peter thus accompanies the gentile delegation but not alone. He is in turn accompanied by a group of his own Jewish associates, believing brothers.

Peter's exit (ἐξῆλθεν) out of the Jewish household where he shared the hospitality that includes meal fellowship with Gentiles (10:23) is complemented by his entrance (εἰσῆλθεν) the next day into Caesarea where Cornelius is awaiting them (10:24). But Cornelius, like Peter, is not alone. He has *called together* his relatives and close friends (10:24). This expands the communal dimension beyond Cornelius with all his household (10:2) to include a wider circle of his gentile relatives and friends.

As Peter was entering the gentile domain, Cornelius's association with him is underscored as he *met with* Peter, and falling at his feet, worshiped him (10:25). The God-fearing gentile centurion acknowledges the status of Peter as a leader of God's specially chosen people. That Peter made him rise with the words, "Rise, I myself am also a human being" (10:26) indicates to the audience Peter's developing understanding of the significance of his vision

---

[20] Polhill, *Acts*, 257: "That Peter was beginning to understand is exemplified by his inviting them to spend the evening as guests. Already he was beginning to have fellowship with Gentiles he formerly considered unclean." Barrett, *Acts*, 512: "Peter gives proof of his readiness to have dealings with Gentiles, and to enter a Gentile house, by inviting Gentiles into the house where he is staying." See also Matson, *Household Conversion*, 106.

regarding the eating of clean and unclean animals (10:11-15).[21] Just as he is not to distinguish between clean and unclean animals, so Peter does not distinguish himself as a Jew to be separate and superior to this Gentile. The Jewish leader and the gentile centurion, as well as their respective Jewish and gentile associates, share a common humanity.

Peter's *speaking with* Cornelius (10:27) further underlines their association as it complements Cornelius's *meeting with* Peter (10:25). When Peter finally entered Cornelius's household, the coming together and association of Jewish and gentile groups reaches a climax. Peter found many who had *come together* (10:27).[22] This completes the series of συν ("with, together") words that emphasizes the coming together and association of the Jewish leader with the gentile centurion and their respective constituencies: Peter went *with* Cornelius's men (σὺν αὐτοῖς) while the brothers from Joppa went *with* (συνῆλθον) Peter (10:23); Cornelius, who called *together* (συγκαλεσάμενος) those related *with* (συγγενεῖς) him and his close friends (10:24), met *with* (συναντήσας) Peter (10:25), who in turn spoke *with* (συνομιλῶν) Cornelius as he entered the Gentile's house and found many who had come *together* (συνεληλυθότας) awaiting him (10:27).

Peter pointed out to this gentile assembly in the house of Cornelius how forbidden it is for a Jewish man to associate with or visit someone of another race (cf. Luke 7:6-7).[23] His announcement, "But God has shown me not to call any human being profane or unclean" (10:28), further indicates to the audience his understanding of the vision regarding the eating of clean and

---

[21] The command to "rise" (ἀνάστηθι) that Peter issued to the Jewish man Aeneas in healing him (9:34) and to the Jewish woman Tabitha in raising her from death (9:40) he now issues to the gentile Cornelius in recognizing their common humanity (10:26).

[22] On the three-fold "entering" (εἰσέρχομαι in 10:24, 25, 27) of Peter that progresses from his entry into Caesarea, the predominantly gentile capital of Judea, to his gradual and climactic entry into the gentile household of Cornelius, see Matson, *Household Conversion*, 106-8.

[23] Polhill, *Acts*, 258 n. 94: "No specific law forbade Jews to associate with Gentiles, but the purity regulations rendered close social interaction virtually impossible."

unclean animals (10:11-15).[24] That Peter, the Jew, is not to call any *human being* profane or unclean (10:28) complements his directive that Cornelius, the Gentile, should consider Peter a fellow *human being* rather than worship him (10:26). Since Peter is not to distinguish between clean and unclean animals or human beings, there is nothing preventing his entrance into the gentile household of Cornelius and sharing the meal hospitality and fellowship of these Gentiles, even if it involves the eating of animals previously considered unclean.[25]

After Peter inquired as to why Cornelius summoned him (10:29), Cornelius's reply provides the audience with another report of his vision (10:30-33), which confirms and develops that of the narrator (10:3-6) and that of Cornelius's men to Peter (10:22). The focus on the progression from Peter's hospitality and meal fellowship in the Jewish household to that in the gentile household continues. Cornelius reports that when he received his vision he was praying "in my house" (10:30), "his house" to which his men invited Peter (10:22), where the God-fearing Cornelius "with all his household" (10:2), now broadened to include his relatives and close friends (10:24), are gathered to receive Peter. For the third time the audience hears that Peter was receiving the hospitality that includes meals (10:6, 18, 32) in the house (10:6, 17, 32) of Simon, the Jewish tanner, when he was summoned to the household of the Gentile. After Cornelius expressed his gratitude and appreciation for Peter's kindness in coming, he sets the stage for Peter's address to this climactic meeting of all the Jewish and gentile groups brought together in his house by God himself: "Now therefore we are all ($\pi\acute{\alpha}\nu\tau\epsilon\varsigma$) present before God to hear everything ($\pi\acute{\alpha}\nu\tau\alpha$) that has been commanded to you by the Lord" (10:33).[26]

---

[24] Rather than declaring all animal food clean and eliminating the category of dietary purity, Peter's vision only allows for Jews to eat with Gentiles, who are now declared clean, according to M. Pettem, "Luke's Great Omission and His View of the Law," *NTS* 42 (1996) 42-44. But it was the eating of animals considered unclean that rendered a Jew unclean, so that the cleansing of animals was necessary to allow Jews to eat freely with Gentiles without the risk of incurring impurity. See also Humphrey, "Collision," 81.

[25] Johnson, *Acts*, 190: "Peter's characterization represents an advance in learning; he now has made a connection between the vision and the events in which he is involved: the terms 'common and unclean' apply not only to foods but also to categories of persons. God 'showed him' not only through the vision but also through his interaction with these Gentiles, and hearing their story." See also Matson, *Household Conversion*, 108.

[26] Witherup ("Cornelius," 56) notes that "now Cornelius has assembled his *whole* household (cf. v. 24) together to hear *all* that God has commanded Peter" (his emphasis).

Peter was one of the witnesses who ate and drank with the risen Jesus (10:34-43)

Peter's solemn statement, "In truth I understand that God is not partial, but that in every nation whoever fears him and acts uprightly is acceptable to him" (10:34-35), expresses for the audience how Cornelius's report of his vision (10:30-33) has confirmed and developed Peter's understanding of his vision about eating clean and unclean animals (10:11-15). Peter is declaring God's acceptance not only specifically of Cornelius, who has been described as God-fearing and upright (10:2, 22), but more generally of anyone "*in every nation*" (10:35) who fears God and acts uprightly.[27] This not only justifies the association of the Jewish Peter (10:28) with the gentile Cornelius, but opens the way for the mission to Gentiles, allowing any Jewish believer to receive hospitality and share meal fellowship with any God-fearing and upright Gentile.

According to Peter's proclamation of the gospel about Jesus Christ to Cornelius and all the other Gentiles gathered in his house (10:36-43) God granted that the risen Jesus become visible (10:40) not to all the Jewish people but to witnesses designated beforehand by God, namely, "us, those who ate and drank with him after he rose from the dead" (10:41).[28] This recalls for the audience the meals that Peter and the other disciples shared with the risen Jesus in the previous narrative (Luke 24:30-35, 41-43; Acts 1:4). These meals not only demonstrated the reality of Jesus' resurrection but continued the meal

---

[27] Barrett, *Acts*, 519: "The words ἐν παντὶ ἔθνει are emphatic. Appropriately qualified persons are acceptable to God whether they are Jews or belong to some other race." On Peter's generalization here, see also M. Dumais, "Le salut en dehors de la foi en Jésus-Christ?: Observations sur trois passages des Actes des Apôtres," *Église et Théologie* 28 (1997) 167.

[28] On the eating and drinking of the witnesses, Gaventa (*From Darkness*, 119) notes: "None of the other speeches in Acts refers to this qualification of the witnesses, but it is especially appropriate for a story that concerns itself with hospitality for Gentiles." See also Soards, *Speeches in Acts*, 75.

fellowship he shared with his disciples during his ministry.[29] They anticipated his invisible presence with them in the eucharistic meals he commanded them to keep doing in remembrance of him (Luke 22:19). At his final meal on earth with his disciples (Luke 24:41-43; Acts 1:4) the risen Jesus bestowed upon them the mission of expanding the proclamation of repentance for the forgiveness of sins to all peoples (Luke 24:47). Peter now carries out this mission in the context of meal hospitality with Gentiles as he concludes his proclamation with the appeal that all who believe in Jesus receive forgiveness of sins through his name (10:43).[30]

By accepting the hospitality that includes meal fellowship from Cornelius, Peter is extending to this gentile assembly the meal fellowship he shared with the risen Jesus as one of those who ate and drank with him. Cornelius and all those Gentiles gathered together with Peter will eat and drink with one of the witnesses who ate and drank with the risen Lord. After Peter went *with* Cornelius's men (σὺν αὐτοῖς) while the brothers from Joppa went *with* (συνῆλθον) Peter (10:23), Cornelius, who called *together* (συγκαλεσάμενος) his relatives and close friends (10:24), met *with* (συναντήσας) Peter (10:25), who in turn spoke *with* (συνομιλῶν) Cornelius as he entered his house and found many who had come *together* (συνεληλυθότας) awaiting him (10:27). The meal fellowship that Peter brings to this assembly as one of the witnesses who ate *with* (συνεφάγομεν) and drank *with* (συνεπίομεν) the risen Jesus (10:41) climaxes this dramatic coming together of Jewish and gentile groups.

---

[29] Matson, *Household Conversion*, 111-12: "Peter's reference to 'eating and drinking' at 10.41 not only recalls Jesus' post-resurrection eating activity with his disciples (Lk. 24.30, 41-43; Acts 1.4) but the table-fellowship practice of his earthly career which becomes part of the charge to the Seventy-two (Lk. 10.7). Peter himself will re-enact this table-fellowship practice by subsequently dining in the house of Cornelius (10.48; 11.3)." See also Johnson, *Acts*, 193; Barrett, *Acts*, 527.

[30] Conzelmann, *Acts*, 84: "A call to repent is lacking, but it would be unnecessary with this audience." Soards (*Speeches in Acts*, 76) notes: "Although this speech neither levels a charge at the audience nor explicates the necessity of repentance, vv. 42b-43 seem at least implicitly to confront the hearers with their sinfulness and to call for their repentance."

Peter shares meal hospitality with Cornelius's household for some days (10:44-48)

While Peter was still speaking the holy Spirit fell upon all those listening to the word (10:44). Then Peter addresses the audience and the astonished circumcised believers who came *with* (συνῆλθεν) him (10:45; cf. 10:23) to the house of Cornelius, "Can anyone withhold the water for baptizing these people, who have received the holy Spirit just as we have?" (10:47; cf. 2:1-13).[31] After Peter commanded (cf. 10:33) that they be baptized in the name of Jesus Christ, they invited him to stay for some days (10:48), that is, to accept hospitality in the household of Cornelius and share meal fellowship with these Gentiles, who have now become believers.[32] This climactically complements the story's focus on reciprocal meal hospitality. Peter, who received hospitality in the house of Simon the Jewish tanner (10:6, 18), and who extended that hospitality to the gentile men sent by Cornelius (10:23), now receives hospitality in the household of Gentiles.[33] By remaining in the house of Cornelius and accepting meal hospitality for some days Peter models for the audience Jesus' command for missionaries to remain in whatever household they enter, eating and drinking what they are offered (Luke 10:7; cf. 9:4).

---

[31] For an analysis of Peter's entire speech in Cornelius's house, see Soards, *Speeches in Acts*, 70-77. On its kerygmatic summary in relation to other speeches, see R. Bauckham, "Kerygmatic Summaries in the Speeches of Acts," *History, Literature, and Society in the Book of Acts* (ed. B. Witherington; Cambridge: Cambridge University Press, 1996) 185-217.

[32] On the request for Peter to remain for some days, Gaventa (*From Darkness*, 120) remarks that "this request suggests that the inclusion of Gentiles does not have to do merely with a grudging admission to the circle of the baptized. Including Gentiles means receiving them, entering their homes, and accepting hospitality in those homes." According to Polhill (*Acts*, 265), Peter's remaining for some days "inevitably involved table fellowship, but that now presented no problem for Peter." See also Matson, *Household Conversion*, 113-14.

[33] As Matson (*Household Convervsion*, 113) notes: "By story's end, the household, not Cornelius, becomes the primary actor: 'they' invite Peter to stay in the house for hospitable fellowship...In this way, the household gradually supplants Cornelius as the primary focus of the narrative." Witherup ("Cornelius," 60) points out how "Cornelius himself fades into the background, his household becoming symbolic of the Gentile world."

At this point a pattern has developed for the audience involving meal fellowship with the newly baptized that unites them with the broader believing community. Just as meal hospitality in their houses (2:46) united the newly baptized Jerusalem believers with all other believers (2:44), so the newly baptized Saul's meal hospitality in the house of Judas (9:11, 19) united him to the believing community at Damascus. Now Peter's reciprocal meal hospitality in the house of Cornelius (10:48; cf. 10:23) unites these newly baptized Gentiles with him and the Jewish believers who accompanied him (10:45; cf. 10:23).[34]

That Peter stayed in the gentile household "for some days" (10:48) reminds the audience of how Saul not only took the food he was offered in meal fellowship in the house of Judas, but continued to accept the meal hospitality of the disciples in Damascus as he stayed with them "for some days" (9:19). Just as Saul's meal fellowship with the Damascus disciples "for some days" implied his sharing in their eucharistic meals, since the meal fellowship of an ideal believing community includes regular devotion to the eucharistic breaking of the bread (2:42, 46; cf. Luke 22:19), so Peter's meal fellowship with the newly baptized Gentiles in the household of Cornelius "for some days" implies their sharing of the eucharist.[35]

In Jerusalem Peter explains his meal fellowship with Gentiles (11:1-18)

Those who disputed with Peter when he went up to Jerusalem (11:2), after the apostles and brothers throughout Judea heard that the Gentiles too had accepted the word of God (11:1), are described as "those of the circumcision" (11:2).[36] This reminds the audience that those who had come with Peter into the house of Cornelius and were amazed that the gift of the holy Spirit was poured out on the Gentiles were also "those of the circumcision" (10:45). But

---

[34] Barrett, *Acts*, 531: "To stay with them implies that Peter recognized them as Christians, and as 'clean'."

[35] According to Matson (*Household Conversion*, 116), "it is more than likely, given Luke's interest in the symbolic power of food, that the table-fellowship enjoyed by Peter and the newly converted household assumed a eucharistic character. It is scarcely conceivable that Luke did not intend the reader to see in this table-fellowship over the course of 'some days' a reference to the Lord's Supper." See also LaVerdiere, *Eucharist*, 106.

[36] On 11:1-18, see Maloney, *All That God Had Done*, 67-100.

"those of the circumcision" in Jerusalem confront Peter alone: "You entered the house of uncircumcised men and ate with them" (11:3).[37]

The accusation that Peter entered (εἰσῆλθες) the house and ate with (συνέφαγες) uncircumcised men (11:3) reminds the audience of similar accusations leveled against Jesus. After the chief tax collector Zacchaeus welcomed Jesus into his house (Luke 19:5-6), all who saw it kept grumbling, "With a man who is a sinner he has gone in (εἰσῆλθεν) to lodge" (Luke 19:7). When all the tax collectors and the sinners were coming near to hear Jesus (Luke 15:1), the Pharisees and the scribes kept grumbling, "This man welcomes sinners and eats with (συνεσθίει) them" (Luke 15:2). Whereas Jesus shared meal hospitality with sinful Jews who associated with Gentiles, Peter shared meal hospitality with actual, uncircumcised Gentiles.[38]

The circumcised in Jerusalem accuse the Peter who declared himself one of the witnesses who shared meal fellowship with the risen Jesus, who ate *with* and drank *with* him (10:41), of also sharing meal fellowship with the uncircumcised by entering their house and eating *with* them (11:3). That Peter "ate *with*" Gentiles sums up this story's dramatic coming together of Jewish and gentile groups expressed by "*with*" (συν) words (10:23, 24, 25, 27, 41, 45), indicating that the charge centers around meal fellowship.[39] In defense of his "eating *with*" Gentiles (11:3) Peter recounts his vision in which the heavenly voice told him to "eat" (11:7; cf. 10:13) from any of the four classes of animals he saw (11:6).[40] He omits the mention of his hunger and that the

---

[37] Although some (e.g., NRSV) read 11:3 as a question, it is probably best to understand it as a direct accusation; see Matson, *Household Conversion*, 118 n. 140; Barrett, *Acts*, 537-38.

[38] Note the emphasis upon the Jewishness of Zacchaeus as a "son of Abraham" in Luke 19:9.

[39] Matson, *Household Conversion*, 118: "What compels Peter to tell of his experiences in the house of Cornelius is not the general desire to inform but a specific, pointed charge. That charge centers around the sharing of food and shelter, not the baptism of a Gentile." See also Haenchen, *Acts*, 354.

[40] Matson, *Household Conversion*, 119-20: "If Peter has enjoyed indiscriminate table-fellowship in the house of Cornelius, it is because *God* has told him it is now proper for him to kill and 'eat' (11.7)...The expansion in the classification of animals from three to four (cf. 10.12) makes the indiscriminate command to kill and eat even more radical (11.7)..."

vision occurred while food was being prepared (10:10) because the issue is not the satisfaction of his hunger but meal fellowship.[41]

In the narrator's version of the vision Peter says, "Not at all, Lord, for never have I eaten anything profane and unclean" (10:14), emphasizing his personal refusal to eat any food that is profane "*and*" unclean. But in his own version Peter places the focus on whatever is profane "*or*" unclean, as he intensifies his absolute refusal to even taste anything questionable: "Not at all, Lord, for nothing profane or unclean has ever entered into my mouth" (11:8).[42] Then Peter repeats, emphatically reinforcing for the audience, what the voice told him in the narrator's account (10:15): "What God has declared clean, you must not treat as profane" (11:9). That nothing profane or unclean has ever entered into Peter's *mouth* (11:8) reminds the audience of the broader significance of the vision's divine voice as explained when Peter solemnly opened his *mouth* and announced: "In truth I understand that God is not partial, but that in every nation whoever fears him and acts uprightly is acceptable to him" (10:34-35; cf. 15:7).[43] Indeed, Peter has already told Cornelius and those assembled in his house: "But God has shown me not to call any human being profane or unclean" (10:28).

Peter further explains how it was God himself who brought together these Jewish and gentile households to share meal fellowship. Immediately after his vision three gentile men, sent from Caesarea to Peter in Joppa, arrived at the Jewish house of Simon the tanner "where we were" (11:11; cf. 10:17-

---

[41] According to Witherup ("Cornelius," 59) the reason for this omission "lies in the symbolic role of food in the story and the purpose of the defense speech itself. The food functions as symbolic of table fellowship between Jews and Gentiles. The real issue is the social intercourse between Jews and Gentiles but seen through their ability to provide mutual hospitality in the Lord."

[42] On the significance of the variant narrations of the visions of Peter and Cornelius, see Witherup, "Cornelius," 45-66; Kurz, "Variant Narrators," 570-86.

[43] On the second version of Peter's vision Witherup ("Cornelius," 59-60) remarks: "What is essential in the second version is not what one eats or how one satisfies one's hunger but how one views all reality, animal and human alike, which God has declared 'clean'. Indeed, it is the act of Peter opening his mouth in testimony to Cornelius and his household (cf. the expression in 10.34 with 15.7) that shows more importantly the purpose of this

18).[44] Peter eventually ate *with* them (11:3) because the Spirit told him to go *with* them without discriminating (11:12). Peter's report that the Spirit told him to go with Gentiles "without discriminating" (μηδὲν διακρίναντα, 11:12) indicates to the audience his more precise understanding of the vision as it makes more definite the narrator's report that the Spirit told him to go "without hesitating" (μηδὲν διακρινόμενος, 10:20). That the Spirit told Peter to go "without discriminating" between Jew and Gentile hints that his Jewish accusers in Jerusalem are likewise to stop "disputing" or "discriminating" (διεκρίνοντο, 11:2) against him for eating with Gentiles (11:3).[45]

That "these six brothers also went *with* me" (11:12) stresses for his accusers how Peter did not go alone with the Gentiles. Peter's report that "six" brothers also went with him, thus establishing a group of seven Jewish members, a biblical number indicating completion or perfection,[46] makes more precise the narrator's report that "some" of the brothers from Joppa went *with* Peter (10:23). The audience knows that "these six brothers" are "those of the circumcision" who had come *with* Peter into the house of Cornelius and were amazed that the gift of the holy Spirit was poured out on the Gentiles (10:45). Peter's report that "*we* entered (εἰσήλθομεν) into the house of the man" (11:12) expands his opponents' focus from Peter alone, "you entered (εἰσῆλθες)" (11:3), to include "these six brothers," that is, those who are "of the circumcision" just like Peter's opponents.[47] Their entrance into "the house of the man" completes the movement from the Jewish house (οἰκιαν, 11:11; cf.

---

vision."

[44] There is a variant reading, "where I was." Either reading could be original. Johnson (*Acts*, 197) notes that "if the reading is 'we were,' then Peter has implicated his Jewish companions from the beginning."

[45] On the shift to "without discriminating" in 11:12, Matson (*Household Conversion*, 120) states: "This subtle shift to the active voice (cf. 10.20) indicates that Peter is now reflecting on his prior experience, which has taught him to consider no person common or unclean (10.28, 34-35). The instructions of the Spirit also serve to contrast God's salvific intentions with the narrow viewpoint espoused by Peter's opponents in Jerusalem, who 'criticized' (διεκρίνοντο) Peter's actions (11.2)."

[46] J. F. Drinkard, "Numbers," *HarperCollins Bible Dictionary*, 764.

[47] On "these six brothers" Johnson (*Acts*, 198) remarks: "Since they have been identified by the narrator in 10:45 as 'from the circumcision,' Peter has not only made them witnesses to the events (in which capacity they are critical to his defense), but has also implicated them in his own actions; they were participants! They were with him, heard his speech, saw the result of the

10:6, 17, 32) of the tanner Simon to the gentile house (οἶκον, 11:12; cf. 10:2, 22, 30; 11:13, 14) of the centurion Cornelius.[48]

Peter reports to his Jewish accusers how God directed the gentile household as well. The "man" (Cornelius)[49] told not just Peter alone but "*us*," the Jewish group of Peter and the six brothers, how he saw the angel standing "in his house,"[50] directing him to send for Peter (11:13), who will speak words by which "you and all your household" will be saved (11:14; cf. 10:22, 33).[51] Since the holy Spirit fell upon the Gentiles when Peter began to speak just as upon "*us*," the Jews, in the beginning (11:15; cf. 2:1-4; 10:44-46), and God gave the Gentiles the same gift he gave to "*us*," the Jewish believers, Peter asks his accusers how he (and therefore they) could possibly

---

Spirit's outpouring, made no objection *then* to the baptism."

[48] According to P. Weigandt ("οἶκος," *EDNT* 2.501), "in Acts 10:1-11:18 Luke distinguishes between two different houses with the aid of οἶκος and οἰκία: The house of Simon the tanner he calls consistently an οἰκία (10:6, 17, 32; 11:11) and that of the Roman centurion Cornelius is consistently an οἶκος (10:22, 30; 11:12f.)."

[49] Witherup ("Cornelius," 57) notes how Cornelius is never even named in this final version of his vision and concludes that "Cornelius's role has been reduced far into the background to allow the importance of Peter's role (and the action of the Holy Spirit) to come to the fore. The significance of the entire event is the bringing of the Gentiles to salvation through the work of the Holy Spirit and the witness of Peter."

[50] On the detail of God's angel as the first to cross the line into the house of the Gentile but the last to be mentioned for its decisive rhetorical effect, Humphrey ("Collision of Modes," 77) states: "Of real interest is the effortless way in which this detail finds itself worked into the final vision-report. With it the speaker says, but with understated finesse, 'And in case you didn't get it, the angel entered first, so who are you to criticize?'"

[51] On the shift here to salvation terminology, Matson (*Household Conversion*, 122) notes "how the twin issues of 'entering' and 'eating' are closely linked in the minds of Peter's accusers at 11.3" (n. 156) and states that "Peter makes table-fellowship an integral element of gentile salvation. If Peter is to speak the word of salvation to Gentiles, Peter must 'enter' the house of

hinder God (11:17; cf. 10:47).[52] Peter's words silenced his accusers, implying that he was justified to enter and eat with Gentiles (11:3). His Jewish accusers then glorified God, saying, "So then even to the Gentiles God has given the repentance that leads to life!" (11:18).

The audience recalls that Jesus shared meal fellowship with tax collectors and sinners not only to celebrate their repentance and forgiveness of sins but also implicitly to call his "righteous" Jewish opponents to repent of their own sinfulness: "I have not come to invite the righteous but sinners to *repentance!*" (Luke 5:32; cf. 15:7, 10). It was most appropriate for the audience that it was in the context of his restored meal fellowship with the disciples (Luke 24:41-43), including the repentant Peter (Luke 22:31-34; 24:12), that the risen Jesus commissioned them to preach *repentance* for the forgiveness of sins "to all the nations/Gentiles" beginning from Jerusalem (Luke 24:47). Peter began this preaching to those in Jerusalem (2:14) when he called them to *repent*, be baptized and receive the holy Spirit (2:38). Those who repented celebrated with an ideal communal meal fellowship (2:42-47). Now, over the issue of meal hospitality the Jewish believers in Jerusalem acknowledge not only that "even the Gentiles" have received the word of God (11:1), but that "even to the Gentiles" God has given the *repentance* that leads to life (11:18).

This climactic conclusion by the Jewish believers in Jerusalem (11:18) not only refers to the repentance of Gentiles but ironically indicates an additional repentance on the part of Jews with regard to Gentiles. Indeed, the entire story narrates a threefold repentance or conversion both in the context of and over the issue of meal fellowship: 1) After Peter accepts their meal hospitality, Cornelius and his gentile household repent of their sins, are baptized and receive the holy Spirit just like the Jews; 2) Peter and those Jews with him convert from their refusal to eat the unclean food that separates them

---

Cornelius, which implies that he may now 'eat' there as well."

[52] On the apparent discrepancy between when the narrator (10:44) and when Peter (11:15) said the holy Spirit fell on the gentile household, Matson (*Household Conversion*, 122) points out: "By moving the Spirit's descent from the end of his message to the beginning (ἐν δὲ τῷ ἄρξασθαί με λαλεῖν); cf. 10.44), Peter invests the coming of the Spirit with an even more unexpected and decisive effect." See also Kurz, "Variant Narrators," 582-83; J. J. Kilgallen, "Did Peter Actually Fail to Get a Word in? (Acts 11,15)," *Bib* 71

from meal hospitality with Gentiles; 3) the Jewish believers in Jerusalem repent of their objection to Peter sharing meal hospitality with Gentiles.[53]

Meal Fellowship with Gentiles and the Apostolic Decree
(15:9, 19-21, 28-29; 21:25)

The audience hears echoes of the Cornelius episode in Peter's speech at the council of Jerusalem (15:7-11).[54] Peter's statement that God made no discrimination between us Jews and the Gentiles (15:9) climactically concludes the thematic progression from making no discriminations among food to making no discriminations among people.[55] Peter was to go with Gentiles "without hesitating" (μηδὲν διακρινόμενος, 10:20) and then "without discriminating" (μηδὲν διακρίναντα, 11:12), and Peter's Jewish accusers in Jerusalem were likewise to stop disputing or discriminating (διεκρίνοντο, 11:2) against him for eating with Gentiles (11:3), because God himself made no discrimination (οὐθὲν διέκρινεν, 15:9) between Jews and Gentiles. The audience twice heard the heavenly voice tell the Peter who had never eaten any profane and/or unclean (ἀκάθαρτον) food (10:14; 11:8) not to treat as profane what God has declared clean (ἐκαθάρισεν, 10:15; 11:9). Now Peter himself reinforces for the audience that God has indeed cleansed (καθαρίσας) the

---

(1990) 405-10.

[53] Gaventa, *From Darkness*, 109: "By means of the issue of *hospitality*, Luke demonstrates that the conversion of the first Gentile required the conversion of the church as well. Indeed, in Luke's account, Peter and company undergo a change that is more wrenching by far than the change experienced by Cornelius." See also Matson, *Household Conversion*, 123-24.

[54] On Peter's speech in 15:7-11, see F. Refoulé, "Le discours de Pierre à l'assemblée de Jérusalem," *RB* 100 (1993) 239-51; Witherup, "Cornelius," 60-62; Soards, *Speeches in Acts*, 90-92; Matson, *Household Conversion*, 124-26.

[55] On the progression from the Cornelius episode to the council of Jerusalem, see J. J. Scott, "The Church's Progress to the Council of Jerusalem According to the Book of Acts," *Bulletin for Biblical Research* 7 (1997) 205-

hearts of believing Gentiles (15:9),[56] implying the justification of meal fellowship between believing Jews and Gentiles.[57]

After Peter's speech Barnabas and Paul expound on all the signs and wonders God did among the Gentiles through them (15:12; cf. 14:27; 15:4), indicating to the audience how the conversion of Gentiles has extended well beyond that of Cornelius and his household. Indeed, James explains how God has acquired from among the Gentiles a people for his name in accord with the scriptural words of the prophets (15:13-18).[58] Rather than require Gentiles to be circumcised and keep the law of Moses, as demanded by some of the party of the Pharisees who had become believers (15:5), James announces the apostolic decree by the whole church (15:22) that they should not trouble those from among the Gentiles who are turning to God (15:19).[59] All the Gentiles must do is avoid the eating of food polluted by idols, sexual immorality,[60] the eating of the meat of strangled animals, and the eating/drinking of blood

---

24.

[56] Matson, *Household Conversion*, 126: "Peter now interprets the cleansing of the Gentiles (καθαρίσας), as well as God's refusal to make distinctions (οὐθὲν διέκρινεν), no longer in a ceremonial sense (foods) but in a moral one: God has cleansed their hearts by faith (15.9)."

[57] Esler, *Community and Gospel*, 98: "The question of table-fellowship between Jew and Gentile is not explicitly raised in Acts 15, but its presence is everywhere implied."

[58] For an analysis of James's speech and its relation to the apostolic decree (15:19-21), see Soards, *Speeches in Acts*, 92-95; R. Bauckham, "James and the Gentiles (Acts 15.13-21)," *History, Literature, and Society in the Book of Acts* (ed. B. Witherington; Cambridge: Cambridge University Press, 1996) 154-84.

[59] On the significance of the apostolic decree as a decision of the whole church, which is formulated in official language and circulated in writing, see H. Cancik, "The History of Culture, Religion, and Institutions in Ancient Historiography: Philological Observations Concerning Luke's History," *JBL* 116 (1997) 677.

[60] On the linking of sexual immorality (πορνεία) with ritual food regulations, Polhill (*Acts*, 330-31) remarks: "It is possible that this category was also originally intended in a mainly ritual sense, referring to those 'defiling' sexual relationships the Old Testament condemns...The boundary between ritual and ethical law is not always distinct, and sexual morality is one of those areas where it is most blurred. For the Jew sexual misbehavior was

(15:20; cf. 15:28-29; 21:25).[61] The observance of these necessary things (15:28), the minimal regulations regarding ritual purity that are well known to believing Gentiles who hear Moses read in the synagogues in every town on every sabbath (15:21),[62] extends meal fellowship between believing Jews and Gentiles well beyond Peter's group and Cornelius's household.[63] It allows the gentile believers in Antioch, Syria, and Cilicia (15:23) to share meal fellowship with Jewish believers, who still practice circumcision and observe the law of Moses (21:20-25).[64]

---

[61] On the background, sources, and interpretive problems regarding the apostolic decree, in addition to the commentaries, see C. Perrot, "Les décisions de l'Assemblée de Jérusalem," *RSR* 69 (1981) 195-208; S. G. Wilson, *Luke and the Law* (SNTSMS 50; Cambridge: Cambridge University Press, 1983) 68-102; Esler, *Community and Gospel*, 97-99; M. A. Seifrid, "Jesus and the Law in Acts," *JSNT* 30 (1987) 39-57; N. Taylor, *Paul, Antioch and Jerusalem: A Study in Relationships and Authority in Earliest Christianity* (JSNTSup 66; Sheffield: Sheffield Academic Press, 1992) 140-42; H. van de Sandt, "An Explanation of Acts 15.6-21 in the Light of Deuteronomy 4.29-35 (LXX)," *JSNT* 46 (1992) 73-97; T. Callan, "The Background of the Apostolic Decree (Acts 15:20,29; 21:25)," *CBQ* 55 (1993) 284-97; A. J. M. Wedderburn, "The 'Apostolic Decree': Tradition and Redaction," *NovT* 35 (1993) 362-89; B. Witherington, "Not So Idle Thoughts About *Eidolothuton*," *TynBul* 44 (1993) 237-54; M. Bockmuehl, "The Noachide Commandments and New Testament Ethics with Special Reference to Acts 15 and Pauline Halakhah," *RB* 102 (1995) 72-101; H. R. Johne, "The Prohibitions in the Jerusalem Council's Letter to Gentile Believers," *Wisconsin Lutheran Quarterly* 94 (1997) 47-48. For a survey of the various interpretive positions, see J. Proctor, "Proselytes and Pressure Cookers: The Meaning and Application of Acts 15:20," *International Review of Mission* 85 (1996) 469-83.

[62] Acts 15:21 is related to the larger Lukan argument against the imposition of the law of Moses according to D. R. Schwartz, "The Futility of Preaching Moses (Acts 15,21)," *Bib* 67 (1986) 276-81.

[63] The apostolic decree does not contradict or place limits on the earlier elimination of the distinction between clean and unclean animals/people (10:11-15, 20, 28, 34-35; 11:5-9, 12). While certain animals and people are no longer to be considered unclean in themselves, the apostolic decree concerns other ways that food and people can be considered unclean or defiled.

[64] Matson, *Household Conversion*, 129: "Salvation of the Gentiles in Acts, therefore, consists not solely in freeing them from the constraints of circumcision and the law but in making them fellow members of the covenant community, sharing a common table with Jews."

Relation of Acts 10:1-11:18 to Previous Meal Scenes

1) Peter's meal fellowship with Cornelius and his household advances the *theme of meal hospitality offered to traveling missionaries*. Jesus instructed the twelve apostles (Luke 9:1-4) and the seventy-two disciples (10:6-8) not to take food for their missionary journeys, but to stay in whatever house welcomes them, accepting their meal hospitality. Jesus himself modeled these instructions when he accepted meal hospitality from Martha and Mary (Luke 10:38-42), from Zacchaeus (19:1-10), and from his disciples (24:41-43). Now Peter, as a traveling missionary (Acts 9:32-43), accepted meal hospitality in the Jewish household of Simon the tanner (9:43; 10:6, 18); he in turn extended that Jewish meal hospitality to those Gentiles sent by Cornelius (10:23). Then Peter and his Jewish companions (10:23, 45) accepted meal hospitality in the gentile household of Cornelius (10:48; 11:3). This opens the way for a reciprocal expansion of meal hospitality offered to and by missionaries. Not only may Gentiles enter Jewish households and share meal fellowship with Jews, but Jews may enter gentile households and share meal fellowship with Gentiles.

2) Peter's meal fellowship with Cornelius and his household develops the *theme of meals as contexts for conversion*. Jesus shared meal fellowship with Jewish tax collectors and sinners to call them to repentance (Luke 5:32; 15:7, 10; 19:5-10). In the context of the risen Jesus' restored meal fellowship with his disciples (24:41-43), including the repentant Peter (22:31-34; 24:12), he commissioned them to preach repentance for the forgiveness of sins to all the nations (24:47). Peter began this preaching to Jews in Jerusalem (Acts 2:14) when he called them to repent, be baptized and receive the holy Spirit (2:38). Those who repented celebrated with an ideal communal meal fellowship (2:42-47). Now, after Peter accepted meal hospitality from Cornelius and his household and preached the gospel to them, these Gentiles in Caesarea repented of their sins, were baptized and received the holy Spirit just like the Jews (10:43-48; 11:15-18). Whereas Jesus brought Jews to repentance by eating with them, Peter brought Gentiles to repentance by eating with them. Indeed, as the Jewish believers in Jerusalem acknowledged, "even to the Gentiles God has given the repentance that leads to life" (11:18). That means that even Gentiles will participate in the eschatological banquet.

Although Jesus also called to repentance those objecting to his meal fellowship with social outcasts and public sinners (Luke 5:30-32; 7:34; 15:1-2, 7, 10; 19:7, 10), they never expressed their repentance in the narrative. But now, not only did Peter and those Jews with him convert from their refusal to eat the unclean food that separates them from meal hospitality with Gentiles

(Acts 10:14-15, 23, 28; 11:8-9), but the Jewish believers in Jerusalem repented of their objection to Peter sharing meal hospitality with Gentiles. After Peter's words silenced their objection to his eating with the uncircumcised (11:3; cf. 15:7-9), their conclusion that "even to the Gentiles God has given the repentance that leads to life" (11:18) ironically expressed their own repentance.

3) Peter's meal fellowship with Cornelius and his household develops the *theme of meal fellowship with the newly baptized that unites them with the broader believing community*. Just as meal hospitality in their houses (Acts 2:46) united the newly baptized Jerusalem believers with all other believers (2:44), so the newly baptized Saul's meal hospitality in the house of Judas (9:11, 19) united him to the believing community at Damascus. Saul continued to accept the meal hospitality of the disciples in Damascus as he stayed with them "for some days" (9:19). This implied his sharing in their eucharistic meals, since the meal fellowship of an ideal believing community includes regular devotion to the eucharistic breaking of the bread (2:42, 46; cf. Luke 22:19). Now, Peter's sharing of meal hospitality in the house of Cornelius "for some days" (10:48) united these newly baptized Gentiles with him and the Jewish believers who accompanied him (10:45; cf. 10:23), implying their sharing of the eucharist.

4) Peter's meal fellowship with Cornelius and his household expands the *theme of eucharistic meal fellowship with the risen Jesus*. The meals that Peter and the other disciples shared with the risen Jesus (Luke 24:30-35, 41-43; Acts 1:4) not only demonstrated the reality of Jesus' resurrection but continued the meal fellowship he shared with his disciples during his ministry. They anticipated his invisible presence with them in the eucharistic meals he commanded them to keep doing in remembrance of him (Luke 22:19). Now, Peter has extended to the believing gentile assembly in Cornelius's household the eucharistic meal fellowship he shared with the risen Jesus as one of those who ate and drank with him (Acts 10:41).

Pragmatics of the Meal Scene in Acts 10:1-11:18

1) God's activity brought together Peter and his believing Jewish companions with Cornelius and his household in the sharing of meal fellowship that resulted in this community of Gentiles in Caesarea coming to faith. The audience is called *to imitate the openness and cooperation of Peter and Cornelius with God's activity* in bringing people of different racial, social, ethnic, religious and cultural backgrounds to faith in the gospel and leveling any barriers that prevent new believers from full social interaction, including meal fellowship, with the broader believing community.

2) By identifying with the conversion of Peter and the Jewish believers in Jerusalem, the audience shares the conviction that God does not consider any food or person unclean or profane in themselves (10:15, 26, 28; 11:9; 15:9), shows no partiality, and accepts those who fear God and act uprightly like Cornelius and his household (10:34-35; 11:18). This conviction empowers the audience to imitate Peter by *socially interacting with and preaching to any receptive people* the gospel of repentance for the forgiveness of sins (10:36-43).

3) The mutual and reciprocal meal hospitality shared by Peter and his Jewish household with Cornelius and his gentile household provides the audience with a *model for missionary strategy*. The audience is called not only to preach the gospel of repentance for the forgiveness of sins to all peoples but also to extend to the people to whom they preach the full social acceptance that the sharing of meal hospitality with them represents (11:18; 15:9, 19-21, 28-29; 21:25). Such meal hospitality can be the social context for their repentance and coming to faith.

4) The meal fellowship that Peter and his believing Jewish companions shared "for some days" (10:48) with Cornelius and the gentile assembly who came to faith in his house, implying their celebration of the eucharist, presents the audience with a *model for their own eucharistic celebrations*. The audience, like Peter, who ate and drank with the risen Lord (10:41), anticipating the Lord's invisible presence with those who celebrate the eucharistic meals he commanded them to keep doing in remembrance of him (Luke 22:19), is called to share the eucharist with the newly baptized in celebration of their entrance into the community of believers.

CHAPTER 16

PAUL'S REVIVAL OF EUTYCHUS AT A MEAL
ACTS 20:7-12

In the section dealing with turning to the Gentiles (11:19-14:28), the audience hears of a food shortage. Agabus, one of the prophets who came from Jerusalem to Antioch, predicted that there would be a severe famine all over the world, which happened under the Roman emperor Claudias. So the disciples decided to send relief in the care of Saul and Barnabas to the brothers who lived in Judea (11:28-30).[1] Also in this section the audience hears again how fasting is coupled with prayer to enhance its effectiveness at particularly decisive moments (13:2-3; 14:23; cf. Luke 2:37; 5:33). And, after Paul and Barnabas are mistaken for gods by the crowds at Lystra (14:11-12), they try to persuade them to turn from their idols to the living God of creation (14:15), who "fills you with food" (14:17).

In the section dealing with Paul's missionary preaching to the Greek world (15:36-18:22), the audience hears of a couple of instances of meal fellowship that Paul shares with newly baptized households at Philippi, first with the household of Lydia (16:11-15, 40) and then with the household of the Roman jailer (16:30-34). In the section dealing with Paul's reassurance and farewell (18:23-21:17) the audience meets the next major meal scene, Paul's revival of Eutychus at a meal (20:7-12).[2]

Paul's Meal Fellowship with the Baptized Household of Lydia at Philippi (16:11-15, 40)

The meal fellowship that Paul and his companions share with the newly baptized Lydia and her household at Philippi (16:11-15, 40) presents the audience with notable narrative progressions of the meal fellowship that Peter and his companions shared with the newly baptized household of Cornelius at

---

[1] B. W. Winter, "Acts and Food Shortages," *The Book of Acts in Its Graeco-Roman Setting* (The Book of Acts in Its First Century Setting 2; eds. D. W. J. Gill and C. Gempf; Grand Rapids: Eerdmans, 1994) 59-78.

[2] For a discussion of the above structural sections in Acts, see O'Fearghail, *Introduction to Luke-Acts*, 80-82.

Caesarea (10:1-11:18).[3] First, meal fellowship with Gentiles progresses from that of the missionary Peter to that of the missionary *Paul*. Second, missionary meal fellowship with Gentiles progresses geographically from Caesarea in Palestine to *Philippi* in Europe, a leading city in that district of Macedonia and a Roman colony (16:12).[4] Indeed, Lydia's hosting of Paul is the first meal fellowship mentioned since the beginning of Paul's mission in Acts 13 and the decision of the council of Jerusalem in Acts 15, which opened the way for Jewish believers to share meals with gentile believers.[5] Third, missionary meal fellowship progresses from a primary focus on gentile men to a primary focus on gentile *women*.

At a dramatic turning point in Paul's mission his "vision" (16:9, 10) at Troas of a Macedonian calling for help led him and his companions to conclude that God had called "us" to proclaim the gospel to the Macedonians

---

[3] On Paul's meal fellowship with the household of Lydia, in addition to the commentaries, see F. M. Gillman, "Early Christian Women at Philippi," *Journal of Gender in World Religions* 1 (1990) 59-79; F. Martin, "Le geôlier et la marchande de pourpre: Actes des Apôtres 16,6-40 (Première partie)," *Sémiotique et Bible* 59 (1990) 9-29; J. Gillman, "Hospitality in Acts 16," *LS* 17 (1992) 185-91; I. Richter Reimer, *Women in the Acts of the Apostles: A Feminist Liberation Perspective* (Minneapolis: Fortress, 1995) 71-149; J. Rius-Camps, "Pablo y el grupo 'nosotros' en Filipos: dos proyectos de evangelización en conflicto (Hch 16,11-40)," *Laurentianum* 36 (1995) 35-59; Matson, *Household Conversion*, 136-54.

[4] A case is made for accepting the most widely attested reading, "a first (leading) city of the district of Macedonia," by R. S. Ascough, "Civic Pride at Philippi: The Text-Critical Problem of Acts 16.12," *NTS* 44 (1998) 93-103. He concludes: "Whether the claim was known to be true or not, the title of 'first city' would have been heard as making this claim in the context of the competition for civic honour in antiquity" (p. 103).

[5] Matson, *Household Conversion*, 153: "Accepting Lydia's hospitality effectively marks a new direction for Paul...The way in which Lydia implores the missionary party to accept lodging in her house underscores the apparent novelty of the event."

(16:9-10).[6] After arriving in Philippi, they spent "some days" in that city (16:12).[7] This reminds the audience of the "vision" (10:3) of Cornelius at Caesarea and that of Peter at Joppa (10:17, 19; 11:5), by which God brought together these groups of Jewish and gentile believers for meal fellowship in the household of Cornelius for "some days" (10:48; cf. 9:19).[8]

While in Philippi on the day of the sabbath Paul and his companions went outside the city gate beside the river where they thought there would be a place of prayer (16:13).[9] "We" sat and spoke, which presumably included proclaiming the gospel (cf. 16:10), with "the women who came together"

---

[6] This introduces the first of the so-called "we" sections in Acts (16:10-17; 20:5-15; 21:1-18; 27:1-28:16), where the narrator speaks as one of Paul's companions. For the interpretive problems of these "we" passages, see S. M. Praeder, "The Problem of First Person Narration in Acts," *NovT* 29 (1987) 193-218; J. Wehnert, *Die Wir-Passagen der Apostelgeschichte: Ein lukanisches Stilmittel aus jüdischer Tradition* (GTA 40; Göttingen: Vandenhoeck & Ruprecht, 1989); S. E. Porter, "The 'We' Passages," *The Book of Acts in Its Graeco-Roman Setting* (The Book of Acts in Its First Century Setting 2; eds. D. W. J. Gill and C. Gempf; Grand Rapids: Eerdmans, 1994) 545-74. For a narrative-critical solution, see Kurz, *Reading Luke-Acts*, 111-24. Tannehill (*Narrative Unity*, 2.246-47) points out that "an anonymous and plural first-person narrator is well suited to increase imaginative participation in the narrative by readers or hearers of it. The anonymous 'we'--a participant narrator--is a special opportunity for us and others to enter the narrative as participants and to see ourselves as companions of Paul..."

[7] For recent archaeological, epigraphical, and historical discussions of Philippi, see L. Bormann, *Philippi: Stadt und Christengemeinde zur Zeit des Paulus* (NovTSup 78; Leiden: Brill, 1995); P. Pilhofer, *Philippi: Die erste christliche Gemeinde Europas* (WUNT 87; Tübingen: Mohr-Siebeck, 1995).

[8] On the similar function of these various visions to advance the narrative's plot, see Matson, *Household Conversion*, 141 n. 32.

[9] On the likelihood that this "place of prayer" ($\pi\rho o\sigma\epsilon\upsilon\chi\acute{\eta}$, in Acts only in 16:13, 16) was the synonymous equivalent of a synagogue, see Matson, *Household Conversion*, 144-45. After Richter Reimer's (*Women*, 72-92) extensive discussion of the question, she concludes: "The $\pi\rho o\sigma\epsilon\upsilon\chi\acute{\eta}$ in Philippi that is mentioned in Acts 16:13-16 can be no different from all the other $\pi\rho o\sigma\epsilon\upsilon\chi\alpha\acute{\iota}$ mentioned in the literary and inscriptional evidence. They are all synagogue buildings in which the Jewish community of a particular town or city gathers, primarily on the Sabbath, to worship God" (pp. 90-91).

there (16:13).[10] This focus on speaking with gathered *women* complements for the audience Peter's speaking (10:44) of the words of the gospel (10:36-43) primarily to the "many men who had come together" in the house of Cornelius (10:27).[11]

Furthermore, the focus on the prominent gentile man, the centurion Cornelius of the cohort called Italica (10:1), progresses to a complementary focus on the prominent gentile woman, Lydia, a dealer in purple cloth, from the city of Thyatira (16:14).[12] Whereas Cornelius was a devout and God-fearing Gentile with all his household (10:2), Lydia was likewise a gentile

---

[10] After Richter Reimer's (*Women*, 72-78) discussion of the significance of "speaking" that refers to preaching to a gathered assembly at a place of prayer, she concludes "that the missionaries spent their Sabbath in the same way as in the other places where, according to their custom, they participated in Jewish worship" (p. 78).

[11] That the primary focus is on the gentile *men* in the Cornelius story is confirmed by the charge of "those of the circumcision" in Jerusalem that Peter entered the house and ate with "uncircumcised men" (11:2-3).

[12] Thyatira was located in the Asian region of Lydia, so that the name "Lydia" could also be a designation of origin. On the name "Lydia," see Gillman, "Hospitality," 185-86. On Thyatira as a center of the purple-dye industry, see Richter Reimer, *Women*, 104; Matson, *Household Conversion*, 143. Most commentators deduce that Lydia, as a dealer in purple-cloth, which was a luxury item worn by the rich (see Luke 16:19), must have been a person of some economic status, since she is able to offer hospitality to missionaries. But after pointing out that Lydia's profession was considered the dirty work of slaves and freed persons, Richter Reimer (*Women*, 112) concludes that "it is probable that the income of her house made possible a better economic state of things than the lot of beggars. But still, as foreigners from the East who carried on a despised trade and also practiced the Jewish religion in that Roman colony, they belonged to the *plebs urbana*, the common people...They are not to be equated with the great merchants of the period." Although perhaps not a "rich" merchant, Lydia nevertheless "acts as a kind of patron to Paul" according to J. H. Neyrey, "Luke's Social Location of Paul: Cultural Anthropology and the Status of Paul in Acts," *History, Literature, and Society in the Book of Acts* (ed. B. Witherington; Cambridge: Cambridge University Press, 1996) 265. See also B. Blue, "Acts and the House Church," *The Book of Acts in Its Graeco-Roman Setting* (The Book of Acts in Its First Century Setting 2; eds. D. W. J. Gill and C. Gempf; Grand Rapids: Eerdmans, 1994) 184-86; Osiek and Balch, *Families*, 97-98.

worshiper of God (16:14).[13] Cornelius and all those gathered in his house were eager "to listen" to everything commanded to Peter by the Lord (10:33). Similarly, as Lydia "was listening," the Lord opened her heart to pay attention to the things spoken by Paul (16:14). After Peter commanded that Cornelius and those gathered in his house be baptized, they asked him to stay (ἐπιμεῖναι) for some days (10:48), which includes their sharing of meal fellowship. Similarly, after Lydia and her house were baptized, she prevailed upon Paul and his companions to enter and stay (μένετε) in her gentile house, implying their sharing of meal fellowship (16:15).

By "entering into the house" of Lydia and staying (μένετε) there (16:15), the missionary Paul and his companions, like the missionary Peter and his companions in the Cornelius story (10:48), model for the audience the obedient fulfillment of Jesus' instructions regarding the reliance upon and acceptance of meal hospitality offered to traveling missionaries. As the audience recalls, Jesus instructed missionaries that "in whatever house you enter you are to stay (μένετε)" there (Luke 9:4), and that they are to eat and drink whatever is offered them "in the same house in which you stay (μένετε)" (Luke 10:7; see also 10:8). By entering into Lydia's house and staying there, Paul and his associates accept her hospitality toward them as traveling missionaries, which includes their sharing of meal fellowship with her and her household.[14]

---

[13] On the designation of Lydia as a "worshiper of God" (σεβομένη τὸν θεόν), Johnson (Acts, 293) states: "Luke's usage is sufficiently flexible to make it impossible to know for certain whether the designation in this case means that she was a Gentile attracted to the synagogue's teachings, or whether she was in fact a pious Jew." But whenever the participial forms of σέβομαι (worship) or its synonymous variant φοβέομαι (fear) are used with God as object in Acts (10:2, 22, 35; 13:16, 26, 43, 50; 16:14; 17:4, 17; 18:6-7), they always distinguish Gentiles from Jews and are never used to describe Jews. On Lydia and other "God-fearers/worshipers" as gentile adherents of Jewish synagogues in Acts, see H. Balz, "φοβέομαι," EDNT 3.431; I. Levinskaya, "The Inscription from Aphrodisias and the Problem of God-Fearers," TynBul 41 (1990) 312-18; idem, Diaspora Setting, 120-26; Blue, "House Church," 182; Matson, Household Conversion, 144.

[14] The combination of "entering a house" and "staying" there is a signal to the audience of the sharing of meal fellowship (see also Luke 19:5; 24:29). According to Matson (Household Conversion, 148), "As a word belonging to the table-fellowship matrix in the Gospel of Luke, μένω implies a fellowship meal."

The hosting of the traveling Paul by Lydia reminds the audience of the hosting of Jesus on his final journey to Jerusalem by the sisters Martha and Mary (Luke 10:38-42). Martha and Mary were complementary models of discipleship for the audience, as they respectively demonstrated the listening and doing of the word of the gospel. Mary's necessary listening (ἤκουεν) of the word of Jesus (10:39), her choice of the "best portion" (10:42), complemented Martha's serving of the meal.[15] By herself Lydia models for the audience both the listening and doing of the word by a disciple. After intently listening (ἤκουεν), so that the Lord opened her heart to pay attention to the things spoken by Paul (Acts 16:14), that is, the gospel (16:10), the baptized Lydia urged and prevailed upon Paul to accept her hospitality, implying her serving him a meal (16:15).[16]

The meal fellowship shared by Paul and his companions with Lydia and her household develops for the audience the theme of meal fellowship with the newly baptized that unites them with the broader believing community. Meal fellowship in their houses (2:46) united the newly baptized Jerusalem believers with all other believers (2:44); the newly baptized Saul's meal fellowship in the house of Judas (9:11, 19) united him to the believing community at Damascus; Peter's meal fellowship in the house of Cornelius (10:48) united these newly baptized Gentiles with him and the Jewish believers who accompanied him (10:45; cf. 10:23). Now, Lydia desires for herself and her household, as newly baptized gentile converts, the meal fellowship with Paul and his companions that will incorporate them into the believing community as full participants. She "urged" (παρεκάλεσεν) Paul and his company, "If you have judged me to be a believer in the Lord" (16:15), that is, as no longer just a "worshiper of God" (16:14) but now as a true believer in the Lord Jesus (cf. 16:31), then they must enter into her house and stay for meal fellowship (16:15).[17]

---

[15] For a full discussion of Jesus' meal with Martha and Mary, see chapter 5.

[16] Matson, *Household Conversion*, 148: "Like Mary before her, Lydia's 'listening' is followed in due course by the celebration of a meal." See also Richter Reimer, *Women*, 126.

[17] Lydia's use of the word "believer" (πιστὴν) to designate herself as a believer in the Lord previously designated the Jewish men accompanying Peter (πιστοὶ, 10:45) and the Jewish mother (πιστῆς, 16:1) of Timothy, who had become believers in the Lord Jesus. Now Lydia uses it to underline her conversion from a gentile "worshiper of God" to a true Christian believer. As Conzelmann (*Acts*, 130) notes, "πιστήν, 'faithful,' is used here instead of σεβομένη, 'worshiper' (cf. vs 14), to reflect the change which has occurred in the life of this woman." See also Gillman, "Hospitality," 187 n. 17, 188-89.

Saul's meal fellowship with the Damascus disciples "for some days" (9:19) and Peter's meal fellowship with the gentile household of Cornelius "for some days" (10:48) implied their sharing of eucharistic meals, since, as the audience recalls, the meal fellowship of an ideal believing community includes regular devotion to the eucharistic breaking of the bread (2:42, 46; cf. Luke 22:19). So also the staying of Paul and his companions for meal fellowship with the household of Lydia at Philippi "for some days" (16:12) implies their sharing of the eucharist.[18]

The way Paul's meal fellowship with the household of Lydia resonates for the audience with Jesus' eucharistic breaking of bread for the Emmaus disciples (Luke 24:28-35) strengthens its eucharistic implications. After the Emmaus disciples "prevailed upon" (παρεβιάσαντο) Jesus, he entered (εἰσῆλθεν) to stay (μεῖναι) with them (Luke 24:29). Similarly, Lydia "prevailed upon" (παρεβιάσατο) Paul and his companions to enter (εἰσελθόντες) into her house and stay (μένετε) (Acts 16:15).[19] After the eyes of the Emmaus disciples were opened (διηνοίχθησαν) and they recognized the risen Jesus (Luke 24:31) in his eucharistic breaking of the bread for them (Luke 24:30, 35; cf. 22:19), they remarked how their heart (καρδία) was burning within them as he spoke (ἐλάλει) to them on the way, as he opened (διήνοιγεν) for them the scriptures (Luke 24:32). Similarly, the Lord opened the heart (διήνοιξεν τὴν καρδίαν) of Lydia to pay attention to the things spoken (λαλουμένοις) by Paul (Acts 16:14) before he shared meal fellowship with her and her household (Acts 16:15).[20]

That Lydia had to "urge" and "force" or "prevail upon" Paul and his companions to enter and stay in her house (16:15) indicates to the audience the reluctance of these Jewish believers to share meal fellowship with Gentiles,

---

[18] Matson, *Household Conversion*, 148: "As in the story of Cornelius, the meals celebrated in the house of Lydia no doubt involved the Eucharist."

[19] That these are the only two occurrences of the verb "prevail upon" (παραβιάζομαι) in the whole of Luke-Acts (as well as in the NT) enhances the connection. See also Johnson, *Acts*, 293. Richter Reimer (*Women*, 124) suggests that Lydia's "prevailing upon" Paul and his companions is an attempt to protect them as guests of her household from the Roman authorities.

[20] According to Matson (*Household Conversion*, 148-49), the "fascinating parallels" between the Emmaus account and the story of Lydia "suggest that Paul's eating in the house of Lydia was similarly eucharistic in nature."

even newly-baptized Gentiles.[21] But just as Peter, the Jewish believers accompanying him, and his Jewish accusers in Jerusalem came to realize that God had broken down the barriers preventing Jewish believing men from sharing meal fellowship with gentile believing men (10:1-11:18), so now Paul and his companions realize that God has broken down the barriers preventing them as believing Jewish men from sharing meal fellowship with believing gentile women.[22] Indeed, Lydia's house seems to have become a gathering place for the believers at Philippi, whether they be Jew or Gentile, male or female. When the Jewish believers, Paul and his companions, came out of the prison, they again entered Lydia's gentile house where they saw and encouraged the brothers (ἀδελφοὺς), that is, the entire believing community gathered there (16:40).[23]

Paul's Meal with the Baptized Roman Jailer and His Household at Philippi (16:30-34)

The celebratory meal that Paul and Silas share with the newly baptized Roman jailer and his whole household marks for the audience another significant advance in missionary meal fellowship with Gentiles. The missionary Peter and his Jewish companions shared meal fellowship with a

---

[21] Esler, *Community and Gospel*, 100-101; Gillman, "Hospitality," 188: "The missionaries are reluctant to accept Lydia's offer because she is a gentile. To accept the invitation would also put them in a position of sharing table fellowship with gentiles."

[22] Matson, *Household Conversion*, 152: "By placing the story of Lydia in such close proximity to the Jerusalem Council, the narrator extends the community's decision to include gentile women as well. In this way Lydia functions as a kind of female 'Cornelius', who is accepted by the Lord for hearing the word of God and heeding it."

[23] On the term "brothers" here, Matson (*Household Conversion*, 149 n. 69) states: "Here is an example where the text itself demands inclusive gender translation (NRSV: 'brothers and sisters') of a masculine term. The 'brothers' certainly included Lydia!" According to Gillman ("Hospitality," 190), "For the first time those in Lydia's household are called *adelphoi*, 'brothers and sisters,' a familial term commonly used for believers...If the missionaries have been portrayed as hesitant about accepting Lydia's initial offer of hospitality, they are no longer so depicted on their return visit. This return visit suggests that initially they were not simply yielding to pressure, but were sincere about staying with a gentile convert."

newly baptized gentile centurion named Cornelius and his household (10:1-11:18), who had been God-fearers associated with Jews (10:2). Then the missionary Paul and his Jewish companions shared meal fellowship with the newly baptized gentile household of a prominent woman named Lydia, who had worshiped God along with Jews (16:11-15). Now, Paul and Silas share a meal with the newly baptized household of an *anonymous* Roman jailer, who had been not a God-fearer but a *pagan Gentile* unassociated with the Jewish worship of God (16:30-34).[24]

Unlike Cornelius and Lydia, named Gentiles who were already notable God-fearers when they converted, the Roman jailer converted as an anonymous pagan Gentile after experiencing a worship-induced, miraculous earthquake, which freed Paul and Silas (16:25-26), the prisoners the jailer was specifically instructed by his Roman superiors to guard securely (16:23-24). When the shaken Roman jailer was about to dutifully kill himself, thinking that his prisoners had escaped, Paul assured him that they were all still within the prison (16:27-28). Overcome with fearful awe for Paul and Silas (16:29), the jailer led them out of the prison and indicated his willingness to convert by asking, "Sirs, what must I do to be saved?" (16:30).[25]

The reply of Paul and Silas includes not only the jailer but his entire household. After Paul and Silas exhort the jailer to believe in the Lord Jesus to be saved, their emphatic expression that "you will be saved--*you and your household*" (16:31) accentuates for the audience the communal dimension of the Roman jailer's conversion. It reminds the audience of the conversion of Cornelius with its similar emphatic inclusion of his entire household. The angel told Cornelius that Peter would speak words to him by which "you will be saved--*you and all your household*" (11:14).

---

[24] On the scene of Paul's meal with the Roman jailer and his household, in addition to the commentaries, see Menoud, "Acts of the Apostles and the Eucharist," 89-90; Martin, "Le geôlier," 9-29; Tannehill, *Narrative Unity*, 2.198-201; Gillman, "Hospitality," 192-94; C. S. de Vos, "The Significance of the Change from οἶκος to οἰκία in Luke's Account of the Philippian Gaoler (Acts 16.30-4)," *NTS* 41 (1995) 292-96; Matson, *Household Conversion*, 154-68.

[25] Discussing the similarities between this episode involving the mission to Gentiles in Philippi and the apostles' mission to Jews in Jerusalem (Acts 2-5), Tannehill (*Narrative Unity*, 2.200) notes that the jailer's question "combines the question following the Pentecost sermon (2:37: 'What should we do, brothers?') with Peter's reply (2:40: 'Be saved from this crooked generation')."

That Paul and Silas then spoke the word of the Lord to the Roman jailer "together with all those in his house" (16:32) continues the emphatic inclusion of the jailer's *entire household* in his conversion.[26] In correspondence to the emphatic expression that "you will be saved--*you and hour household*" (16:31), the jailer "was baptized--*he and all his*" (ἐβαπτίσθη αὐτὸς καὶ οἱ αὐτοῦ πάντες, 16:33). In this emphatic inclusion of the jailer's entire household to make this a communal baptism the audience hears the echo of how Lydia's baptism likewise included her household (ἐβαπτίσθη καὶ ὁ οἶκος αὐτῆς, 16:15), and how all those in the household of Cornelius were baptized with him (10:47-48).

The emphasis upon the conversion not only of the Roman jailer but of his *entire household* reaches its climax as the jailer brought Paul and Silas up "into the house," provided a meal, and rejoiced "with all the household" at coming to believe in God (16:34).[27] The Roman jailer, who compassionately washed the wounds of Paul and Silas (16:33; cf. 16:22-23), completes his hospitable care for his former prisoners as he provides them a much needed

---

[26] According to de Vos ("Philippian Gaoler," 292-96), the change from οἶκος in 16:31 to οἰκία in 16:32 indicates a reference to two different groups. A simpler, more likely explanation is that οἶκος in 16:31 refers to the personified household of the jailer whereas οἰκία in 16:32 refers to the architectural dwelling of the jailer's house. "All those in his house" simply designates all those who live in the house of the jailer, that is, the members of his household. It does not necessarily indicate that the missionary proclamation took place in the house. Indeed, the entrance into the house is not narrated until after the baptism in 16:34; cf. Gillman, "Hospitality," 193; Matson, *Household Conversion*, 160-61.

[27] For the plausible suggestion that ἀναγαγών ("brought up") is used here because the rooms in the cellar below the house proper served as the prison, see BAGD, 53. Whereas οἰκία was used for the reference to all those who live in the house of the jailer (16:32), οἶκος, which earlier referred to the personified household of the jailer (16:31), is now used for the climactic entrance of Paul and Silas into the jailer's house (16:34; cf. 16:15). The term πανοικεὶ is strategically situated between the words "rejoiced" (ἠγαλλιάσατο) and "come to believe" (πεπιστευκὼς) to indicate that "all the household" both rejoiced with and came to believe with the Roman jailer. That the jailer and all his household came to believe in God (16:34) complements the exhortation for the jailer to believe (πίστευσον) in the Lord Jesus in order for him and his household to be saved (16:31).

meal.[28] But the meal also serves as the setting for the jubilant celebration of the conversion of this newly baptized household. That the jailer rejoiced with all the household at coming to believe in God underscores for the audience that these are *pagan* Gentiles who now for the first time truly believe in God. Unlike the gentile households of Cornelius and of Lydia, who already believed in God but came to believe in the Lord Jesus, the household of the Roman jailer, in coming to believe in the Lord Jesus to be saved (16:31), also finally came to believe in the true God.[29] These newly baptized pagan converts appropriately celebrate their new found faith during a meal with Paul and Silas, the missionaries who brought them to faith.

The celebratory meal shared by Paul and Silas with the Roman jailer and his whole household continues to develop for the audience the pattern of meal fellowship with the newly baptized, which completes their initiation into the believing community as fellow members. Meal fellowship with already believing communities closely followed upon the baptisms of the first Jewish believers in Jerusalem (2:44, 46), of the Jewish Saul in Damascus (9:11, 19), of the gentile but God-fearing Cornelius and his household in Caesarea (10:23, 45, 48), of the gentile but God-worshiping Lydia and her household in Philippi (16:15), and now of the Roman jailer and his household in Philippi (16:34). But with the meal of the jailer and his household the audience for the first time experiences the meal fellowship that initiates a formerly *pagan* and thoroughly *Roman* gentile household into the believing community.

Although the expression "provided a meal," literally "set a table" (16:34), is not in itself a designation for the eucharist, the combination of all the special circumstances as well as the total narrative context of this meal

---

[28] Gillman ("Hospitality," 193) draws an interesting comparison between the Roman jailer and the good Samaritan, who likewise demonstrated remarkable hospitality toward a wounded traveler (Luke 10:30-37). Just as the Samaritan, after caring for the wounds of the traveler, generously provided for his lodging at an inn (10:34-35), which implies the provision of meals, so the Roman jailer, after washing the wounds of Paul and Silas, brought them into his house and provided them a meal.

[29] Whereas the newly baptized Lydia, already a "worhsiper of God" (16:14), wanted to be confirmed as a "believer in the Lord (Jesus)" (16:15), the newly baptized jailer and his household, having been exhorted "to believe in the Lord Jesus" (16:31), rejoiced at "coming to believe in God" (16:34).

causes it to resonate with eucharistic overtones in the ears of the audience.[30] The special circumstances of this meal point to a eucharist: That it occurs at an unusual time--past midnight (cf. 16:25, 33)--underscores its character as a spontaneous celebration of salvation.[31] Indeed, the very nature of the meal as a celebration of faith in God (16:34) and in the Lord Jesus for salvation (16:31) indicates the appropriateness of a eucharist. That all of the previous instances of meal fellowship with the newly baptized exhibited eucharistic connotations makes a eucharistic meal likely here as well.

The noteworthy expression for the meal, "set a table" ($\pi\alpha\rho\acute{\epsilon}\theta\eta\kappa\epsilon\nu$ $\tau\rho\acute{\alpha}\pi\epsilon\zeta\alpha\nu$, 16:34), reminds the audience of the institution of the eucharist at Jesus' last supper, which contains two significant occurrences of the word "table" ($\tau\rho\acute{\alpha}\pi\epsilon\zeta\alpha$).[32] Luke uses the word "table" at Jesus' institution of the eucharist not only as a figurative reference to the meal but to accentuate the special meal or table fellowship involved in sharing at a common table the bread and wine designated as Jesus' sacrificial body and blood.[33] Jesus' pronouncement that "the hand of the one betraying me is with me at the table ($\dot{\epsilon}\pi\grave{\iota}$ $\tau\hat{\eta}\varsigma$ $\tau\rho\alpha\pi\acute{\epsilon}\zeta\eta\varsigma$)" (Luke 22:21) is especially horrifying for the audience, because it indicates that Judas's betrayal violates not just ordinary table fellowship but *eucharistic* table fellowship. But the disciples who have remained with Jesus throughout his trials (22:28) and have shared in the table

---

[30] That the expression for the meal does not in itself designate a eucharist is noted by Conzelmann, *Acts*, 133; R. Pesch, *Die Apostelgeschichte (Apg 13-28)* (EKK V/2; Zürich: Benziger, 1986) 116; Polhill, *Acts*, 356 n. 40. I cannot, however, agree with Polhill's wording: "The *text* gives no warrant for seeing the 'meal' as the Lord's Supper" (my emphasis). I will argue below that the text and context does imply a eucharistic meal. As R. I. Pervo (*Luke's Story of Paul* [Minneapolis: Fortress, 1990] 58) states: "This is not explicitly described as a eucharist, but the allusions are plain. Every meal in Luke-Acts has dimensions that intimate the Eucharist."

[31] Tannehill, *Narrative Unity*, 2.200; Matson, *Household Conversion*, 163: "The lateness of the hour suggests that the food served on this occasion was more than a meal; it was, in fact, a celebration of salvation."

[32] That among the four Gospels only Luke employs the word "table" ($\tau\rho\acute{\alpha}\pi\epsilon\zeta\alpha$) at Jesus' institution of the eucharist (Luke 22:21, 30) enhances the connection and thus the eucharistic connotation of the Roman jailer's "table" (Acts 16:34); see Matson, *Household Conversion*, 164.

[33] Paul uses the expression "table of the Lord" ($\tau\rho\alpha\pi\acute{\epsilon}\zeta\eta\varsigma$ $\kappa\upsilon\rho\acute{\iota}o\upsilon$) for the eucharist (1 Cor 10:21) in a context underlining its special meal or table fellowship; see Matson, *Household Conversion*, 164 n. 131.

fellowship of the eucharist (22:19-20) will again share table fellowship with Jesus by eating and drinking "at my table" (ἐπὶ τῆς τραπέζης μου) at the eschatological banquet in "my kingdom" (22:30).[34] The Roman jailer's "table" (Acts 16:34) thus recalls for the audience the special eucharistic "table" fellowship of Jesus' last supper, which anticipates the final "table" fellowship with Jesus at the eschatological banquet.[35]

That the meal was the setting at which the jailer "rejoiced" (ἠγαλλιάσατο) with all the household at coming to believe in God (16:34) echoes for the audience how the newly baptized believers in Jerusalem were sharing food and the eucharistic breaking of bread "with gladness" (ἐν ἀγαλλιάσει, 2:46).[36] Just as the Jerusalem believers celebrated their salvation with eschatological joy at eucharistic meals (2:42, 46), so the rejoicing of the Roman jailer and all his household in coming to the faith that means their salvation (16:30-31) imbues their special meal with a eucharistic association.

Like the missionary Peter and his companions (10:48) and the missionary Paul and his companions (16:15), the missionaries Paul and Silas model for the audience the obedient fulfillment of Jesus' instructions regarding the acceptance of meal hospitality offered to traveling missionaries. By readily accepting the meal the jailer "set before" (παρέθηκεν) them in his house which they had entered (16:34), Paul and Silas fulfill Jesus' instruction that missionaries are to eat and drink whatever is "set before" (παρατιθέμενα) them in whatever house they enter and are welcomed (Luke 10:8).[37]

---

[34] On the references to the eucharistic "table" at Jesus' last supper, see chapter 11.

[35] Matson, *Household Conversion*, 164: "Every meal in Luke and Acts is a proleptic celebration of the coming kingdom of God, including that of the jailer and his household."

[36] In reference to the verb used for the "rejoicing" of the jailer and his household, Tannehill (*Narrative Unity*, 2.200) points out: "The description of the jailer's joy with this unusual and strong verb (it and the related noun occur in Acts only in 2:46; 16:34; and in a Scripture quotation in 2:26) links the jailer with the early converts in Jerusalem...In both the early Jerusalem church and in the jailer's house this exultation accompanies a meal that is evidently a celebration of salvation." See also Matson, *Household Conversion*, 164. For more on the eucharistic breaking of bread "with gladness" in Jerusalem (2:42, 46), see chapter 14.

[37] As Trummer ("παρατίθημι," 22) notes, the verb παρατίθημι in Luke 10:8 and Acts 16:34 "designates the serving of food as a sign of

Peter demonstrated great hesitancy before sharing meal fellowship with the God-fearing Cornelius because he was a Gentile. Because the God-worshiping Lydia was a gentile woman, she had to urge and prevail upon an apparently hesitant Paul and his companions to enter "into my house" and stay for an implied meal (16:15). Now, in a most remarkable and striking contrast for the audience, Paul and Silas show absolutely no hesitancy whatsoever when the Roman jailer brought them up "into the house," the house of a formerly *pagan* Gentile, for the hospitality of an explicitly provided meal (16:34).[38] This indicates to the audience a further stunning advance in the breaking down of the social and dietary barriers preventing Jews from sharing meal fellowship with Gentiles. Indeed, concern for the Jewish food laws no longer seems to be an issue.[39] Paul and Silas show that Jewish missionaries can share meal fellowship not only with God-worshiping Gentiles like Lydia and her household but even with pagan Gentiles like the Roman jailer and his household.[40]

The meal at the house of the Roman jailer benefits both parties. From the side of the newly baptized jailer and his household the meal completes their initiation into the believing community. From the side of Paul and Silas the meal in the house of the Roman jailer proves that the accusation which imprisoned them was false. Their accusers had charged: "These men are disturbing our city, being Jews, and are proclaiming customs that are not

---

hospitality."

[38] As Matson (*Household Conversion*, 166) perceptively points out, "the story of the jailer contains an explicit meal scene that is lacking in the story of Lydia: the jailer 'set a table' before them (16.34). This expression makes explicit what was only implicit in the story of Lydia, namely, Paul's stay in the house for the purpose of 'table-fellowship'." See also Blue, "House Church," 186.

[39] In the words of Matson (*Household Conversion*, 167), "the conversion of the Roman jailer stands as a radical act on the pages of Acts. It not only entails preaching to an outright pagan but a flagrant disregard of Jewish dietary concerns."

[40] Blue, "House Church," 186 n. 260. According to Matson (*Household Conversion*, 166), "if Lydia and her household become Paul's first

permitted for us to receive or do, being Romans" (16:20-21).[41] But Paul and
Silas have been accepted into the house of a Roman official for a meal without
observance of the Jewish dietary customs.[42] The Roman jailer and his
household became believers without receiving or doing Jewish customs
contrary to Roman law. Indeed, by sharing a meal with the Roman jailer and
his household, Paul and Silas have demonstrated that they are not only Jews
but Romans as well.[43] The meal that the missionaries Paul and Silas share
with the newly baptized Roman jailer and his household indicates to the
audience that God has now opened the way for the gospel to enter into pagan
Roman society.

Paul Revives Eutychus at the Breaking of the Bread (20:7-12)

*7 On the first day of the week when we gathered to break bread, Paul
was speaking with them; because he was going to depart the next day, he
prolonged the speech until midnight. 8 There were, however, enough lamps in
the upstairs room where we were gathered.*

*9 A young man named Eutychus, who was sitting in the window, was
sinking into a deep sleep as Paul was speaking at great length. Overcome by
sleep, he fell down from the third floor and was taken up dead. 10 But going
down, Paul fell upon him, and embracing him, said, "Do not be alarmed, for
his life is in him."*

(gentile) hosts, the jailer and his household become his first pagan hosts."

[41] The accusers at Philippi were Jews who claimed to be loyal Romans,
according to D. R. Schwartz, "The Accusation and the Accusers at Philippi
(Acts 16,20-21)," *Bib* 65 (1984) 357-63. But according to Tannehill
(*Narrative Unity*, 2.201), "there is no indication of Jewish opposition. The
role of stirring up opposition, attributed to Jews in 13:50 and 14:2, 19, is
taken by the Gentile owners of the slave girl, who speak as Romans opposed to
subversive Jewish preachers."

[42] Matson, *Household Conversion*, 167: "The 'customs' (ἔθη) which
they are accused of bringing to Philippi almost certainly included the Jewish
food laws since these were part and parcel of the Jewish faith and one of its
most distinguishing features."

[43] Tannehill, *Narrative Unity*, 2.201: "Paul and Silas belong to Roman
society in spite of the fact that their accusers dismissed them as Jews."
Matson, *Household Conversion*, 167: "Paul and Silas show themselves to be
Romans by staying in a Roman house and eating Roman food. They are not

11 Then going upstairs, he broke bread and ate, continuing to talk at length until daybreak. Thus he departed. 12 They took the boy away alive and were encouraged immeasurably.[44]

They gathered with Paul in the upstairs room for the breaking of the bread (20:7-8)

In Paul's farewell meal with the community at Troas echoes both of Jesus' last supper, at which he instituted the eucharist, and of the risen Jesus' eucharistic meals with his disciples reverberate in the ears of the audience. Jesus' last supper, a farewell Passover meal with his disciples, was occasioned by the plot of the Jewish leaders to put him to death (Luke 22:2, 15) and took place on the day of the feast of Unleavened Bread (Luke 22:7; cf. 22:1). Similarly, Paul's last, farewell meal with the community at Troas was occasioned by a travel change due to the plot made against him by the Jews in Greece (20:3) and took place after the days of Unleavened Bread (20:6; cf. 12:3).

That the meal at Troas occurred "on the first day of the week" (20:7) reminds the audience that not only the revelation of Jesus' resurrection but also the meals at which the disciples experienced eucharistic table fellowship with the risen Jesus (Luke 24:28-35, 41-43) likewise occurred "on the first day of the week" (Luke 24:1).[45] Reminiscent of the eucharistic "breaking of the bread" (2:42, 46) by the first believers in Jerusalem in fulfillment of Jesus' instruction to "keep doing this in remembrance of me" after he "broke" the bread while instituting the eucharist (Luke 22:19), the believers at Troas gathered together on the first day of the week "to break bread" (20:7). As the audience recalls, it was in the eucharistic "breaking of the bread" that the Emmaus disciples first experienced Jesus as risen from the dead (Luke 24:35).

The notice that "we" gathered on the first day of the week to break bread (20:7) underscores the communal dimension of this meal scene and

---

simply Romans politically, they are Romans culturally as well."

[44] On the meal scene in 20:7-12, in addition to the commentaries, see Menoud, "Acts of the Apostles and the Eucharist," 90-95; B. Trémel, "A propos d'Actes 20,7-12: Puissance du thaumaturge ou du témoin?" *RTP* 112 (1980) 359-69; Tannehill, *Narrative Unity*, 2.247-51; A. D. Bulley, "Hanging in the Balance: A Semiotic Study of Acts 20:7-12," *Église et Théologie* 25 (1994) 171-88.

[45] That these are the only occurrences of the phrase, "on the first day

facilitates the imaginative participation of the audience.[46] In the context of a communal gathering for the eucharistic breaking of the bread Paul extends his speech until midnight because he was going to depart the next day (20:7). There were enough lamps in the room to allow for this extension into the darkness of midnight (20:8).

That the gathering for the meal took place in the upstairs room (ἐν τῷ ὑπερῴῳ, 20:8) provides the audience with yet another allusion to Jesus' institution of the eucharist, which similarly took place in an upper room (ἀνάγαιον, Luke 22:12). The upstairs room for the eucharistic meal at Troas also reminds the audience of Peter's restoration to life of the dead Tabitha in Joppa in an upstairs room (ὑπερῴῳ, 9:37, 39; cf. 1:13).[47] The double notice that "we gathered" (20:7, 8), which forms a literary inclusion defining this introductory unit of the meal scene, reinforces the audience's participation in the communal setting of the meal with Paul.[48]

At the eucharistic meal Paul restores Eutychus to life (20:9-10)

One of those who had gathered for the meal and farewell speech of Paul was a young man whose noteworthy name of Eutychus, meaning "lucky" or "fortunate one," may already give the audience a hint of his significance for this meal scene.[49] Sitting in the window of the upstairs room, Eutychus was

---

of the week," in Luke-Acts enhances the connection.

[46] The meal scene at Troas occurs within the second (20:5-15) of the so-called "we" sections in Acts. On the "we" sections and their function of facilitating audience participation, see n. 6 above.

[47] On the similarities between Peter's raising of Tabitha (9:36-42) and Paul's raising of Eutychus (20:7-12), Tannehill (*Narrative Unity*, 2.247) states: "Both are stories of death and life, both concern a Christian disciple who is named, and both refer to an 'upper room (ὑπερῷον).'"

[48] Tannehill, *Narrative Unity*, 2.247: "A first-person narrator is a focalizing channel through whom the story is experienced. Our experience of events is limited to the experience of the first-person narrator, and this common experience creates a bond of identification. The anonymous 'we' is a focalizing channel without clear definition, except as companions of Paul, making it easy for many individuals, and even a community, to identify with the narrator."

[49] On the meaning of the name Eutychus, see Pesch, *Apostelgeschichte*, 2.191; Johnson, *Acts*, 356. Recall the similar appropriateness of the name Lazarus, meaning "he whom God helps" (Luke 16:20), for the meal scene in

sinking into a deep sleep as Paul continued to speak at great length. Finally overcome by sleep, he fell down from the third floor and was taken up dead (20:9).[50] That Eutychus was taken up "dead" allows the audience to assimilate him to the dead Tabitha, whom Peter restored to life (9:36-41), as well as to the dead daughter of Jairus and the dead son of the widow at Nain, both of whom Jesus restored to life (Luke 8:49-56; 7:11-15).[51]

The noteworthy gestures of Paul toward the dead body as well as his reassuring words indicate to the audience that the life of Eutychus has been miraculously restored. Going down from the upstairs room, Paul "fell upon" the body of the dead Eutychus, and "embracing him," said to those gathered for the meal, "Do not be alarmed, for his life is in him" (20:10).[52] The audience recalls Peter's similar gesture of "turning to the body" of the dead Tabitha when he uttered the powerful words that miraculously restored her to life, "Tabitha, rise up!" (9:40). The audience also recalls the life-restoring gestures and words of Jesus, who took the dead daughter of Jairus by the hand and called to her, "Child, arise!" (Luke 8:54), and who came forward and

---

Luke 16:19-31 (see chapter 8).

[50] The ground floor is to be counted as the first of the three floors or stories; see D. F. Deer, "Getting the 'Story' Straight in Acts 20.9," *BT* 39 (1988) 246-47.

[51] On the possibility that the statement, "he was taken up dead," is an example of "free indirect discourse" rather than a statement of the omniscient narrator, so that the statement expresses only the judgment by those who took up Eutychus, see Tannehill, *Narrative Unity*, 2.248-49. But the use of the passive verb "was taken up" ($\mathring{\eta}\rho\theta\eta$) seems to place the audience's focus not on the subjective perspective of those who took up but on the objective status of the one taken up, namely, that Eutychus was actually "dead" (for a similar use of $\mathring{\eta}\rho\theta\eta$ in this regard, see Luke 9:17). If the author wanted to express that Eutychus was not really dead, but only thought to be dead by those who picked him up, he would probably express it differently (cf. Luke 3:23: Jesus "was the son, as was thought, of Joseph"). It seems best and most natural, then, to consider the statement that "he was taken up dead" as an unambiguous statement of the omniscient narrator; see also Haenchen, *Acts*, 585; Conzelmann, *Acts*, 169; Polhill, *Acts*, 419 n. 64; Bulley, "Hanging in the Balance," 176 n. 16.

[52] On the significance of Paul's words here, Bulley ("Hanging in the Balance," 177) notes that "they represent the only words spoken in the piece. For all the importance given to Paul's discussion with the people at Troas and for all his urgency to speak with them before he has to leave, only this one

touched the coffin of the widow's dead son, when he said, "Young man, I say to you, arise!" (Luke 7:14).[53] Paul's confident assurance to the gathered community that Eutychus is no longer dead (20:10) reminds the audience of Jesus' similar reassurance to those mourning the dead daughter of Jairus, "Do not weep, for she is not dead but sleeping" (Luke 8:52).

After Paul broke bread and ate, they took away Eutychus alive (20:11-12)

That Paul, after he went back up to the upstairs room, broke bread and ate places the miraculous restoration of Eutychus to life squarely within the context of the eucharistic breaking of the bread. The audience, who heard that the community at Troas had gathered specifically "to break bread" (20:7), now hears that the Paul who miraculously restored the dead Eutychus to life performs as both the host and fellow participant of this eucharistic meal, as he both "broke the bread and ate" (20:11).[54]

The reminiscences of the eucharistic meals with the risen Jesus continue for the audience. Just as the risen Jesus performed as the host of the eucharistic meal with the Emmaus disciples, as he broke (κλάσας) the bread and distributed it to them (Luke 24:30), so now Paul performs as the host of the eucharistic meal with the community of disciples at Troas, as he broke (κλάσας) the bread and ate (20:11). As the risen Jesus became a participant of the eucharistic meal he shared with the group of disciples gathered together in Jerusalem by eating a piece of baked fish before them (Luke 24:42-43; see also Acts 1:3-4), so now Paul becomes a participant of the eucharistic meal he shares with the community gathered together in Troas by eating the broken bread with them (20:11).

The emphasis upon Paul's lengthy speaking during the eucharistic meal at Troas--"he was *speaking* with them" and "prolonged his *speech* until

---

sentence is reported."

[53] These life-restoring gestures and words toward those who have died have their dramatic precedents in Elijah's miraculous restoration to life of a widow's dead son (1 Kgs 17:19-23) and in Elisha's miraculous restoration to life of the dead son of the Shunammite woman (2 Kgs 4:32-37). Both of these restorations involve especially elaborate, life-restoring gestures performed on the bodies of dead youths.

[54] The close coordination of the participles, "breaking" (κλάσας) the bread and "eating" (γευσάμενος), renders the suggestion by Polhill (*Acts*, 420 n. 66) of two different meals here highly unlikely. As Haenchen (*Acts*, 585) points out: "Naturally it is not Paul alone who partakes of the Lord's Supper, but everyone. Paul however stands in the centre of the narrative, and is

midnight" (20:7), "as Paul was *speaking* at great length" (20:9), and "continuing to *talk* at length until daybreak" (20:11)--reminds the audience of a similar emphasis on speaking in conjunction with the risen Jesus' eucharistic meal at Emmaus.[55] When the Emmaus disciples were *talking* about all the things that had occurred, it happened that while they were *talking* and debating, the risen Jesus himself drew near and walked with them (Luke 24:14-15). After Jesus asked them about the *words* they were discussing (Luke 24:17), they gave a lengthy report (Luke 24:18-24). Then, beginning with Moses and *all* the prophets, Jesus interpreted to them what referred to him in *all* the scriptures (Luke 24:27). An interpretation dealing with *all* the prophets in *all* the scriptures must have been lengthy. Indeed, that all of this was lengthy speaking is confirmed by the Emmaus disciples' urging of Jesus, "Stay with us, for it is towards evening and the day has already declined" (Luke 24:29; cf. "until midnight" and "until daybreak" in Acts 20:7, 11).

As the audience recalls, when the eyes of the Emmaus disciples were opened and they recognized the risen Jesus in the eucharistic breaking of the bread, he abruptly disappeared from them (Luke 24:31, 35). Now, somewhat similarly, Paul rather abruptly disappeared, "thus he departed" (20:11), after his eucharistic breaking of the bread and eating with the community at Troas. That Paul departed so abruptly, before they took Eutychus away alive (20:12), underscores for the audience Paul's complete confidence that the life of Eutychus has been restored (20:10).[56]

But with regard to the celebration of the eucharist the abrupt departure of Paul also functions much like the sudden disappearance of the risen Jesus. While the sudden disappearance of the risen Jesus at Emmaus prepared the audience for his future physical absence, it also assured them of his invisible presence at future celebrations of the eucharist, which makes present for the community the life-giving effects of his death and resurrection (cf. Luke 22:19-20). Now, while the abrupt departure of Paul prepares the community at Troas for his absence, it also leaves them and the audience with a unique experience of the life-giving effects of the eucharist he hosted and ate with them, during which Eutychus died but was restored to life (20:9-10).

---

[55] M. Lattke, "ὁμιλέω," *EDNT* 2.509-10: "The section of the 'we'-source in Acts 20:7-12 has the same juxtaposition of διαλέγομαι (v. 7) and ὁμιλέω (v. 11) that is unique to the literary style of Luke. If 'break bread' is here a technical term for the Lord's Supper, then ὁμιλέω could also already have the meaning 'preach' that established itself in the patristic era...

[56] On Paul's abrupt departure as a sign of his conviction that Eutychus was indeed alive, see Pesch, *Apostelgeschichte*, 2.192.

That "they took the boy away alive (ζῶντα)" (20:12) confirms for the audience Paul's miraculous restoration of the dead Eutychus to life. It further reminds the audience of Peter's miraculous restoration of the dead Tabitha, when "he presented her alive (ζῶσαν)" (9:41). But that they took Eutychus away alive in the context of the eucharistic breaking of the bread (20:7, 11-12) especially reminds the audience how the risen Jesus presented himself alive (ζῶντα) to the apostles (1:3) in close conjunction with his farewell eucharistic meal fellowship with them (1:4).[57] Indeed, before the Emmaus disciples shared in the eucharistic breaking of the bread with the risen Jesus, they told him about the women who claimed that they had seen a vision of angels, "who say he is alive (ζῆν)" (Luke 24:23), recalling the angels' question to the women, "Why do you seek the living one (τὸν ζῶντα) among the dead?" (Luke 24:5).[58] Whereas the Emmaus disciples experienced the Jesus who had died as "the living one" in the eucharistic breaking of the bread (Luke 24:30-35), the community at Troas had another life-from-death experience during the eucharistic breaking of the bread, as they took the Eutychus who had died away "alive" (20:12).[59]

The eucharistic breaking of the bread has not only given the Emmaus disciples an experience of the presence of the risen Jesus (Luke 24:30-35), but has empowered Paul to extend the life-giving effects of the death and resurrection of Jesus, continually commemorated at the eucharist (Luke 22:19-20), to an individual member of the community. But there are also communal consequences. Not only was Eutychus restored to life, but those who took him away alive "were encouraged immeasurably" (20:12; cf. 20:1, 2), after Paul assured them, "Do not be alarmed, for his life is in him" (20:10). Paul's farewell eucharistic breaking of the bread and eating with the community at Troas has left them with a uniquely memorable life-from-death experience, which dramatically develops for the audience the life-giving and salvific benefits of the communal celebration of the eucharistic meal. Eutychus's restoration to physical life at the eucharist points to the eucharistic community's participation in final, eschatological life of meal fellowship in the kingdom of God.

---

[57] On Acts 1:3-4, see chapter 14.

[58] L. Schottroff, "ζῶ," *EDNT* 2.108: "The life of the resurrected one means, most importantly, that he again has a physical life, like that of Tabitha or Eutychus after they were miraculously raised from the dead (Acts 9:41; 20:12)."

[59] For another celebration in communal meal fellowship of a metaphorical rather than literal life-from-death experience, see Luke 15:24, 32.

Relation of Acts 20:7-12 to Previous Meal Scenes

1) Paul's revival of Eutychus at a eucharistic meal develops the *theme of eucharistic meal fellowship with the risen Jesus*. The meals that the disciples shared with the risen Jesus (Luke 24:30-35, 41-43; Acts 1:3-4) not only demonstrated that Jesus was alive but anticipated his invisible presence with them in the eucharistic meal fellowship he commanded them to keep doing in remembrance of him (Luke 22:19). The ideal Jerusalem community regularly celebrated the eucharistic breaking of the bread (Acts 2:42-47). Peter extended to the household of Cornelius the eucharistic meal fellowship he shared with the risen Jesus as one of those who ate and drank with him (Acts 10:41). Now, Paul's eucharistic breaking of the bread with the community at Troas leaves them with an experience not only of the invisible presence of the risen Jesus but of the miraculous life-giving effects of that presence upon one of the members of the community. It anticipates the ultimate salvific and life-giving meal fellowship they will share with the risen and exalted Jesus at the eschatological banquet in the kingdom of God (Luke 22:16-18, 29-30).

2) Paul's revival of Eutychus at a eucharistic meal continues the *theme of eucharistic meal fellowship with traveling missionaries*. The missionary Peter, as one of those who ate and drank in eucharistic meal fellowship with the risen Jesus (Acts 10:41), shared that eucharistic meal fellowship with the household of Cornelius (10:48; 11:3). At the beginning of his missionary activity Paul shared eucharistic meal fellowship at Philippi with the household of Lydia (16:11-15, 40) and with the household of the converted Roman jailer (16:30-34). Now, towards the end of his missionary activity, Paul shares the eucharistic breaking of the bread with the community at Troas.

3) Paul's revival of Eutychus at a eucharistic meal advances the *theme of eucharistic farewell meals*. At his farewell Passover supper with his disciples Jesus not only instituted the eucharist to be continually celebrated in remembrance of him (Luke 22:19-20), but left his disciples with extensive instructions preparing them for the future (22:21-38). The risen Jesus shared eucharistic farewell meals with his disciples, which prepared them for his future absence but invisible presence with them (Luke 24:30-35, 41-43; Acts 1:3-4). Now, Paul shares a eucharistic farewell meal with the community at Troas, in which he prepares them for his absence by leaving them with a lengthy discourse and the memorable encouragement of the miraculous restoration of Eutychus to life.

Pragmatics of the Meal Scene in Acts 20:7-12

1) By identifying with Eutychus, the audience gains a deeper appreciation of the *life-giving effects of the eucharist for their own lives*. The miraculous revival of Eutychus from death, as a consequence of Jesus' resurrection from the dead commemorated and made present in the eucharist, invites the audience to celebrate the eucharist as a hopeful anticipation of their own ultimate participation in the salvific death and resurrection of Jesus at the eschatological banquet in the kingdom of God.

2) By identifying with the community at Troas, the audience gains a deeper appreciation of the *life-giving effects of the eucharist for the fellow members of their own community*. That Eutychus was restored to life at the eucharist "immeasurably encourages" (20:12) and comforts the audience that their fellow members who have died will ultimately share in the life of the risen Jesus at the final banquet.

3) By identifying with Paul, the audience gains a deeper appreciation of the *life-giving effects of the eucharist for its pastoral leadership*. The missionary Paul's revival of Eutychus's physical life and his spiritual encouragement of the community at his farewell eucharistic breaking of the bread serve as a model for the audience's eucharistic celebrations. The eucharist empowers the audience, like Paul, to apply the life-giving effects of the death and resurrection of Jesus to both the physical and spiritual needs of the members of the community.

CHAPTER 17

PAUL USES A MEAL FOR ENCOURAGEMENT
ACTS 27:33-38

The final section of Acts, focused in general on Paul's climactic journey to Rome (21:18-28:31), is divided into three sections: Paul in Jerusalem (21:18-23:11), the plot against Paul (23:12-26:32), and Paul's journey to Rome (27:1-28:31).[1] The audience encounters the theme of eating and drinking in each of these sections.

At the beginning of the section dealing with Paul in Jerusalem (21:18-23:11) James reiterates to Paul the apostolic decree allowing believing Gentiles to share table fellowship with Jews: "Concerning the Gentiles who have come to believe, we have sent a letter with our decision that they should abstain from meat sacrificed to idols, from blood, from the meat of strangled animals, and from sexual immorality" (21:25; cf. 15:20, 29).[2]

At the beginning of the section concerning the plot against Paul (23:12-26:32) the narrator tells the audience that the Jews bound themselves by oath not to eat or drink until they had killed Paul (23:12). Then the audience hears the Jews themselves state: "We have bound ourselves by a solemn oath to taste nothing until we have killed Paul" (23:14). The report of the son of Paul's sister to the Roman commander reiterates that the Jews will not eat or drink until they have killed Paul (23:21). This threefold expression of the Jews' oath not to eat or drink emphatically underscores for the audience the extreme urgency and seriousness of their decision to kill Paul.[3]

In the section narrating Paul's voyage to Rome (27:1-28:31) the audience encounters the final major meal scene in Luke-Acts. In the midst of a life-threatening storm at sea Paul encourages his fellow travelers with a meal that alludes to the eucharist (27:33-38).

---

[1] For a discussion of these structural sections, see O'Fearghail, *Introduction to Luke-Acts*, 82-83. For a recent treatment of the journeys in Acts, see D. Marguerat, "Voyages et voyageurs dans le livre des Actes et la culture gréco-romaine," *RHPR* 78 (1998) 33-59.

[2] Polhill, *Acts*, 449: "The words of v. 25 are to be seen as an assurance to Paul that the basic decision of the Jerusalem Conference had not been changed. Gentiles still were not being asked to live by the Jewish Torah--only to observe those basic ritual matters that made table fellowship and social interaction possible between Jewish and Gentile Christians." On the apostolic decree at Jerusalem, see chapter 15.

[3] On the oath of not eating or drinking here, Johnson (*Acts*, 404) states that "taking an oath to kill someone or else starve to death is an extreme form." For Haenchen (*Acts*, 645) not eating or drinking indicates that the oath "was completely serious."

During a Sea Storm Paul Encourages His Fellow Passengers with a Meal (27:33-38)

33 Until day was about to come, Paul was encouraging all to share food, saying, "Today is the fourteenth day that you have continued without food, waiting in suspense, taking nothing. 34 Therefore I encourage you to share food. For it is for your salvation, for from the head of no one of you will a hair be lost."

35 Having said these things and taking bread, he thanked God before all, and breaking it, began to eat. 36 Becoming reassured, they all also took food.

37 We were--all the persons on the ship--two hundred seventy-six. 38 Having been satisfied with food, they lightened the ship by throwing the wheat into the sea.[4]

Paul urges all on the ship to share food in order to be saved (27:33-34)

After the sailors dropped four anchors from the stern out of fear that the ship might run aground on a rocky coast, they prayed for "day to come" (27:29). This focus upon daybreak provides the temporal setting for the next meal scene, which is introduced with a subsequent notice of time and duration, "until day was about to come" (27:33). The temporal framework reminds the audience of the previous meal scene, in which Paul saved Eutychus from death (20:7-12). That meal scene likewise took place during a long night (20:7) and lasted until daybreak (20:11).

While the sailors were praying, "until day was about to come," Paul was urging all on the ship to share food (27:33) for a double reason. First, it will keep all on the ship *communally united*, so that they can all be saved from the shipwreck Paul predicted (27:22, 26). This is important because some of

---

[4] On the meal scene in 27:33-38, in addition to the commentaries, see Menoud, "Acts of the Apsotles and the Eucharist," 95-97; S. M. Praeder, "Acts 27:1-28:16: Sea Voyages in Ancient Literature and the Theology of Luke-Acts," *CBQ* 46 (1984) 695-700; Esler, *Community and Gospel*, 101-4; M. Oberweis, "Ps. 23 als Interpretationsmodell für Act 27," *NovT* 30 (1988) 169-83; Tannehill, *Narrative Unity*, 2.334-37; T. Hawthorne, "A Discourse Analysis of Paul's Shipwreck: Acts 27:1-44," *Journal of Translation and Textlinguistics* 6 (1993) 253-73; A. Moda, "Paolo prigioniero e martire: Gli avvenimenti romani," *BeO* 35 (1993) 89-118.

the sailors have already attempted to abandon the ship in a boat (27:30). But Paul told the Roman centurion and soldiers in charge, "Unless these remain on the ship, you cannot be saved!" (27:31). By cutting the boat loose, the soldiers prevented the sailors from abandoning the rest of the people on the ship (27:32). And now, by sharing food (μεταλαβεῖν τροφῆς), *all* (ἄπαντας) on the ship (27:33) will remain communally united, reminding the audience how *all* (πάντες, 2:44) of the first believers in Jerusalem remained communally united by sharing food (μετελάμβανον τροφῆς) with gladness and generosity of heart (2:46), while devoting themselves to the communal fellowship of the eucharistic breaking of the bread in their houses (2:42, 46).[5]

Secondly, the communal sharing of food by all on the ship will *strengthen* them to be saved from the shipwreck. Out of despair of being saved from death in the sea storm, those on the ship had gone for a long time without food (27:20-21). That Paul encouraged them all to share food (μεταλαβεῖν τροφῆς) reminds the audience how Paul himself at the time of his conversion, after fasting for three days (9:9), took food (λαβὼν τροφὴν) and was strengthened (9:19). And that Paul encouraged (παρεκάλει) all those in danger of dying in the sea storm to share food (27:33) recalls for the audience how the community at Troas were encouraged (παρεκλήθησαν) immeasurably when they took Eutychus away alive after Paul revived him from death during the eucharistic meal (20:12).

The narrator's earlier notice that it was the fourteenth night of the sea storm (27:27) is complemented by the words of Paul: "Today is the fourteenth day that you have continued without food, waiting in suspense, taking nothing" (27:33). That those on the ship have continued without food (ἄσιτοι) while waiting in suspense and taking nothing to eat underlines for the audience the great need for them to eat now, as it reinforces the narrator's statement that they had been without food (ἀσιτίας) for a long time (27:21), having lost all hope of being saved (27:20).

With his own words, "Therefore I encourage you to share food," Paul not only reinforces the report of the narrator (27:33), but states the goal of their communal eating to regain strength: "For it is for your salvation, for from the head of no one of you will a hair be lost" (27:34). The rhetorical exaggeration that not even a hair from the head of anyone will be lost (ἀπολεῖται) accentuates for the audience Paul's promise that there will be the loss (ἀποβολὴ) of no one, only the ship (27:22). That their communal sharing of food is for their *salvation* aims at restoring their hope of being *saved*

---

[5] The verb used here, μεταλαμβάνω, connotes not just the "taking" but the "sharing" of food; see BAGD, 511; *EDNT* 2.414.

(27:20). Indeed, unless they all remain communally united on the ship, they cannot be *saved* (27:31).

That their sharing of food to remain communally united and to regain strength is for their salvation (27:34) refers, first of all, to their immediate salvation from death in the sea storm. But, based on what the audience has already heard about "salvation" in the previous narrative of Luke-Acts, their immediate salvation from the sea storm also seems to point to and anticipate their participation in the eschatological salvation from death accomplished by the death and resurrection of Jesus that is commemorated in the eucharistic sharing of food.[6] Indeed, the double and deeper sense of salvation involved in this final meal scene in Luke-Acts climaxes for the audience a progressive development of the theme of salvation in previous meal scenes.

Jesus concluded his first meal with a Pharisee (Luke 7:36-50) by climactically announcing to the sinful woman whose many sins were forgiven because she so hospitably demonstrated such great love toward him (7:47): "Your faith *has saved* you; go in peace" (7:50). That the repentant woman's faith in Jesus as the forgiver of sins "has saved" her and placed her in a present state of salvation (σέσωκέν, in the perfect tense expressing the continuing effect of a past act) so that she can go "in peace" has meant that Jesus has extended meal fellowship to her in the form of the eschatological salvation and peace that he brings. By her participation at the meal this Jewish woman individually received God's salvation from Jesus, God's "savior" (σωτήρ, Luke 2:11; Acts 5:31; 13:23).[7]

Employing both the verb (σῶσαι) and the noun (σωτηρία) for an emphatic focus on "salvation," Jesus climactically concluded the scene of his meal with Zacchaeus (Luke 19:1-10) by announcing: "Today *salvation* has

---

[6] On the double meaning of "salvation" in 27:34, see Menoud, "Acts of the Apostles and the Eucharist," 97. Tannehill (*Narrative Unity*, 2.336-37) states that salvation here "is not only the hope of those in a storm at sea but the purpose of God for all humanity, as announced at the beginning of Luke (2:30-32; 3:6). The emphasis on salvation in Luke-Acts gives to the emphasis on salvation in this sea voyage a second, symbolic sense." See also Soards, *Speeches in Acts*, 129-30. For the references to and meaning of salvation in Luke-Acts, see also W. Radl, "σῴζω," *EDNT* 3.319-21; K. H. Schelkle, "σωτηρία," *EDNT* 3.327-29; idem, "σωτήριος," *EDNT* 3.329; Spicq, *Theological Lexicon*, 3.344-57.

[7] In reference to Jesus as "savior" in Luke-Acts, K. H. Schelkle ("σωτήρ," *EDNT* 3.327) states: "Σωτήρ summarizes Christ's entire ministry and purpose."

arrived in this house, because he too is a son of Abraham. For the Son of Man has come to seek and *to save* what was lost" (19:9-10). By repenting of his sinfulness, the chief tax collector and rich man Zacchaeus, like the sinful woman (7:50), experienced God's eschatological salvation brought by Jesus in the context of meal hospitality. Whereas the sinful woman's repentance brought her salvation as an individual, Zacchaeus's repentance brought salvation not only to himself but to his entire household--"salvation has arrived *in this house*" (19:9). That Zacchaeus was saved as one who was "lost" is metaphorically equivalent to being saved from "death." The audience knows that the Greek word for "lost" (ἀπολωλός) often connotes "dead," as confirmed by the parallels between being "dead" and "lost" in the parable of the prodigal son (Luke 15:24, 32).[8]

The theme of salvation through meal fellowship progresses to the salvation of the entire community of the first Jewish believers in Jerusalem. In correspondence to Peter's exhortation that those in Jerusalem "*be saved* from this crooked generation" (Acts 2:40) by repenting and being baptized for the forgiveness of their sins (2:38), the Lord was daily adding "*those who were being saved*" to the community (2:47). The community of those being saved experienced, celebrated, and demonstrated their salvation in and through their communal sharing of meal fellowship (2:42-47).

In the scene of Peter's hospitable meal fellowship with Cornelius and his household (Acts 10:1-11:18) the theme of salvation through meals advances to include a community of believing Gentiles. Peter reported to his Jewish accusers in Jerusalem how God directed the gentile God-fearer Cornelius to tell Peter and his Jewish companions how he saw an angel standing in his house, directing him to send for Peter (11:13), who will speak words by which "you and all your household will be *saved*" (11:14). Peter's words silenced the accusation, implying that he was justified to enter and eat with a household of Gentiles (11:3) in order to bring them salvation.[9] The concluding exclamation of the Jewish accusers, "So then even to the Gentiles God has given the repentance that leads to life!" (11:18), indicates to the audience how "salvation" experienced through meal fellowship includes a share in eschatological "life."[10]

With the scene of the meal shared by Paul and Silas with the baptized Roman jailer and his household at Philippi (16:30-34) the theme of salvation

---

[8] BAGD, 95; A. Kretzer, "ἀπόλλυμι," *EDNT* 1.135-36.

[9] On table fellowship with believing Jews as an integral element of gentile salvation here, see Matson, *Household Conversion*, 122.

[10] On "life" here as an expression of eternal, eschatological "life," see Schottroff, "ζῶ," 109.

through meal fellowship moves from the Petrine to the Pauline mission and from a household of God-fearing Palestinian Gentiles in Caesarea to a household of pagan Roman Gentiles in Philippi. When the jailer led Paul and Silas out of prison, he indicated his willingness to convert by asking, "Sirs, what must I do to be *saved*?" (16:30; cf. 2:37, 40). Paul and Silas exhorted the jailer to believe in the Lord Jesus to be saved. Their emphatic expression that "you will be *saved*--you and your household" (16:31), echoing what the angel told Cornelius (11:14), accentuates for the audience the communal dimension of the Roman jailer's conversion. Just as the Jerusalem believers celebrated their coming to salvation "with gladness" at eucharistic meals (2:42, 46), so the "rejoicing" of the Roman jailer and all his household in coming to the faith that means their salvation (16:30-31) occurs at a special meal with eucharistic associations (16:34).[11]

Although not employing the vocabulary of "salvation," the scene of Paul's revival of Eutychus at a eucharistic meal (20:7-12) nevertheless advances the theme of salvation through meal fellowship. The salvation involved is that of the rescue of life from death.[12] When Eutychus fell and was taken up "dead" (20:9), Paul assured the community gathered for the meal that his "life" is in him (20:10). After the eucharistic breaking of bread and eating (20:11) they took Eutychus away "alive" (20:12). In the previous meal scenes salvation was experienced and celebrated in table fellowship by those who had repented and become new believers. But here an already believing member of the community receives salvation in the form of the life-giving effects of the death and resurrection of Jesus that is continually commemorated in the eucharist (Luke 22:19-20). This miraculous life-from-death experience at a eucharistic meal, which "immeasurably encouraged" (20:12) the community at Troas, indicates to the audience how the communal celebration of the eucharist anticipates the future and final salvation of eschatological life after earthly death.

Whereas Eutychus alone was saved from death during the communal meal at Troas (20:7-12), Paul now urges "all" on board the ship (27:33), including the many non-believers, to share food for their salvation (27:34). That this "salvation" includes but also transcends their immediate rescue from death in the sea storm and points to their eschatological salvation is confirmed by Paul's additional reason for their sharing of food: "For from the head of no one of you will a hair be lost" (27:34). This proverbial expression (cf. 1 Sam

---

[11] For the eucharistic associations of the meal in 16:34, see chapter 16.

[12] Note how "salvation" is paralleled with "life" in 11:14, 18 and with "eternal life" in 13:46-48.

14:45; 2 Sam 14:11; 1 Kgs 1:52) promises, first of all, the complete physical safety of each and every individual on the ship--"*no one*" (οὐδενὸς in emphatic position) will be lost in death.[13] But it also reminds the audience of Jesus' previous promise to the disciples: "But not a hair from your head will ever be lost" (Luke 21:18; cf. 12:7). Since this promise closely follows upon Jesus' warning that "they will put some of you to death" (21:16), it refers not just to immediate, physical safety but also assures ultimate, eschatological salvation in eternal life.[14]

After Paul himself began to eat, all on the ship also took food (27:35-36)

That Paul took bread (λαβὼν ἄρτον), thanked (εὐχαρίστησεν) God before all, and broke (κλάσας) it before he began to eat (27:35) reminds the audience of the similar pattern of meal gestures in previous eucharistic meals with Jesus.[15] When the risen Jesus reclined at table for a eucharistic meal with the disciples at Emmaus, he took the bread (λαβὼν τὸν ἄρτον), blessed (εὐλόγησεν) and broke (κλάσας) it, before giving it over to them (Luke 24:30).[16] When Jesus instituted the eucharist at his last supper, he took bread

---

[13] See "θρίξ," *EDNT* 2.156: "Matt 5:36; Luke 21:18; Acts 27:34 speak of a single *hair* in emphasizing God's protecting care for the most trifling object."

[14] In reference to Jesus' proverbial promise in Luke 21:18 Green (*Luke*, 738) states: "Jesus promises that persecution, even death, does not spell the end of life for the faithful." And the word "lost" here, referring immediately to "hair" but by extension to the whole individual (Luke 21:18; Acts 27:34), often connotes or points to eschatological destruction (Luke 9:24; 13:3, 5; 15:24, 32; 17:33; 19:10). See also Kretzer, "ἀπόλλυμι," 1.135-36.

[15] On the word "take" (λαβὼν) here, A. Kretzer ("λαμβάνω," *EDNT* 2.336) notes: "The active meaning *take, grasp* is characteristic in the Synoptic Gospels of feeding and meal terminology and receives a eucharistic stamp through the celebration in the early Church (Mark 14:22f. par.; cf. 1 Cor 11:23f.; Luke 24:30, 43; John 21:13)." Wanke ("κλάω," 2.296) also notes: "In Christian usage 'breaking of bread' took on the specific sense of 'eucharistic' breaking of bread...According to Acts 27:35 Paul acted in accordance with Jewish table customs. For Luke, however, an allusion to the nearness of the Lord experienced in the eucharist is not to be excluded."

[16] On the interchangeability of the words "thank" (εὐχαριστέω) and "bless" (εὐλογέω) in reference to the table benediction, see H. Patsch, "εὐχαριστία," *EDNT* 2.88.

(λαβὼν ἄρτον), gave thanks (εὐχαριστήσας), and broke (ἔκλασεν) it, before he gave it to his disciples (Luke 22:19). And when Jesus overabundantly fed the great crowd in the desert, he took (λαβὼν) the five loaves (ἄρτους) and the two fish, and looking up to heaven, he blessed (εὐλόγησεν) and broke (κατέκλασεν) them, before giving them to the disciples to set before the crowd (Luke 9:16).[17]

Whereas Jesus gave the eucharistic bread to the disciples and crowds to eat (Luke 9:16; 22:19; 24:30), Paul significantly began to eat it himself (27:35). Although Paul did not share the eucharist with the non-believers on the ship, his own eating of a eucharistic meal provided an example that transformed all the others: "Becoming reassured, they all also took food" (27:36).[18] That they all took food (προσελάβοντο τροφῆς) finally fulfills Paul's urgent exhortation that they all share food (μεταλαβεῖν τροφῆς, 27:33, 34). Paul's eating of the eucharist thus encouraged them to share food for their salvation (27:34), that is, for their immediate salvation from death, which anticipates the eschatological salvation of all on the ship--believers and non-believers--made possible by the life-giving death and resurrection of Jesus commemorated in the eucharist.[19]

That Paul took (λαβὼν) bread, thanked God before all (ἐνώπιον πάντων), and breaking it, began to eat (ἐσθίειν) (27:35) reminds the audience how the risen Jesus, when the disciples gave him a piece of baked fish in Jerusalem (Luke 24:42), took it and ate it before them (λαβὼν ἐνώπιον αὐτῶν ἔφαγεν, 24:43). By eating before them, the risen Jesus encouraged the startled, terrified, troubled, and doubting disciples (Luke 24:37-38, 41) to

---

[17] Praeder, "Sea Voyages," 699: "Luke-Acts lacks references to blessings or thanksgivings at ordinary meals. Taking bread, blessing or thanksgiving, breaking bread, and distributing of bread are reported only at the extraordinary meals of the feeding of the five thousand, the last supper, and the evening meal at Emmaus (Luke 9:16; 22:19; 24:30). All three meals are supposed to be seen in relation to Christian eucharistic meals."

[18] On the meaning of εὐθυμέω in 27:22, 25, 36 as being "reassured," recovering confidence and composure, see Spicq, Theological Lexicon, 2.114.

[19] LaVerdiere, Eucharist, 109-10: "Paul gave them an example of what everyone needed to do in order to be saved. The reference to the Eucharist is unmistakable. The event, however, should not be interpreted as describing an actual Eucharist, but as a literary analogy. Just as Paul, the sailors, and the passengers had to eat in order to have the strength they needed to survive, so also the Christians needed to join in the Eucharistic meal if they wished to be saved."

believe that he has been raised from the dead as a living person. By eating before all on the ship, Paul similarly encouraged the distraught and frightened (27:20, 24) people on the ship to take food in order to be saved (27:34).

Paul's eating of the eucharist for the encouragement of the others on the ship (27:35-36) also reminds the audience of his eucharistic meal with the believing community at Troas (20:7-12). After he broke bread for the eucharist and ate (20:11), the community took Eutychus away alive and were greatly encouraged (20:12). Whereas Paul's eating of the eucharist at Troas led to the encouragement of believers, his eating of the eucharist on the ship encourages even and especially non-believers.[20] All on the ship will be saved because Paul was with them and ate the eucharist on their behalf. That Paul gave thanks ($\varepsilon\dot{v}\chi\alpha\rho\acute{\iota}\sigma\tau\eta\sigma\varepsilon\nu$) to God before all ($\pi\acute{\alpha}\nu\tau\omega\nu$) as he ate the eucharist (27:35) confirms the angel's promise that God has graciously given ($\kappa\varepsilon\chi\acute{\alpha}\rho\iota\sigma\tau\alpha\acute{\iota}$) to Paul all ($\pi\acute{\alpha}\nu\tau\alpha\varsigma$) those sailing with him (27:24).[21]

After all were satisfied with food, they lightened the ship (27:37-38)

The abrupt and brief return of the first person plural narration, "We were--all the persons on the ship--two hundred seventy-six" (27:37), enhances the audience's imaginative participation in this meal scene.[22] The exact numbering of two hundred and seventy-six for all on board reinforces Paul's promise of a complete and total salvation of each and every individual on the ship, "from the head of no one of you will a hair be lost" (27:34).[23] The reference to "*all* the persons" climaxes the scene's emphasis on the salvation of all on the ship: Paul was encouraging *all* to share food (v 33), he promised that *no one* of them would be lost (v 34), he thanked God before *all* (v 35), and they *all* also took food (v 36). Paul's eating of the eucharist unified and

---

[20] Tannehill, *Narrative Unity*, 2.336: "Even though the others do not share Paul's food, celebrating the Eucharist 'before all' so that all will eat shows a remarkable concern to benefit non-Christians through a central Christian practice."

[21] On the connection and word play here, see Praeder, "Sea Voyages," 698; Tannehill, *Narrative Unity*, 2.335-36.

[22] Tannehill, *Narrative Unity*, 2.246-47; Porter, "The 'We' Passages," 566.

[23] Some have suggested an additional mysterious or mystical ring to the number two hundred and seventy-six because it is a triangular number--the sum of the numbers from one to twenty-three. See Polhill, *Acts*, 528 n. 45.

strengthened the total number of persons on the ship--both believers and non-believers--for salvation.[24]

Having been satisfied with food, those on board now had the strength to lighten the ship for the enhancement of their rescue by throwing the leftover food, the wheat, into the sea (27:38).[25] The reference to "all" two hundred seventy-six persons who were satisfied (κορεσθέντες) with food (27:37-38) further reminds the audience of Jesus' miraculously overabundant feeding of the crowd (Luke 9:10-17). In that meal scene the people numbered "about five thousand men" (9:14), "all" of whom ate and were satisfied (ἐχορτάσθησαν) (9:17). Jesus' overabundant satisfaction of the whole crowd with food anticipated their participation in the eschatological banquet. Similarly, that all on the ship were satisfied with food as a result of Paul's eating of the eucharist not only nourishes them for immediate salvation from the sea storm (27:34) but anticipates their eschatological salvation in meal fellowship at the ultimate banquet.

Because of Paul's eating of the eucharist, which led to all on the ship being satisfied and thus strengthened with food, eventually, although the ship itself was lost as Paul predicted (27:22), "all," who had remained united by sharing food on the ship, were "saved" (πάντας διασωθῆναι) on the land (27:44).[26] By eating the eucharist, which commemorates the death and resurrection of Jesus (Luke 22:19-20), Paul made the salvific, life-giving effects of that death and resurrection present and active not only for the

---

[24] Tannehill, *Narrative Unity*, 2.335: "The 'we' in the voyage to Rome generally refers to a small group of Christians. Here, however, the entire ship's company becomes a single 'we' as the narrator numbers the company so that readers will know what 'all' means. Even though the boundary of the church is not completely eliminated, the meal on the ship is an act that benefits all, Christian and non-Christian, and an act in which community is created across religious lines."

[25] B. M. Rapske, "Acts, Travel and Shipwreck," *The Book of Acts in Its Graeco-Roman Setting* (The Book of Acts in Its First Century Setting 2; eds. D. W. J. Gill and C. Gempf; Grand Rapids: Eerdmans, 1994) 32-33: "The urgent labours of all those aboard (3rd person plural of κουφίζω after mention of the 276: Acts 27:38) in the pre-dawn hours of the morning of the shipwreck might reasonably be thought to have significantly lightened such a smaller grain carrier before its run for shore."

[26] The verb form διασῴζω for "save" is found six times in Luke-Acts (Luke 7:3; Acts 23:24; 27:43, 44; 28:1, 4). See U. Busse, "διασῴζω," *EDNT* 1.313.

believers but even and especially for the non-believers on the ship. This tells the audience that the death and resurrection of Jesus, celebrated and made present in the eucharist, can unify and strengthen all peoples--both believers and non-believers--for salvation in the meal fellowship of the eschatological banquet.[27]

Relation of Acts 27:33-38 to Previous Meal Scenes

1) Paul's encouragement of his fellow passengers with a eucharistic meal climaxes the *theme of salvation in and through meal fellowship*. An anonymous, repentant Jewish woman individually received God's salvation as Jesus forgave her sins at his first meal with a Pharisee (Luke 7:36-50). Then a repentant Jewish man named Zacchaeus, by welcoming Jesus into his home for table fellowship, received salvation not only for himself but for his entire household (19:1-10). Next, the entire community of the first Jewish believers in Jerusalem celebrated their salvation in and through their communal sharing of eucharistic meal fellowship (Acts 2:42-47). Then an entire household of gentile God-fearers headed by Cornelius in Caesarea became believers, receiving salvation in and through their meal fellowship with Peter and his Jewish cohorts (10:1-11:18). Next, an entire household of pagan Roman Gentiles headed by an anonymous jailer in Philippi became believers and celebrated their salvation in a eucharistic meal with Paul and Silas (16:30-34). Then Eutychus, a member of the believing community at Troas, received salvation as Paul revived him from death at a eucharistic meal, greatly encouraging the entire community (20:7-12). Now, all on board the ship, believers as well as non-believers, are saved from the sea storm that foreshadows their eschatological salvation at the banquet in God's kingdom, because they were encouraged to take food by Paul's eating of the eucharist.

2) Paul's eating of a eucharistic meal on the ship culminates the *theme of the transformative effects of the eucharist*. After Jesus instituted and shared the first eucharist with his disciples (Luke 22:7-38), they were enabled to play their respective roles in his passion, death and resurrection. The eucharistic meal that the unrecognized Jesus served to the Emmaus disciples opened their eyes to recognize him as the risen Lord (24:28-35), who then, by receiving a piece of fish and eating it before all the disciples in Jerusalem (24:41-43),

---

[27] According to Tannehill (*Narrative Unity*, 2.338), "this section of Acts represents a new boldness of hope that anticipates salvation (in some sense) for every individual of a pluralistic community and views persons such as Paul as mediators of this promise."

transformed his troubled and terrified disciples into future hosts of the eucharist. The eucharistic meals celebrated by the first believers in Jerusalem united them into an ideally joyful and sharing community (Acts 2:42-47). The eucharistic meals that Peter shared with the household of Cornelius (10:41), and that Paul shared with the households of Lydia (16:11-15) and of the Roman jailer (16:30-34), brought these gentile believers into fellowship with Jewish believers. The eucharistic meal that Paul celebrated with the believers at Troas revived Eutychus from death and immeasurably encouraged the community (20:7-12). Now, the eucharist that Paul eats on the ship transforms the despairing believers as well as non-believers into a unified group, strengthened with food for their salvation from the sea storm that anticipates their salvation at the eschatological banquet.

3) Paul's encouragement of his fellow passengers with a eucharistic meal completes *the theme of eucharistic meal fellowship with Gentiles*. Peter and his Jewish companions shared eucharistic meal fellowship with the gentile God-fearers who became believers in the household of Cornelius at Caesarea (10:1-11:18). Then Paul and his Jewish companions shared eucharistic meal fellowship with the gentile household of Lydia who became believers at Philippi (16:11-15). This progressed to Paul and Silas sharing eucharistic meal fellowship with the pagan household of the Roman jailer who became believers at Philippi (16:30-34). And now, Paul, by eating the eucharist himself, unites the believers and non-believing Gentiles on the ship into a meal fellowship that satisfies and strengthens them for the salvation that anticipates the final banquet in the kingdom of God.

4) Paul's eating of a eucharistic meal on the ship concludes *the theme of the eucharistic meals that empower Paul for his mission*. After Paul converted and was baptized, he took food, alluding to the eucharist, and was strengthened to carry out his mission (9:17-22). The eucharistic meals that Paul shared in the households of Lydia and of the Roman jailer (16:11-15, 30-34) strengthened him and his companions to carry out his mission, endure imprisonment, and encourage the believers at Philippi (16:40). The eucharistic meal that Paul celebrated with the community at Troas enabled him to greatly encourage them by reviving Eutychus (20:7-12). Now, Paul's own eating of the eucharist empowers him to encourage all the others on the ship to take food for their salvation now and at the final banquet.

Pragmatics of the Meal Scene in Acts 27:33-38

1) The eating of the eucharist can empower the audience, like it did Paul, to extend the life-giving, salvific effects of the death and resurrection of Jesus, which is commemorated and made present at the eucharist, *to both believers and non-believers*.

2) The celebration of the eucharist not only anticipates future eschatological salvation at the eschatological banquet, but can have *salvific and life-giving effects in present situations* of distress and despair.

3) The eating of the eucharist can *strengthen* the individual members of the audience, like it did Paul, *to encourage, help, and rescue all who are in need.*

4) The celebration of the eucharist can *unite* the audience, like all of those on the ship with Paul, not only with one another but with non-believers to work together *for the present and future salvation of all peoples* to be completed at the eschatological banquet in the kingdom of God.

CHAPTER 18

CONCLUSION

The rich and varied theme of eating and drinking spans the entire narrative of Luke-Acts. The many different meal scenes often occur at pivotal points in the overall narrative strategy. Luke's preparatory narrative (Luke 1:1-4:44) whets the audience's appetite for the subsequent meal scenes by introducing certain aspects of the theme of eating and drinking (1:15, 53; 2:7, 12, 16, 37; 3:11; 4:1-4, 39). (Chapter 1)

As Jesus gathered his disciples at the beginning of his ministry in Galilee, the audience encounters the first meal scenes--a successive series of three controversial meals involving Jesus and his disciples, each pointing to the final, eschatological banquet that has begun with Jesus. The first controversial meal introduces the issue of sharing meal fellowship with public sinners and social outcasts. By provocatively inviting the Pharisees and their scribes to repent, Jesus reminds the audience of their continual need to humbly *repent* of their own sinfulness in order to share in the *inclusive meal fellowship* of the great eschatological banquet that Jesus will host (5:27-32). The second controversial meal concerns the religious practice of fasting. It invites the audience to practice a *new kind of fasting* that anticipates the eschatological wedding feast Jesus has ushered in (5:33-39). The third controversial meal raises the question of doing the work necessary to satisfy one's hunger on the sabbath. As the lord of the sabbath, Jesus calls for the audience not to deprive themselves or others of such basic and fundamental human needs as the *satisfaction of their hunger*, which actually fulfills the divine intention of the sabbath observance as a sacred time of rest and refreshment in anticipation of the final, eschatological sabbath (6:1-5). (Chapter 2)

In the midst of Jesus' ministry in Galilee (5:1-9:50) the audience meets the next meal scene, Jesus' meal with a sinful woman and Simon the Pharisee. This meal scene continues the theme of meals as calls to repentance in order to experience the meal fellowship that anticipates the eschatological banquet. It calls for the audience, like the woman whose many sins were forgiven and unlike the recalcitrant Pharisee, to repent of their sins in order to experience the *new meal fellowship of God's salvation and peace that Jesus' forgiveness offers*. The audience is to welcome into that meal fellowship those sinners who, like the sinful woman and themselves, have repented and been forgiven (7:36-50). (Chapter 3)

Toward the end of Jesus' ministry in Galilee (5:1-9:50) his overabundant feeding of the crowds advances the theme of the meal scenes as anticipations of the overabundant satisfaction of hunger, both physical and spiritual, at the eschatological banquet. Jesus' miraculous empowerment of the disciples to hospitably welcome and overabundantly feed the vast crowd invites the audience not only to experience the *overabundant satisfaction of hunger*

Jesus offers but to hospitably extend this overabundance to others (9:10-17). (Chapter 4)

At the beginning of the second section (10:38-11:54) of the travel narrative in which Jesus journeys to his destiny in Jerusalem (9:51-19:48), Jesus' meal with the sisters Martha and Mary (10:38-42) adds an important element to the theme of the meal scenes as anticipations of the eschatological banquet: It is by his divinely determined death and resurrection that Jesus will bring about the ultimate banquet of the kingdom of God. Jesus' meal with Martha and Mary reminds the audience that discipleship includes both men and women who not only hear but do the word of God. It encourages the audience to be disciples who imitate not only Martha by welcoming and hospitably serving one another, but also Mary by listening to the word of Jesus about the *divine necessity of his suffering and death* in Jerusalem before being raised (9:22, 35, 44). This word, the "one thing necessary" and "best portion" (10:42) for the banquet, also calls all in the audience to follow Jesus by denying themselves, taking up their cross daily, and losing their lives for his sake in order to save them (9:23-25) and inherit eternal life (10:25). (Chapter 5)

At the end of the second section (10:38-11:54) of the journey to Jerusalem Jesus' second meal with a Pharisee (11:37-54) advances the theme of meals as calls to repentance in order to experience the meal fellowship that anticipates the eschatological banquet. Instead of repenting, however, the Pharisees and lawyers become extremely hostile and plot to trap Jesus in his speech (11:53-54). In contrast to the Pharisees and lawyers, those in the audience are to be *authentic leaders* by giving alms to the poor and hungry (11:39-41), by working for social justice (11:42), by using their knowledge to assist others to serve God (11:43-46, 52), and by recognizing, welcoming, and heeding the prophets who speak God's word to them (11:47-51). Although, as disciples of Jesus, the audience can expect to be rejected, persecuted, and possibly even killed like Jesus, they can be encouraged by the promise of God's ultimate vindication (11:47-51). (Chapter 6)

At the end of the fourth section (13:22-14:24) of the journey to Jerusalem Jesus' third meal with a Pharisee (14:1-24) further develops the theme of meals as calls to repentance in order to experience the meal fellowship that anticipates the eschatological banquet. In contrast to the lawyers and Pharisees, those in the audience are to be *authentic and compassionate leaders* by repenting and being healed of their moral "dropsy," their craving desires to acquire wealth and honor for themselves (14:1-6, 18-20, 24), by humbling themselves in their social behavior (14:7-11, 15), and by completely rejecting the system of social reciprocity by sharing meal fellowship with society's poor, sick, and lowly (14:12-24). As disciples of

Jesus, the audience is advised to invite to the banquet of God's kingdom those who are not selfishly absorbed with acquiring possessions and social honors (14:15-24). (Chapter 7)

In the fifth section (14:25-17:10) of the journey to Jerusalem Jesus' parables celebrating the finding of the lost with festive meals (15:1-32) continue the theme of the meals as calls to repentance in order to experience the meal fellowship that anticipates the eschatological banquet. Jesus' three parables invite the audience, in contrast to the Pharisees and the scribes, to empathize with the shepherd (15:3-7), the woman (15:8-10), and the father (15:11-32), who *joyfully celebrate most appropriately with communal and festive meals the repentance of any sinner*. When the audience repents of their own sinfulness, which can render them "lost" and "dying" of hunger in their relationship to God, they can expect to be received with the overwhelming forgiveness, abundantly satisfying nourishment, and tremendous joy of God as their loving and merciful Father. Jesus prods the audience to further repentance by relating to God not merely as a faithful and obedient servant but as a cherished child of a lovingly compassionate father, and by relating to any sinner who repents as their fellow brothers and sisters. (Chapter 8)

Also in the fifth section (14:25-17:10) of the journey to Jerusalem, Jesus' parable of the reversed meals of a rich man and Lazarus (Luke 16:19-31) extends the theme of meals as calls to repentance in order to experience the meal fellowship that anticipates the eschatological banquet. Instead of being lovers of money like the Pharisees, the audience is invited to repent *by relying upon God as the only one who can and will completely satisfy all their hungers* in the eschatological banquet, *by sharing the food they have to rectify social injustice* toward their fellow human beings in need, and *by relating to the hungry poor so compassionately and hospitably as their fellow human beings* that they themselves have the courageous faith to become as the poor, the hungry, and the weeping, whom God will fully satisfy and make happy at the eschatological banquet in the kingdom of God (6:20-21). (Chapter 9)

In the seventh and concluding section (18:31-19:48) of the journey to Jerusalem Jesus' meal with a chief tax collector and rich man named Zacchaeus (19:1-10) further promotes the theme of meals as calls to repentance in order to experience the meal hospitality that anticipates the eschatological banquet. Like Zacchaeus the audience is called *to repent of their sinfulness*, especially their neglect of the poor and wrongdoing toward others, in order to see and experience Jesus as the Son of Man who came to seek and to save what was lost. They will thereby anticipate the salvation Jesus will complete by his suffering, death and resurrection. Unlike those who grumbled that Jesus went to lodge with a sinner, the audience is called *to include social outcasts and public sinners in their meal fellowship* in order both to motivate and celebrate their repentance. Like Jesus the audience is *to rely upon the meal hospitality* of those to whom they proclaim the good news of the kingdom of God. (Chapter 10)

In Jerusalem Jesus' last Passover supper with his disciples before his death (22:7-38) provides a preliminary climax to the themes of the previous meals as anticipations of the eschatological banquet, as preparations for the time after Jesus' death, and as challenges to authentic leadership. Jesus' command to "keep doing this in remembrance of me" (22:19) empowers the audience, by obeying him as their authoritative teacher (22:7-13), *to continue to anticipate the eschatological banquet* by sharing the new Passover bread that is his sacrificial body given for their salvation and the new Passover cup of wine that is his sacrificial blood of the new covenant that atones for and forgives sins (22:19-20). Jesus' last supper calls the audience *to avoid betraying him* like Judas (22:21-23), to imitate the greatness of Jesus' servant leadership by humbly and selflessly *serving the needs of one another* (22:24-27), *to persevere through trials* in order to eat and drink with Jesus as well as serve others at the eschatological banquet (22:14-18, 28-30), to become true servant leaders not only by returning to Jesus after failures but also by *strengthening the faithfulness of others who likewise fail* (22:31-34), and *to endure any hostility* they encounter as they follow Jesus on his way to suffering and death (22:35-38). (Chapter 11)

The risen Jesus' meal with the Emmaus disciples (24:28-35) advances the themes of the meal fellowship formed by Jesus breaking and distributing bread to his disciples, of meal hospitality offered to traveling missionaries, of the dual role of Jesus as both the guest and the host of meals, and of Jesus bringing about the eschatological banquet of God's kingdom by his death and resurrection. Whenever the audience celebrates the eucharist, they will be united in *meal fellowship with the risen Jesus* by remembering the scriptural teaching that explains Jesus' prophetic predictions of the divine necessity of his death and resurrection, so that they can recognize and experience his invisible presence with them when they give to one another the bread and wine that have become his sacrificial body and blood. The audience is *to share with those who welcome them their faith and hope* in the resurrection of Jesus. The audience's experience of the risen Lord in the eucharist *reinforces their hope* of being united with him in the meal fellowship of the final eschatological banquet. (Chapter 12)

The risen Jesus' meal with the disciples in Jerusalem (24:41-43) develops the themes of Jesus' meals as celebrations of joy, of his empowerment of the disciples to be the hosts of his special meals, of meal hospitality offered to traveling missionaries, and of his meals as anticipations of the eschatological banquet. Like Jesus the audience is to *depend upon the meal hospitality* of those to whom they bring the message of the peace and joy of God's kingdom and to extend meal hospitality to others. The celebration of the eucharist *unites the audience in meal fellowship* with their invisibly present host and guest, the risen Jesus, *empowers them to feed others from the overabundance* with which he feeds them in the bread and wine of his sacrificial body and blood, *further reinforces their hope* of sharing meal fellowship with him at the eschatological banquet, and *qualifies the audience to be witnesses* for the mission of proclaiming repentance for the forgiveness of sins to all nations. (Chapter 13)

In the section of the Acts of the Apostles focusing on Jerusalem, the communal meals of new believers in Jerusalem (Acts 2:42-47) serve as a transition from Jesus' breaking of the bread with his disciples to the believing community's eucharistic breaking of the bread. The table fellowship of the Jerusalem believers continues the themes of meals as celebrations of joy, as demonstrations of the ideals of meal fellowship that Jesus taught, and as anticipations of the eschatological banquet. The eucharistic table fellowship of the audience should result in a *glad and generous sharing of their food and possessions* with one another (Acts 2:42-46), especially those who are most needy among them (Acts 6:1-3). Through the eucharistic meal fellowship by which they celebrate their own repentance for the forgiveness of sins, the audience can be *witnesses who attract others to repent and be forgiven*, and so anticipate the joy and generosity of the eschatological banquet. (Chapter 14)

In the first subsection (8:4-11:18) of the section of Acts focusing on missionary preaching (8:4-21:17), Peter's meal fellowship with Cornelius and his household (10:1-11:18) advances the themes of meals as calls to repentance in order to experience the meal hospitality that anticipates the eschatological banquet, of meal hospitality offered to traveling missionaries, of meal fellowship with the newly baptized, and of eucharistic meal fellowship with the risen Jesus. This scene of meal fellowship between believing Jews and Gentiles challenges the audience to bring people of different racial, social, ethnic, religious and cultural backgrounds to faith in the gospel by *leveling any barriers that prevent new believers from the meal fellowship that anticipates the eschatological banquet*. It empowers the audience to socially interact with and preach to any receptive people the gospel of repentance for the forgiveness of sins. It calls the audience to extend to the people to whom they preach the full social acceptance that the sharing of meal hospitality with them represents and to share the eucharist with the newly baptized in order to unite them with the risen Lord and the broader believing community. (Chapter 15)

In the section of Acts dealing with Paul's reassurance and farewell (18:23-21:17), Paul's revival of Eutychus at a eucharistic meal (Acts 20:7-12) develops the themes of eucharistic meal fellowship with the risen Jesus in anticipation of the eschatological banquet, of eucharistic meal fellowship with traveling missionaries, and of eucharistic farewell meals. It invites the audience to celebrate the eucharist as a hopeful anticipation of their ultimate *participation in the salvific death and resurrection of Jesus at the eschatological banquet*. The eucharist empowers the audience to apply the life-giving effects of the death and resurrection of Jesus to both the physical and spiritual needs of the members of the community. (Chapter 16)

In the final section of Acts, dealing with Paul's journey to Rome (27:1-28:31), Paul's encouragement of his fellow passengers with a eucharistic meal (Acts 27:33-38) climaxes the themes of salvation in and through the meal fellowship that anticipates the eschatological banquet, of the transformative effects of the eucharist, of eucharistic meal fellowship with Gentiles, and of eucharistic meals that empower Paul for his mission. The eucharist empowers the audience *to extend the life-giving, salvific effects of the death and resurrection of Jesus to both believers and non-believers* in situations of distress and despair. The eucharist strengthens and unites the members of the audience *to work not only with one another but with non-believers for the present and future salvation of all peoples* to be completed at the eschatological banquet in the kingdom of God. (Chapter 17)

In conclusion, all of the meals in Luke-Acts, in one way or another, anticipate the ultimate meal fellowship to be enjoyed at the *eschatological banquet* in the kingdom of God. In this regard *Jesus' last Passover supper* with his disciples (Luke 22:7-38), at which he instituted the eucharist, *serves as the focal point for all of the other meals in Luke-Acts*. All of the many meals that call for the Jewish leaders to repent of their uncompassionate and selfish style of leadership (5:27-6:5; 7:36-50; 11:37-54; 14:1-24; 15:1-32; 16:19-31; 19:1-10) in order to share in the meal fellowship with repentant and forgiven sinners that anticipates the eschatological banquet find their climax in Jesus' last supper. Here Jesus calls his disciples to imitate his own servant leadership by humbly and selflessly serving the needs of one another (22:24-27) and by not only returning to Jesus after their own failures but also by compassionately strengthening others who likewise fail in faithfulness (22:31-34).

The overabundant food (9:10-17) and "best portion" (10:38-42) of the ultimate banquet will be brought about by the *death and resurrection of Jesus to be made present and commemorated at the eucharist* (22:19-20). All of the meals in Luke-Acts after Jesus' last supper are eucharistic meals of fellowship with the risen Lord (Luke 24:28-35, 41-43) that anticipate the joy and harmony (Acts 2:42-47), the unity (10:1-11:18), and the eternal life (20:7-12) and salvation (27:33-38) that all peoples will share in the meal fellowship of the eschatological banquet in the kingdom of God.

BIBLIOGRAPHY

Aletti, J.-N. "Luc 24,13-33: Signes, accomplissement et temps." *RSR* 75 (1987) 305-20.

Alexander, L. "Sisters in Adversity: Retelling Martha's Story." *Women in the Biblical Tradition*. Ed. G. J. Brooke. Studies in Women and Religion 31. Lewiston: Mellen, 1992. 167-86.

Alexander, L. *The Preface to Luke's Gospel: Literary Convention and Social Context in Luke 1.1-4 and Acts 1.1*. SNTSMS 78. Cambridge: Cambridge University Press, 1993.

---. "The Preface to Acts and the Historians." *History, Literature, and Society in the Book of Acts*. Ed. B. Witherington. Cambridge: Cambridge University Press, 1996. 73-103.

Andersen, T. D. "The Meaning of EXONTES CHARIN PROS in Acts 2.47." *NTS* 34 (1988) 604-10.

Arlandson, J. M. *Women, Class, and Society in Early Christianity: Models from Luke-Acts*. Peabody: Hendrickson, 1997.

Ascough, R. S. "Narrative Technique and Generic Designation: Crowd Scenes in Luke-Acts and in Chariton." *CBQ* 58 (1996) 69-81.

---. "Civic Pride at Philippi: The Text-Critical Problem of Acts 16.12." *NTS* 44 (1998) 93-103.

Aus, R. D. "Luke 15:11-32 and R. Eliezer Ben Hyrcanus's Rise to Fame." *JBL* 104 (1985) 443-69.

Bailey, K. E. *Finding the Lost: Cultural Keys to Luke 15*. St. Louis: Concordia, 1992.

Balz, H. "ἄρτος." *EDNT* 1.159-60.

---. "κλαίω." *EDNT* 2.293-94.

---. "μαμωνᾶς." *EDNT* 2.382-83.

---. "μερίς." *EDNT* 2.409.

---. "οὐαί." *EDNT* 2.540.

---. "παροικέω." *EDNT* 3.42.

---. "φοβέομαι," *EDNT* 3.429-32.

Barrett, C. K. *The Acts of the Apostles: Volume I: Preliminary Introduction and Commentary on Acts I-XIV*. ICC. Edinburgh: Clark, 1994.

Batten, A. "Dishonour, Gender and the Parable of the Prodigal Son." *Toronto Journal of Theology* 13 (1997) 187-200.

Bauckham, R. "The Rich Man and Lazarus: The Parable and the Parallels." *NTS* 37 (1991) 225-46.

---. "James and the Gentiles (Acts 15.13-21)." *History, Literature, and Society in the Book of Acts*. Ed. B. Witherington. Cambridge: Cambridge University Press, 1996. 154-84.

---. "Kerygmatic Summaries in the Speeches of Acts." *History, Literature, and Society in the Book of Acts*. Ed. B. Witherington. Cambridge: Cambridge University Press, 1996. 185-217.

Baumbach, G. "γραμματεύς." *EDNT* 1.259-60.

---. "Φαρισαῖος." *EDNT* 3.415-17.

Baumgarten, A. I. *The Flourishing of Jewish Sects in the Maccabean Era: An Interpretation.* JSJSup 55. Leiden: Brill, 1997.

Bergmeier, R. "πούς." *EDNT* 3.143-44.

Betz, H. D. *The Sermon on the Mount: A Commentary on the Sermon on the Mount, Including the Sermon on the Plain (Matthew 5:3-7:27 and Luke 6:20-49).* Hermeneia. Minneapolis: Fortress, 1995.

Betz, O. "'Αβραάμ." *EDNT* 1.2-4.

Beutler, J. "μάρτυς." *EDNT* 2.393-95.

Beydon, F. "A temps nouveau, nouvelles questions: Luc 10,38-42." *Foi et Vie* 88 (1989) 25-32.

Blue, B. "Acts and the House Church." *The Book of Acts in Its Graeco-Roman Setting.* Eds. D. W. J. Gill and C. Gempf. The Book of Acts in Its First Century Setting 2. Grand Rapids: Eerdmans, 1994. 119-89.

Böcher, O. "ᾅδης." *EDNT* 1.30-31.

---. "αἷμα." *EDNT* 1.37-39.

---. "διάβολος." *EDNT* 1.297-98.

---. "σατανᾶς." *EDNT* 3.234.

Bock, D. L. *Proclamation from Prophecy and Pattern: Lucan Old Testament Christology.* JSNTSup 12. Sheffield: JSOT, 1987.

---. "Understanding Luke's Task: Carefully Building on Precedent (Luke 1:1-4)." *Criswell Theological Review* 5 (1991) 183-201.

---. *Luke 1:1-9:50.* BECNT 3A. Grand Rapids: Baker Books, 1994.

Bockmuehl, M. "The Noachide Commandments and New Testament Ethics with Special Reference to Acts 15 and Pauline Halakhah." *RB* 102 (1995) 72-101.

Böhlemann, P. *Jesus und der Täufer: Schlüssel zur Theologie und Ethik des Lukas.* SNTSMS 99. Cambridge: Cambridge University Press, 1997.

Borghi, E. "Lc 15,11-32: Linee esegetiche globali." *RivB* 44 (1996) 279-308.

Bormann, L. *Philippi: Stadt und Christengemeinde zur Zeit des Paulus.* NovTSup 78. Leiden: Brill, 1995.

Borse, U. "Der Evangelist als Verfasser der Emmauserzählung." *SNT(SU)* 12 (1987) 35-67.

Botha, J. E. *Jesus and the Samaritan Woman: A Speech Act Reading of John 4:1-42.* NovTSup 65. Leiden: Brill, 1991.

Botha, P. J. J. "Community and Conviction in Luke-Acts." *Neot* 29 (1995) 145-65.

Bovon, F. *Das Evangelium nach Lukas (Lk 1,1-9,50).* EKKNT 3. Zürich: Benziger, 1989.

Braun, W. "Symposium or Anti-Symposium? Reflections on Luke 14:1-24." *Toronto Journal of Theology* 8 (1992) 70-84.

---. *Feasting and Social Rhetoric in Luke 14.* SNTSMS 85. Cambridge: Cambridge University Press, 1995.

Brawley, R. L. "Canon and Community: Intertextuality, Canon, Interpretation, Christology, Theology, and Persuasive Rhetoric in Luke 4:1-13." *SBLASP* 31 (1992) 419-34.

Brock, A. G. "The Significance of φιλέω and φίλος in the Tradition of Jesus Sayings and in the Early Christian Communities." *HTR* 90 (1997) 393-409.

Brodie, T. L. "Again Not Q: Luke 7:18-35 as an Acts-Oriented Transformation of the Vindication of the Prophet Micaiah (1 Kings 22:1-38)." *IBS* 16 (1994) 2-30.

Brown, R. E. *The Birth of the Messiah: A Commentary on the Infancy Narratives in the Gospels of Matthew and Luke.* New Updated ed. ABRL. New York: Doubleday, 1993.

Brutscheck, J. *Die Maria-Marta Erzählung: Eine redaktionskritische Untersuchung zu Lk 10, 38-42.* BBB 64. Frankfurt: Hanstein, 1986.

---. "Lukanische Anliegen in der Maria-Marta Erzählung: Zu Lk 10,38-42." *Geist und Leben* 62 (1989) 84-96.

Büchele, A. *Der Tod Jesu im Lukasevangelium: Eine redaktionsgeschichtliche Untersuchung zu Lk 23.* Frankfurter Theologische Studien 26. Frankfurt: Knecht, 1978.

Bulley, A. D. "Hanging in the Balance: A Semiotic Study of Acts 20:7-12." *Église et Théologie* 25 (1994) 171-88.

Busse, U. "διασῴζω." *EDNT* 1.313.

Callan, T. "The Background of the Apostolic Decree (Acts 15:20,29; 21:25)." *CBQ* 55 (1993) 284-97.

Cancik, H. "The History of Culture, Religion, and Institutions in Ancient Historiography: Philological Observations Concerning Luke's History." *JBL* 116 (1997) 673-95.

Caragounis, C. C. *The Son of Man: Vision and Interpretation.* WUNT 38. Tübingen: Mohr-Siebeck, 1986.

Carey, W. G. "Excuses, Excuses: The Parable of the Banquet (Luke 14:15-24) Within the Larger Context of Luke." *IBS* 17 (1995) 177-87.

Carroll, J. T. "Luke's Portrayal of the Pharisees." *CBQ* 50 (1988) 604-21.

---. "Jesus as Healer in Luke-Acts." *SBLASP* 33 (1994) 269-85.

---. "Sickness and Healing in the New Testament Gospels." *Int* 49 (1995) 130-42.

Carter, W. and J. P. Heil. *Matthew's Parables: Audience-Oriented Perspectives.* CBQMS 30; Washington: Catholic Biblical Association, 1998.

Carter, W. "Getting Martha Out of the Kitchen: Luke 10:38-42 Again." *CBQ* 58 (1996) 264-80.

Castelot, J. J. and A. Cody. "Religious Institutions of Israel." *NJBC*. 1253-83.

Cavalcanti, T. "Jesus, the Pentitent Woman, and the Pharisee." *Journal of Hispanic/Latino Theology* 2 (1994) 28-40.

Coleridge, M. *The Birth of the Lukan Narrative: Narrative as Christology in Luke 1-2*. JSNTSup 88. Sheffield: JSOT, 1993.

---. "'You Are Witnesses' (Luke 24:48): Who Sees What in Luke." *AusBR* 45 (1997) 1-19.

Co, M. A. "The Major Summaries in Acts: Acts 2,42-47; 4,32-35; 5,12-16: Linguistic and Literary Relationship." *ETL* 68 (1992) 49-85.

Combet-Galland, C. and F. Smyth-Florentin. "Le pain qui fait lever les Écritures: Emmaüs, Luc 24/13-35." *ETR* 68 (1993) 323-32.

Contreras Molina, F. "El Relato de Zaqueo en el Evangelio de Lucas." *Communio* 21 (1988) 3-47.

Conzelmann, H. *Acts of the Apostles*. Hermeneia. Philadelphia: Fortress, 1987.

Cook, C. "The Sense of Audience in Luke: A Literary Examination." *New Blackfriars* 72 (1991) 19-30.

Corley, K. E. *Private Women, Public Meals: Social Conflict in the Synoptic Tradition*. Peabody: Hendrickson, 1993.

Cosgrove, C. H. "The Divine *Dei* in Luke-Acts: Investigations into the Lukan Understanding of God's Providence," *NovT* 26 (1984) 168-90.

Cotter, W. J. "The Parable of the Children in the Marketplace, Q (Lk) 7:31-35: An Examination of the Parable's Image and Significance." *NovT* 29 (1987) 289-304.

Couffignal, R. "Un père au coeur d'or: Approches nouvelles de Luc 15,11-32." *RevThom* 91 (1991) 95-111.

---. "Du jumelage des paraboles: Approches nouvelles de Luc XV,3-10." *BLE* 94 (1993) 3-18.

Crump, D. *Jesus the Intercessor: Prayer and Christology in Luke-Acts*. WUNT 2. Tübingen: Mohr, 1992.

Cunningham, S. *'Through Many Tribulations': The Theology of Persecution in Luke-Acts*. JSNTSup 142. Sheffield: Sheffield Academic Press, 1997.

Danker, F. W. *Benefactor: Epigraphic Study of a Graeco-Roman and New Testament Semantic Field*. St. Louis: Clayton, 1982.

---. *Jesus and the New Age: A Commentary on St. Luke's Gospel*. Philadelphia: Fortress, 1988.

Darr, J. A. *On Character Building: The Reader and the Rhetoric of Characterization in Luke-Acts*. Louisville: Westminster/Knox, 1992.

---. "Narrator as Character: Mapping a Reader-Oriented Approach to Narration in Luke-Acts." *Characterization in Biblical Literature*.

Eds. E. S. Malbon and A. Berlin. *Semeia* 63. Atlanta: Scholars Press, 1993. 43-60.

---. "'Watch How You Listen' (Lk. 8.18): Jesus and the Rhetoric of Perception in Luke-Acts." *The New Literary Criticism and the New Testament*. Eds. E. S. Malbon and E. V. McKnight. JSNTSup 109. Sheffield: Sheffield Academic Press, 1994. 87-107.

Dautzenberg, G. "διακρίνω." *EDNT* 1.305-7.

Deer, D. F. "Getting the 'Story' Straight in Acts 20.9." *BT* 39 (1988) 246-47.

Delobel, J. "Lk 7,47 in Its Context: An Old Crux Revisited." *The Four Gospels 1992: Festschrift Frans Neirynck*. Ed. F. Van Segbroeck, et al. BETL 100. Leuven: Leuven University Press, 1992. 1581-90.

Delzant, A. "Les disciples d'Emmaüs (Luc 24,13-35)." *RSR* 73 (1985) 177-85.

de Meeûs, X. "Composition de Lc., XIV et genre symposiaque." *ETL* 37 (1961) 847-70.

Denova, R. I. *The Things Accomplished Among Us: Prophetic Tradition in the Structural Pattern of Luke-Acts*. JSNTSup 141. Sheffield: Sheffield Academic Press, 1997.

Derrett, J. D. M. "Clean and Unclean Animals (Acts 10:15, 11:9): Peter's Pronouncing Power Observed." *HeyJ* 29 (1988) 205-21.

---. "The Walk to Emmaus (Lk 24,13-35): The Lost Dimension." *EstBib* 54 (1996) 183-93.

de Vos, C. S. "The Significance of the Change from οἶκος to οἰκία in Luke's Account of the Philippian Gaoler (Acts 16.30-4)." *NTS* 41 (1995) 292-96.

Dillman, R. "Das Lukasevangelium als Tendenzschrift: Leserlenkung und Leseintention in Lk 1,1-4." *BZ* 38 (1994) 86-93.

Dillon, R. J. *From Eye-Witnesses to Ministers of the Word*. AnBib 82. Rome: Biblical Institute, 1978.

---. "Previewing Luke's Project from His Prologue (Luke 1:1-4)." *CBQ* 43 (1981) 205-27.

---. "Ravens, Lilies, and the Kingdom of God (Matthew 6:25-33/Luke 12:22-31)." *CBQ* 53 (1991) 605-27.

Doble, P. *The Paradox of Salvation: Luke's Theology of the Cross*. SNTSMS 87. Cambridge: Cambridge University Press, 1996.

Donahue, J. R. *The Gospel in Parable: Metaphor, Narrative, and Theology in the Synoptic Gospels*. Philadelphia: Fortress, 1988.

---. "Tax Collector." *ABD* 6.337-38.

Downing, F. G. "The Ambiguity of 'The Pharisee and the Toll-Collector' (Luke 18:9-14) in the Greco-Roman World of Late Antiquity." *CBQ* 54 (1992) 80-99.

---. "Theophilus's First Reading of Luke-Acts." *Luke's Literary Achievement: Collected Essays*. Ed. C. M. Tuckett. JSNTSup 116. Sheffield: Sheffield Academic Press, 1995. 91-109.

Drinkard, J. F. "Numbers." *HarperCollins Bible Dictionary*. 763-64.

Dumais, M. "Le salut en dehors de la foi en Jésus-Christ?: Observations sur trois passages des Actes des Apôtres." *Église et Théologie* 28 (1997) 161-90.

du Plessis, I. J. "The Saving Significance of Jesus and His Death on the Cross in Luke's Gospel--Focusing on Luke 22:19b-20." *Neot* 28 (1994) 523-40.

---. "Applying the Results of Social-Historical Research to Narrative Exegesis: Luke as a Case Study." *Neot* 30 (1996) 335-58.

Durber, S. "The Female Reader of the Parables of the Lost." *JSNT* 45 (1992) 59-78.

Dussaut, L. "Le triptyque des apparitions en Luc 24 (Analyse structurelle)." *RB* 94 (1987) 161-213.

Eckert, J. "καλέω," *EDNT* 2.240-44.

Ehrman, B. D. "The Cup, The Bread, and the Salvific Effect of Jesus' Death in Luke-Acts," *SBLASP* 30 (1991) 576-91.

Elliott, J. H. "Household and Meals Vs. Temple Purity: Replication Patterns in Luke-Acts." *BTB* 21 (1991) 102-8.

Elliott, J. K. "Anna's Age (Luke 2:36-37)." *NovT* 30 (1988) 100-02.

Esler, P. F. *Community and Gospel in Luke-Acts: The Social and Political Motivations of Lucan Theology*. SNTSMS 57. Cambridge: Cambridge University Press, 1987.

Farris, S. *The Hymns of Luke's Infancy Narratives: Their Origin, Meaning and Significance*. JSNTSup 9. Sheffield: JSOT, 1985.

Fee, G. D. "'One Thing Needful?' Luke 10:42." *New Testament Textual Criticism: Its Significance for Exegesis: Essays in Honour of Bruce M. Metzger*. Eds. E. J. Epp and G. D. Fee. Oxford: Clarendon, 1981. 61-75.

---. "The Use of Greek Patristic Citations in New Testament Textual Criticism: The State of the Question." *Studies in the Theory and Method of New Testament Textual Criticism*. Eds. E. J. Epp and G. D. Fee. SD 45. Grand Rapids: Eerdmans, 1993. 356-57.

Feeley-Harnik, G. *The Lord's Table: The Meaning of Food in Early Judaism and Christianity*. Washington: Smithsonian Institution, 1994.

Feldkämper, L. *Der betende Jesus als Heilsmittler nach Lukas*. Veröffentlichungen Des Missionspriesterseminars St. Augustin bei Bonn 29. St. Augustin, West Germany: Steyler, 1978.

Fiedler, P. "Die Gegenwart als österliche Zeit--erfahrbar im Gottesdienst: Die 'Emmausgeschichte' Lk 24,13-35." *Auferstehung Jesu--Auferstehung der Christen: Deutungen des Osterglaubens*. Ed. L. Oberlinner. QD 105. Freiburg: Herder, 1986. 124-44.

Fitzmyer, J. A. *The Gospel According to Luke I-IX*. AB 28. Garden City: Doubleday, 1981.

---. *The Gospel According to Luke X-XXIV*. AB 28A. Garden City: Doubleday, 1985.

Fornari-Carbonell, I. M. *La escucha del huésped (Lc 10,38-42): La hospitalidad en el horizonte de la communicación*. Institución San Jerónimo 30. Estella: Verbo Divino, 1995.

Frankemölle, H. "λαός." *EDNT* 2.339-44.

Frein, B. C."The Literary and Theological Significance of Misunderstanding in the Gospel of Luke." *Bib* 74 (1993) 328-48.

---. "Narrative Predictions, Old Testament Prophecies and Luke's Sense of Fulfilment." *NTS* 40 (1994) 22-37.

Friedrich, J. H. "κληρονομέω." *EDNT* 2.298-99.

---. "κλῆρος." *EDNT* 2.299-300.

---. "ξενίζω." *EDNT* 2.485.

Garrett, S. R. *The Demise of the Devil: Magic and the Demonic in Luke's Writings*. Minneapolis: Fortress, 1989.

---. "'Lest the Light in You Be Darkness': Luke 11:33-36 and the Question of Commitment." *JBL* 110 (1991) 93-105.

Garrison, R. *The Graeco-Roman Context of Early Christian Literature*. JSNTSup 137. Sheffield: Sheffield Academic Press, 1997.

Gaventa, B. R. *From Darkness to Light: Aspects of Conversion in the New Testament*. OBT 20. Philadelphia: Fortress, 1986.

Geddert, T. J. "The Parable of the Prodigal: Priorities (Luke 15:11-32)." *Direction* 24 (1995) 28-36.

Gérard, J.-P. "Les riches dans la communauté lucanienne." *ETL* 71 (1995) 71-106.

Gerhardsson, B. *The Testing of God's Son (Matt 4:1-11 & Par)*. ConBNT 2. Lund: Gleerup, 1966.

Giesen, H. "ταπεινός." *EDNT* 3.333.

---. "ταπεινόω." *EDNT* 3.334-35.

Gillman, F. M. "Early Christian Women at Philippi." *Journal of Gender in World Religions* 1 (1990) 59-79.

Gillman, J. "A Temptation to Violence: The Two Swords in Lk 22:35-38." *LS* 9 (1982) 142-53.

---. "Hospitality in Acts 16." *LS* 17 (1992) 181-96.

Glatt, D. A. and J. H. Tigay, "Sabbath." *HarperCollins Bible Dictionary*. 954-55.

Goldberg, G. J. "The Coincidences of the Emmaus Narrative of Luke and the Testimonium of Josephus." *JSP* 13 (1995) 59-77.

Gourgues, M. "Le père prodigue (Lc 15,11-32): De l'exégèse à l'actualisation." *NRT* 114 (1992) 3-20.

Gowler, D. B. *Host, Guest, Enemy, and Friend: Portraits of the Pharisees in Luke and Acts*. New York: Lang, 1991.

---. "Hospitality and Characterization in Luke 11:37-54: A Socio-Narratological Approach." *The Rhetoric of Pronouncement*. Ed. V. K. Robbins. *Semeia* 64. Atlanta: Scholars Press, 1994. 213-51.

Green, J. B. *The Death of Jesus: Tradition and Interpretation in the Passion Narrative*. WUNT 2. Tübingen: Mohr-Siebeck, 1988.

---. "The Social Status of Mary in Luke 1,5-2,52: A Plea for Methodological Integration." *Bib* 73 (1992) 457-72.

---. "Internal Repetition in Luke-Acts: Contemporary Narratology and Lucan Historiography." *History, Literature, and Society in the Book of Acts*. Ed. B. Witherington. Cambridge: Cambridge University Press, 1996. 283-99.

---. *The Gospel of Luke*. NICNT. Grand Rapids: Eerdmans, 1997.

Grelot, P. "Les tentations de Jésus." *NRT* 117 (1995) 501-16.

Griffiths, J. G. "Cross-Cultural Eschatology with Dives and Lazarus." *ExpTim* 105 (1993) 7-12.

Grundmann, W. "σύν-μετά." *TDNT* 7.766-97.

Haenchen, E. *The Acts of the Apostles: A Commentary*. Philadelphia: Westminster, 1971.

Hamm, D. "Sight to the Blind: Vision as Metaphor in Luke." *Bib* 67 (1986) 457-77.

---. "Luke 19:8 Once Again: Does Zacchaeus Defend or Resolve?" *JBL* 107 (1988) 431-37.

---. "Zacchaeus Revisited Once More: A Story of Vindication or Conversion?" *Bib* 72 (1991) 249-52.

Harrill, J. A. "The Indentured Labor of the Prodigal Son (Luke 15:15)." *JBL* 115 (1996) 714-17.

Hartman, L. "Reading Luke 17,20-37." *The Four Gospels 1992: Festschrift Frans Neirynck*. Ed. F. Van Segbroeck, et al. BETL 100. Leuven: Leuven University Press, 1992. 1663-75.

Hasel, G. F. "Sabbath." *ABD* 5.849-56.

Hasler, V. "γενεά." *EDNT* 1.241-42.

---. "εἰρήνη." *EDNT* 1.394-97.

Hassold, M. J. "Eyes to See: Reflections on Luke 19:1-10." *Lutheran Theological Journal* 29 (1995) 68-73.

Hauck, F. "καθαρός." *TDNT* 3.413-17.

Haufe, G. "παραβολή." *EDNT* 3.15-16.

Hawthorne, T. "A Discourse Analysis of Paul's Shipwreck: Acts 27:1-44." *Journal of Translation and Textlinguistics* 6 (1993) 253-73.

Hegermann, H. "διαθήκη." *EDNT* 1.299-301.

---. "σοφία" *EDNT* 3.258-61.

Heil, C. *Die Ablehnung der Speisegebote durch Paulus: Zur Frage nach der Stellung des Apostels zum Gesetz.* BBB 96. Weinheim: Beltz Athenäum, 1994.

Heil, J. P. *Jesus Walking on the Sea: Meaning and Gospel Functions of Matt 14:22-33, Mark 6:45-52 and John 6:15b-21.* AnBib 87. Rome: Biblical Institute, 1981.

---. "Interpreting the Miracles of Jesus." *McKendree Pastoral Review* 3 (1986) 15-45.

---. "Reader-Response and the Irony of Jesus Before the Sanhedrin in Luke 22:66-71." *CBQ* 51 (1989) 271-84.

---. "Reader-Response and the Irony of the Trial of Jesus in Luke 23:1-25." *ScEs* 43 (1991) 175-86.

---. "Ezekiel 34 and the Narrative Strategy of the Shepherd and Sheep Metaphor in Matthew." *CBQ* 55 (1993) 698-708.

---. "Miracles." *HarperCollins Bible Dictionary.* 687-89.

Heiligenthal, R. "Wehrlosigkeit oder Selbstschutz?: Aspekte zum Verständnis des lukanischen Schwertwortes." *NTS* 41 (1995) 39-58.

Heininger, B. *Metaphorik, Erzählstruktur und Szenisch-Dramatische Gestaltung in den Sondergutgleichnissen bei Lukas.* NTAbh 24. Münster: Aschendorff, 1991.

Herzog, W. R. *Parables as Subversive Speech: Jesus as Pedagogue of the Oppressed.* Louisville: Westminster/Knox, 1994.

Hess, A. J. "γογγύζω." *EDNT* 1.256-57.

Hock, R. F. "Lazarus and Micyllus: Greco-Roman Backgrounds to Luke 16:19-31." *JBL* 106 (1987) 447-63.

Hofius, O. "Fusswaschung als Erweis der Liebe: Sprachliche und sachliche Anmerkungung zu Lk 7,44b." *ZNW* 81 (1990) 171-77.

---. "βάλλω." *EDNT* 1.191-92.

Holtz, T. "δώδεκα." *EDNT* 1.361-63.

House, C. "Defilement by Association: Some Insights from the Usage of κοινός/κοινόω in Acts 10 and 11." *AUSS* 21 (1983) 143-53.

Houzet, P. "Les Serviteurs de l'Évangile (Luc 17,5-10) sont-ils inutiles? Ou un contresens traditionnel." *RB* 99 (1992) 335-72.

Hübner, H. "καταλύω." *EDNT* 2.264.

---. "νομικός." *EDNT* 2.470-71.

---. "τελέω." *EDNT* 3.346-47.

---. "τέλος." *EDNT* 3.347-48.

Humphrey, E. M. "Collision of Modes?--Vision and Determining Argument in Acts 10:1-11:18." *Textual Determinacy Volume II.* Eds. R. B.

Robinson and R. C. Culley. *Semeia* 71. Atlanta: Scholars Press, 1995. 65-84.

Ireland, D. J. *Stewardship and the Kingdom of God: An Historical, Exegetical, and Contextual Study of the Parable of the Unjust Steward in Luke 16:1-13*. NovTSup 70. Leiden: Brill, 1992.

Johne, H. R. "The Prohibitions in the Jerusalem Council's Letter to Gentile Believers." *Wisconsin Lutheran Quarterly* 94 (1997) 47-48.

Johnson, L. T. *The Gospel of Luke*. Sacra Pagina 3. Collegeville: Liturgical Press, 1991.

---. *The Acts of the Apostles*. SacPag 5. Collegeville: Liturgical Press, 1992.

Jones, J. N. "'Think of the Lilies' and Prov 6:6-11." *HTR* 88 (1995) 175-77.

Just, A. A. *The Ongoing Feast: Table Fellowship and Eschatology at Emmaus*. Collegeville: Liturgical Press, 1993.

Karris, R. J. *Luke: Artist and Theologian: Luke's Passion Account as Literature*. New York: Paulist, 1985.

---. "Women and Discipleship in Luke." *CBQ* 56 (1994) 1-20.

Kerr, A. J. "Zacchaeus's Decision to Make Fourfold Restitution." *ExpTim* 98 (1986) 68-71.

Kilgallen, J. J. "What Kind of Servants Are We? (Luke 17,10)." *Bib* 63 (1982) 549-51.

---. "John the Baptist, the Sinful Woman, and the Pharisee." *JBL* 104 (1985) 675-79.

---. "Did Peter Actually Fail to Get a Word in? (Acts 11,15)." *Bib* 71 (1990) 405-10.

---. "A Proposal for Interpreting Luke 7,36-50." *Bib* 72 (1991) 305-30.

---. "A Suggestion Regarding *Gar* in Luke 10,42." *Bib* 73 (1992) 255-58.

---. "The Purpose of Luke's Divorce Text (16,18)." *Bib* 76 (1995) 229-38.

---. "Luke 15 and 16: A Connection." *Bib* 78 (1997) 369-76.

---. "Forgiveness of Sins (Luke 7:36-50)." *NovT* 40 (1998) 105-16.

Kilpatrick, G. D. "Luke 24:42-43." *NovT* 28 (1986) 306-8.

Kimball, C. A. *Jesus' Exposition of the Old Testament in Luke's Gospel*. JSNTSup 94. Sheffield: JSOT, 1994.

Kingsbury, J. D. "The Pharisees in Luke-Acts." *The Four Gospels 1992: Festschrift Frans Neirynck*. Ed. F. Van Segbroeck, et al. BETL 100. Leuven: Leuven University Press, 1992. 1497-512.

Kitzberger, I. R. "Love and Footwashing: John 13:1-20 and Luke 7:36-50 Read Intertextually." *Biblical Interpretation* 2 (1994) 190-206.

Kloppenborg, J. S. "*Exitus Clari Viri*: The Death of Jesus in Luke." *Toronto Journal of Theology* 8 (1992) 106-20.

Kodell, J. *The Eucharist in the New Testament*. Collegeville: Liturgical Press, 1988.

Köhler, W. "περί." *EDNT* 3.71-73.

Kozar, J. V. "Absent Joy: An Investigation of the Narrative Pattern of Repetition and Variation in the Parables of Luke 15." *Toronto Journal of Theology* 8 (1992) 85-94.

Krämer, H. "ἐνώπιον." *EDNT* 1.462.

Kreitzer, L. "Luke 16:19-31 and 1 Enoch 22." *ExpTim* 103 (1992) 139-42.

Kremer, J. "Die Bezeugung der Auferstehung Christi in Form von Geschichten: Zu Schwierigkeiten und Chancen heutigen Verstehens von Lk 24,13-53." *Geist und Leben* 61 (1988) 172-87.

Kretzer, A. "ἀπόλλυμι." *EDNT* 1.135-36.

---. "λαμβάνω." *EDNT* 2.336-38.

Kurz, W. S. "Luke 22:14-38 and Greco-Roman and Biblical Farewell Addresses." *JBL* 104 (1985) 251-68.

---. "Narrative Approaches to Luke-Acts." *Bib* 68 (1987) 195-220.

---. *Reading Luke-Acts: Dynamics of Biblical Narrative.* Louisville: Westminster/Knox, 1993.

---. "Effects of Variant Narrators in Acts 10-11." *NTS* 43 (1997) 570-86.

Làconi, M. "Ricchi davanti a Dio (Lc 12,13-21)." *Sacra Doctrina* 34 (1989) 5-41.

Lafon, G. "Le repas chez Simon." *Études* 377 (1992) 651-60.

Lampe, G. W. H. "The Two Swords (Luke 22:35-38)." *Jesus and the Politics of His Day.* Eds. E. Bammel and C. F. D. Moule. Cambridge: Cambridge University Press, 1984. 335-51.

Larsson, E. "συζητέω." *EDNT* 3.284.

Lattke, M. "ὁμιλέω." *EDNT* 2.509-10.

LaVerdiere, E. *The Eucharist in the New Testament and the Early Church.* Collegeville: Liturgical Press, 1996.

Lee, D. A. "Women as 'Sinners': Three Narratives of Salvation in Luke and John." *AusBR* 44 (1996) 1-15.

Légasse, S. "ἐπιστρέφω." *EDNT* 2.40-41.

Leivestad, R. "ἰατρός." *EDNT* 2.171.

Léon-Dufour, X. *Sharing the Eucharistic Bread: The Witness of the New Testament.* New York: Paulist, 1987.

Leroy, H. "ἀφίημι." *EDNT* 1.181-83.

Levinskaya, I. "The Inscription from Aphrodisias and the Problem of God-Fearers." *TynBul* 41 (1990) 312-18.

---. *The Book of Acts in Its Diaspora Setting.* The Book of Acts in Its First Century Setting 5. Grand Rapids: Eerdmans, 1996.

Linton, O. "The Parable of the Children's Game: Baptist and Son of Man (Matt. XI.16-19=Luke VII.31-5): A Synoptic Text-Critical, Structural and Exegetical Investigation." *NTS* 22 (1975-76) 159-79.

Lohse, E. "σάββατον." *TDNT* 7.1-35.

Lukasz, C. *Evangelizzazione e conflitto: Indagine sulla coerenza letteraria e tematica della pericope di Cornelio (Atti 10,1-11,18)*. Europälsche Hochschulschriften 23. Frankfurt: Lang, 1993.

Lull, D. J. "The Servant-Benefactor as a Model of Greatness (Luke 22:24-30)." *NovT* 28 (1986) 289-305.

Macina, M. "Fonction liturgique et eschatologique de l'anamnèse eucharistique (Lc 22,19; 1 Co 11,24.25): Réexamen de la question à la lumière des Ecritures et des sources juives." *Ephemerides Liturgicae* 102 (1988) 3-25.

Mack, B. L. "The Anointing of Jesus: Elaboration Within a Chreia." *Patterns of Persuasion in the Gospels*. Eds. B. L. Mack and V. K. Robbins. FFNT. Sonoma: Polebridge, 1989. 100-04.

Malherbe, A. J. "The Christianization of a *Topos* (Luke 12:13-34)." *NovT* 38 (1996) 123-35.

Malina, B. J. and J. H. Neyrey. "Honor and Shame in Luke-Acts: Pivotal Values of the Mediterranean World." *The Social World of Luke-Acts: Models for Interpretation*. Ed. J. H. Neyrey. Peabody: Hendrickson, 1991. 25-65.

Maloney, L. M. *"All That God Had Done with Them": The Narration of the Works of God in the Early Christian Community as Described in the Acts of the Apostles*. American University Studies VII/91. New York: Lang, 1991.

Marguerat, D. "Voyages et voyageurs dans le livre des Actes et la culture gréco-romaine." *RHPR* 78 (1998) 33-59.

Marshall, I. H. *The Gospel of Luke*. Grand Rapids: Eerdmans, 1978.

---. *Last Supper and Lord's Supper*. Grand Rapids: Eerdmans, 1980.

Martin, F. "Le geôlier et la marchande de pourpre: Actes des Apôtres 16,6-40 (Première partie)." *Sémiotique et Bible* 59 (1990) 9-29.

Matera, F. J. *Passion Narratives and Gospel Theologies: Interpreting the Synoptics Through Their Passion Stories*. Mahwah: Paulist, 1986.

Matson, D. L. *Household Conversion Narratives in Acts: Pattern and Interpretation*. JSNTSup 123. Sheffield: Sheffield Academic Press, 1996.

McConaughy, D. L. "An Old Syriac Reading of Acts 1:4 and More Light on Jesus' Last Meal before His Ascension." *Oriens Christianus* 72 (1988) 63-67.

McKay, K. L. *A New Syntax of the Verb in New Testament Greek: An Aspectual Approach*. Studies in Biblical Greek 5. New York: Lang, 1994.

Menoud, P. H. "The Acts of the Apostles and the Eucharist," *Jesus Christ and the Faith*. PTMS 18. Pittsburgh: Pickwick, 1978. 84-106.

Menzies, R. P. "Spirit and Power in Luke-Acts: A Response to Max Turner." *JSNT* 49 (1993) 11-20.

Merkel, H. "τελώνης," *EDNT* 3.348-50.

Merklein, H. "μετάνοια." *EDNT* 2.415-19.

---. "πλούσιος." *EDNT* 3.114-17.

---. "πτωχός." *EDNT* 3.193-95.

Metzger, B. M. *A Textual Commentary on the Greek New Testament.* New York: United Bible Societies, 1971.

Meynet, R. "'Celui à qui est remis peu, aime un peu..' (Lc 7,36-50)." *Greg* 75 (1994) 267-80.

Mitchell, A. C. "Zacchaeus Revisited: Luke 19,8 as a Defense." *Bib* 71 (1990) 153-76.

---. "The Use of συκοφαντεῖν in Luke 19:8: Further Evidence for Zacchaeus's Defense." *Bib* 72 (1991) 546-47.

---. "The Social Function of Friendship in Acts 2:44-47 and 4:32-37." *JBL* 111 (1992) 255-72.

Moda, A. "Paolo prigioniero e martire: Gli avvenimenti romani." *BeO* 35 (1993) 89-118.

Moessner, D. P. *Lord of the Banquet: The Literary and Theological Significance of the Lukan Travel Narrative.* Minneapolis: Fortress, 1989.

---. "The Meaning of ΚΑΘΕΞΗΣ in the Lukan Prologue as a Key to the Distinctive Contribution of Luke's Narrative among the 'Many'." *The Four Gospels 1992: Festschrift Frans Neirynck.* Ed. F. Van Segbroeck, et al. BETL 100. Leuven: Leuven University Press, 1992. 1513-28.

---. "'Eyewitnesses,' 'Informed Contemporaries,' and 'Unknowing Inquirers': Josephus' Criteria for Authentic Historiography and the Meaning of παρακολουθέω." *NovT* 38 (1996) 105-22.

Montagnini, F. "La communità primitiva come luogo cultuale: Nota da *At* 2,42-46." *RivB* 35 (1988) 477-84.

Moo, D. J. *The Old Testament in the Gospel Passion Narratives.* Sheffield: Almond, 1983.

Moore, T. S. "The Lucan Great Commission and the Isaianic Servant." *BSac* 154 (1997) 47-60.

Moxnes, H. "Meals and the New Community in Luke." *SEÅ* 51 (1986) 158-67.

---. *The Economy of the Kingdom: Social Conflict and Economic Relations in Luke's Gospel.* Philadelphia: Fortress, 1988.

Müller, C. "ἐπιούσιος." *EDNT* 2.31-32.

Neale, D. A. *None But the Sinners: Religious Categories in the Gospel of Luke.* JSNTSup 58. Sheffield: JSOT, 1991.

Nebe, G. "μέρος." *EDNT* 2.409-10.

Nelson, P. K. "The Flow of Thought in Luke 22.24-27." *JSNT* 43 (1991) 113-23.

---. "Luke 22:29-30 and the Time Frame for Dining and Ruling." *TynBul* 44 (1993) 351-61.

---. *Leadership and Discipleship: A Study of Luke 22:24-30*. SBLDS 138. Atlanta: Scholars Press, 1994.

---. "The Unitary Character of Luke 22.24-30." *NTS* 40 (1994) 609-19.

Neufeld, D. *Reconceiving Texts as Speech Acts: An Analysis of 1 John*. Biblical Interpretation Series 7. Leiden: Brill, 1994.

Neyrey, J. H. "Ceremonies in Luke-Acts: The Case of Meals and Table Fellowship." *The Social World of Luke-Acts: Models for Interpretation*. Ed. J. H. Neyrey. Peabody: Hendrickson, 1991. 361-87.

---. "Luke's Social Location of Paul: Cultural Anthropology and the Status of Paul in Acts." *History, Literature, and Society in the Book of Acts*. Ed. B. Witherington. Cambridge: Cambridge University Press, 1996. 251-79.

Niebuhr, K.-W. "Kommunikationsebenen im Gleichnis vom verlorenen Sohn." *TLZ* 116 (1991) 481-94.

Noël, T. "The Parable of the Wedding Feast: A Narrative-Critical Interpretation." *Perspectives in Religious Studies* 16 (1989) 17-27.

Nolland, J. *Luke 1-9:20*. WBC 35A. Dallas: Word Books, 1989.

---. *Luke 9:21-18:34*. WBC 35B. Dallas: Word Books, 1993.

---. *Luke 18:35-24:53*. WBC 35C. Dallas: Word Books, 1993.

North, J. L. "ὀλίγων δέ ἐστιν χρεία ἤ ἑνός (Luke 10.42): Text, Subtext and Context." *JSNT* 66 (1997) 3-13.

Oberweis, M. "Ps. 23 als Interpretationsmodell für Act 27." *NovT* 30 (1988) 169-83.

O'Collins, G. "Did Jesus Eat the Fish (Luke 24:42-43)?" *Greg* 69 (1988) 65-76.

Oepke, A. "νόσος." *TDNT* 4.1091-98.

O'Fearghail, F. *The Introduction to Luke-Acts: A Study of the Role of Lk 1,1-4,44 in the Composition of Luke's Two-Volume Work*. AnBib 126. Rome: Biblical Institute, 1991.

O'Hanlon, J. "The Story of Zacchaeus and the Lukan Ethic." *JSNT* 12 (1981) 2-26.

Osborne, G. R. *The Resurrection Narratives: A Redactional Study*. Grand Rapids: Baker, 1984.

Osiek, C. and D. L. Balch. *Families in the New Testament World: Households and House Churches*. Louisville: Westminster John Knox, 1997.

O'Toole, R. F. *The Unity of Luke's Theology: An Analysis of Luke-Acts.* GNS 9. Wilmington: Glazier, 1984.

---. "The Literary Form of Luke 19:1-10." *JBL* 110 (1991) 107-16.

---. "Does Luke Also Portray Jesus as the Christ in Luke 4,16-30?" *Bib* 76 (1995) 498-522.

Palzkill, A. "προσδέχομαι." *EDNT* 3.162-63.

Parsons, M. C. and R. I. Pervo. *Rethinking the Unity of Luke and Acts.* Minneapolis: Fortress, 1993.

Parsons, M. C. *The Departure of Jesus in Luke-Acts: The Ascension Narratives in Context.* JSNTSup 21. Sheffield: JSOT, 1987.

---. "The Prodigal's Elder Brother: The History and Ethics of Reading Luke 15:25-32." *Perspectives in Religious Studies* 23 (1996) 147-74.

Patsch, H. "ἀνάμνησις." *EDNT* 1.85-86.

---. "εὐλογέω." *EDNT* 2.79-80.

---. "εὐχαριστία." *EDNT* 2.88.

---. "πάσχα." *EDNT* 3.49-51.

---. "ὑπέρ." *EDNT* 3.396-97.

Paulsen, H. "ἐνδυναμόω." *EDNT* 1.451.

Pedersen, S. "εὐφραίνω." *EDNT* 2.86-87.

---. "κύων." *EDNT* 2.332.

Perrot, C. "Les décisions de l'Assemblée de Jérusalem." *RSR* 69 (1981) 195-208.

Pervo, R. I. *Luke's Story of Paul.* Minneapolis: Fortress, 1990.

Pesch, R. *Die Apostelgeschichte (Apg 1-12).* EKK V/1. Zürich: Benziger, 1986.

---. *Die Apostelgeschichte (Apg 13-28).* EKK V/2. Zürich: Benziger, 1986.

Pesch, W. "δραχμή." *EDNT* 1.353-54.

Pettem, M. "Luke's Great Omission and His View of the Law." *NTS* 42 (1996) 35-54.

Petzer, K. "Style and Text in the Lucan Narrative of the Institution of the Lord's Supper (Luke 22.19b-20)." *NTS* 37 (1991) 113-29.

Pilch, J. J. "Sickness and Healing in Luke-Acts." *The Social World of Luke-Acts: Models for Interpretation.* Ed. J. H. Neyrey. Peabody: Hendrickson, 1991. 181-209.

Pilgrim, W. E. *Good News to the Poor: Wealth and Poverty in Luke-Acts.* Minneapolis: Augsburg, 1981.

Pilhofer, P. *Philippi: Die erste christliche Gemeinde Europas.* WUNT 87. Tübingen: Mohr-Siebeck, 1995.

Piper, R. A. "Social Background and Thematic Structure in Luke 16." *The Four Gospels 1992: Festschrift Frans Neirynck.* Ed. F. Van Segbroeck, et al. BETL 100. Leuven: Leuven University Press, 1992. 1637-62.

Plummer, A. *The Gospel According to S. Luke*. ICC. Edinburgh: Clark, 1922.

Plymale, S. F. *The Prayer Texts of Luke-Acts*. New York: Lang, 1991.

Pöhlmann, W. *Der verlorene Sohn und das Haus: Studien zu Lukas 15,11-32 im Horizont der antiken Lehre von Haus, Erziehung und Ackerbau*. WUNT 68. Tübingen: Mohr-Siebeck, 1993.

Polhill, J. B. *Acts*. NAC 26. Nashville: Broadman, 1992.

Popkes, W. "παραδίδωμι." *EDNT* 3.18-20.

---. "πειράζω." *EDNT* 3.64-67.

Porter, S. E. *Verbal Aspect in the Greek of the New Testament, with Reference to Tense and Mood*. Studies in Biblical Greek 1. New York: Lang, 1993.

---. "The 'We' Passages." *The Book of Acts in Its Graeco-Roman Setting*. Eds. D. W. J. Gill and C. Gempf. The Book of Acts in Its First Century Setting 2. Grand Rapids: Eerdmans, 1994. 545-74.

Powell, M. A. "The Religious Leaders in Luke: A Literary-Critical Study." *JBL* 109 (1990) 93-110.

---. "Toward a Narrative-Critical Understanding of Luke." *Int* 48 (1994) 341-46.

Praeder, S. M. "Acts 27:1-28:16: Sea Voyages in Ancient Literature and the Theology of Luke-Acts." *CBQ* 46 (1984) 683-706.

---. "The Problem of First Person Narration in Acts." *NovT* 29 (1987) 193-218.

Price, R. M. *The Widow Traditions in Luke-Acts: A Feminist-Critical Scrutiny*. SBLDS 155. Atlanta: Scholars Press, 1997.

Priest, J. F. "Messianic Banquet." *IDBSup*, 591-92.

Proctor, J. "Proselytes and Pressure Cookers: The Meaning and Application of Acts 15:20." *International Review of Mission* 85 (1996) 469-83.

Quesnell, Q. "The Women at Luke's Supper." *Political Issues in Luke-Acts*. Eds. R. J. Cassidy and P. J. Scharper. Maryknoll: Orbis, 1983. 59-79.

Radl, W. "σῴζω." *EDNT* 3.319-21.

---. "χείρ." *EDNT* 3.462-63.

Ramaroson, L. "'Le premier, c'est l'amour' (Lc 7,47a)." *ScEs* 39 (1987) 319-29.

---. "La première question posée aux disciples d'Emmaüs en Lc 24,17." *ScEs* 47 (1995) 299-303.

Ramsey, G. W. "Plots, Gaps, Repetitions, and Ambiguity in Luke 15." *Perspectives in Religious Studies* 17 (1990) 33-42.

Rapske, B. M. "Acts, Travel and Shipwreck," *The Book of Acts in Its Graeco-Roman Setting*. The Book of Acts in Its First Century Setting 2. Eds. D. W. J. Gill and C. Gempf. Grand Rapids: Eerdmans, 1994.

Ravens, D. A. S. "The Setting of Luke's Account of the Anointing: Luke 7.2-8.3." *NTS* 34 (1988) 282-92.

---. "Zacchaeus: The Final Part of a Lucan Triptych?" *JSNT* 41 (1991) 19-32.

---. *Luke and the Restoration of Israel.* JSNTSup 119. Sheffield: Sheffield Academic Press, 1995.

Refoulé, F. "Le discours de Pierre à l'assemblée de Jérusalem." *RB* 100 (1993) 239-51.

Reid, B. E. "'Do You See This Woman?': Luke 7:36-50 as a Paradigm for Feminist Hermeneutics." *BR* 40 (1995) 37-49.

---. *Choosing the Better Part?: Women in the Gospel of Luke.* Collegeville: Liturgical Press, 1996.

Reinmuth, E. "Ps.-Philo, *Liber Antiquitatum Biblicarum* 33,1-5 und die Auslegung der Parabel Lk 16:19-31." *NovT* 31 (1989) 16-38.

Resseguie, J. L. "Automatization and Defamiliarization in Luke 7:36-50." *Literature & Theology* 5 (1991) 137-50.

Richter Reimer, I. *Women in the Acts of the Apostles: A Feminist Liberation Perspective.* Minneapolis: Fortress, 1995.

Rigato, M. L. "'Mosè e i profeti' in chiave cristiana: un pronunciamento e un midrash (Lc 16,16-18 + 19-31)." *RivB* 45 (1997) 143-77.

Riley, G. J. "Influence of Thomas Christianity on Luke 12:14 and 5:39." *HTR* 88 (1995) 229-35.

Ringe, S. H. *Jesus, Liberation, and the Biblical Jubilee.* OBT 19. Philadelphia: Fortress, 1985.

Rissi, M. "κρίνω." *EDNT* 2.318-21.

Rius-Camps, J. "Las variantes de la Recensión Occidental de los Hechos de los Apóstoles (VI) (Hch 2,41-47)." *Filologia Neotestamentaria* 8 (1995) 199-208.

---. "Pablo y el grupo 'nosotros' en Filipos: dos proyectos de evangelización en conflicto (Hch 16,11-40)." *Laurentianum* 36 (1995) 35-59.

Robbins, V. K. "Pronouncement Stories from a Rhetorical Perspective." *Forum* 4,2 (1988) 3-32.

---. "The Social Location of the Implied Author of Luke-Acts." *The Social World of Luke-Acts: Models for Interpretation.* Ed. J. H. Neyrey. Peabody: Hendrickson, 1991. 305-32.

---. "Socio-Rhetorical Criticism: Mary, Elizabeth and the Magnificat as a Test Case." *The New Literary Criticism and the New Testament.* Eds. E. S. Malbon and E. V. McKnight. JSNTSup 109. Sheffield: Sheffield Academic Press, 1994. 164-209.

Robinson, B. P. "The Place of the Emmaus Story in Luke-Acts." *NTS* 30 (1984) 481-97.

Rohrbaugh, R. L. "The Pre-Industrial City in Luke-Acts: Urban Social Relations." *The Social World of Luke-Acts: Models for Interpretation.* Ed. J. H. Neyrey. Peabody: Hendrickson, 1991. 125-49.

Roloff, J. "θυσιαστήριον." *EDNT* 2.163-64.

Roth, S. J. *The Blind, the Lame, and the Poor: Character Types in Luke-Acts.* JSNTSup 144. Sheffield: Sheffield Academic Press, 1997.

Rousseau, F. "Un phénomène particulier d'inclusions dans Luc 24.13-35." *SR* 18 (1989) 67-79.

Saldarini, A. J. "Pharisees." *ABD* 5.289-303.

---. "Scribes." *ABD* 5.1012-16.

Sand, A. "χρεία." *EDNT* 3.472-73.

Sanders, J. A. "The Ethic of Election in Luke's Great Banquet Parable." *Luke and Scripture: The Function of Sacred Tradition in Luke-Acts.* Eds. C. A. Evans and J. A. Sanders. Minneapolis: Fortress, 1993. 106-20.

Sanger, D. "θρόνος." *EDNT* 2.156-58.

Schelkle, K. H. "σωτήρ." *EDNT* 3.325-27.

---. "σωτηρία." *EDNT* 3.327-29.

---. "σωτήριος." *EDNT* 3.329.

Schneider, G. "εὐεργετέω." *EDNT* 2.76-77.

---. "θόρυβος." *EDNT* 2.153-54.

---. "νέος." *EDNT* 2.462-63.

---. "ὁρίζω." *EDNT* 2.531-32.

Schoenborn, U. "δέομαι." *EDNT* 1.286-87.

Schottroff, L. "ζῶ." *EDNT* 2.105-9.

Schramm, T. "ἁπλοῦς." *EDNT* 1.123-24.

---. "ἡγέομαι." *EDNT* 2.113.

Schürmann, H. "Der Abendmahlsbericht Lk 22,7-38 als Gottesdienstordnung, Gemeindeordnung, Lebensordnung." *Ursprung und Gestalt: Erörterungen und Besinnungen zum Neuen Testament.* Düsseldorf: Patmos, 1970. 108-50.

---. "Der Dienst des Petrus und Johannes (Lk 22,8)." *Ursprung und Gestalt: Erörterungen und Besinnungen zum Neuen Testament.* Düsseldorf: Patmos, 1970. 274-76.

Schüssler Fiorenza, E. "A Feminist Critical Interpretation for Liberation: Martha and Mary: Lk. 10:38-42." *Religion and Intellectual Life* 3 (1986) 21-36.

---. "Theological Criteria and Historical Reconstruction: Martha and Mary: Luke 10:38-42." *Center for Hermeneutical Studies Protocol Series* 53 (1987) 1-12.

Schwartz, D. R. "The Accusation and the Accusers at Philippi (Acts 16,20-21)." *Bib* 65 (1984) 357-63.

---. "The Futility of Preaching Moses (Acts 15,21)." *Bib* 67 (1986) 276-81.

Scobel, G. "Das Gleichnis vom verlorenen Sohn als metakommunikativer Text: Überlegungen zur Verständigungsproblematik in Lukas 15." *Freiburger Zeitschrift für Philosophie und Theologie* 35 (1988) 21-67.

Scott, B. B. *Hear Then the Parable: A Commentary on the Parables of Jesus.* Minneapolis: Fortress, 1989.

Scott, J. J. "The Cornelius Incident in the Light of Its Jewish Setting." *JETS* 34 (1991) 475-84.

---. "The Church's Progress to the Council of Jerusalem According to the Book of Acts." *Bulletin for Biblical Research* 7 (1997) 205-24.

Seccombe, D. P. *Possessions and the Poor in Luke-Acts.* SNT(SU) 6. Linz: Fuchs, 1982.

Seethaler, A. "Die Brotvermehrung--ein Kirchenspiegel?" *BZ* 34 (1990) 108-12.

Seifrid, M. A. "Jesus and the Law in Acts." *JSNT* 30 (1987) 39-57.

Seim, T. K. *The Double Message: Patterns of Gender in Luke-Acts.* Nashville: Abingdon, 1994.

Sellew, P. "The Last Supper Discourse in Luke 22:21-38." *Forum* 3 (1987) 70-95.

Senior, D. *The Passion of Jesus in the Gospel of Luke.* Collegeville: Liturgical Press, 1989.

Sheeley, S. M. *Narrative Asides in Luke-Acts.* JSNTSup 72. Sheffield: JSOT, 1992.

Shepherd, W. H. *The Narrative Function of the Holy Spirit as a Character in Luke-Acts.* SBLDS 147. Atlanta: Scholars Press, 1994.

Sloan, I. "The Greatest and the Youngest: Greco-Roman Reciprocity in the Farewell Address, Luke 22:24-30." *SR* 22 (1993) 63-73.

Sloan, R. B. *The Favorable Year of the Lord: A Study of Jubilary Theology in the Gospel of Luke.* Austin: Schola, 1977.

Smith, D. E. "Table Fellowship as a Literary Motif in the Gospel of Luke." *JBL* 106 (1987) 613-38.

---. "Messianic Banquet." *ABD* 4.788-91.

---. "Table Fellowship." *ABD* 6.302-4.

Soards, M. L. *The Speeches in Acts: Their Content, Context, and Concerns.* Louisville: Knox, 1994.

Spencer, F. S. "Neglected Widows in Acts 6:1-7." *CBQ* 56 (1994) 715-33.

Spicq, C. *Theological Lexicon of the New Testament.* 3 vols. Peabody: Hendrickson, 1994.

Squires, J. T. *The Plan of God in Luke-Acts.* SNTSMS 76. Cambridge: Cambridge University Press, 1993.

Staudinger, F. "ἐλεημοσύνη." *EDNT* 1.428-29.

Steele, E. S. "Luke 11:37-54--A Modified Hellenistic Symposium?" *JBL* 103 (1984) 379-94.

Stenger, W. "βιάζομαι." *EDNT* 1.216-17.

Sterling, G. E. *Historiography and Self-Definition: Josephos, Luke-Acts and Apologetic Historiography.* NovTSup 64. Leiden: Brill, 1992.

---. "'Athletes of Virtue': An Analysis of the Summaries in Acts (2:41-47; 4:32-35; 5:12-16)." *JBL* 113 (1994) 679-96.

Steyn, G. J. *Septuagint Quotations in the Context of the Petrine and Pauline Speeches of the Acta Apostolorum.* CBET 12. Kampen: Pharos, 1995.

Strauss, M. L. *The Davidic Messiah in Luke-Acts: The Promise and Its Fulfillment in Lukan Christology.* JSNTSup 110. Sheffield: Sheffield Academic Press, 1995.

Sweetland, D. M. "The Lord's Supper and the Lukan Community." *BTB* 13 (1983) 23-27.

Tannehill, R. C. *The Narrative Unity of Luke-Acts.* Vol. 1. FFNT. Philadelphia: Fortress, 1986.

---. *The Narrative Unity of Luke-Acts.* Vol. 2. FFNT. Minneapolis: Fortress, 1990.

---. "The Lukan Discourse on Invitations (Luke 14,7-24)." *The Four Gospels 1992: Festschrift Frans Neirynck.* Ed. F. Van Segbroeck, et al. BETL 100. Leuven: Leuven University Press, 1992. 1603-16.

---. "Should We Love Simon the Pharisee?: Hermeneutical Reflections on the Pharisees in Luke." *CurTM* 21 (1994) 424-33.

---. "The Story of Zacchaeus as Rhetoric: Luke 19:1-10." *The Rhetoric of Pronouncement.* Ed. V. K. Robbins. *Semeia* 64. Atlanta: Scholars Press, 1994. 201-11.

---. *Luke.* Abingdon New Testament Commentaries. Nashville: Abingdon, 1996.

Taylor, N. *Paul, Antioch and Jerusalem: A Study in Relationships and Authority in Earliest Christianity.* JSNTSup 66. Sheffield: Sheffield Academic Press, 1992.

Thibeaux, E. R. "'Known To Be a Sinner': The Narrative Rhetoric of Luke 7:36-50." *BTB* 23 (1993) 151-60.

Trémel, B. "A propos d'Actes 20,7-12: Puissance du thaumaturge ou du témoin?" *RTP* 112 (1980) 359-69.

Trummer, P. "ἱκανός." *EDNT* 2.184-85.

---. "παρατίθημι." *EDNT* 3.22.

Tuckett, C. M. "The Lukan Son of Man." *Luke's Literary Achievement: Collected Essays.* Ed. C. M. Tuckett. JSNTSup 116. Sheffield: Sheffield Academic Press, 1995. 198-217.

Turner, M. "The Spirit and the Power of Jesus' Miracles in the Lucan Conception." *NovT* 33 (1991) 124-52.

---. "The Spirit of Prophecy and the Power of Authoritative Preaching in Luke-Acts: A Question of Origins." *NTS* 38 (1992) 66-88.

Tyson, J. B. *Images of Judaism in Luke-Acts.* Columbia: University of South Carolina Press, 1992.

Untergassmair, F. G. "ἐκχέω." *EDNT*, 1.424.

---. "κλείς." *EDNT* 2.296-97.

van der Minde, H.-J. "γεύομαι." *EDNT* 1.245-46.

van de Sandt, H. "An Explanation of Acts 15.6-21 in the Light of Deuteronomy 4.29-35 (LXX)." *JSNT* 46 (1992) 73-97.

Via, E. J. "Women, the Discipleship of Service, and the Early Christian Ritual Meal in the Gospel of Luke." *St. Luke's Journal of Theology* 29 (1985) 37-60.

Vogels, W. "Having or Longing: A Semiotic Analysis of Luke 16:19-31." *Église et Théologie* 20 (1989) 27-46.

Völkel, M. "μνημεῖον." *EDNT* 2.434-35.

---. "ὀφθαλμός." *EDNT* 2.552-53.

---. "σήμερον." *EDNT* 3.241.

Wall, R. W. "Peter, 'Son' of Jonah: The Conversion of Cornelius in the Context of Canon." *JSNT* 29 (1987) 79-90.

---. "Martha and Mary (Luke 10.38-42) in the Context of a Christian Deuteronomy." *JSNT* 35 (1989) 19-35.

Wanke, J. *Die Emmauserzählung: Eine redaktionsgeschichtliche Untersuchung zu Lk 24,13-35.* ETS 31. Leipzig: St. Benno, 1973.

---. "'...wie sie ihn beim Brotbrechen erkannten': Zur Auslegung der Emmauserzählung Lk 24,13-35." *BZ* 18 (1974) 180-92.

---. "κλάω." *EDNT* 2.295-96.

Wedderburn, A. J. M. "The 'Apostolic Decree': Tradition and Redaction." *NovT* 35 (1993) 362-89.

Wehnert, J. *Die Wir-Passagen der Apostelgeschichte: Ein lukanisches Stilmittel aus jüdischer Tradition.* GTA 40. Göttingen: Vandenhoeck & Ruprecht, 1989.

Weigandt, P. "οἶκος." *EDNT* 2.500-503.

Weiser, A. "ἀγαλλιάω." *EDNT* 1.7-8.

---. "διακονέω." *EDNT* 1.302-4.

Wendland, E. R. "Finding Some Lost Aspects of Meaning in Christ's Parables of the Lost--and Found (Luke 15)." *Trinity Journal* 17 (1996) 19-65.

Wilcox, M. "Luke 2,36-38: 'Anna Bat Phanuel, of the Tribe of Asher, a Prophetess..': A Study in Midrash in Material Special to Luke." *The Four Gospels 1992: Festschrift Frans Neirynck.* Ed. F. Van Segbroeck, et al. BETL 100. Leuven: Leuven University Press, 1992. 1571-79.

Wilson, J. C. "Tithe." *ABD* 6.578-80.

Wilson, S. G. *Luke and the Law*. SNTSMS 50. Cambridge: Cambridge University Press, 1983.

Wimmer, J. F. *Fasting in the New Testament: A Study in Biblical Theology*. New York: Paulist, 1982.

Winter, B. W. "Acts and Food Shortages." *The Book of Acts in Its Graeco-Roman Setting*. Eds. D. W. J. Gill and C. Gempf. The Book of Acts in Its First Century Setting 2. Grand Rapids: Eerdmans, 1994. 59-78.

Wischmeyer, O. "Matthäus 6,25-34 par: Die Spruchreihe vom Sorgen." *ZNW* 85 (1994) 1-22.

Witherington, B. *Women in the Ministry of Jesus: A Study of Jesus' Attitude to Women and Their Roles as Reflected in His Earthly Life*. SNTSMS 51. Cambridge: Cambridge University Press, 1984.

---. "Not So Idle Thoughts About *Eidolothuton*." *TynBul* 44 (1993) 237-54.

Witherup, R. D. "Cornelius Over and Over and Over Again: 'Functional Redundancy' in the Acts of the Apostles." *JSNT* 49 (1993) 45-66.

Wright, C. J. H. "Sabbatical Year." *ABD* 5.857-61.

York, J. O. *The Last Shall Be First: The Rhetoric of Reversal in Luke*. JSNTSup 46. Sheffield: JSOT, 1991.

Zeller, D. "ἀφροσύνη." *EDNT* 1.184-85.

Zerwick, M. and M. Grosvenor. *A Grammatical Analysis of the Greek New Testament*. Vol. 1. Rome: Biblical Institute, 1974.

Zerwick, M. *Biblical Greek*. Rome: Biblical Institute, 1963.

Zmijewski, J. "βδέλυγμα." *EDNT* 1.209-10.

---. "νηστεύω." *EDNT* 2.465-67.

Zwiep, A. W. "The Text of the Ascension Narratives (Luke 24.50-3; Acts 1.1-2, 9-11)." *NTS* 42 (1996) 219-44.

---. *The Ascension of the Messiah in Lukan Christology*. NovTSup 87. Leiden: Brill, 1997.

SCRIPTURE INDEX